DO IT IN THE DARK

Tom Burk

You must know that there are many darkroom books on the market. Nevertheless, when choosing subjects for the series of HP Books on photography, we decided to add one more good book on darkroom technique. One with a *difference.*

There are so many different chemicals, procedures and tricks. Many books present all of the bewildering array of alternatives to the beginner. This is like giving a world map to the uncertain traveler and saying, "Go somewhere."

We asked author Tom Burk to very carefully describe *one good way* to do each thing. To explicitly list *one set* of chemicals and equipment by brand name and quantity needed. To give *one exact procedure* with no detail omitted even though seemingly trivial. To write a fool-proof fail-proof single good method of developing and printing and then add on some of the fancy stuff.

Most of the needed darkroom skills are manipulative things you learn to do with your hands and fingers. The elegantly practical way to show you these procedures is to *show them to you* with pictures. Many, many pictures.

We carefully defined the purpose of this book—to get you started in home lab technique with a solid base of experience and success. Then you can start exploring other ways confidently and without confusion.

I think you'll agree, author Burk met the challenge and this book will lead you straight-arrow into successful darkroom methods.

Carl Shipman
Editor

Publisher: Bill Fisher
Editors: Bill Fisher and Carl Shipman
Design: Josh Young
Photography: Tom Burk
Book Assembly: Nancy Fisher
Typography: Debbie McMillian, Ellen L. Duerr

Contents

ISBN: 0-912656-28-X
Library of Congress Catalog Card Number 74-82516

P.O. Box 5367, Tucson, AZ 85703
602/888-2150
Printed in U.S.A.

It Starts in Your Camera

Before we get into the darkroom, let's take a few moments to consider how you can help or hinder with your camera work before you ever get there.

Properly exposed film is a definite help. Over- or underexposure is certainly a hindrance. A great many wonders can be worked in the darkroom, but make it easy on yourself to start with. Take some time to get acquainted with your camera equipment so you can be relatively sure of correct exposure. Stick to the manufacturer's recommendations concerning film speed—at least at the beginning.

It's a good idea to think about the type of subject matter you will usually be shooting and pick a film which will cover most situations. If you are photographing scenery or still life in black-and-white, a film with a slower speed rating and fine grain, such as Kodak Panatomic-X, is a good choice. If you prefer people pictures, Plus-X will do nicely. In low-light situations or when you need to stop action, a higher-speed film like Tri-X is essential. Whichever film you choose, try to stay with it as much as possible.

Standardization is the key. If you learn to use your materials well and to their best advantage, you're ahead of the game to start. More problems are caused by switching from film to film than can be imagined. It's difficult for you to get really familiar with what a particular film can do for you if you only use it now and again.

When making exposure readings be sure you know what your meter is seeing and reading. For instance, if your subject of interest is a small bright object in the center of a large black area, the meter will give a reading leading to overexposure. The meter sees the black part as a large area needing considerable exposure. This will overexpose the small bright area so it *blocks* up on the negative and has no detail.

The opposite is true of a scene where a small black object is surrounded by a large bright background. Underexposure results if you follow the meter indication. The flat dull negative makes a flat, overall gray print.

Either of these situations calls for metering on a substitute subject to obtain the correct expo-

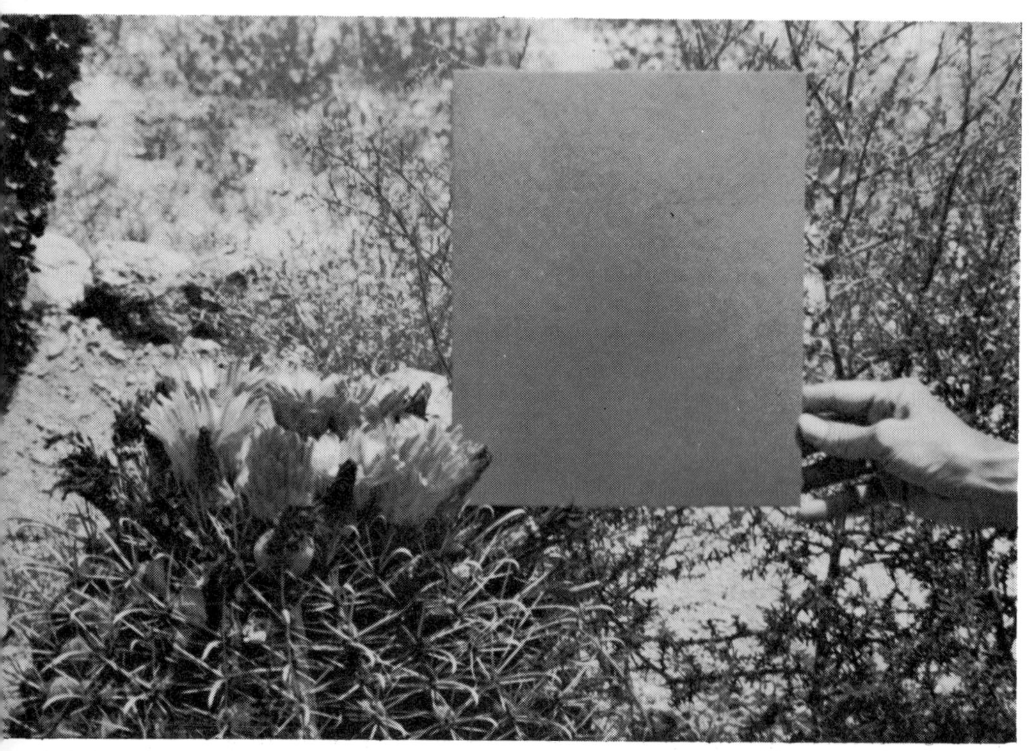

For best results when making a meter reading before exposing, read from a Kodak 18% gray card. This will eliminate the problem of having the meter influenced by large dark or light areas.

sure reading. A Kodak 18% gray card is the answer. Hold the gray card in front of the meter, in the same light as the subject to be photographed, and you'll get an accurate exposure reading. The gray card is 18% gray because that's the amount of light reflected by an average outdoor scene, and your exposure meter is *designed* to see all scenes at that value.

Should you run across a scene with excessive contrast, it's a good idea to expose to favor the brighter areas so they don't block and lose detail. Conversely, a dull flat scene is best exposed for the shadow or darker parts. In either case—with normal development—your negative will be closer to the density necessary to make a pleasing print.

Remember your hand-held or in-camera meter looks at every scene as if it were 18% gray. If you meter on a white building, the meter tells you how to expose to make the subject 18% gray. That's why it's handy to carry an 18% gray card with you to meter on as a substitute subject.

Of nearly equal importance is proper focus. If you're using a roll-film camera, you will usually want enlargements from your negatives. An unsharp image is just that much more unsharp when magnified through enlargement. Aside from being unpleasant to look at, an out-of-focus image degrades print quality.

If the image is not sharp, tone separation is not well defined and the print has an overall gray appearance. There is a definite difference between out-of-focus and soft-focus. A soft-focus image is actually a sharp-focus image with the edge knocked off, see Special Techniques chapter.

Learn to use your camera and exposure meter; pay attention to exposure settings, focus and holding the camera steady. Then the hours you spend in the darkroom will be very rewarding. An extra few moments of thought and care when taking the photograph will save much effort when it's time to make your final print. Remember what I told you when you're trying to save a photo you forgot to be careful in exposing. *There is no magic substitute for proper exposure when you take the picture.*

OK, roll up your sleeves, put on your see-through plastic apron and let's get to what we all came for . . .

Pictures not sharp? One of the most common causes is camera shake. Some photographers use the shutter release button like a punching bag. Jab! Click—Wind. Jab! Click—Wind. With each Jab! the camera moves. The shutter speed can be very fast and camera movement may still produce an unsharp negative, even if the subject is as immobile as a gravestone.

Practice squeezing down on the shutter release ever so gently. With practice, you'll get so good you can do it deliberately without bouncing your camera around.

Another reason for unsharp pictures is not being able to focus on the viewing screen, assuming you have a camera where you do the focusing by watching how sharp the image gets on the viewing screen—as with an SLR (single-lens reflex) or TLR (twin-lens reflex). In the case of the TLR, there is usually a magnifier in the focusing hood that you can slip into position to observe whether you are getting the image really sharp or not. But with the SLR, there's no such aid and you either see it or you don't. If you think you have the shutter-release squeeze down pat and have stopped jabbing at the camera—and you are still getting unsharp pictures—have your eyes examined. You may need glasses to be able to focus your camera. Or, you may need a prescription eyepiece or corrective eyepiece to install over the viewing port of your camera in place of the present plain-glass cover lens. If yours is a simple correction requiring only so many plus or minus diopters to be able to see straight, you may be able to adapt the finder lenses made by Canon, Konica, Minolta or Nikon. If your correction is complex, involving astigmatism and such like, you have no choice but to order a viewing lens ground to your prescription—or else wear your glasses when focusing your camera. I'll vote for the corrective eyepiece because it will usually let you see more of the picture. One manufacturer of custom eyepieces is Olympia Optical Devices, P.O. Box 2266-H, S. Hackensack, NJ 07606.

Developing Film

The picture is on the film. You focused the camera, set the *f*-stop and shutter speed for the correct exposure, composed the way you wanted the scene to appear on the film and clicked the shutter. You can't see the picture until the film is developed. If you unrolled the film and looked at it, nothing would be there to indicate any picture had ever been imposed onto the emulsion. Once you have an exposed roll of film, you want to convert it into negatives from which you can make paper prints to be able to enjoy the original scenes as you saw them.

A negative is a reversed image on sensitized material. Light-colored areas in the original scene appear dark or less-transparent on the negative. Due to the sensitizing effect of light, the silver material in the film emulsion can be changed to dense deposits of metallic silver during chemical development. These silver deposits then keep light from striking the paper during printing. This reverses the image once more and the paper print shows approximately the same tone values as the original scene.

Developing film is really easy and you can get outstanding results by following the directions I am going to provide. Every step has been thoroughly covered. In some cases you may even feel I've been too thorough by telling you more than you wanted

A simplified sketch showing the cross section of a typical black-and-white film. (1) supercoat to help prevent damage to the emulsion, (2) emulsion layer which forms the negative image through exposure to light and chemical development, (3) film base to provide support for the emulsion and (4) antihalation backing to prevent light from passing through the film and bouncing back to produce multiple images.

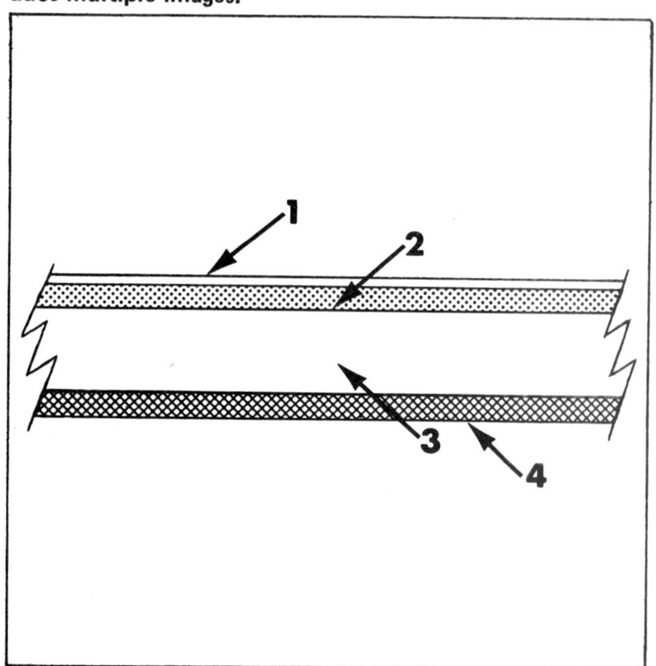

The data sheet provided with the film gives all necessary information regarding exposure and processing with a number of common developers. KEEP IT AND REFER TO IT OFTEN!

Processing

Handle in total darkness. However, a KODAK Safelight Filter, No. 3 (dark green) or its equivalent in a suitable safelight lamp with a 15-watt bulb can be used for a few seconds after development is half completed, provided it is kept at least 4 feet from the film.

Develop for the approximate times given.

NEW DATA

KODAK Packaged Developers	Developing Times (in Minutes)*									
	SMALL TANK—(Agitation at 30-Second Intervals)					**LARGE TANK**—(Agitation at 1-Minute Intervals)				
	65 F 18 C	**68 F 20 C**	70 F 21 C	72 F 22 C	75 F 24 C	65 F 18 C	**68 F 20 C**	70 F 21 C	72 F 22 C	75 F 24 C
HC-110 (Dilution B)	6	**5**	4½	4	3½	6½	**5½**	5	4¾	4
POLYDOL	6½	**5½**	4¾	4¼	3¼	7½	**6**	5½	4¾	3¾
D-76	6½	**5½**	5	4½	3¾	7½	**6½**	6	5½	4½
D-76 (1:1)	8	**7**	6½	6	5	10	**9**	8	7½	7
MICRODOL-X	8	**7**	6½	6	5½	10	**9**	8	7½	7
MICRODOL-X (1:3)	—	—	11	10	**9½**	—	—	14	13	**11**

*Avoid development times of less than 5 minutes if possible, because poor uniformity may result.
Note: Do not use developers containing silver halide solvents.

Rinse at 65 to 75 F (18 to 24 C) with agitation.
KODAK Indicator Stop Bath—30 seconds
or KODAK Stop Bath SB-5 —30 seconds

Fix at 65 to 75 F (18 to 24 C) with agitation.
KODAK Fixer —5 to 10 minutes
or KODAK Fixing Bath F-5—5 to 10 minutes
or KODAK Rapid Fixer —2 to 4 minutes
or KODAFIX Solution —2 to 4 minutes

Wash for 20 to 30 minutes in running water at 65 to 75 F (18 to 24 C). To minimize drying marks, treat in KODAK PHOTO-FLO Solution after washing. To save time and conserve water, use KODAK Hypo Clearing Agent.

Dry in a dust-free place.

Storage Keep unexposed film at 75 F (24 C) or lower. Process film as soon as possible after exposure.

Clipped from Kodak Plus-X Pan Professional instruction sheet for 120 & 220 films.

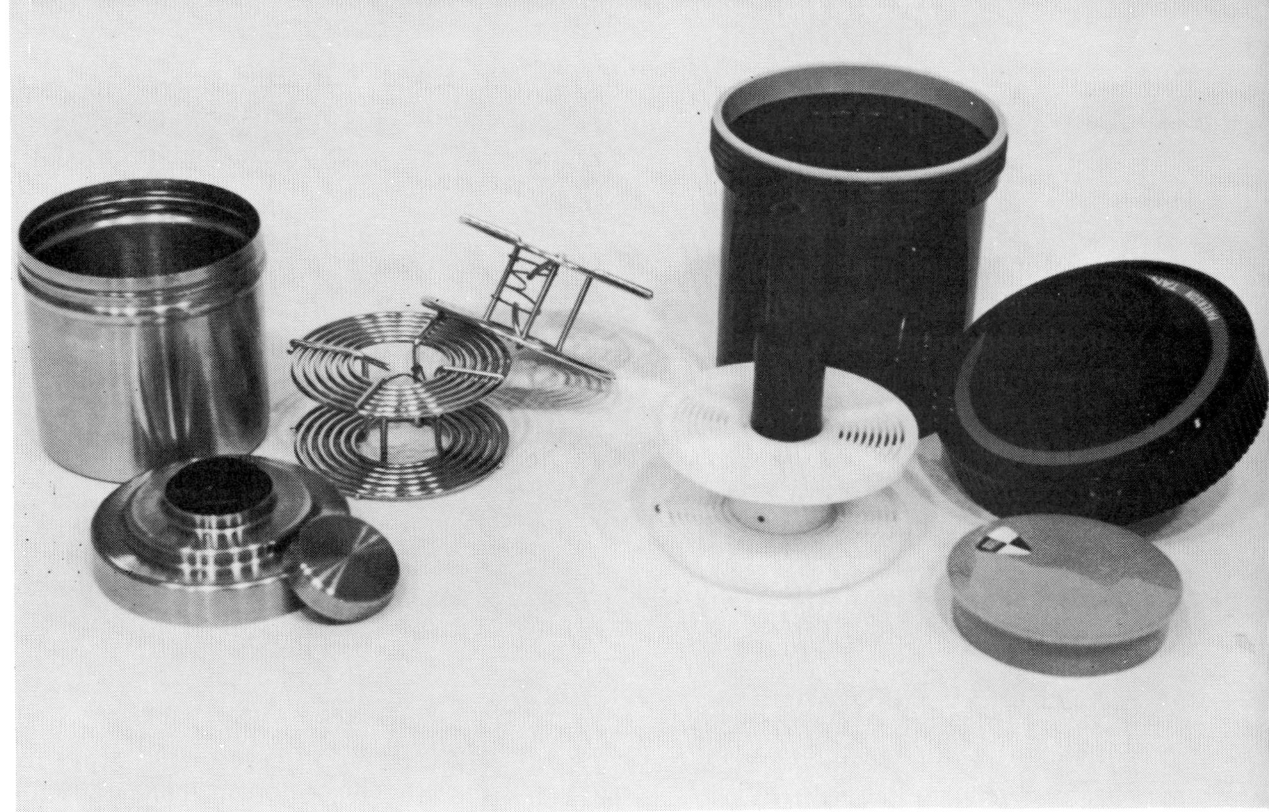

You can process 35mm film in either stainless-steel or plastic tanks. Nikor and Paterson types shown here.

to know about that. And some things are so important I may tell you about them several times, just to make sure you get the idea of how important those things are, too.

There is really nothing very tricky about the developing process. It is just paying attention to the details so you end up with beautiful negatives: Correctly developed and fixed, washed to ensure permanence and then dried in a dust-free area. The nice thing about doing your own is that you can see whether you got what you wanted when you clicked the shutter. In some cases you'll be able to go back later the same day—or the next day—to get the light at a different angle or reshoot to enhance some portion of the scene you'd like to show in a different way. There's no waiting for the film and prints to come back from a processor to find out whether you "got some good ones."

EQUIPMENT YOU NEED

There are equipment musts, so let's start with what you'll need to develop film. First you need a container to hold and support the film so all of its surface can be contacted by the developing and fixing solutions. A number of processing tanks are available—from inexpensive plastic ones—to those made of Type 316 stainless steel which will last a lifetime. Plastic tanks and reels are somewhat easier to load with film and the Paterson type I've illustrated has the added advantage of filling and dumping more quickly than the stainless-steel Nikor tanks. With a little practice you can load the stainless-steel reels with relative ease. Some people can load them faster than the plastic reels.

Both types are serviceable but I recommend the stainless-steel Nikor ones, even though the initial cost is greater. Some of the ones I have are now 25 years old and they still look and work like brand-new. A 16-ounce tank will process one roll of 120 or two rolls of 135 film.

Both plastic and steel tanks are called *daylight type,* meaning once the film is loaded onto the reels and placed in the tank and the lid installed—further procedures can be done in normal room light. Processing chemicals are poured into the tank through a baffled opening in the lid and emptied the same way. It takes about 10 seconds to fill or empty a 16-ounce Nikor tank—about 4 seconds to fill or empty the Paterson.

A thermometer is necessary because development depends on a time-and-temperature balance.

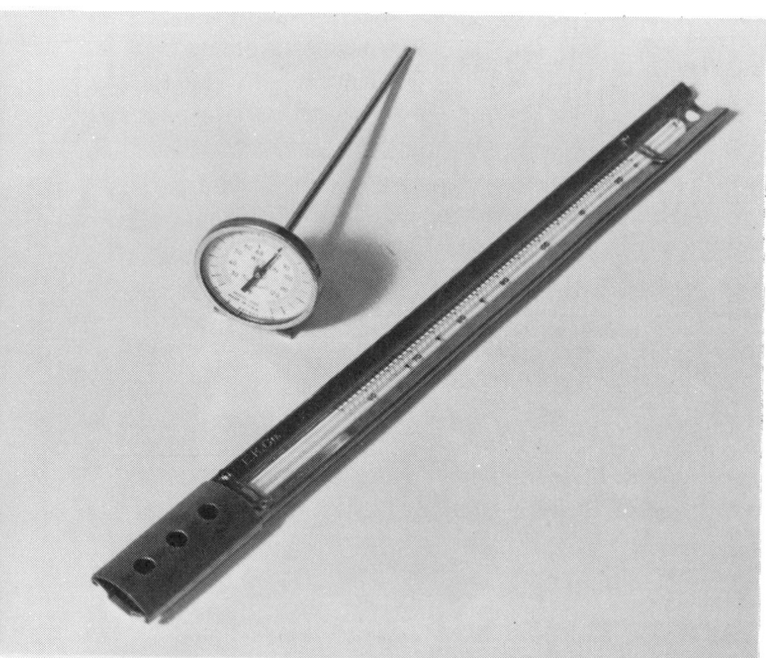

Two types of process thermometers, both the immersion type. The dial type by Weston is less expensive and somewhat handier but the Kodak Process thermometer is a bit more accurate. Weston also makes a "Mirroband" dial model. It is easier to read accurately because the mirror behind the pointer helps you to avoid parallax errors.

You have noticed the data sheet in the carton with the film. It gives processing instructions, together with several developers compatible with that film and developing times required for *specified* temperatures.

The manufacturer has determined that temperatures should range from a low of 65°F (19°C) to a high of 75°F (24°C) for each film and developer combination. Lower temperatures require excessively long developing times because chemical activity is slowed down. Higher temperatures speed up chemical activity, shortening developing time—possibly too short to work with easily—and cutting your margin for error. High temperatures also tend to soften the emulsion, increasing the chance for damage due to the slightest scrape on the film. Chunks of emulsion loosened during the wet processes are impossible to repair and they make black spots on your prints which you won't like.

The ideal processing temperature is 68°F (20°C) and all solutions should be kept as close as possible to this temperature. I'll say a lot more about this later because it is super-important.

Now you need a method of timing the process and several timers are available. For many years I used the simplest and most available timer—my wrist watch with a sweep-second hand. There are both windup and electric lab timers on the market, and I recommend the GraLab electric model. Its large dial glows in the dark and is equally useful for film processing and printing. Remember time—as well as temperature—is critical for most processes, so get a timer you can rely on. The GraLab reads time left to finish the interval you set on it. This eliminates remembering what time you started, always a problem with ordinary clocks or wrist watches.

A couple of plastic graduates, either 16- or 32-ounce, and a strainer-type funnel, round out the necessary hardware. I like 32-ounce graduates even when using only 16 ounces of solution, because they are handy when you get to the print making. You'll probably be happier with the white-plastic type because the clear rigid ones have a tendency to crack and chip with repeated use. Graduations marked in dark figures on white plastic are much easier to read than the clear raised markings on clear graduates. I avoid glass because it breaks so easily. It's hard to cut yourself on plastic!

Other items of equipment you'll need to process film are bottles to mix and store the chemical solutions in. It's handy to have an assortment of bottles in quarts, half-gallons and gallons. Actually you only need as many bottles of the appropriate size as you have solutions, but a few extra bottles will be put to use quicker than you might first imagine. There's always something else to try, as you'll see.

Bottles, whether plastic or glass, should be dark-brown to decrease the amount of light reaching the chemicals. Strong light and exposure to air greatly shorten the lives of processing solutions, *especially developer.*

The cheapest way to get bottles for chemical storage is to visit your local drugstore and ask for them. The druggist may give them to you or charge a small amount, depending on store policy. Such bottles probably contained concentrated syrups. They are usually one-gallon size, dark-brown glass, with handles on the necks and securely fitting screw-on plastic tops.

I personally prefer plastic bottles because there is less chance of getting cut on them if they should break accidentally. I have never met a

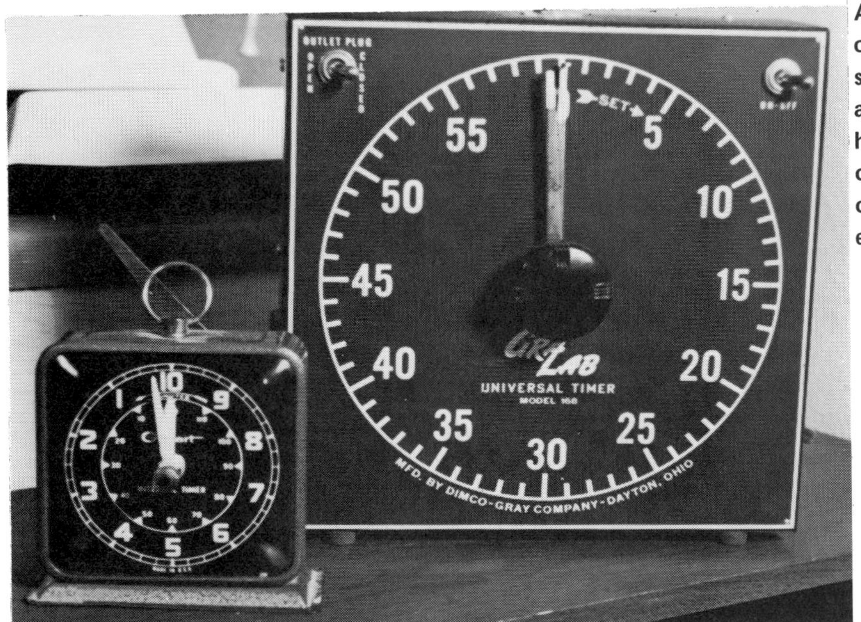

A pair of reliable processing timers. Smaller one by Gilbert sounds a bell alarm and is spring-operated. GraLab unit sounds a buzzer alarm if desired. It's electrically operated and has provision for timing your enlarger or other printing operations. Both can be obtained with luminous dials to make it easier to read them in complete darkness.

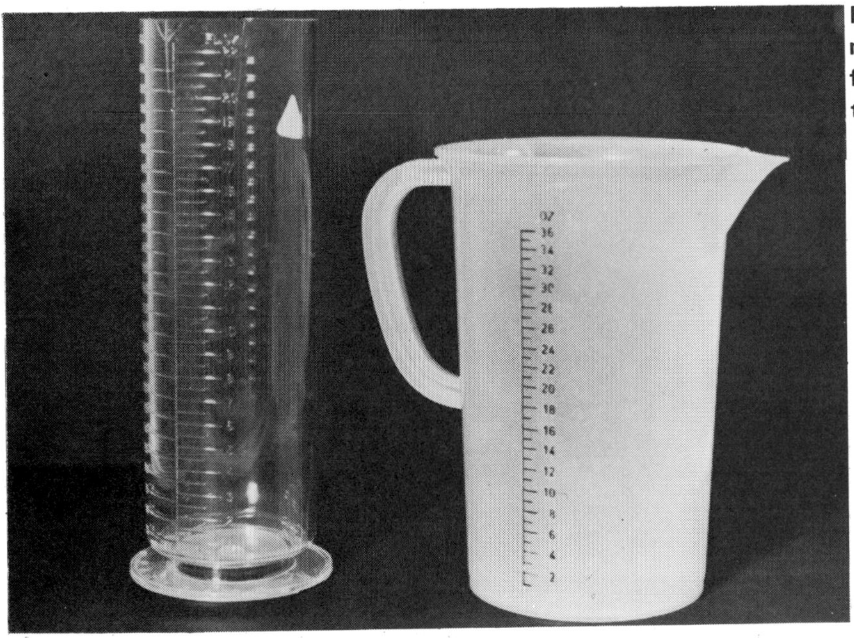

Darkroom graduates. White plastic with dark markings is easiest to read. Clear raised figures used on the clear graduate are sometimes hard to decipher.

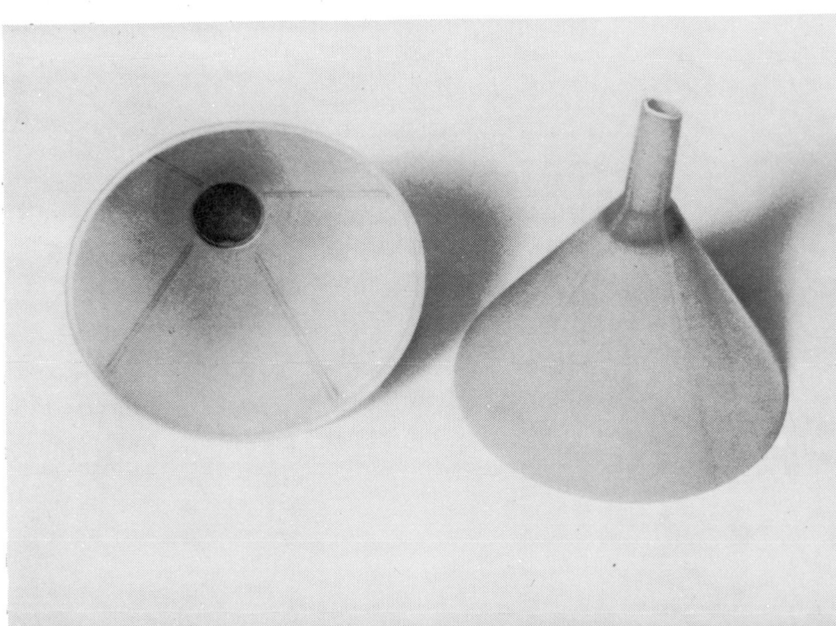

Always use a funnel with a screen strainer. It keeps out foreign material which may be abrasive or cause spots on the next roll of film developed.

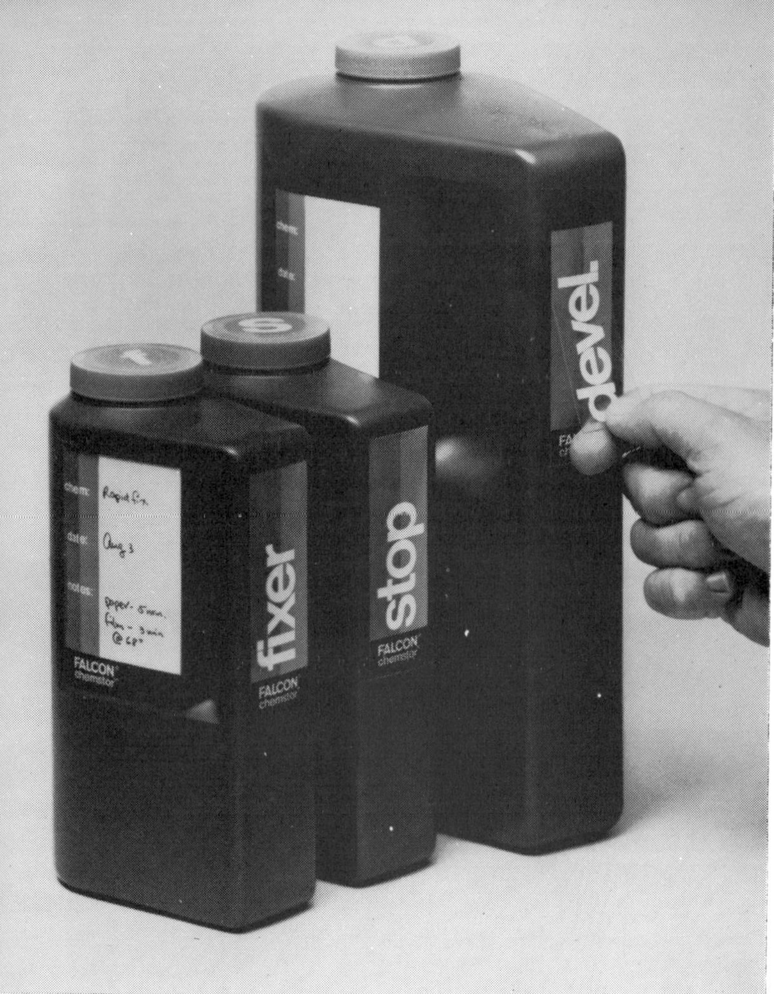

Chemstor brown polyethylene bottles for chemical storage. Flat sides permit space-saving storage and the preprinted labels ensure that the chemicals are returned to the proper bottle after use.

The chemicals needed to process your first roll of film. Developer D-76, fixer and Photo-flo-wetting agent. As always, FOLLOW DIRECTIONS for mixing.

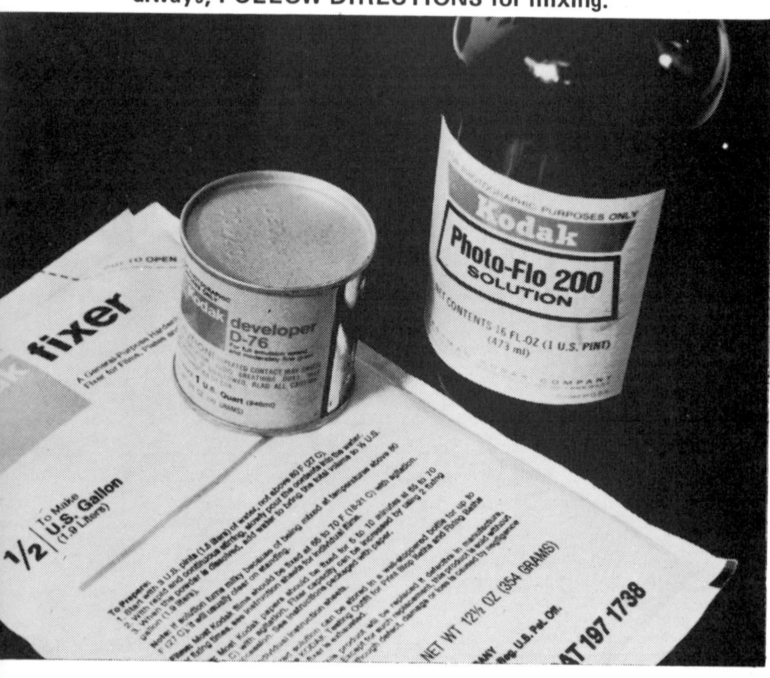

photographer who could claim he or she had not dropped a jug on the floor. Plastic containers are available in quart, half-gallon and gallon sizes at your camera store.

Falcon Safety Products, Inc. makes flat-sided polyethylene containers called *Chemstor* in quart and gallon sizes. They come with preprinted labels for the chemicals you will use: Developer, Stop, Fixer, Bleach, Toner and Stabilizer. Blank data labels are included for your own notations. Other manufacturers make plastic bottles in the usual round shape. For developer storage you'll want Falcon's *air-evac* collapsible plastic bottles which I'll say more about later.

Another item you'll find helpful is a one-gallon salad-dressing or mustard jar. Its wide-mouth opening works well for mixing solutions. Ask your favorite restaurant or lunch counter for one.

Having acquired the film tank, reels, thermometer, timer, graduate, funnel and storage bottles, get the chemicals you need.

PROCESSING CHEMICALS YOU NEED

Developer—This first chemical turns the exposed silver halides of the photographic emulsion into metallic silver and makes a visible image on the film. There are probably as many developers as there are films and the choice is largely a matter of personal preference. You should consider: Is it readily available locally; what are its keeping qualities; what are the processing times; what quantities are available; does the manufacturer recommend it for the film I'm using? It should be easy to obtain because it's a poor idea to switch formulas often. Again, standardize and know your materials!

Keeping qualities are important, especially if your processing adventures are separated by long periods. It's a waste to mix a gallon of chemical, use it once and let it sit for two or three months. Most developers will deteriorate during that time. If your processing schedule runs that way, you'll be better off to use one of the liquid-concentrate developers where you mix only as much working solution as you need. Or store your exposed film in the refrigerator until you have enough to warrant the purchase of a quart of developer which you'll dump down the drain at the end of the processing session.

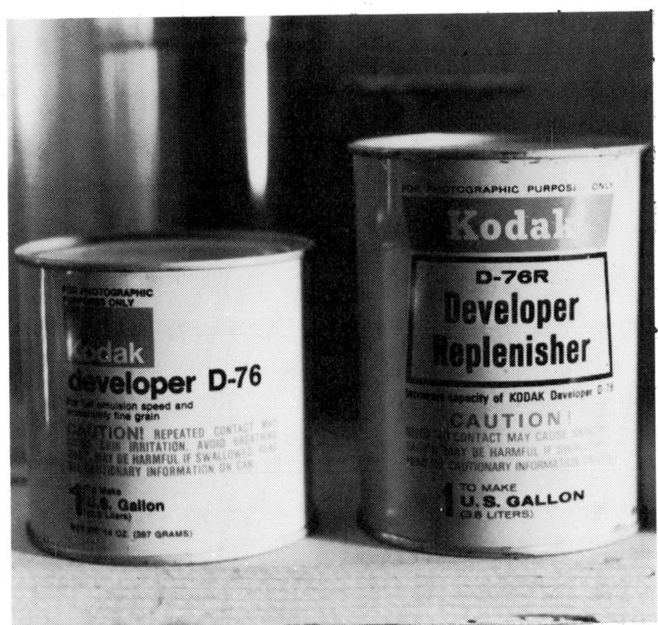

Kodak Developer D-76 is readily available and one of the most versatile developers on the market. You see here the most popular film developer around today. Also shown is D-76R replenisher, which is designed to prolong the life of the film developer when it is not used on a one-shot basis as I've recommended.

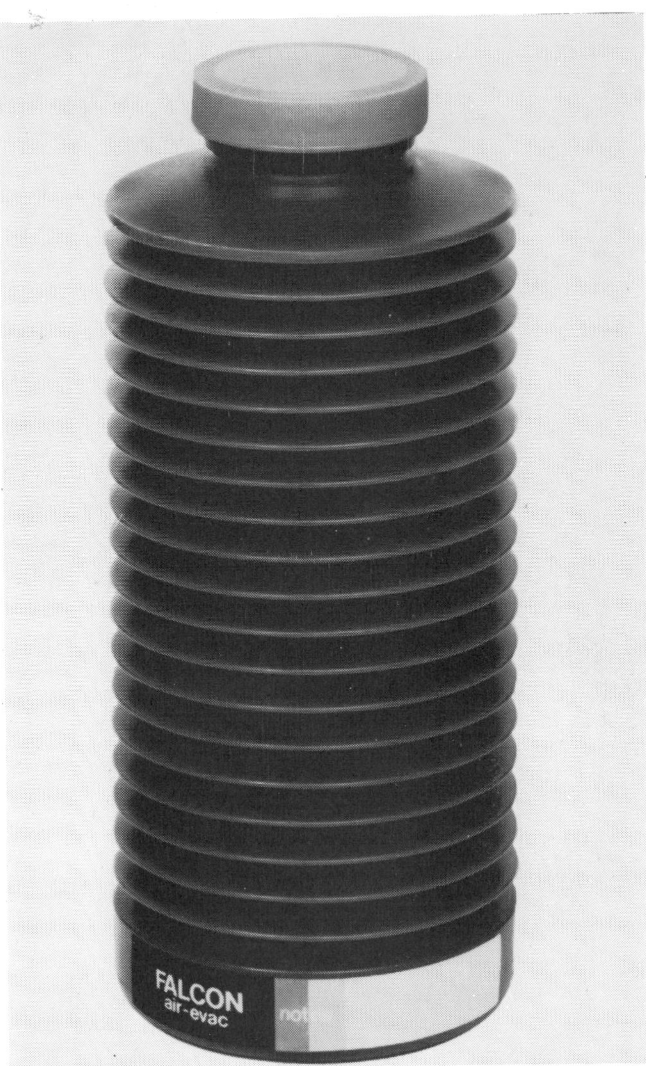

The air-evac chemical storage bottle is designed so air can be squeezed from a partially full bottle. Developers last longer when they are not weakened by oxidation due to exposure to trapped air.

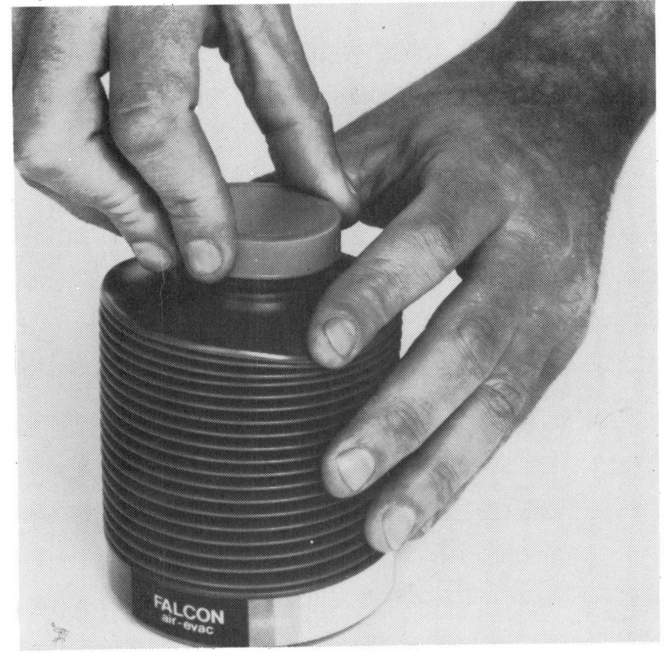

It is important to keep air out of the developer bottle. This can be done by gently squeezing the sides of the plastic bottle until the liquid reaches the pouring lip. While holding the solution at this level, screw on the cap securely. If you are using a glass or rigid-plastic storage containers, pick up a bag of marbles from your local variety store. After taking out the desired quantity of developer for your 1:1 solution, drop in a sufficient number of marbles to raise the solution level to the top.

The neatest solution I've seen for the problem of keeping air out of developer is a collapsible one-quart plastic bottle called *air-evac.* As you use developer, you just squeeze the accordion-fold until the liquid is level with the opening and screw on the cap. It's made by Falcon Safety Products and most camera stores carry it.

Shelf life of unused developer solutions is normally six months in a *full* bottle stored between 65°–75°F (18°–24°C) when stored in a dark place. Shelf life is about six weeks once you've started using the developer or if you keep the unused soup in a partially-filled bottle. If you store developer at higher temperatures, its life will be drastically reduced because it will deteriorate quicker. If you

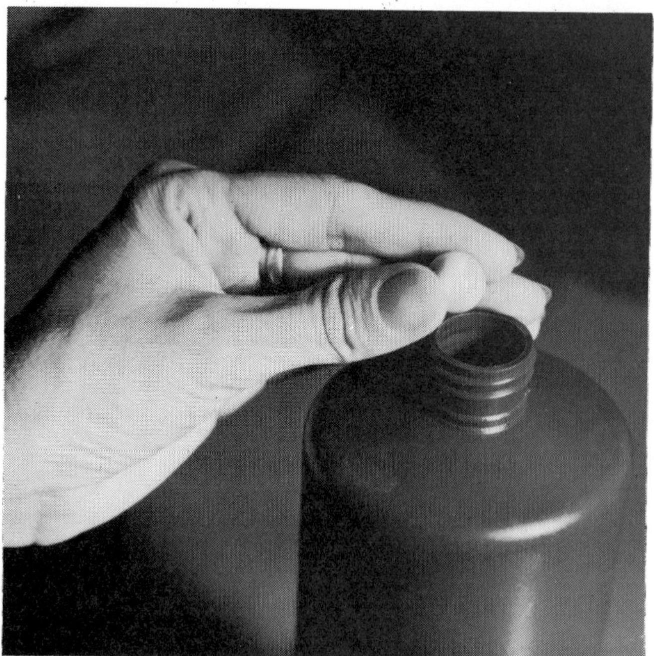

Keep a supply of marbles on hand to keep the developer level up in its bottle. This prevents loss of developer strength due to contact with air.

> **Plastic bottles**—Regular low-density polyethylene bottles should not be used for long term storage because oxygen diffuses through the polyethylene wall and will ruin the developer.

Always be sure that each chemical bottle is labeled. Include the date. Developer may keep up to two months in a full bottle with a tight cap. Throw it out if it turns dark and cloudy as that means it has oxidized and is no longer good.

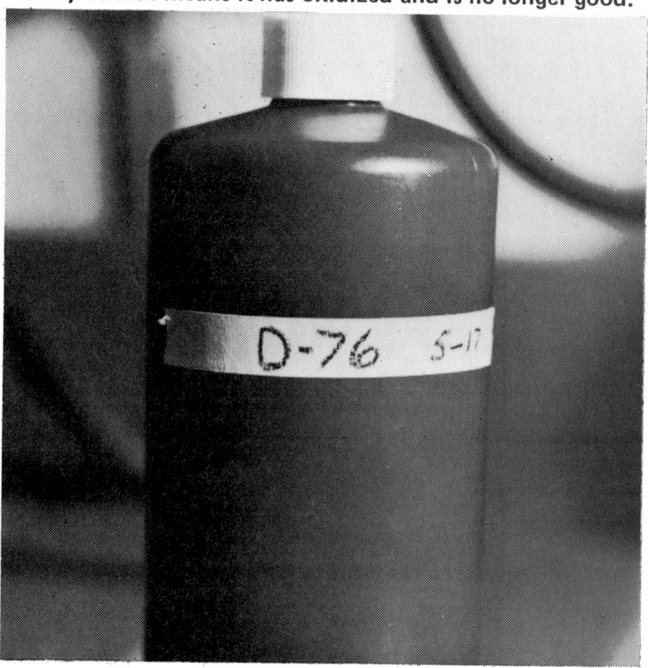

process only a couple of rolls per month it is foolish to mix chemicals in the gallon size, so buy chemicals in the smaller quart or half-gallon sizes if these fit your photographic way of life. Mark the label with the date you mixed the developer.

Processing times should be reasonable. Twenty minutes or so in the developer is an unnecessarily long time and can create a chemical fog on the film. Times shorter than five minutes indicate a rapid-working developing agent with the chance of increased grain, loss of shadow detail and possible uneven development. Times between five and ten minutes are normal and give the film normal development without excessive chemical action. The manufacturer of the film has spent countless dollars testing his product and has carefully weighed all of these factors so you can trust his recommendations.

Rinse or Stop-Bath—Next you need a plain-water rinse or a stop bath. I prefer the tap-water rinse at 68°F (20°C) because I find it effective and it gives me one less processing chemical to mess with and store. A water rinse dilutes the chemical the film emulsion absorbed and stops its action gradually. Developer action takes place when the solution is alkaline and an acid bath stops developer action just as soon as it covers the film.

If you choose to use the acid stop bath you will want a weak solution of acetic acid and water. The camera store sells glacial acetic acid. It is nearly pure at approximately 100% strength. In a well-ventilated area, mix this by slowly pouring three parts acid in 11 parts water to make a 28% *stock solution.* Label it POISON. Keep it in your

> **Don't get skinned**—Your skin may be sensitive to some developing agents. Direct contact may cause skin irritation. I suggest you keep your hands washed with a neutralizing soap such as Neutrogena when developing or printing. Better yet, wear a pair of household rubber gloves. Chapped, cracking hands are painful and ugly.
>
> This warning applies both to film processing and print making. The most common culprit is the chemical *Metol,* so read labels and heed warnings.

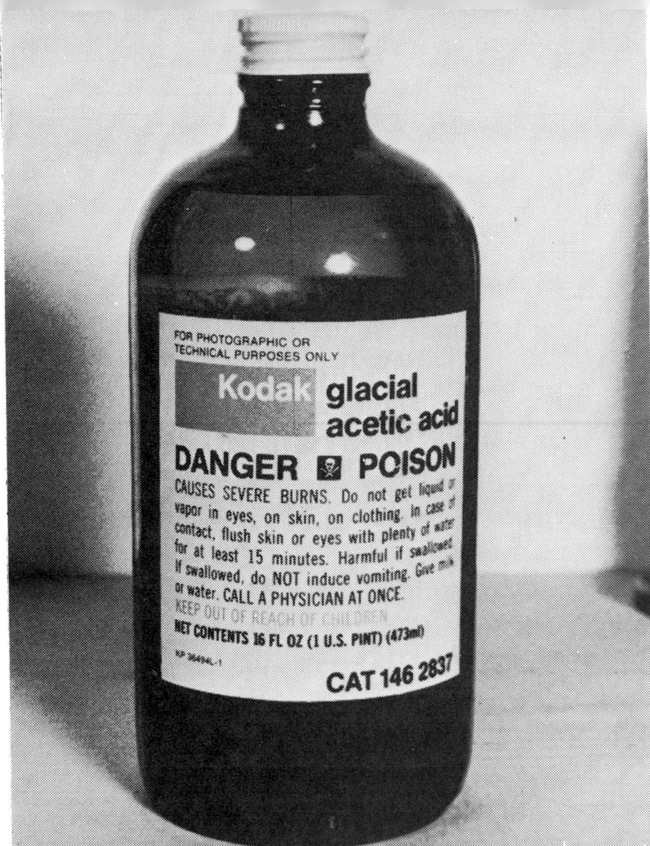

Glacial acetic acid makes stop baths for film and paper. It solidifies or "freezes" at 61°F. (16°C.). Crystals expand on melting; warm the bottle from the top gently to avoid breaking it.

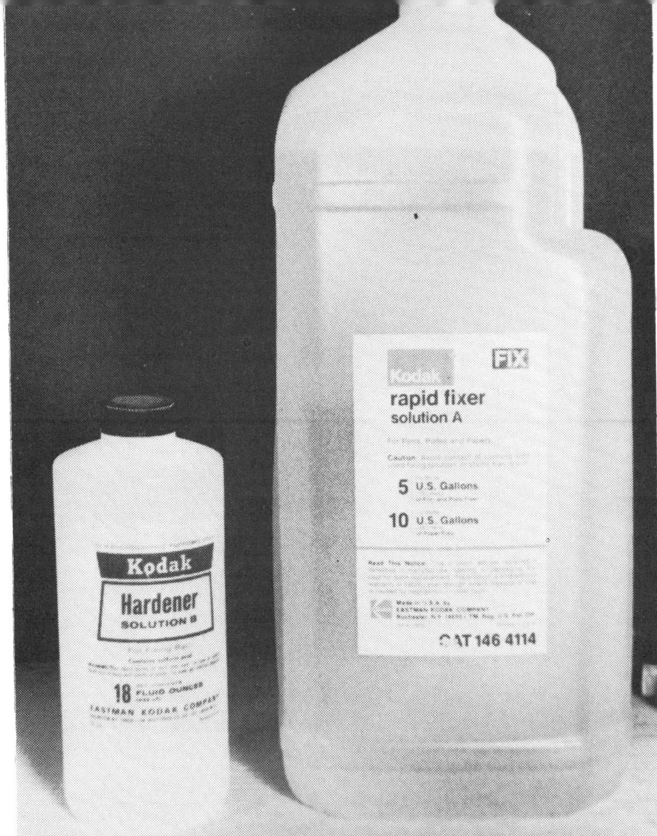

I prefer Kodak rapid fixer to the powdered form of hypo because it is easier to mix, works faster and has a longer life. Follow mixing instructions on container. REMINDER: Always follow the recommendations of the manufacturer.

darkroom, out of the way of your children. Lock up the glacial acetic acid and the stock solution so no one else can get to it as it is really potent stuff. Dilute the 28% stock solution by adding 1¾ ounces to 1 quart of water for the working stop bath solution. Always add acid to water. If you do the opposite the solution could boil and spatter the acid on you, causing burns or other damage.

Acetic acid may cause skin irritation. When you use either glacial or stock solutions, do so carefully in a well-ventilated area. The fumes are toxic. It smells like very strong vinegar.

If you use too much acid in your stop bath it can cause gas bubbles in the film emulsion, making small black spots on your prints.

Fixer—Next is the chemical which fixes or makes the developed image permanent. Commonly called *hypo,* the active ingredient is sodium thiosulfate or, in the case of rapid fix, ammonium thiosulfate. Good terms to throw out across the coffee table to make friends think you're pretty sharp.

Fixer dissolves the *unexposed* silver salts in the film emulsion and dissolves the antihalation backing—the dark-gray or bluish material on the base side of the film. During exposure of the film the antihalation backing keeps light which passes through the film from reflecting back to create fog or a double image in the emulsion.

The fixer works its wonders in two to ten minutes, depending on the type you use and how new it is. Kodak Fixer will clear film in five to ten minutes. Kodak Rapid-Fix takes only two to four minutes and should be considered when time is important. Regardless of what fixer you use, a good rule is to leave your film in the fixer for twice the time it takes for the film's milky appearance to be removed. This is called *clearing.* This ensures that all unexposed silver has been dissolved and the negatives will be permanent if you wash them correctly. If you've seen negatives with a brownish cast they were probably fixed wrong and all unexposed silver was not removed.

Wetting Agent—The only other chemical you will use is something like Kodak Photo-Flo or liquid dishwashing detergent. Water contains dissolved minerals which will remain as deposits on the film

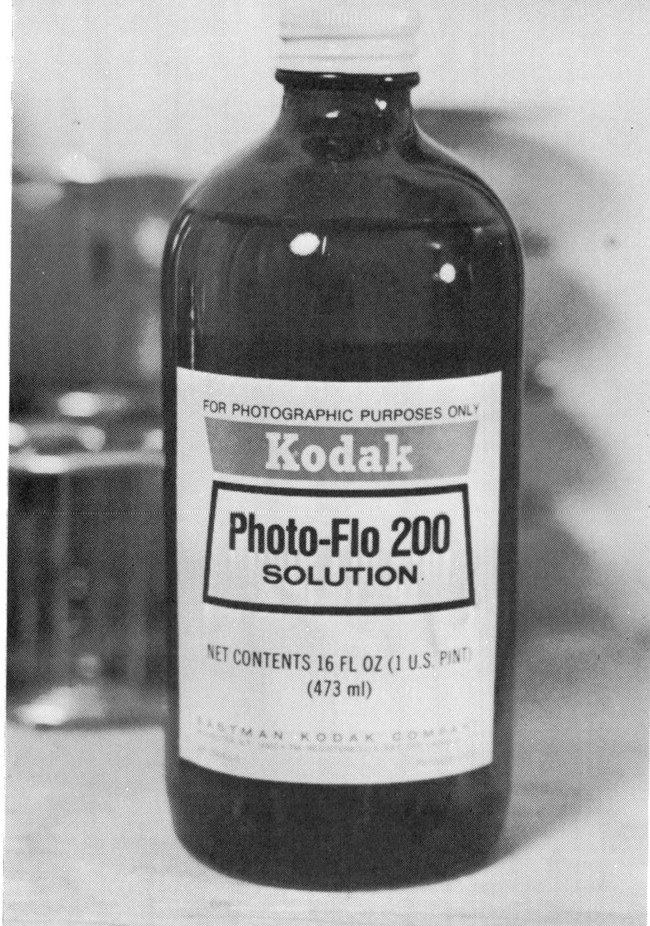

A little bit goes a long way. Two or three drops to the pint will suffice. A good investment to help keep film free of waterspots while drying. But use it sparingly. Too strong a mixture will cause a build-up of sludge on the film.

surface after drying wherever water drops did not run off. The wetting agent reduces the surface tension of the remaining water on the film surface so it tends to run down to the bottom of the film. Because the wetting agent helps the water to run off the film, it also helps the film to dry faster. Quicker drying may reduce dust-spot accumulation on the film surface, so the wetting agent reduces the possibility of water spots, water streaks *and* dust particles on the dried film. It promotes cleaner, faster drying at the same time. If the water in your area is very hard, this step will be essential. If you notice a white film, spots or streaking on your film after drying, use a wetting agent.

If you have these deposits they will be apparent on the base or shiny side of the film. Wipe them off with very gentle strokes of a dry long-staple cotton ball. Kodak and others make film cleaners for this purpose. But regardless of the cleaning technique, *gentleness* is the watch word.

Remember: Magnification of the image through enlargement means *magnification of any blemishes.*

THE ESSENTIAL VIRTUE

I should emphasize the cardinal rule of darkroom technique—CLEANLINESS. Have some old towels to wipe counter tops and dry tanks, reels and any other hardware you use. Everything used for processing film or prints must be rinsed and dried after use. Take care with all chemicals. Don't spill or splash them on the working surfaces. Chemicals will dry as white spots and are easily transferred to sensitized materials such as film and paper, especially if you live in an area with high humidity. Wash your towels often.

The same goes for your hands. Always wash after contact with any chemical to avoid contaminating materials, utensils or other chemical solutions. Even when your hands are dry and clean, handle film only by the edges. Fingerprints are tough to eliminate and if you are one of those unfortunates who has high skin acidity, the oil in *your* fingerprints can etch the film permanently.

Even if you've never washed a dish or pan in your life, this is the place to start. It's a must. Warm water and soap such as Neutrogena will do the job. Make sure your hands are dried thoroughly after washing.

If you get into technical photographic literature you will encounter the expression *pH,* a measure of relative acidity or alkalinity. Water is neutral with a pH of 7. Smaller numbers indicate acid, down to a pH of 1. Higher numbers are alkaline up to pH 14. Because photographic chemicals are very sensitive to pH, it's important not only to be clean but also to avoid the possibility of dirt or pollutants causing pH changes in the solutions.

It's also important to keep your hands chemically neutral which is why I recommend a neutral soap such as the brand Neutrogena. There are other solid and liquid hand soaps with a pH value near 7, because some skin conditions require it.

The curious term *pH* comes from the German *potenz Hydrogen* if memory serves me. It is scientifically complicated but anybody can remember that it's a scale from 1 to 14 with 7 in the middle. Chemists also use the word *basic* to mean alkalinity so you can remember that as the numbers go up from 1, the nature of the solution changes alphabetically—from Acid to Basic or A to B. That

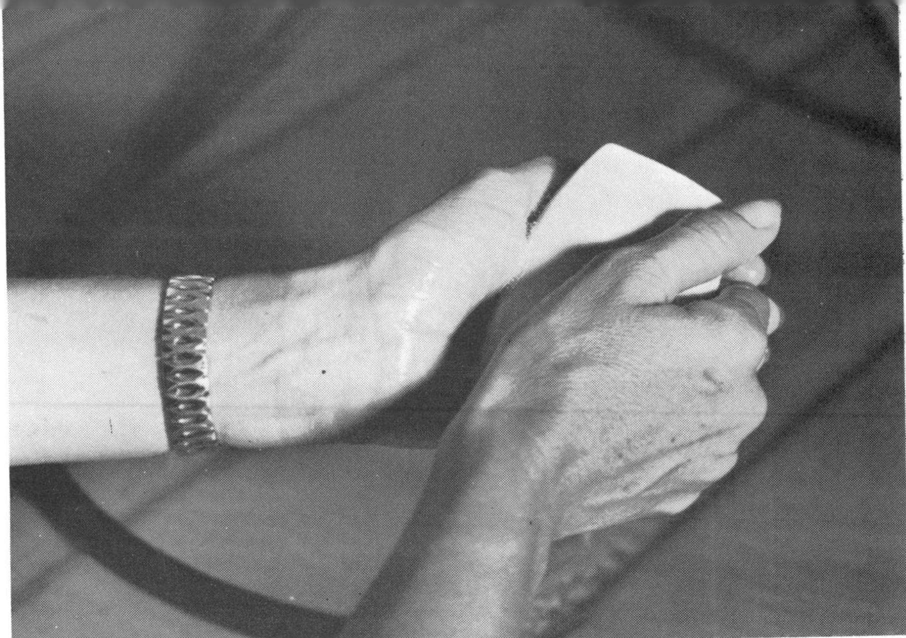

KEEP YOUR HANDS CLEAN AND FREE FROM CHEMICALS! Wash after contact with developer, stop bath or fixer.

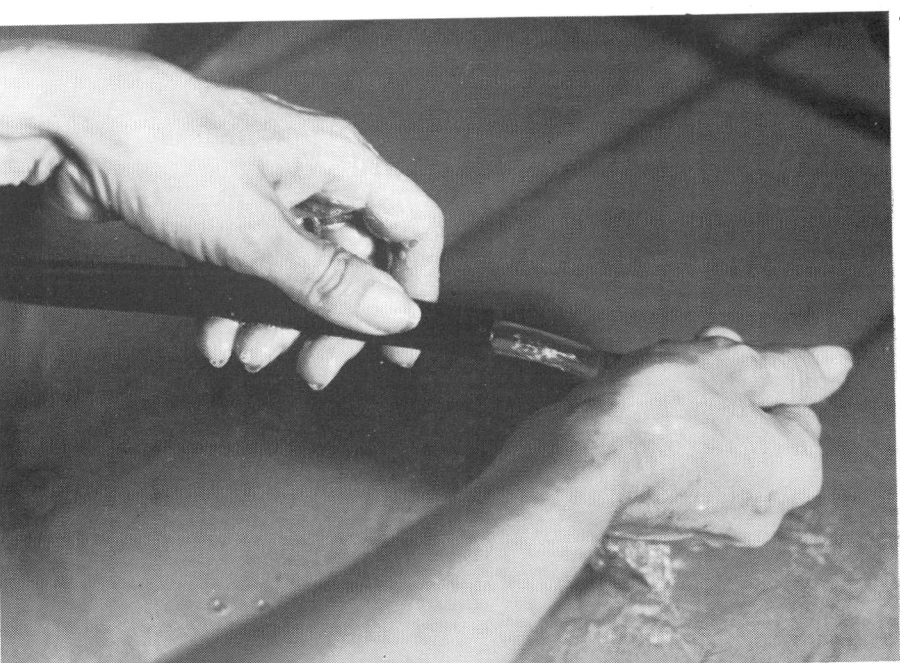

. . . rinse . . .

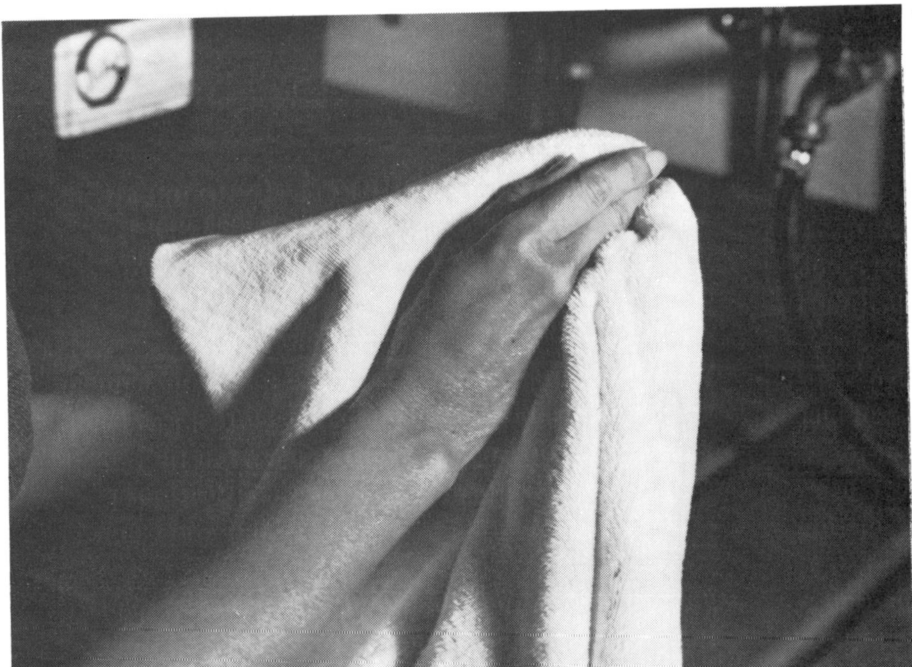

. . . dry!

After working, use a hand lotion. Massage it into your finger tips and around the nails to avoid skin problems from photo chemicals.

---

bunch of incidental information should certainly improve your image at cocktail parties among chemists and other types of drinkers.

Now you know about the hardware and chemicals to develop your film. I've given you data and helpful hints as we've gone along so you have an idea of what to do. I'll give a summary and some hints first and then go through the process step-by-step.

HINTS AND TIPS

You'll find practically anything photographic has an instruction sheet or manual with it. It's well worth your time to go through this information. Some instruction sheets are not as clear as they should be, but the instructions will start you in the right direction. READ ALL INSTRUCTIONS.

When loading film onto reels for developing, plastic reels must be completely dry, and you must hold the reel lightly so the reel edges are not warped. With steel reels you can manage even though they are slightly damp, but don't try to put a lot of pull on the film. Allow it to wind itself onto the reel once it is started squarely. Too much pressure will cause the film to miss a guide and double over itself. Where film comes in contact with itself, that area will not develop or fix and that portion of the picture will be lost.

If by some chance your camera has damaged an area along the edge of the film, great care is necessary in loading the film on the reel. Just be deliberate and gentle when loading the reels and all will be well.

In the dark, use a regular beer-can opener to pry the flat end off the 35mm film magazine. Cut off the tapered end of 35mm film and load the reel. At the end of the roll, cut off the taped-on spool and you're ready to load the reel into the tank. If you are using roll film with a paper backing, separate the film from the paper backing as you load the reel. Cut the film at the taped end end and discard the paper.

Instant-load plastic film magazines have the exposed film in the larger end which is simply broken off and pulled apart. Again, there is a paper backing to separate from the film and throw away. Although the negative size of this film is different than 35mm negatives, 126 film is processed on the same size developing reel. It is rather short, so don't be alarmed when you run out of film before you run out of reel. Practice loading

DO IT IN THE DARK! All film-loading steps pictured on these pages are done in total darkness until the reel is in the tank and the lid is installed.

Loading 35mm Film

A series of steps to load a daylight tank. Open film canister with the blunt end of a beer-can opener on the flat end, not the end with the film spool projecting.

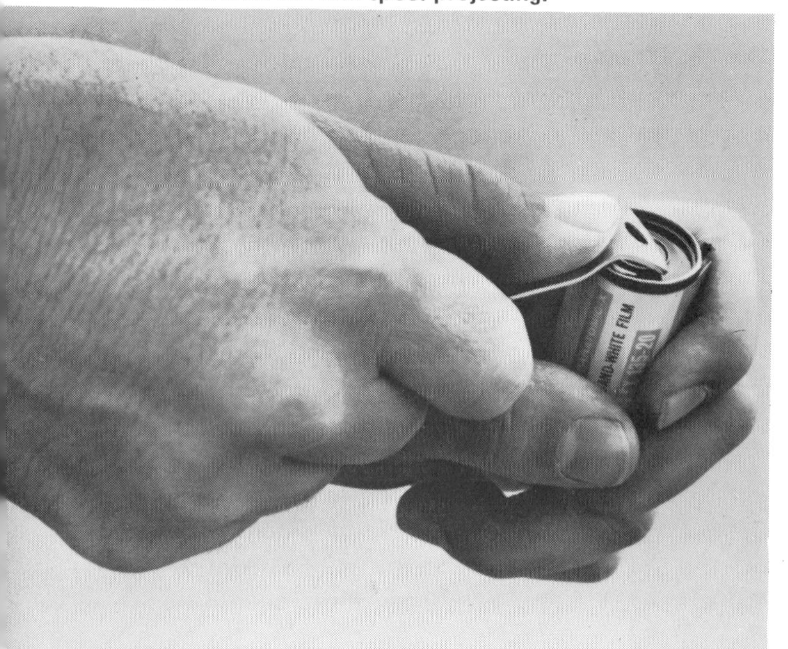

Cut the tapered film end free and discard it.

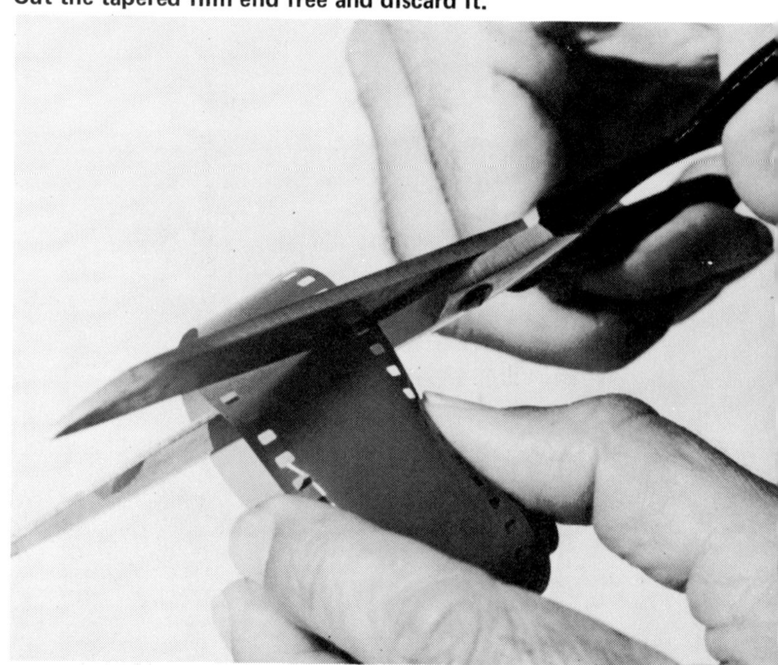

Using a slight bowing pressure, insert the end of the film into the spring clip off the reel. Note which way the film track spirals so you won't be trying to wind the film backwards away from the spiral in the dark.

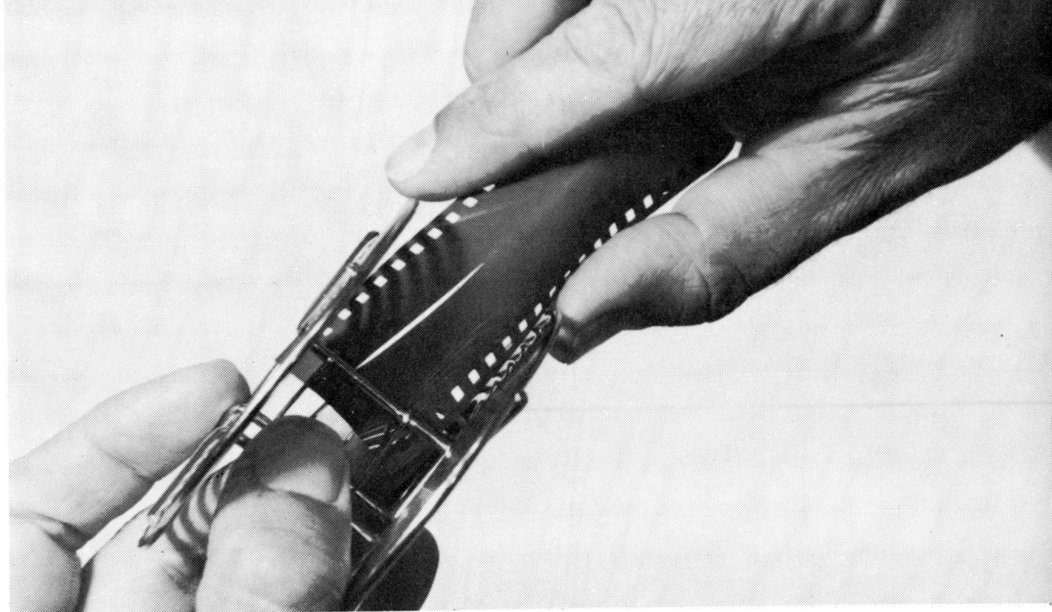

Handle the film only by the edges and still using slight edge pressure, allow the film to flow onto the reel. Turn the reel as you wind the film into the spiral tracks or guides.

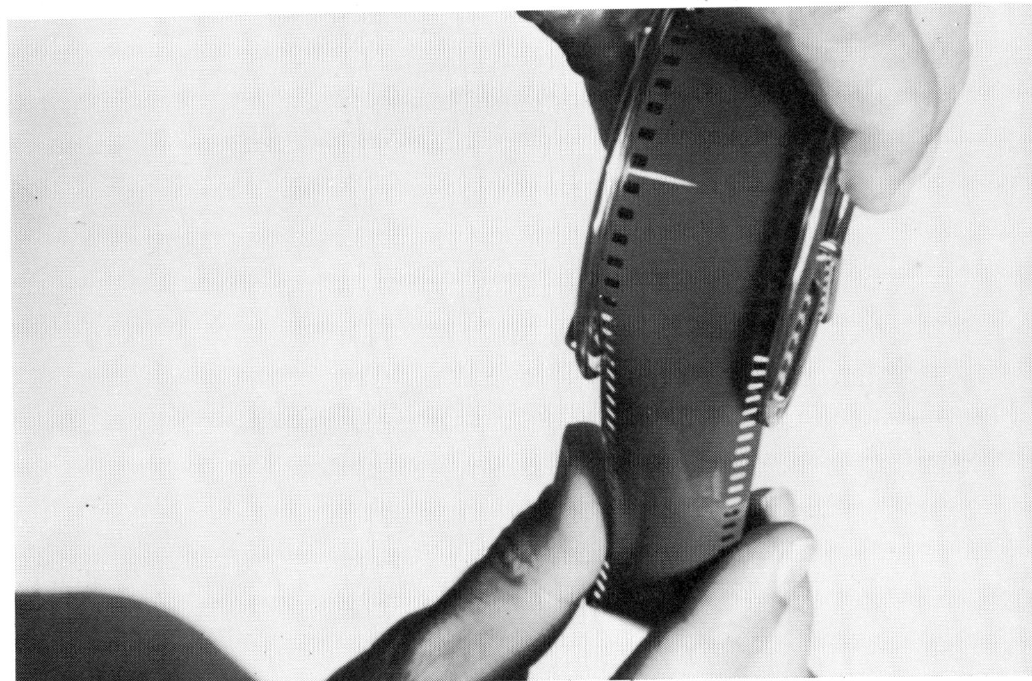

If you have somehow damaged the film edge, go VERY slowly while winding. It will go but only with care! Film torn this badly should probably be trimmed so the protruding piece won't contact the film opposite it in the reel. Such could cause clear spots on the developed film.

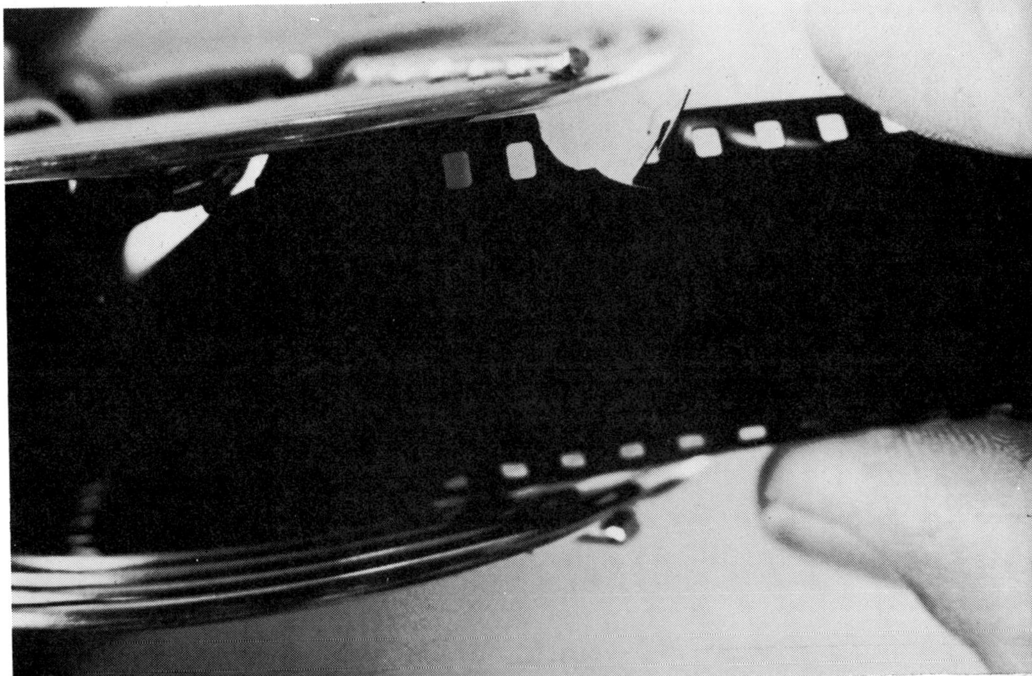

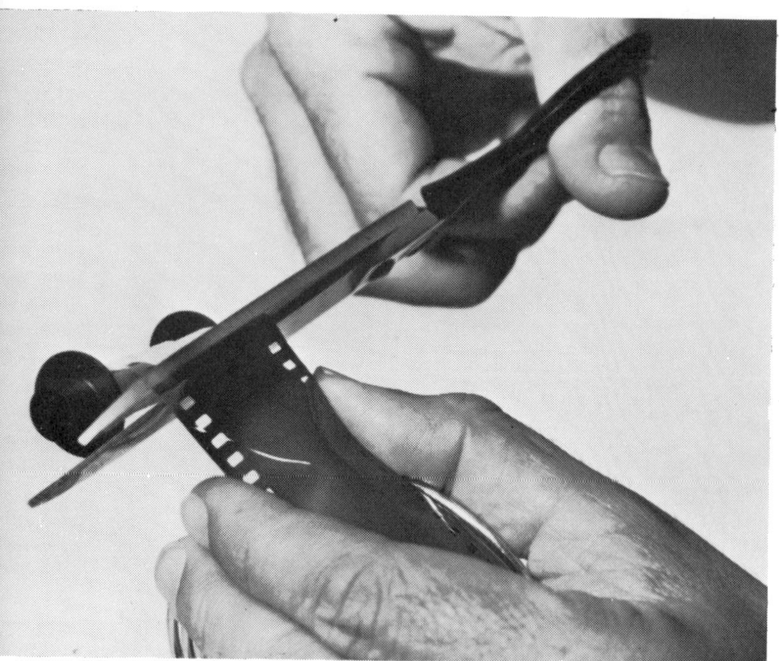

When you reach the spool, cut the film as close to the tape as possible and discard spool. If you like, bend 1/2 inch of the film across the width to stiffen the end of the film so it will tend to stay in the reel.

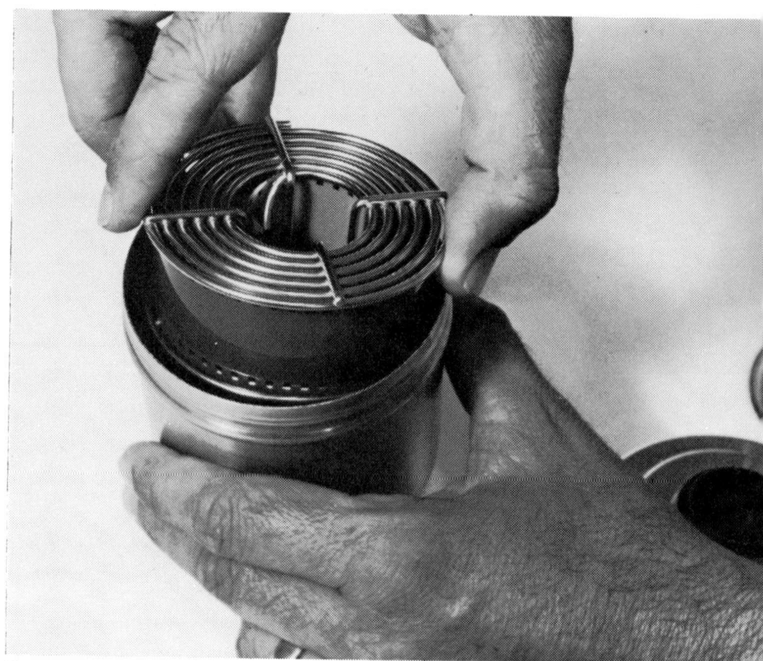

Place the loaded reel into the developing tank.

If you are using a 16-ounce developing tank with two reels place an empty reel on top of the loaded one to restrict the movement of reel during agitation. Overagitation is as harmful as too little.

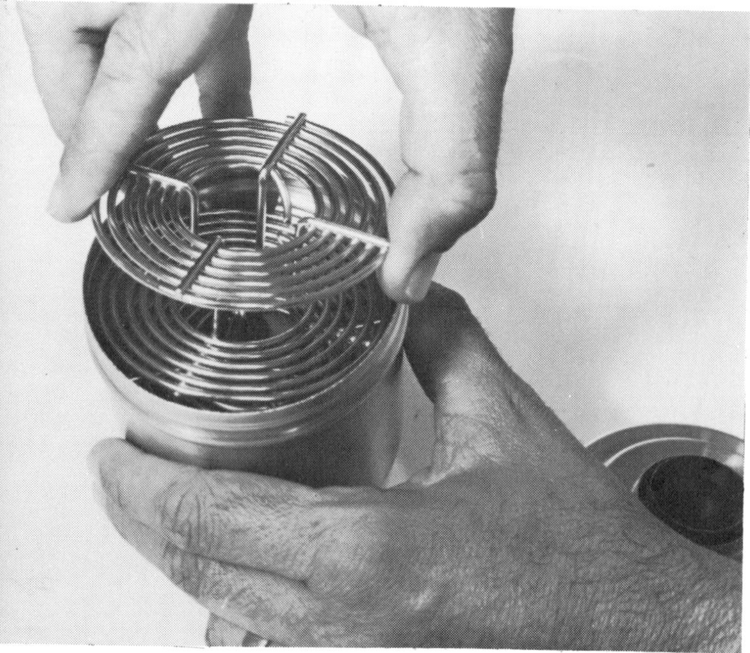

Place the lid on the developing tank and switch on the room light.

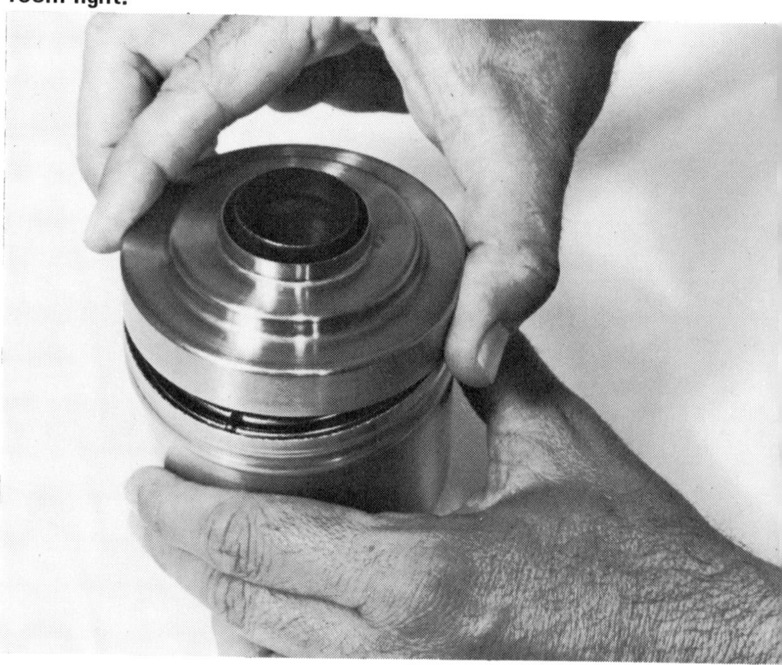

Loading 120 Roll Film

When preparing to load a film with 120 size material, begin in the dark by tearing the sealing strip from the roll using a fingernail.

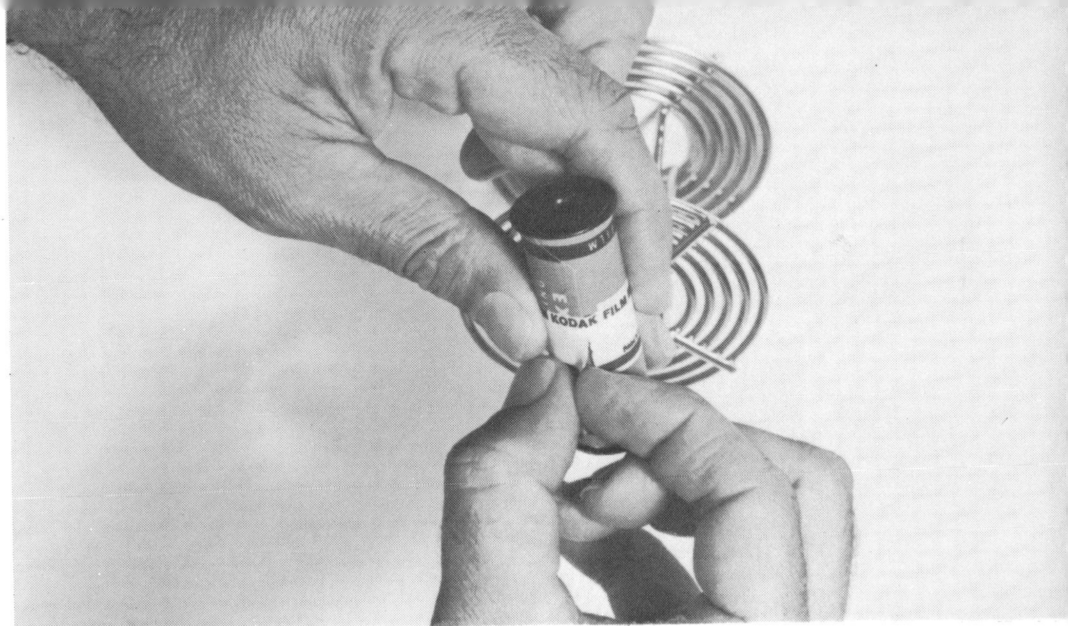

Unroll the film and separate it from the protective paper. Cut the film from the paper at the joining tape. DISCARD THE PAPER SO YOU ARE SURE YOU ARE DEVELOPING THE RIGHT STRIP!

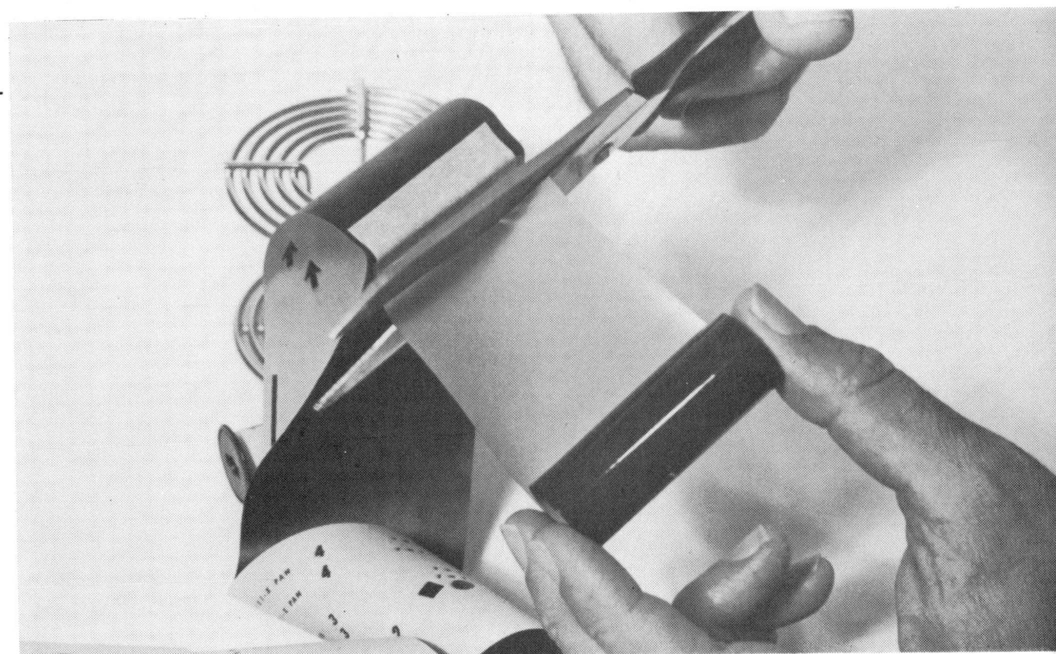

Load the film on the reel by starting it squarely under the spring clip. Observe which way the film track spirals so you won't be trying to wind the film backwards against the spiral in the dark.

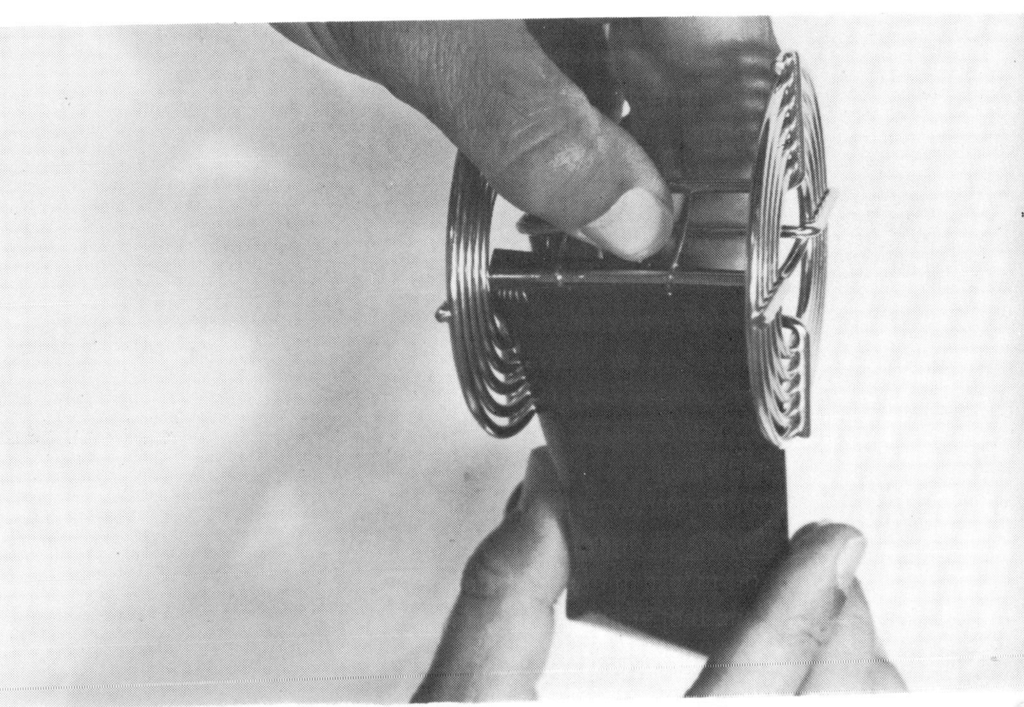

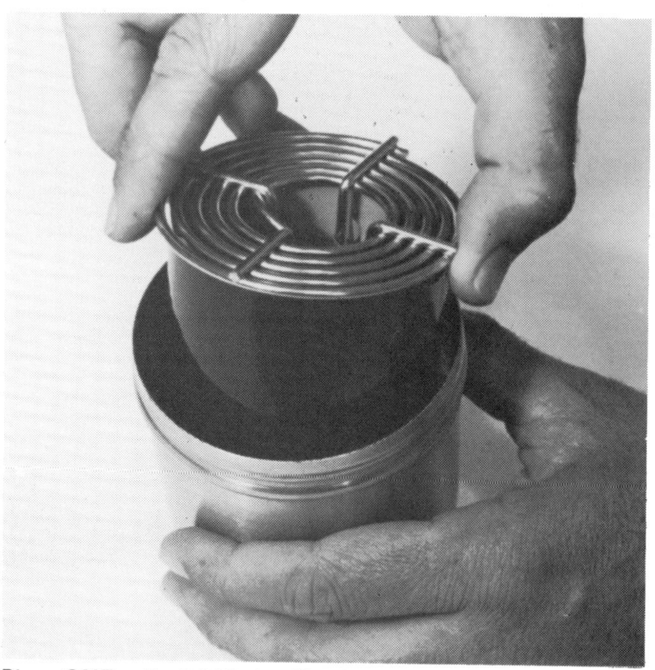

Place ONE roll of 120-size film in a 16-ounce developing tank.

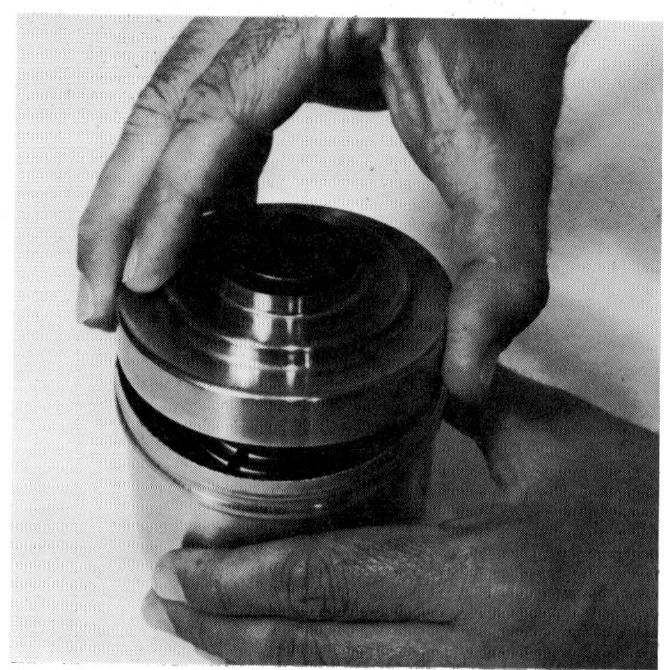

Place the cover on the tank and switch on the room light.

Loading 126 Cartridge Film

To load a processing reel with film from an instant-load cartridge, first break the plastic cartridge in two by hand. The film is in the big end.

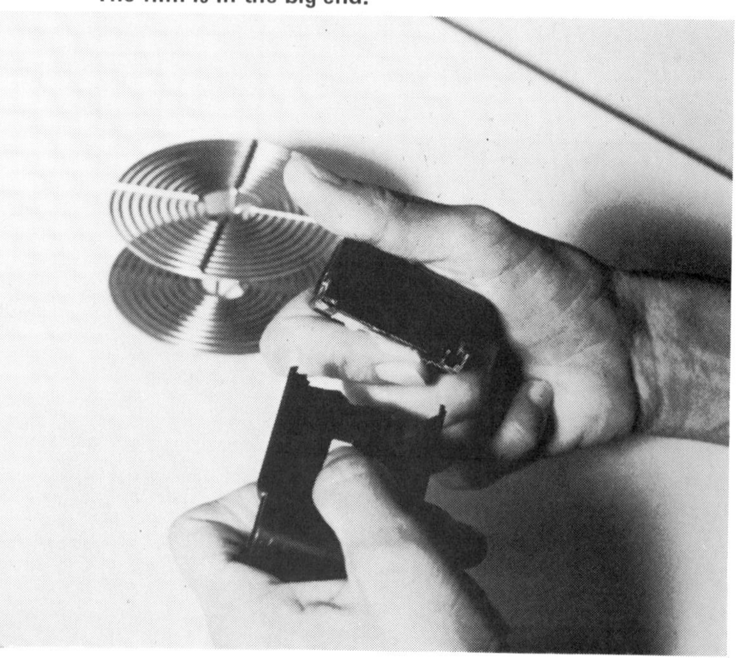

Remove the loose plastic covering the film roll.

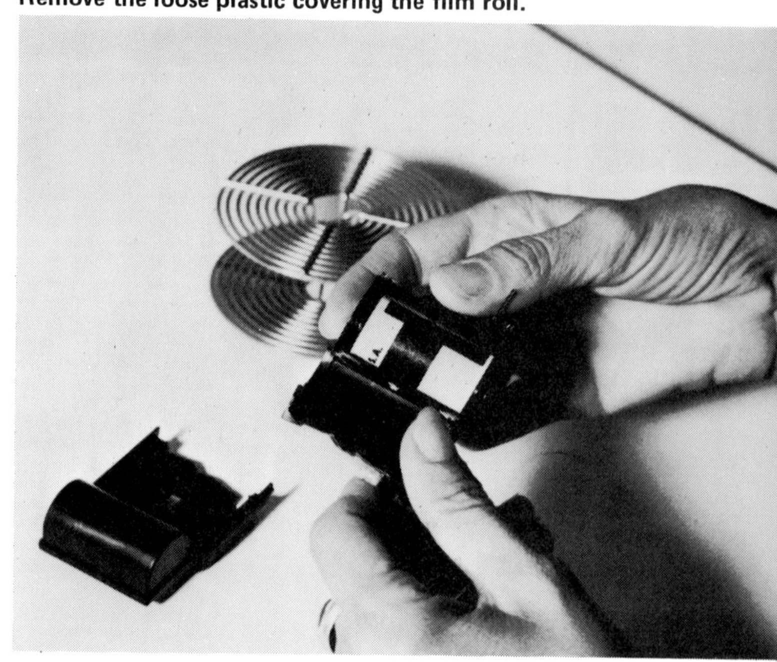

Remove the paper-covered film roll and discard the plastic fragments.

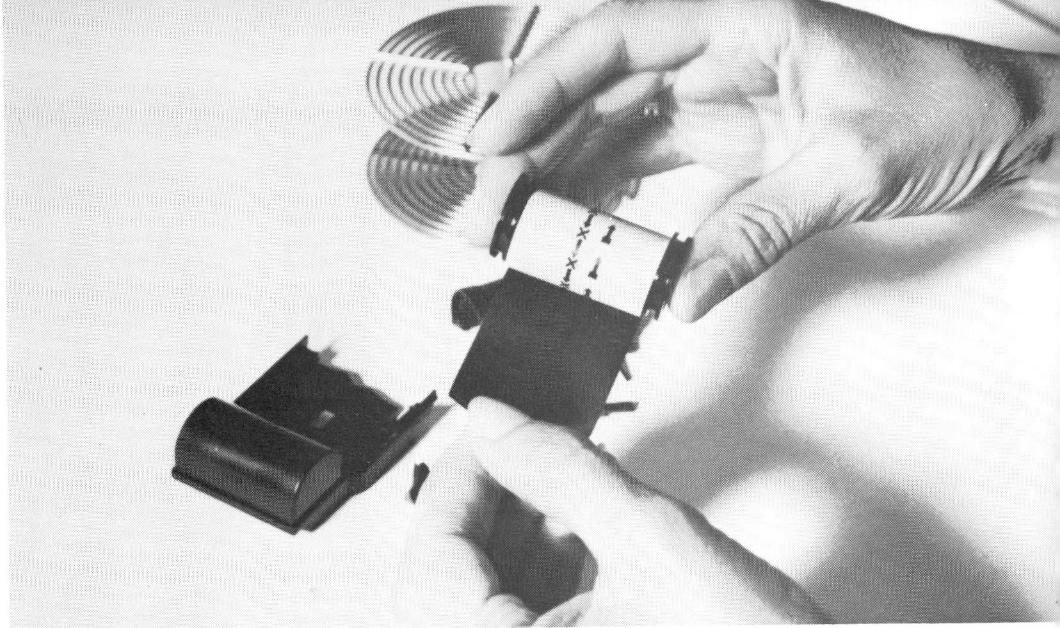

Unroll the film-paper combination and cut the film free at the tape end. Discard the paper so you won't develop the wrong strip!

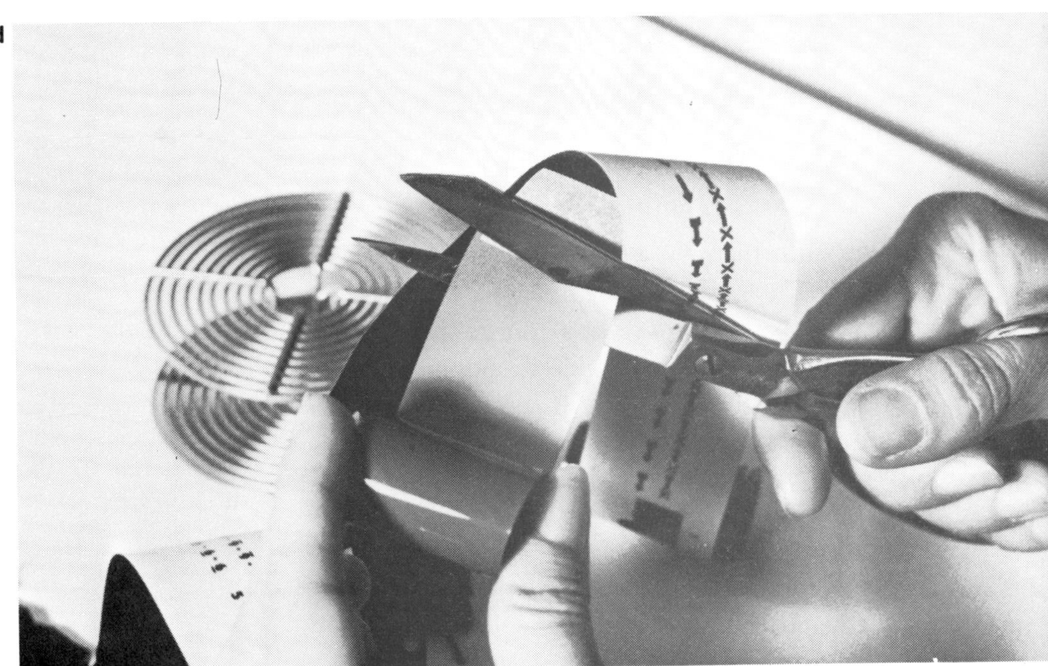

Load the film onto the reel in the same manner as that for 35mm. Don't be alarmed when you feel the film on the loaded reel. It is quite short and won't even begin to fill up the reel. Place the loaded reel in the developing tank, hold in place with an empty reel if only developing one roll, put on tank cover and switch on room light.

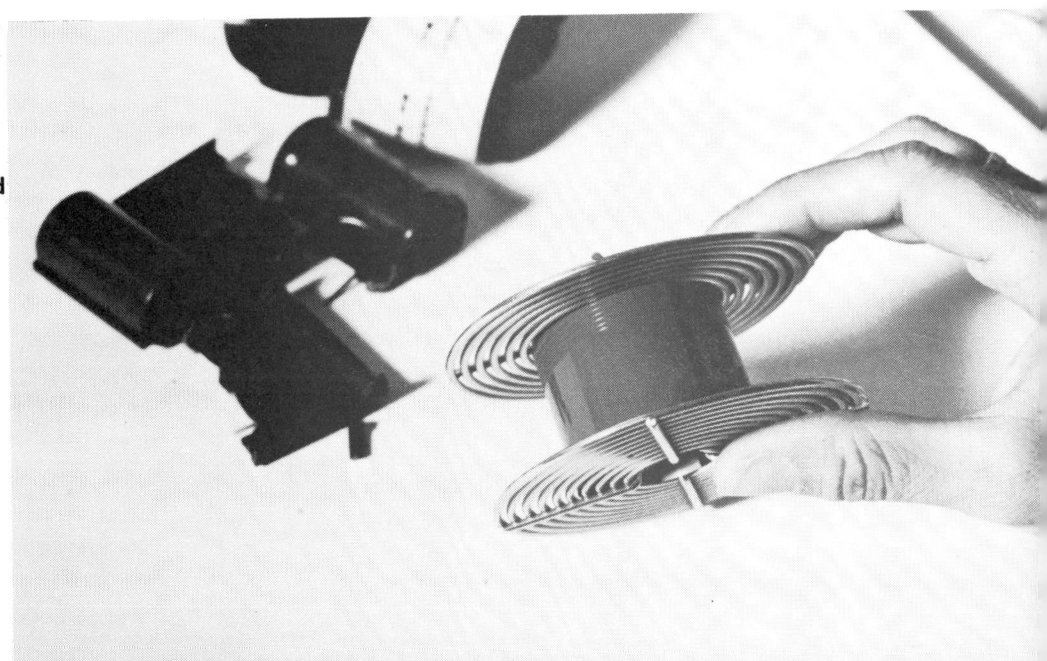

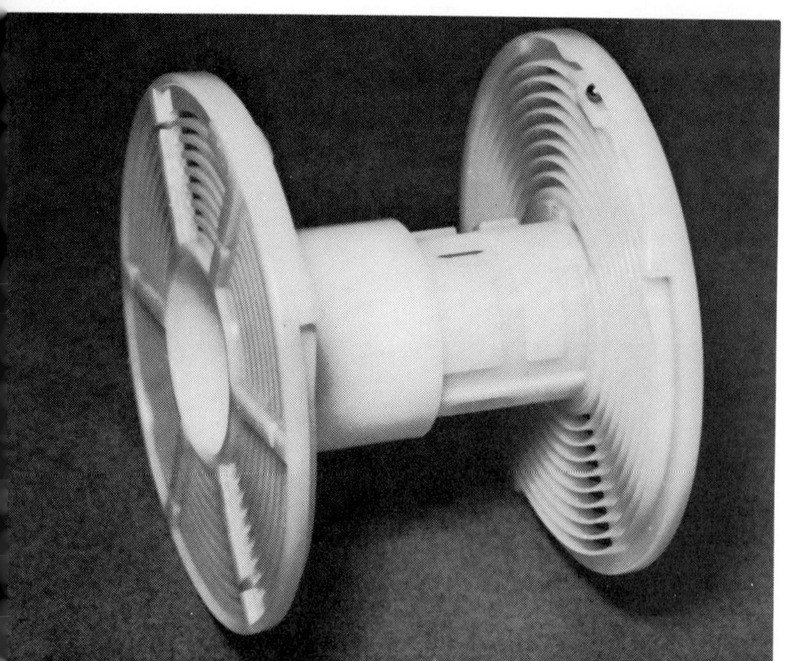

Plastic film reels come with some tanks. This Paterson reel adjusts from 35mm to 120. Stainless-steel reels work with only one film size.

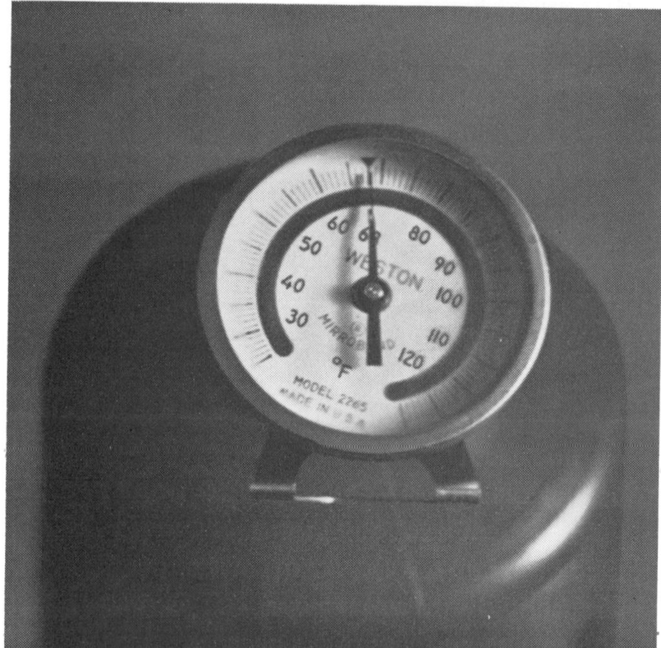

Make sure that the developing solutions are at the correct temperature—68°F. (20°C.). Thermometer is shown inserted into one of the brown-plastic bottles. This Weston Mirroband thermometer is very easy to read. The mirror helps ensure you are looking straight at the needle to get an accurate reading.

the film onto the reel in the daylight. Get a roll of film at the cheapest possible price. Your dealer may even have a roll of out-dated film he'll give you when you buy all this film-developing paraphernalia. Tell him you want it so you can practice loading the reel in daylight. First you do it with your eyes open. Then practice with your eyes shut. Only peek when you get into trouble. Keep doing it until you don't have to peek. Try to visualize how you will tell which way the spiral film track goes when you can't look at the reel. Get good at loading the reel before you try it in the dark with a real exposed roll, because then you are not allowed to peek.

Once the reel is loaded and still in the dark, put it in the developing tank and put the lid on. Now the room lights can be turned on or you can take the tank out of the changing bag. Because you knew you'd be using them, you brought the chemicals to the required temperature of 68°F (20°C), including a bottle with the rinse water or the stop bath. If your chemicals are stored where they get a little warmer than that, a few minutes in the refrigerator will bring them to the working temperature. During the winter a short time in a warm room or in a sink or tray filled with warm water will get them up to temperature. Keep

Pour the required amount of developer into a graduate. Then fill tank from the graduate and you'll know the tank is really full. If tank won't fill fast enough when it is level, tilt it slightly.

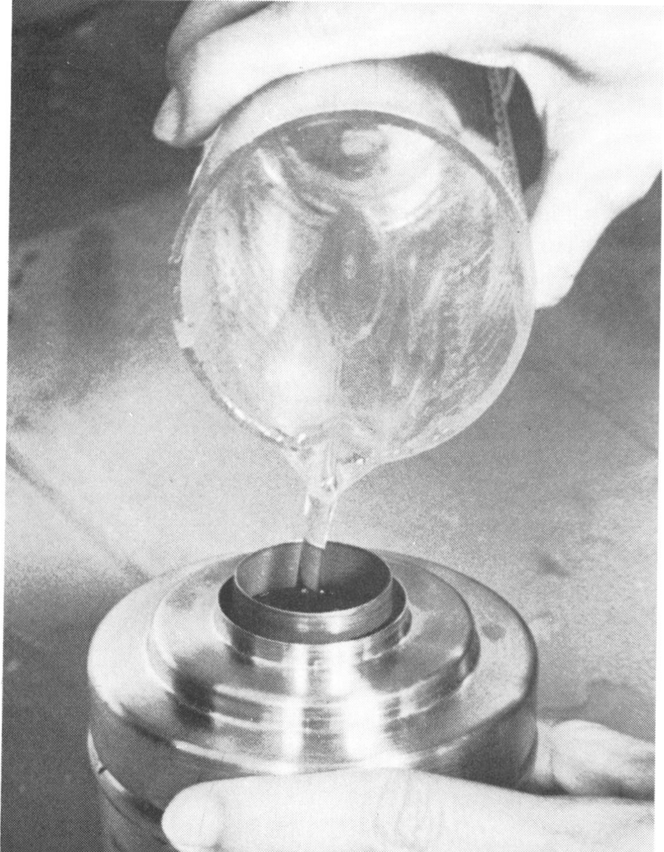

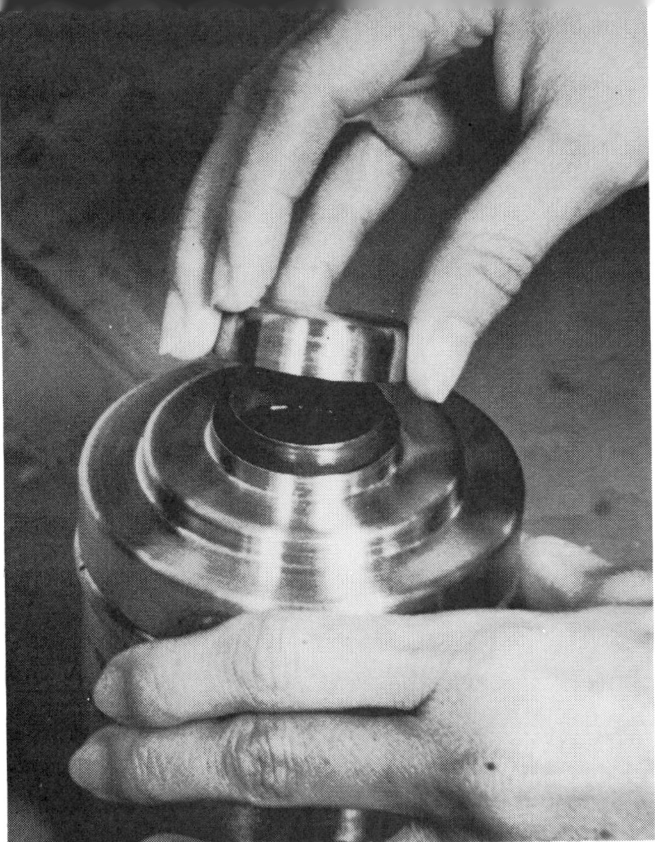

Place the small cap on the tank to avoid spilling chemical during agitation.

Tap the bottom of the developing tank lightly on the sink bottom or edge to dislodge any air bubbles which may have formed as the tank was filled.

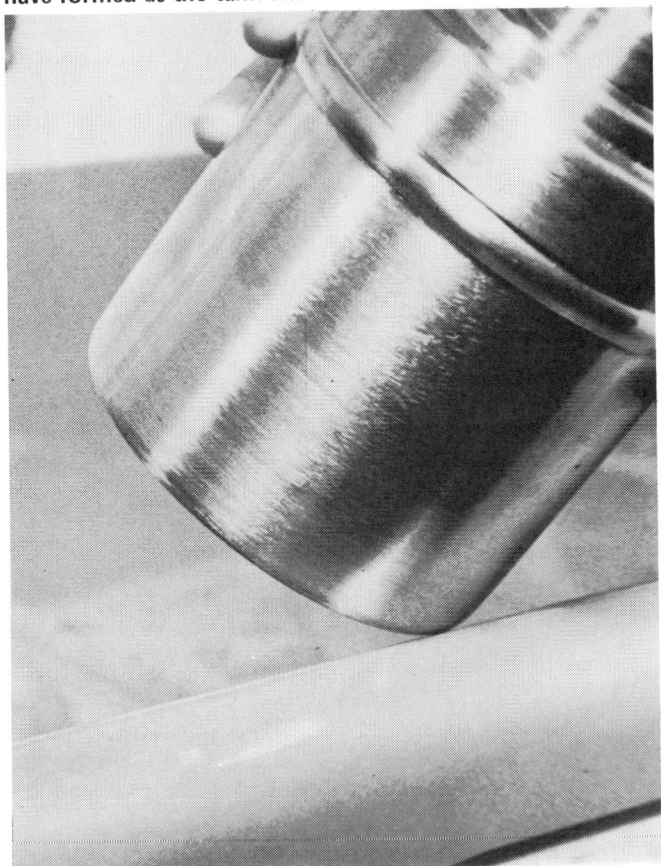

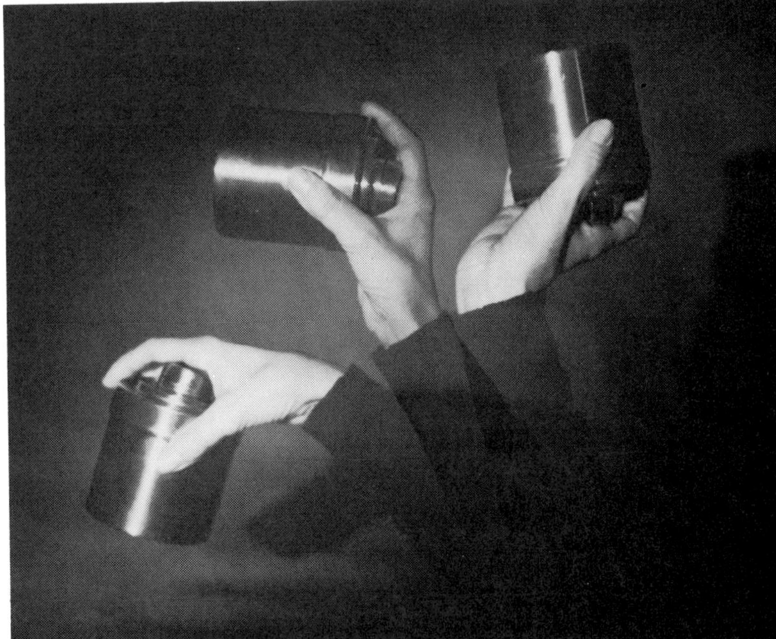

Agitate by lifting and inverting the tank. This requires grasping the tank firmly and holding the lid and cap on, too. Do not ever lift a loaded tank by the lid. The lid may come off, ruining your film.

watching the thermometer because temperatures may go beyond where you want them.

When the desired solution temperature is once reached, there will not usually be enough change during the normal processing time to be harmful. Determine the developing time for the temperature you are using–hopefully 68°F (20°C)–and proceed. This information will be on the developer package, on the data sheet packed with the film, or in a darkroom manual.

Put the developing tank in your sink in case you splash or spill some of the chemicals. Pour the developer through the tank lid opening and start the timer after about five seconds of filling. When the tank is full, rap it gently on the sink bottom at least twice to dislodge any air bubbles which may have formed during the film-chemical contact.

Should bubbles called *air bells* form, the developer will not act on the film where the bubbles are and clear small dots on the film emulsion will result. These print as black spots and are very difficult to eliminate.

Agitation is the next order of business. Not the kind you get from your spouse because of the time you spend in the darkroom, but the shake-it-up kind. If you use plastic developing cans,

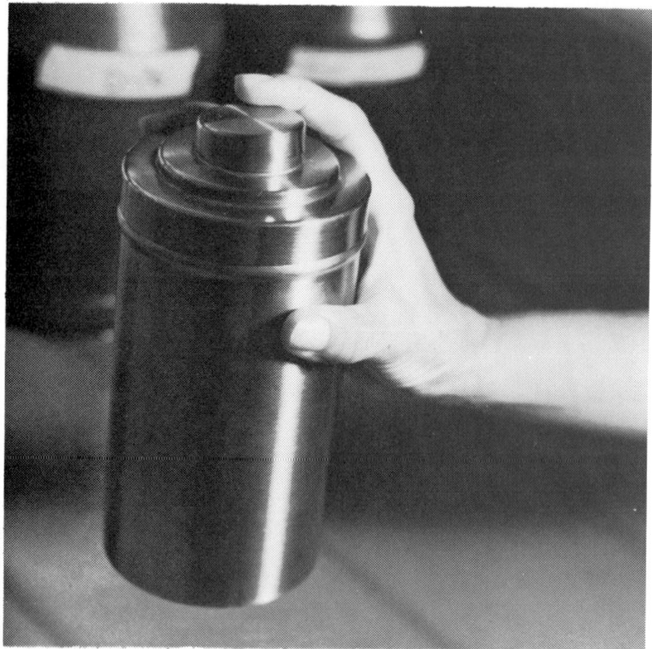

Agitation by lifting and inverting the tank requires holding the cap on with at least one finger. Small leaks around cap are not unusual. Don't worry about the loss of fluid because not much leaks out.

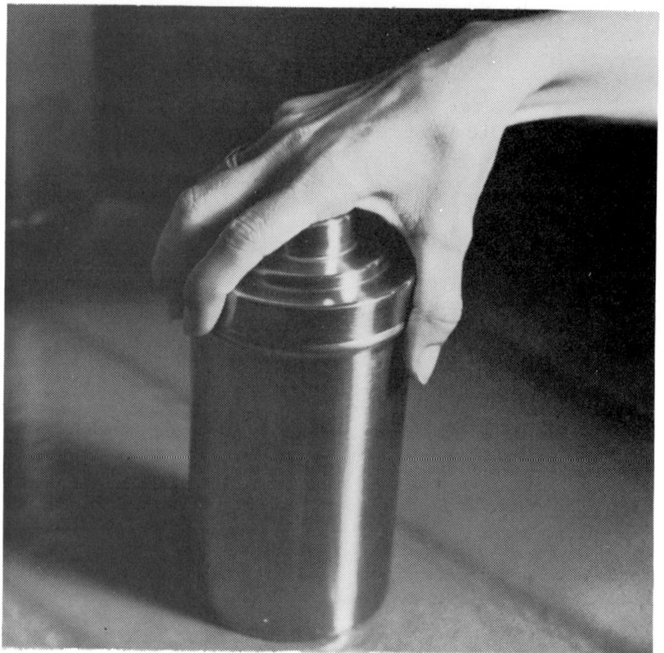

If a little fluid leaking around the cap annoys or worries you, grasp the tank as shown, and—

Don't ever pick up a loaded stainless-steel tank by its top. Get a firm hold on the tank AND the top. Otherwise, the top will come off. Your film will be exposed to light and ruined. Remember — grab the tank securely and hold the top and the cap on whenever you move the tank or agitate it.

—turn it side to side vigorously once each second of the agitation period. This is not as complete agitation as the inversion method, but will do in a pinch.

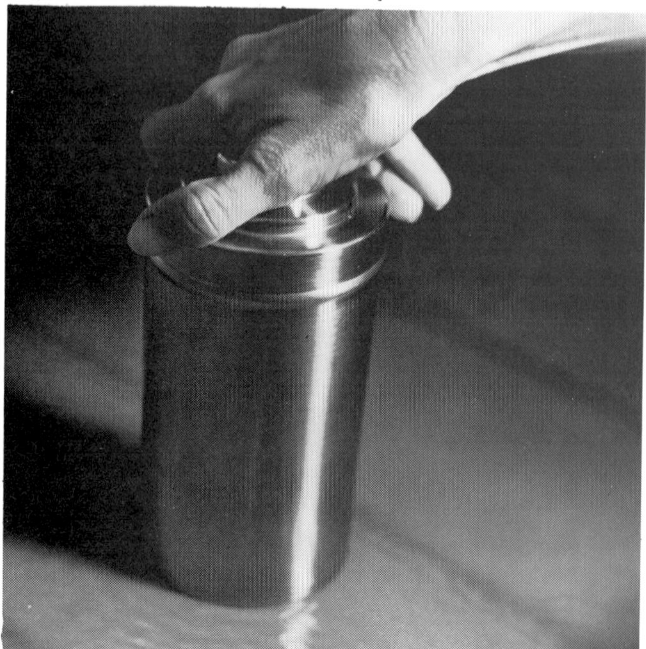

When using plastic developing tanks, agitation is performed by simply rotating the plastic agitator in the center of the tank lid one complete turn in each direction each second of the agitation period.

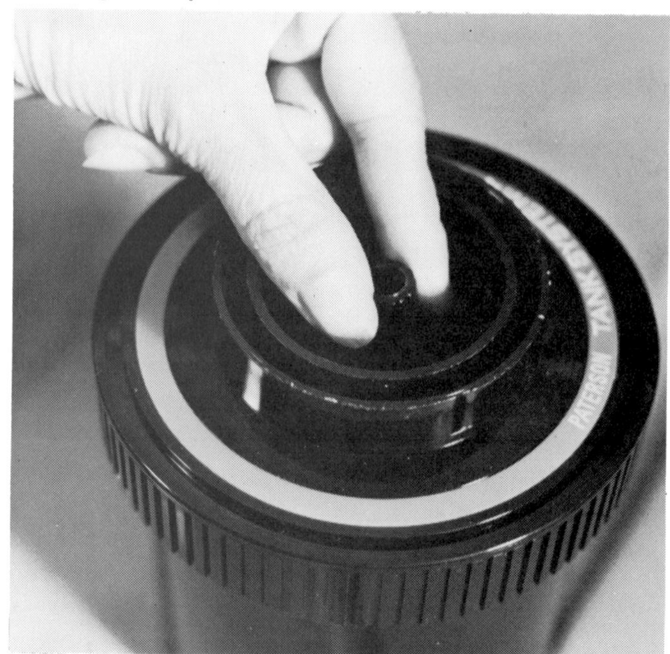

agitate by turning the reel with the agitator in the center of the tank as shown in the photo. With steel cans, turn the entire can upside down and back to agitate properly.

Agitation keeps fresh developer contacting the film at all times. Areas recording the highlights or bright areas cause considerable reaction with the developer and to achieve complete development in these areas, fresh chemical must always be working there. If the developer remains still and the small amount in contact with the film is allowed to exhaust itself, weak highlight areas result and your final prints will lack contrast and brilliance. Tapping probably provides sufficient initial agitation.

Unless the film or developer manufacturer says differently, agitate for five seconds every 30 seconds thereafter. Overagitation results in increased contrast and grain, so don't be too zealous. Steady, even turning of the steel tank or turning the plastic tank reel does the trick.

Remember it takes about 10 seconds to empty a 16-ounce steel film tank and include that in your overall processing time. Ten seconds to zero—start pouring. The Paterson 16-ounce tank empties in about four seconds.

If you have diluted the developer with water as I recommend, pour it down the drain after use. Diluting the developer for the purpose of obtaining finer grain makes it a one-shot deal and it should not be saved. Pour the developer back into the storage bottle only if you have been using it full strength. If you are using developer at full strength without replenishment, mark the number of rolls you just processed on the DEVELOPER label. When using developer full strength with a replenisher refer to the instructions packed with the replenisher and read the accompanying side bar so you'll know how to do it.

Next is the acid stop-bath or water rinse, and it's a shorty! Fill the tank, agitate for 30 seconds and empty. No great time lost here, but it *is* an important step. It reduces the amount of developer carried into the fixer so your fixer lasts longer.

Then to the fixer or hypo. Here you gain either permanent negatives or those which will turn brown and crack with age. Agitation is necessary for at least the first 30 seconds and it won't hurt to go for the first full minute. Thereafter, 10 seconds per minute is plenty. Leave the film in the fixer for about two minutes, open the tank and remove the film reel. Pull a short length off the reel. Look at it while holding it between you and the sink, not against a bright light. If the clear edges have a marked milky appearance, it is not sufficiently cleared. Put the film back on the reel and put the reel back in the fixer for another two minutes, using constant agitation. Don't be shook if it isn't completely cleared as the light won't have an adverse effect at this point. It simply means your fixer is near exhaustion and should be replaced. Remember:Leave the film in

Using developer with a replenisher—If you are not using a develop-and-dump "one-shot" developer as I recommend here, the best method of extending used-solution shelf life is by replenishment. Replenisher is available for most common developers. It is basically the same formula as the standard developer but mixed in a stronger solution. The directions tell you how much to add after processing a roll of film. As a rule of thumb, most recommend adding ¾ ounce of replenisher to the developer for each 80 square inches of film processed. This area is equivalent to one roll of 120 or one 36-exposure roll of 35mm—or one 8x10 sheet of film, or four pieces of 4x5 film. Replenisher is added to the bottle of developer before the developer from the film processing tank is returned to the bottle. Used developer in the processing tank is then returned to fill the bottle to the opening—assuming you began with a full bottle. Any solution left in the tank is discarded. If you mixed your developer in a quart size, mix the replenisher in a quart size also. When you've used the quart of replenisher, dump the developer and remix fresh solutions of both. This is recommended for any size container. As you use the replenisher, add marbles to the bottle or keep squeezing the liquid to the opening in an *air-evac* bottle before screwing on the cap. Replenisher doesn't like to be exposed to air, either.

the fixer for twice the time it takes to clear away the antihalation backing.

Pour the fixer back into its storage bottle. Use the filter funnel as you do so to keep debris from being stored with the good solution. Mark the number of rolls you just processed onto the FIXER label.

After the film is fixed, wash it. Most manufacturers recommend 20 to 30 minutes in running water but I find 10 minutes is entirely satisfactory

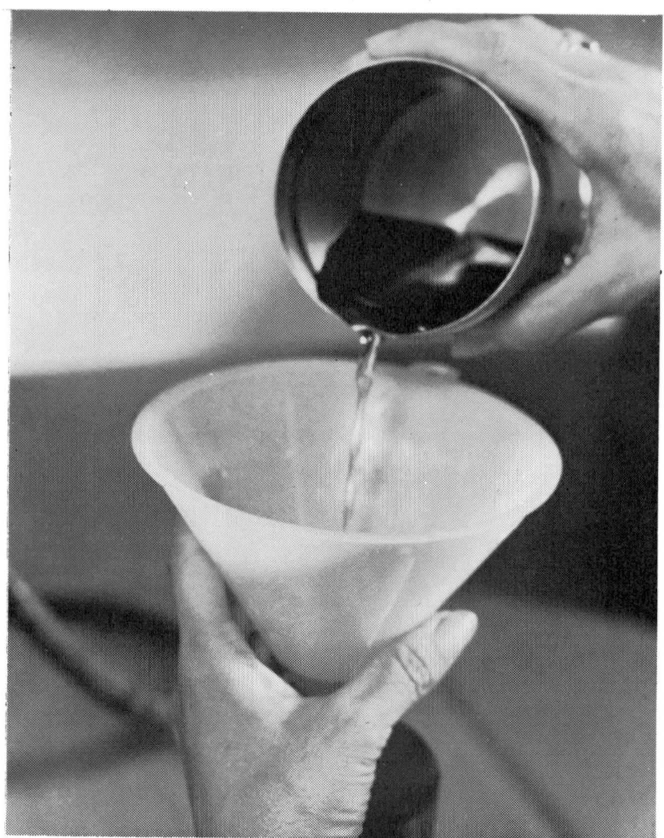

Return the fixer to its storage bottle using a filter funnel. FILTER ALL CHEMICALS WHEN RETURNING TO STORAGE TO AVOID SLUDGE AND FOREIGN MATERIAL FROM CAUSING DAMAGE TO FUTURE FILM PROCESSED!

Developers without replenisher—If you are not using a replenisher to keep up the strength of a developer you are using, keep track of every roll you process. Mark this on the label. The instruction sheet should indicate how many rolls of film the developer can be expected to process before its quality deteriorates seriously. The same instructions may indicate a need for increasing the developing time as the developer has been used. This keeps your negatives looking the same even though the solution is wearing out. But keeping track of the number of rolls developed is not the only consideration. Developer does not keep well once you start using it. This is true even though you take great pains to keep out excess air with marbles or by squeezing plastic bottles to bring the liquid to the opening as you screw on the cap. That's why you will notice a date on my solution labels. I want to know when I mixed them so I can throw them out after a certain length of time—even if I didn't get to develop the number of rolls the manufacturer promised me. Sometimes you may develop a roll or two—then not do any processing for a couple of months. Throw out the developer and make new soup. Even if it is still good, there's no way you can tell whether it really is and you don't want to risk your valuable negatives to find out. Developer is cheap compared with the value of your pictures. I feel you should throw out any used film developer after two months. If the solution turns quite dark and cloudy, throw it out regardless of how young it is. Never mind what it cost, dump it!

with a suitable washer. I have an old 4x5 inch hard-rubber sheet-film tank with two holes drilled in one end near the bottom which works beautifully. Fixer, being heavier than water, runs out these holes and 10 minutes is more than ample. Wat-air has a washing cylinder they claim will wash film in three minutes. I have used it and found it remarkable. I still like my hard-rubber 4x5 tank. One of these can usually be bought used at a low price. All it needs is a few holes drilled at the bottom on one or more sides. Any plastic pitcher or container can be used the same way if you poke holes in the side at the bottom and run water in at the top.

After your film has washed for the prescribed time in water at 68°F (20°C) it is ready to hang up to dry.

I've discussed wash-water temperature more fully in an accompanying sidebar. Now is the time to use a wetting agent if you desire. Use Kodak's Photo-Flo Solution: One capful to a half-gallon of

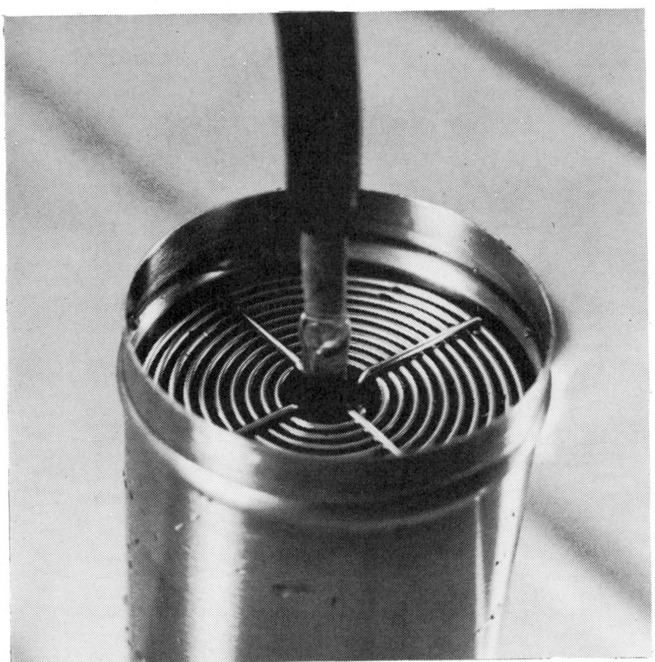

The processed film can be washed in the developing tank by placing a hose over the steel rod supplied with the tank.

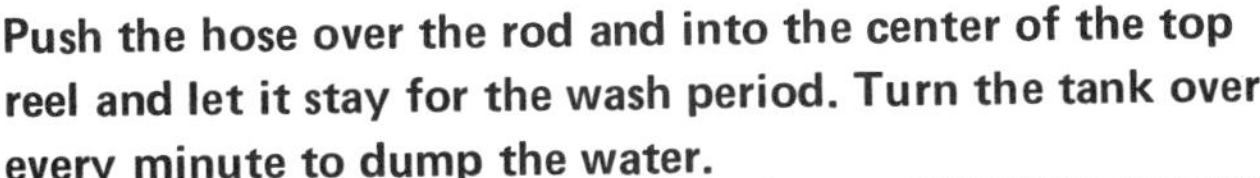

Push the hose over the rod and into the center of the top reel and let it stay for the wash period. Turn the tank over every minute to dump the water.

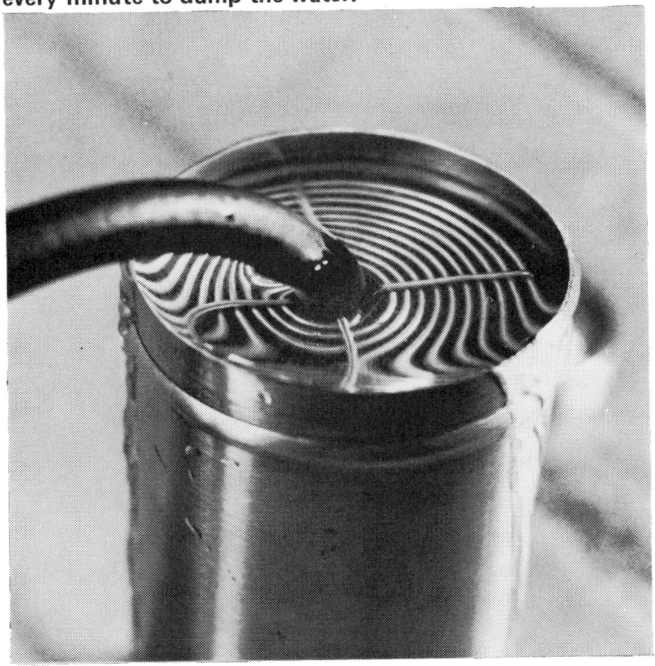

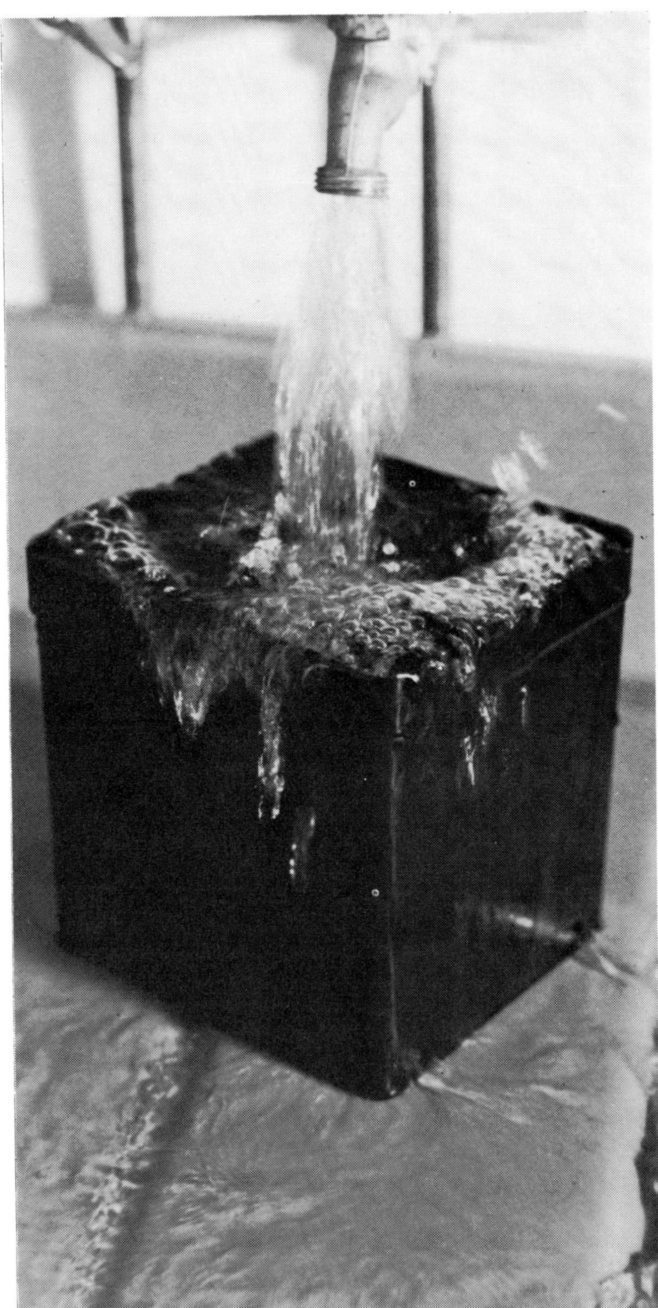

A 4"x5" rubber or plastic tank with two ¼-inch holes drilled at the bottom makes a very efficient and inexpensive wash tank.

Cleaning stainless-steel tanks—Use a household cleanser followed by soap and water. *Never use scouring pads* because small bits of steel may imbed in the stainless-steel surface and cause impossible-to-remove rust spots.

water does it, so even a small bottle lasts a long time. You can also use one or two drops of liquid dishwashing detergent in 16 ounces of water to make your wetting wash. Dunk the film in the wetting agent and agitate it several times, making sure to get rid of any bubbles which might form on the film. Dump the mixed wetting solution down the drain after using it to wet your film. It can be kept but even if you filter it, it often creates its own sludge and growths flourish in it. It's cheap, so throw it out.

Following the wash, or wetting agent if you used it, grip one end of the film in a film clip and pull the film out of the reel. Sandwich the film between two fingers and gently squeegee it as it comes off the reel. Add a film clip to the free end of the film and hang it up in a dust-free place. Go have a cup of coffee and let nature take its course.

Some people prefer to use a photographic squeegee or soft viscose sponge to get excess water off of the film. If you do so, it is necessary to soak either one in the wetting agent and squeeze or

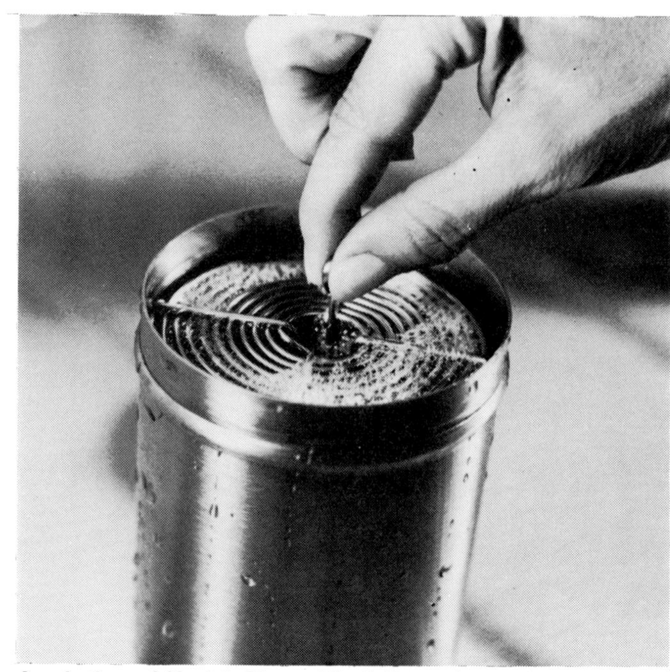

A solution of Kodak Photo-Flo follows the wash step to help eliminate the possibility of water spots after drying. Bounce the film reels in the solution for one minute after the wash is complete.

Hypo Neutralizers—To ensure good washing of the film in a short time, use a hypo-neutralizing solution. Solutions of this sort act on retained hypo in the film, which if allowed to remain would eventually stain and discolor the silver image. You can wash excess hypo out of the film, but this usually involves long wash times. The hypo neutralizer lessens wash time and water consumption by changing the excess hypo complexes into photographically inert compounds that won't stain the image.

A typical neutralizer is Kodak's Hypo Clearing Agent. It keeps for three months in a sealed bottle. It comes in a package containing five envelopes, each good for making a quart of solution. A quart is adequate for processing 30 rolls of film. Just wash the film for about a minute, then slosh it in the Hypo Clearing Agent for 1 to 2 minutes and wash the film for 10 minutes and you are absolutely certain that the hypo has been removed and your negatives will have a long, stain-free life ahead of them. When using the tank with holes in the bottom or one of the other fast-washing methods, chances are that 5 minutes will be a perfectly adequate amount of washing to guarantee hypo-free negatives.

Cold water washes film inefficiently. When water drops below 68° F (20° C) use hypo neutralizer to help get rid of the hypo and remaining silver salts. You'll get best washing if you stick to the recommended temperature because film emulsion may reticulate when the temperature is gradually lowered or raised in the washing process. Don't ever drop wash-water temperature from 68° F (20° C) to a temperature below 60° F (15° C) without placing the film in successively cooler water. This is too much of a hassle for me. I'd rather make sure the wash water is at the recommended temperature and not have to worry about damaging the tender emulsion on my valuable films.

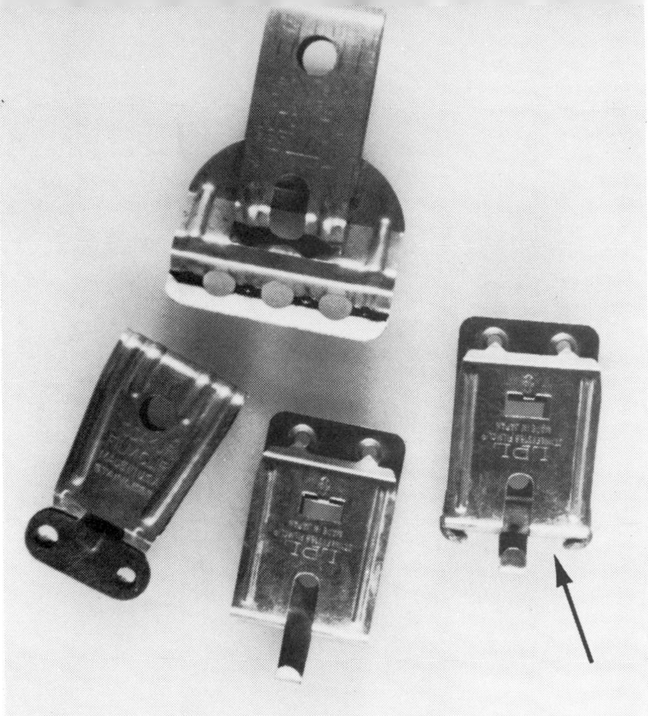

Film hanging clips to help ensure that when drying more than one roll, the rolls do not bend and stick to one another. Weighted ones are sometimes used on the bottom (arrow).

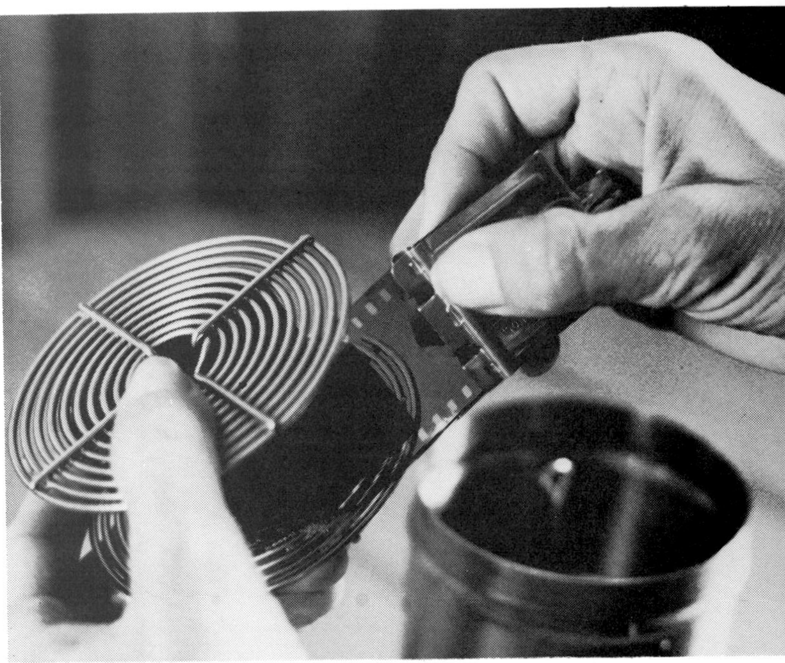

After the wetting solution, the reel is removed from the tank or washer and a film clip attached to the beginning end. Make sure teeth of clip penetrate the film to get a sure grip. You don't want your damp film to fall on the floor.

Pulling the film from the reel to arm's length, place another clip on the other end. Don't touch the film other than by the edge. The emulsion is moisture-filled at this time and easily damaged.

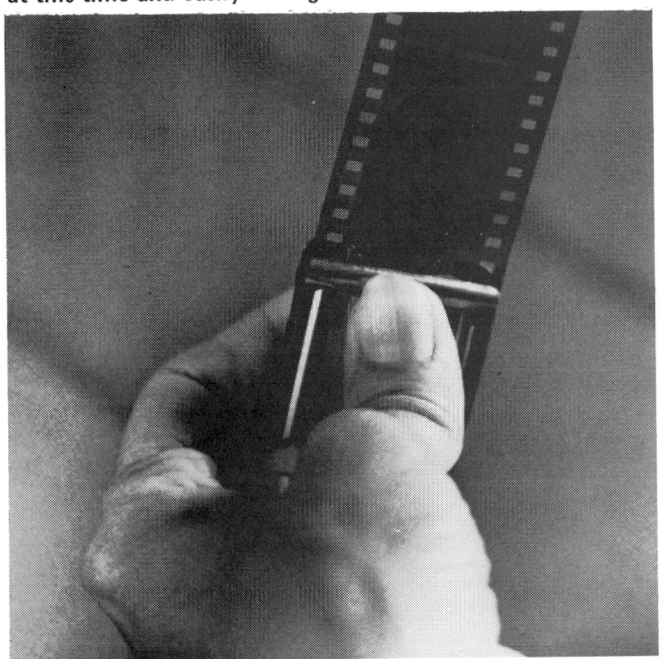

Film squeegees used to remove excess moisture from the film prior to drying. The rubber bladed type is longer lasting than the sponge type which has a tendency to pick up and hold foreign material which may cause severe scratching to future rolls. Either can scratch film if a speck of dirt gets into the act. Fingers are often a safer tool for removing excess water from film.

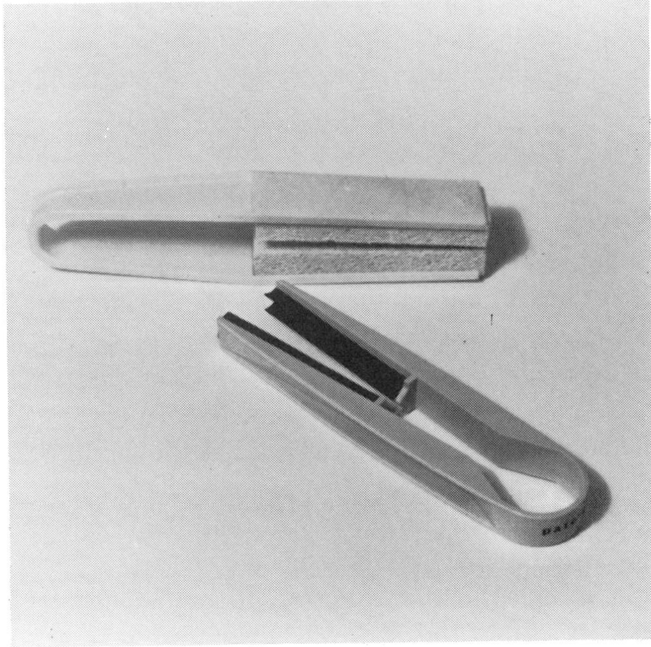

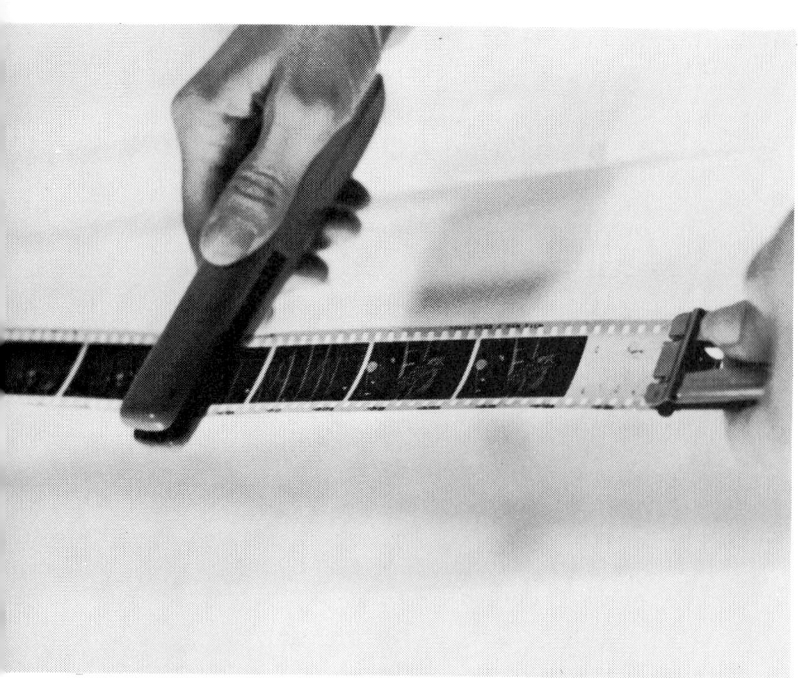

Gently **remove excess moisture from the film if you use a film squeegee. This is a great way to pick up scratches, so make sure the squeegee is clean before use.**

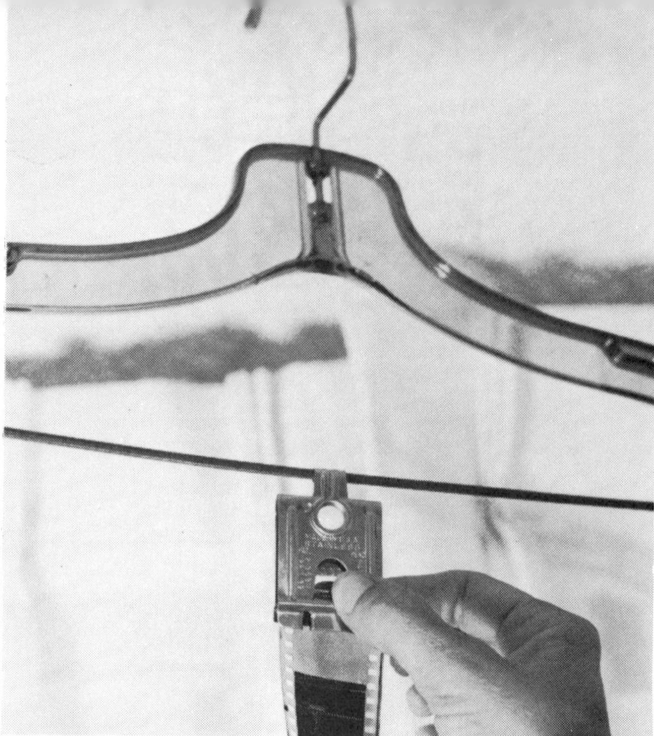

A coat hanger suspended from the ceiling in a dust- and draft-free place serves well as a film-drying support. Make sure teeth of clip penetrate film.

shake off the excess water before using. It is easy for a grain of dirt to get onto the squeegee or sponge and create a scratch right down the full length of the film. This kind of injury is impossible to fix and that's why I prefer to use my fingers.

WHAT'S A DUST-FREE AREA?

You'll note I said to hang the film in a dust-free area. Those are hard to find. Dust is nearly always floating around in the air as you can see when a stray sunbeam cuts through a room. Air currents which carry dust onto the film surface are the main culprits to watch out for. Some rooms are dustier than others because they get more traffic or are not cleaned as often.

Some closets can be used to hang film for drying—*if* the door is opened carefully, the film is hung without entering the closet to brush dirt off of the floor or clothes hanging there—and the door carefully closed. A shower enclosure is a great place to hang film to dry *if* you can keep people out of the bathroom so no air currents are created by traffic into and out of the room. If the bathroom is clean, hang film over the tub to dry. Go out and bar the door until the film is dry. Avoid opening and closing the door.

Hanging film in a doorway to a room where there is a lot of traffic or where windows are open is not recommended. Also, be careful of hot-air or air-conditioning vents which stir up the air in a room or even deposit dirt directly onto the film as it dries.

If you really enjoy photography you may even build a small drying cabinet with a filtered air inlet and a dust-tight door to give your film the best possible chance of drying without getting dust imbedded onto its surfaces.

About all that can go wrong at this point is for dust or other foreign matter to stick to the film before it is completely dry. If that should happen, with all your care, rewash the film and let the dust soak off. Don't try to remove it with a can opener or pocket knife because lots of emulsion will come with it. Once it's rewashed and rewetted, use your fingers to squeegee the roll again. Remove anything still stuck as gently as possible. Find a less-dusty place to dry the film this time!

Standardize!—Before I leave film and its processing, let me make a comment about the kind of film and developer you use. When I say *"Standardize!"* I really mean it! Use the one or two films and one developer which you decide will best handle the bulk of your photography. Learn the capabilities of each and you'll soon have a good reliable basic

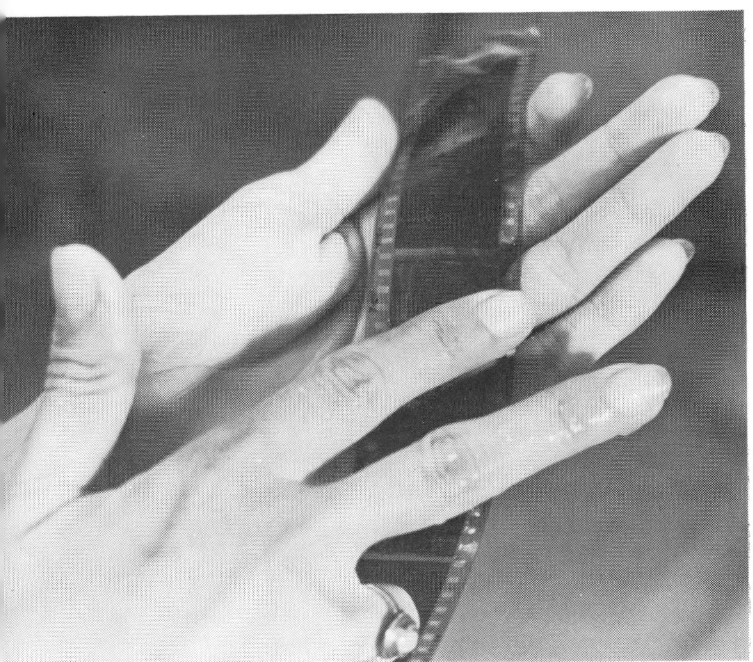

If, after the film has dried, you notice particles of dirt or dust on the film, you will have to re-wash the roll. After the film is completely soaked, about five minutes, very gently remove any material still visible with soft finger action. DO NOT USE A COMMERCIAL FILM CLEANER WITH COTTON OR TISSUE TO REMOVE DIRT PARTICLES! This will cause scratching of the base material or cutting of the emulsion which is impossible to repair.

Fast film driers—There are chemical and mechanical ways to dry film in a hurry if you must. I've already mentioned the possible use of a drying cabinet. Some commercially available ones have heaters and a means of forcing clean air through them. There are also volatile solutions, mostly alcohol-based, into which you can dunk your film after washing. These solutions are miscible with water, so no wetting agent need be used. The film is dunked, then squeegeed and hung up to dry. The film will usually dry in about five minutes unless the atmosphere is terribly humid. I avoid these driers because I have had trouble with streaking when I've used them. Getting the streaks off was either impossible or else took just as long as if I had let the film dry naturally after using a wetting agent.

lab technique you can depend on.

Even so, experimentation is half the fun of photography, so don't hesitate to try special materials for odd situations—*after* you know the basics by heart.

There are films with extremely high contrast, others with very fine grain and some for the times when you have practically no light to speak of at all. Each has its own recommended developer or you can try the mix-and-match angle or secret formulas in the magazines. Results can be very rewarding.

Many an error has turned into a fad. If you do come up with something new and different, do it, then move on. Don't make the mistake of making every picture just like the one before. What is exciting once or twice can become a bore if you keep doing it.

Later on, I'll get into some rather fancy processes and chances are you'll be hard put to come up with something completely new. But don't stop trying to be creative. The camera and darkroom are fantastic tools for the creative process, so absorb the basics and press on.

NOW TO GET SPECIFIC

Because we live in a complex world, we are surrounded by instructions on how to do things. Books like this are supposed to tell you how to do something so you can actually do it when you have read the book.

Most of us have been frustrated by instructions which assume some bit of information or procedure is already known by the reader. The wife can understand the instructions printed on the lid of the washing machine but the husband can't make any sense out of them.

If you have ever ridden a horse just once, you know all the essential basics. But if you never have done it, then you must be told which side to mount from, how to start up the contraption, how to get it stopped, and how to make it turn sometimes. If you can find a book on how to ride a horse, I'll betcha some of those vital details are left out.

There are a lot of photo-lab-technique books on the market and it has seemed to me that many of them are *about* doing it but not specifically *how* to do it. You can't really avoid talking *about* doing it and that's what this has been so far. But I aim to tell and show you *how* with pictures even if it bores somebody who already knows how.

SPECIFIC EQUIPMENT LIST

Here is the equipment you need to develop your first roll of black-and-white film. The equipment listed is what I personally prefer and have found to be very workable. Other manufacturers offer similar items. Your local photo dealer can help you fill out the list if an item I recommend is not available in your area.

1 Beer can opener, any brand
1 Pair scissors, big enough to find and use in the dark
1 Honeywell Nikor 16-ounce stainless-steel tank with lid
2 Honeywell Nikor 35mm stainless steel film reels, or
1 Honeywell Nikor 120 film reel.
1 Weston Model 2265 dial-type thermometer
1 White-plastic graduate, 32-ounce
1 White-plastic graduate, 16-ounce
1 Strainer-type plastic funnel
1 GraLab or Gilbert Interval Timer or wrist watch or clock with sweep-second hand
1 Plastic stirring rod or paddle
1 Salad dressing or mustard jar, one-gallon size with wide mouth
2 Brown-plastic bottles, 32-ounce size
1 Brown-plastic bottle, 64-ounce size
1 Package Kodak D-76 Developer to make one quart
1 Package Kodak Fixer to make one-half gallon
1 Kodak Photo-Flo 4-ounce bottle or bottle of liquid dishwashing detergent
2 Film hanging clips for each roll or film being processed
1 Bag of glass marbles, or substitute an *air evac* bottle for one of the 32-ounce bottles.
1 Darkroom to load film in, or
1 Changing bag (bigger ones are best)
1 Towel or roll of paper towels for drying hands

and last, but not least

1 or 2 Rolls exposed Kodak Plus-X 35mm or 126 black-and-white film, or
1 Roll exposed Kodak Plus-X 120 black-and-white film

SPECIFIC PROCESSING STEPS

1. Mix the D-76 developer according to the instructions on the can, using the 32-ounce graduate, the wide-mouthed jar, the thermometer and the plastic stirring rod. Pour the mixed solution through the strainer funnel into one of the 32-ounce brown-plastic bottles or into an *air evac* bottle. Screw on the lid and set the bottle aside to cool after labeling it DEVELOPER D-76 with the date. Plan now to throw this developer out in two months—or sooner if it starts to discolor. Wash off the graduate, jar, thermometer, stirrer, funnel and your hands, Wash the funnel thoroughly.

Here's what you need to take into a darkroom or put into your gadget bag to load and process either 35mm or 120 size film.

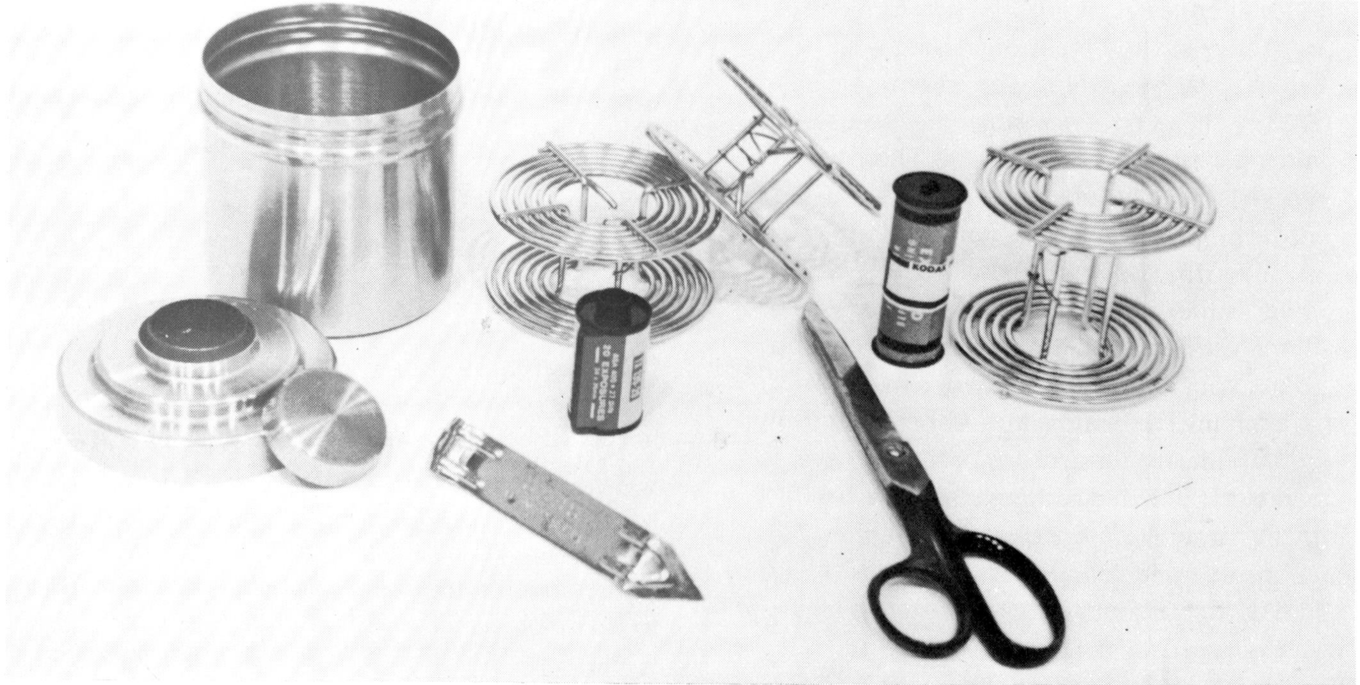

2. Mix Kodak Fixer according to instructions on container, using the 32-ounce graduate, the wide-mouthed jar, the thermometer and the plastic stirring rod. Pour the mixed solution through the strainer funnel into the 64-ounce brown-plastic bottle. Screw on the lid and set bottle aside to cool. Label bottle FIXER. Date the label so you can remember when it was made. Throw out this fixer after processing 25 rolls, or the equivalent area. Wash off the funnel, jar, thermometer, stirrer and your hands.

3. Put 32-ounces of water into a brown-plastic bottle. Label it WASH.

4. Place developing tank, lid, film reel(s), beer-can opener, scissors, and exposed roll(s) of film in unopened rolls, cartridges or cassettes on dry work area in a dark room. Or, put these items into your changing bag, close both zippers and skip steps 5 and 6. Take off your luminous watch.

5. Close and lock door to room. If your door has no lock, take a minute to explain to everyone in the vicinity that they had better stay out if they know what's good for them. Hang a sign on the outside of the door with terrifying blood-curdling threats. If small children are in the area forget the whole idea until you get a lock on the door.

6. Turn off darkroom light. Sit there in the dark for several minutes. Look around for awhile. As your eyes become accustomed to the dark you may find light leaks you did not know existed. Cover these with towels or tape until the room is truly black. You don't want to fog your film, at least not on the first try.

7. Use the can opener to pry off the flat end of the 35mm film container. If you are using a changing bag, put your arms into the sleeves so you can manipulate the stuff in the bag.

8. Cut off tapered end at start of 35mm roll. Load the film onto the reel and cut off the spool when you get nearly all of the film onto the reel. Finish winding the film onto the reel and put the reel in the tank. Or with a paper-backed film, pull away the leader paper until you get to the start of the film. It will not be taped to the backing paper so you will feel the film when you get to it. I bend over the film about ½ inch clear across the width of the film so it tends to make a stiffener. This makes it easier to load into either a steel or a plastic reel. If you have an Instamatic 126 car-

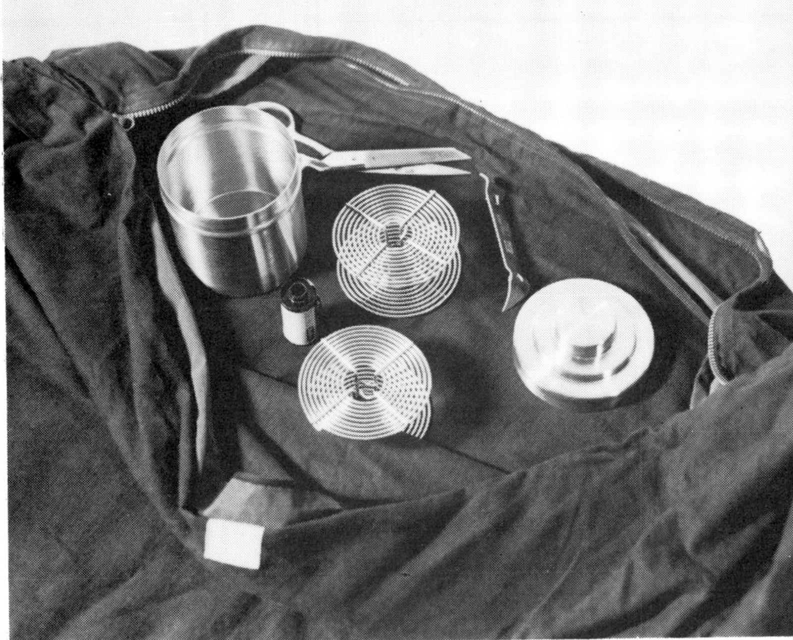

A changing bag is made of two layers of material, one heavy cloth and the other a rubberized material, each zippered in opposite directions so that it is light tight. It is an inexpensive alternative to having a darkroom to load your film into the developing tank. The bag is unzipped and the necessary equipment placed inside. Two elastic closed arm holes are at one end, and—

—after the zippers are closed, the arms are inserted through the arm holes and film loading is carried out in the normal fashion. Unless you are a fast operator, don't try this in the middle of a desert because sweaty fingers leave fingerprints on the film.

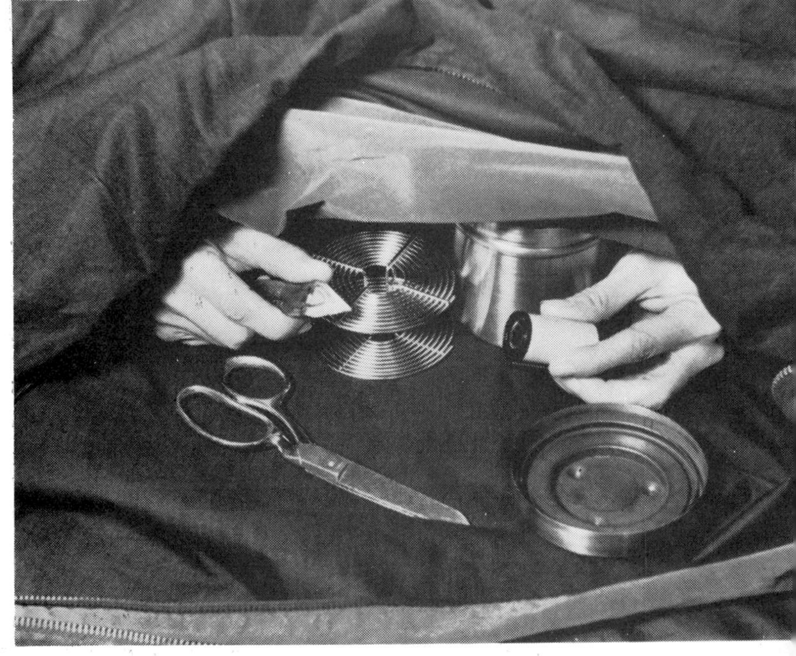

tridge, break it open and unload it as shown in the accompanying photos. If you have a second roll of 35mm or 126 film, load it onto the other reel.

9. Place the loaded film reel(s) into developing tank. If there is an empty reel, put that into the tank, too, and put the tank lid on. This tank will hold two 35mm film reels and should always have both in place to prevent too much agitation during processing. One reel alone has too much travel area when you invert the tank during agitation. One 120 type reel fits in this same tank.

10. Turn on darkroom light or take loaded tank out of changing bag.

11. Check temperature of developer, wash or stop bath and fixer. Bring chemicals to 68°F (20°C) by chilling in refrigerator or heat by immersing bottles in a sink or tray of hot water.

12. Bring 8 ounces of tap water to 68°F (20°C). Use mixing faucet in sink or chill with ice cubes.

13. Using a 16-ounce graduate, mix 8 ounces of D-76 developer and 8 ounces of water to obtain a 1:1 working solution.

14. Check temperature of developer solution to be absolutely sure it is 68°F (20°C).

15. Set timer for 7 minutes.

16. Through the filling hole in the tank lid, add the developer working solution as rapidly as it will go. At first tilt the tank to help entrapped air escape from the tank, thereby allowing developer to enter faster.

17. Start timer or note location of watch or clock second and minute hands.

18. Gently tap bottom of the developer tank on the bench or table top a couple of times to dislodge any air bubbles from the film.

19. At the end of 30 seconds, agitate the developer tank for 5 seconds. Do this again every 30 seconds. Do this by slowly turning the tank upside down and back. Approximately three times. If you have a plastic tank, do it the plastic-tank way.

20. Ten seconds before the timer reaches the end of the 7-minute span, drain the developer into the sink through the hole in the lid. The developer has been diluted with water and is *not* returned to the developer bottle.

21. Pour 68°F (20°C) water from your WASH bottle into the developing tank through the filling hole and agitate briskly for 30 seconds.

22. Empty the water into the sink through the filling hole.

23. Pour 16 ounces of fixer into the developing tank through the filling hole, replace the cap on the hole and agitate for 30 seconds. Set and start timer for 10 minutes. Agitate for 10 seconds each minute for a total of 10 minutes.

24. When the timer stops after 10 minutes, remove the lid from the developing tank and examine the film. There should be no trace of haziness in the clear areas of the film (edges, ends, unexposed areas). If there is, replace the film in the tank, replace the lid and agitate continuously for three minutes. This problem only occurs when fixer is old and exhausted.

25. Using the strainer funnel, return the fixer in the tank to the brown bottle, making sure to check the label so that you are returning solution into the FIXER bottle.

26. Rearrange the film reels in the tank so loaded reel is on top of the empty one.

27. Place the developing tank with reels inside and lid removed, under the faucet with running water at 68° to 70°F (20° to 21°C). Allow the

Getting the developer into the tank—Jillions of rolls of film are successfully developed every year by pouring the developer through the light-baffled lids of daylight tanks. Filling a 16-ounce or smaller tank through the lid opening takes from 10 to 30 seconds. Some of the film is not covered with developer until the tank is full. This does not usually cause any visible uneven development unless you are working with a tank holding more than 16 ounces.

Ideally, if you are working with larger tanks, it is better to work in a darkroom where you can pour the developer into the tank, submerge the loaded film reels into the developer and finally put the lid on the tank before turning on the lights. This gets the developer into contact with all of the film's surface almost at the same time. Practically, most photographers pour the solutions in through the lid and don't worry about it.

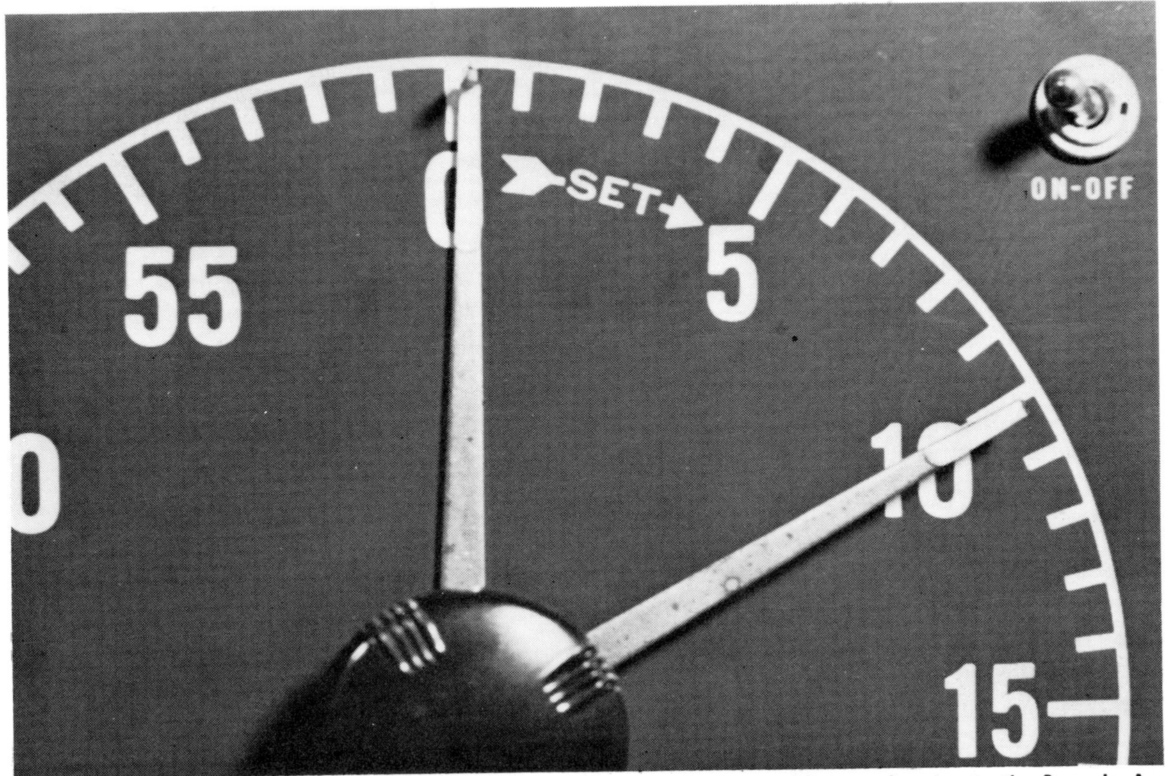

When using a 16-ounce developing tank, begin to empty the solution at 10 seconds prior to the 0 mark. A 32-ounce tank takes another 5 seconds. GraLab Timer's hands move counter-clockwise (backward) from normal clocks or watches. If you must load film close to a timer, cover the timer so the luminous dial won't fog your film.

tank to fill and overflow. Each minute dump the water from the tank by hand and allow the tank to refill. Continue this procedure for 10 minutes. Or, put the reel with film in the washing tank with holes in its bottom and run water in at the top for 10 minutes.

28. Prepare the wetting solution by adding 2 or 3 drops of Photo-Flo 200 or dishwasher detergent to 16 ounces of water.

29. Empty the developing tank of water and add the wetting solution. Agitate the reel in a circular motion for 1 minute, or slosh it up and down in the solution.

30. Remove the loaded film reel from the tank and allow it to drain.

31. Place a film hanging clip on the end of the film and unwind from the reel.

32. Gently run the film between the first and second fingers of your hand to remove excess liquid.

33. Place a second film hanging clip on the opposite end and hang the film to dry.

34. Dry the film in a quiet dust-free place. A wire coat hanger hung over a shower-curtain rod or onto a hook will serve as a support for the film clip. Be sure that the film strip hangs straight and that nothing comes in contact with it.

35. Add marbles to the D-76 bottle to bring the liquid level even with the bottle opening, then screw on the cap. Or squeeze the plastic bottle or collapse your Air-Evac bottle to bring the liquid even with the top before screwing on the cap. Mark 24 OUNCES LEFT on the label.

36. Mark the number of rolls processed on the FIXER label. Check that you have the caps on tightly on both the developer and fixer bottles. Wash up everything and put it all away so it will be ready for the next session. You'll be back soon.

There you have it! If you followed the directions, you have a roll of well-developed negatives. Let's hope you read the camera instruction book with care and made all correct exposures.

Watch the wash-water temperature—A lot of negatives are spoiled because photographers think the temperature of water coming out of the tap will stay where they have adjusted it. The chances of ruining negatives by changes in wash-water temperature are truly great. All it takes is one flushed toilet and cold-water may no longer be available at your mixing faucet. The water pressure also diminishes and your film gets a hot-water bath, maybe hot enough to cause reticulation. Unless you were planning on reticulation as discussed on page 107, you probably don't really want that pattern impressed on all your lovely negatives. In some houses the water can get hot enough to melt the emulsion off the backing! Even if you have built your darkroom with a thermostatically controlled mixing valve, unless the darkroom water supply is directly from the water main, chances are good that water-pressure changes will cause temperature variations. A thermometer in the water line can help you monitor the temperature so you can yank the tank or film-wash gadget away from the water when temperature starts changing rapidly.

To check this in your house, get the tap water adjusted to run at 68°F (20°C). Hold your thermometer in the stream of water and watch it closely while various other things are turned on in the house. These should include flushing the toilets, turning on a shower or bath-water faucet and anything else you can think of. If the temperature does not vary, yours is an unusual house. When it does, you'll know your house is like mine and you'll have to be careful so your negatives don't end up as a heap of emulsion in the bottom of the wash tank.

If you live in an area where the temperature of the water directly from the tap is normally higher than you can use, such as 75° to 90°F (24° to 32°C), try this. Fill a standard two-gallon plastic bucket with tap water and bring the temperature of the water to 68° to 70°F (20° to 21°C), either by putting in a tray or two of ice cubes or by leaving the bucket in the refrigerator for awhile. When you are ready to wash the processed film, dip 16 ounces of water from the bucket and pour it into the developing tank. Agitate the tank with a twisting motion for ten seconds and dump the water into the sink. Repeat this procedure until the entire contents of the bucket have been used.

It's a bit more of a hassle than letting the water tap do the work, but knowing that the film is well washed and has not been abused by temperature extremes makes it worthwhile.

Large changing bags are easier to use than small ones. You need the extra room for manipulating the film, reel, tank and scissors. The elastic in the changing-bag arm holes wears out. Don't throw the bag away—replace the elastic or use rubber bands around the arm holes to keep a snug, light-tight fit.

ABOUT THE AUTHOR

Dedicated photographer Tom Burk is a graduate of the Brooks Institute in Santa Barbara, California. His career in photography has prepared him well to write this book with emphasis on the sure and certain method.

As forensic photographer for the Tucson Police Department, he took and processed photographs for criminal evidence, scene-of-the-crime documentaries, and the identification of people and objects.

As Director of Medical Photography at the Tucson Medical Center, he supervises a staff of field photographers and darkroom technicians in the technically challenging field of recording medical events and procedures. Mr. Burk also conducts popular classes in photography and darkroom technique.

Evaluation & Proofing

Now you have a dry strip of developed film and you can evaluate your negatives. This is the first time you will handle the film dry, so remember to touch all negatives *only at the edges!* No fingerprints on the image itself, please. Any marks such as fingerprints, drying marks, scratches or imbedded dirt will show on the final print and require extra time and effort to eliminate.

At the end of this chapter I will explain all the work you'll have to do if you get careless and get marks on your film.

A GOOD NEGATIVE

It has been said that a properly exposed and developed negative should be just dark enough in the highlight areas so when you lay it on a newspaper, bold type can be read through the highlight area. I personally advise using a somewhat denser negative with highlight areas through which bold newspaper type is a little difficult to read. Remember, you are working with a negative image so the bright areas of the original scene are the dark areas on the film. Also, the shadow or light areas of the film should have perceptible detail. A negative like this will print easily on *normal* printing paper and that's what you are after.

Only flat-black holes or solid-white spots in the original scene should be without detail in the negative. A snow-white plastic safety helmet, for instance, has no texture and will appear quite dense on the negative. A black sweater on a lovely lady on a moonlight night will become a clear area on the negative. If you saw detail clearly in the original scene, it should appear on the negative—and ultimately on the finished print.

Hold the film up to a window or light and have a look. It takes a little practice to read negatives, but it's really not difficult. Two things you don't want to see are areas of solid black or perfectly clear areas where you know detail should be visible. If you can see detail or texture in the white and black areas and a lot of shades of gray in between, you've got it!

NEGATIVE PROBLEMS

If your negatives don't fit the above description, compare them with this list and the accompanying photos to see what went wrong.

1. Negative appears to have a very weak image with no shadow detail—UNDEREXPOSED.

2. Negative appears to have a weak image but you can see detail in important shadow areas—UNDERDEVELOPED.

3. Negative appears very dense with completely blocked-up highlight areas—OVEREXPOSED.

4. Negative appears dense overall, but has detail in lightest and darkest areas—OVERDEVELOPED.

5. Negative lacks any shadow detail, but has dense, blocked-up highlights—UNDEREXPOSED and OVERDEVELOPED.

As a general rule, bold news print should be readable when a properly exposed and processed negative is placed over it.

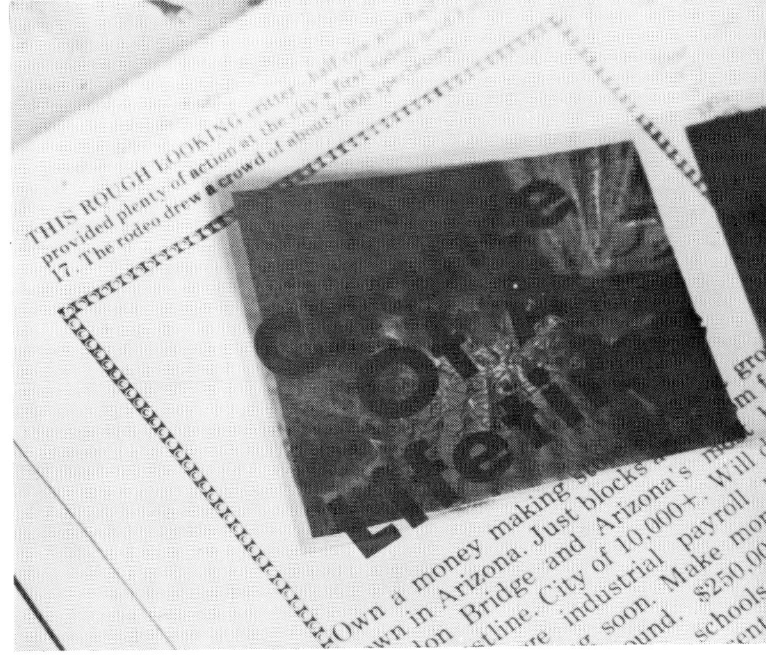

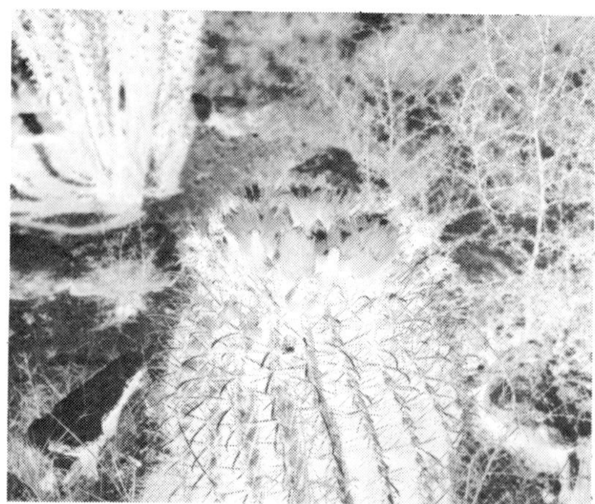

A properly exposed and processed negative will produce a print with good blacks and whites and no areas without discernible detail.

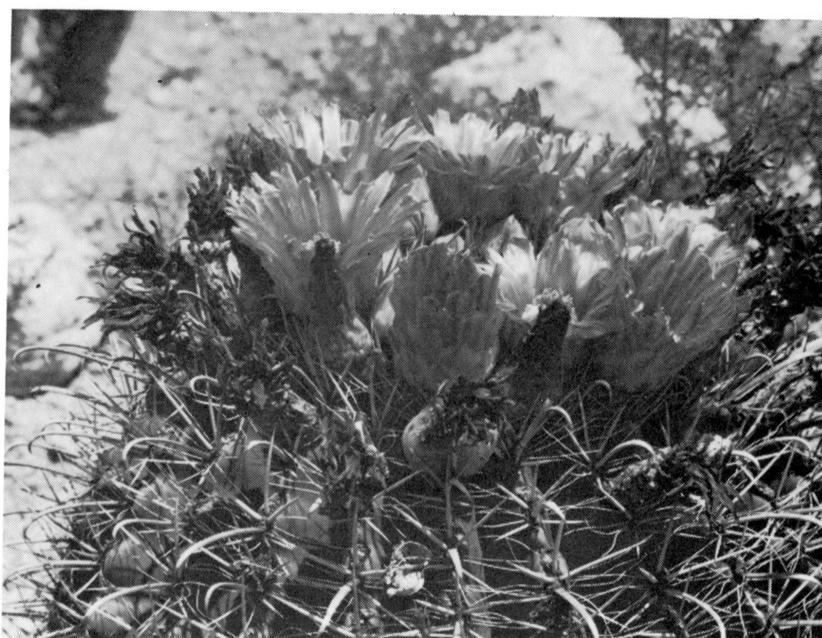

A print from your "normal" negative will show the maximum detail in the scene. Printing it is very easy.

6. Negative shows much shadow detail, but highlight areas are not much darker—OVER-EXPOSED and UNDERDEVELOPED.

That is the range of common errors you can make in the exposure/processing relationship. With a little thought and attention, the remedy to any of these problems is not difficult, after you determine what the problem is from the above list.

Underexposed negatives lack detail in the shadow areas and are flat and dull. They may look uninteresting, but they are difficult to print.

Prints from an underexposed negative are flat and lifeless. Uninteresting, they won't be ones you'll want to hang on your living-room wall.

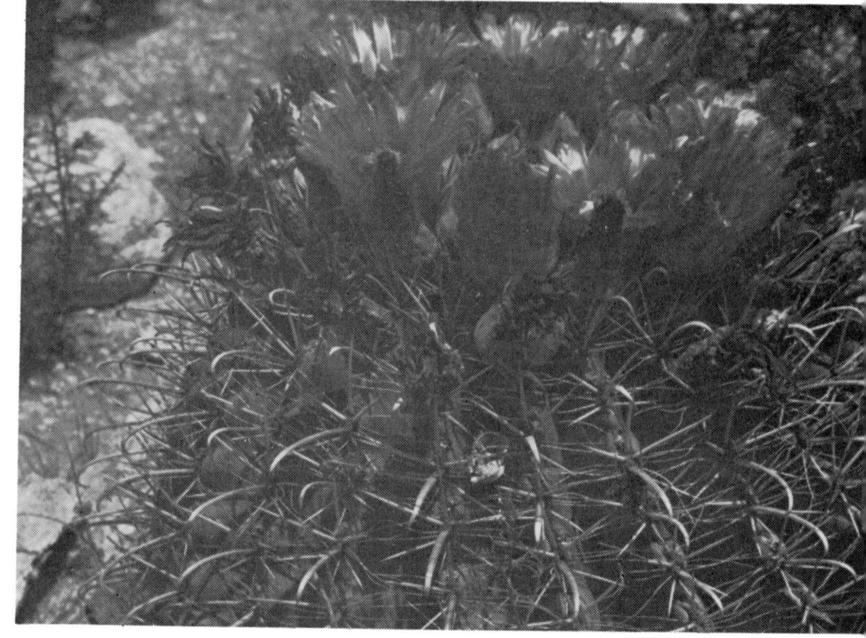

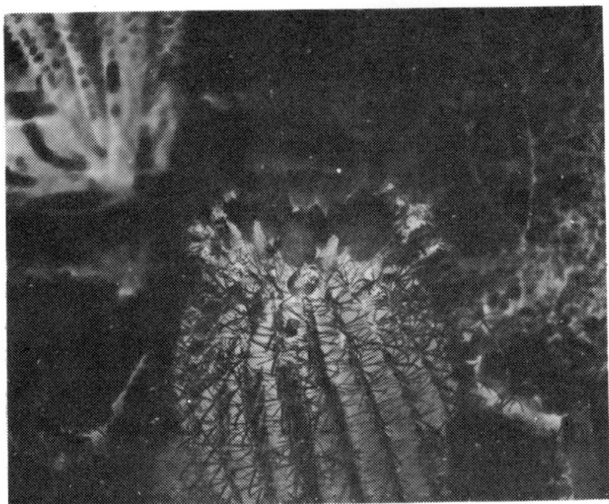

Overexposed negative is void of necessary detail in the highlights or bright areas. A negative like this requires considerable time and effort to print. The resulting print will not usually be something you'd want to show your friends.

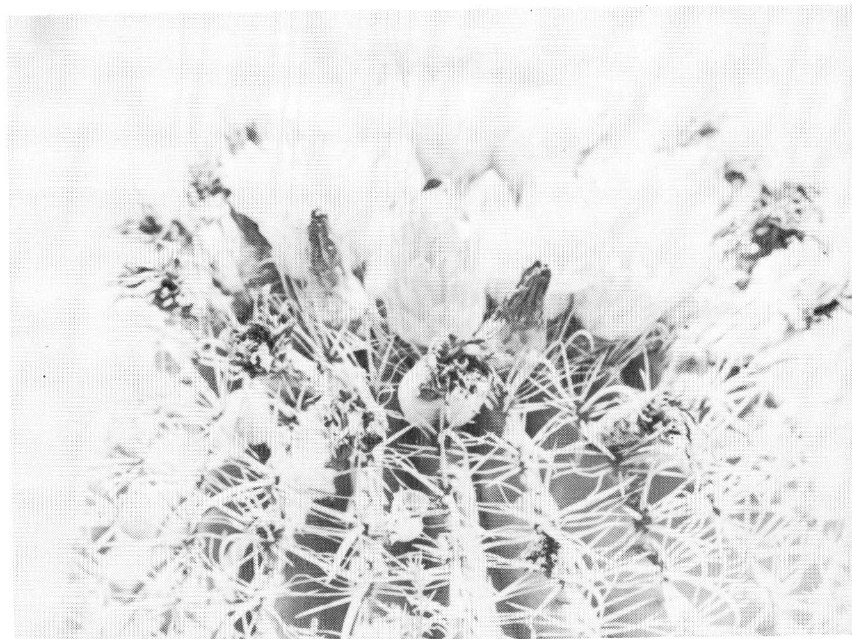

A print from a grossly overexposed negative. It can be desirable and effective, but only for special effects. Notice all highlight details are "washed out."

PROCESSING PROBLEMS

If you feel you've simply gone astray in processing, here is a checklist:

1. Check your timer against another clock or two around the house and make sure it is accurate. If you're using the sweep-second hand on your watch, don't let your attention wander and forget when you started. Write down the starting time.

2. Check the information sheet with the film to verify proper time for the temperature you are using.

3. Check your thermometer with one from your local camera shop. *Don't* check an immersion thermometer against the type used to measure air temperature—it won't prove a thing.

4. Finally, make sure you are using the developer you think you are, and that it was mixed correctly.

If anything on this list must be corrected, do it now. If everything proves out, we can assume the problem lies elsewhere.

EXPOSURE PROBLEMS

I didn't write this book to instruct you in the mechanical operation of your camera and exposure meter. If you're far enough into the act to do your own darkroom work, you're relatively secure in the procedure of exposure-making. If you're not sure and want a good discussion of the

When checking an immersion thermometer don't use an air thermometer as comparison.

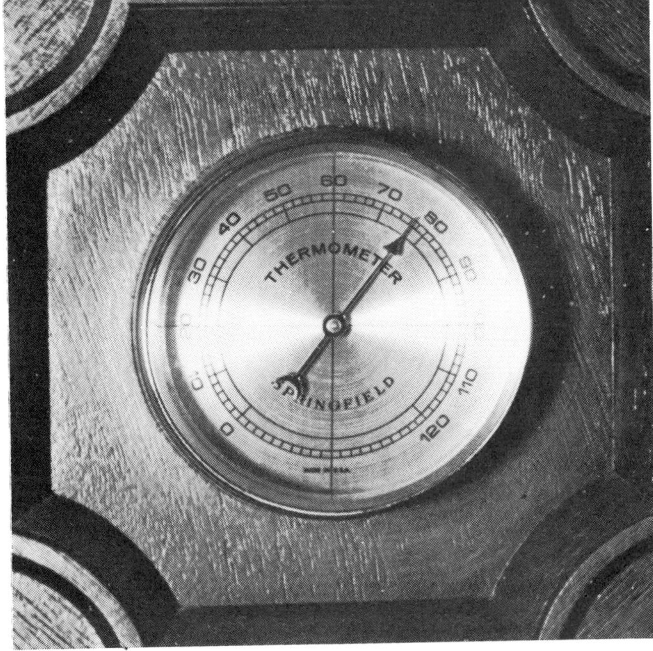

basics, try *Understanding Photography* by Carl Shipman. If your main interest is just shooting pictures and you don't care too much about how things work, read *How To Take Great Pictures With Your SLR* by Lou Jacobs, Jr.

However, if you've been having your negative material processed and printed commercially, you may not have been aware that your exposures have been somewhat in error. Automatic-printing equipment and custom photofinishers can correct a lot of problems. So, now take a minute to check against this list:

1. Read the film information sheet again to be sure you're using the recommended film speed.

2. Check your light-meter-instruction booklet so you know you are using it correctly. If the light meter is built into the camera, this means check camera instructions. Did you change the battery this year?

3. Check your light meter against another meter known to be accurate.

If you found any problems in either the exposure or processing checklist, make the necessary corrections, expose another roll of film and process as I've directed. This time you've got it, right?

MAKING PROOFS

The first thing to do with a roll of processed negatives is to see if any of the images will make the great pictures you want. Now is the time for proofing.

There are several ways to go about proofing, including the contact and enlarging methods. You will undoubtedly use both as time goes along. The contact sheet is the easiest and most popular.

A contact sheet is made simply by placing the negatives in contact with a sensitive paper and exposing to a light source. Done in the darkroom with enlarging-type papers such as Kodak's Kodabrome RC, the exposed paper is processed as any other developable paper. You can use a 15-watt frosted white bulb to expose the paper. If you have an enlarger you can use it as the light source with a normal enlarging paper. I'm going to have you use enlarging paper because you'll need it for enlargements later on. This keeps expenses down and eliminates confusion about which paper does what. Let's assume you don't have an enlarger yet and use the contact method first. Here's what you need:

SPECIFIC EQUIPMENT LIST

1 Light source. A table lamp, reading lamp, or a fixture in the room you are printing in will work fine. Equip the fixture with a 15-watt frosted-white bulb.
1 Contact printing (proof) frame 8x10 size, or
1 Piece 8x10-inch window glass, ¼-inch thick, or
1 Proofing device such as Paterson or Technal Contact Proof Printer
1 25-sheet package, 8x10-inch Kodak Kodabrome RC medium-contrast glossy enlarging paper
3 Processing trays, 11x14 inch
1 Kodak Dektol developer, can to make one quart working solution
1 Kodak Fixer, package to make one-half gallon
1 Brown-plastic bottle, 32-ounce size, to store developer stock solution, or
1 Air-Evac bottle
1 Brown-plastic bottle, 64-ounce size, to store fixer solution
1 Bottle of 28% acetic acid to make short stop. You may have already mixed this when you prepared your materials for developing film. If not, go back to page 10 and read how to make the 28% stock solution.
1 32-ounce white-plastic graduate
1 Thermometer, Weston Model 2265 dial-type
2 Print tongs
1 Scissors, large enough to find easily in dim light
1 Safelight with OC filter
1 Towel or roll of paper towels for drying hands

Buy Dektol in this one-quart can to get started on your black-and-white proofing adventures.

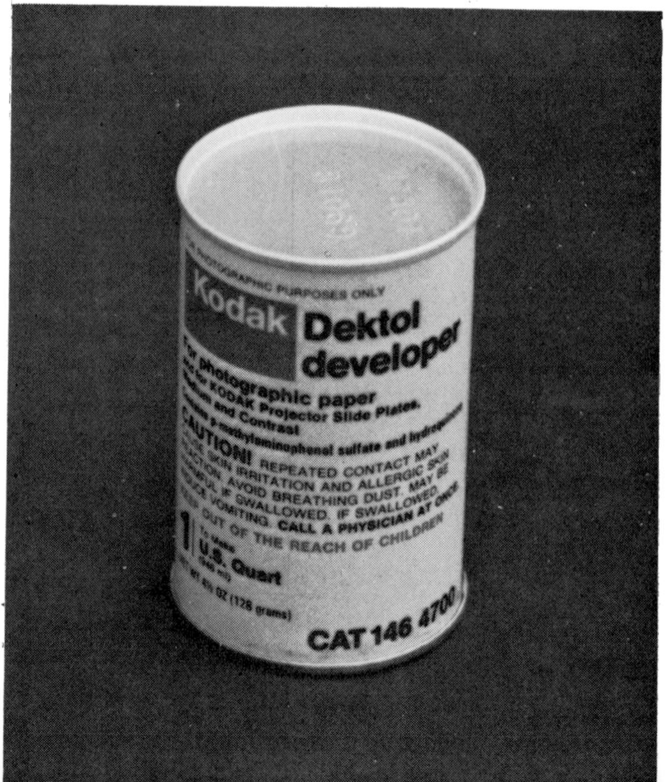

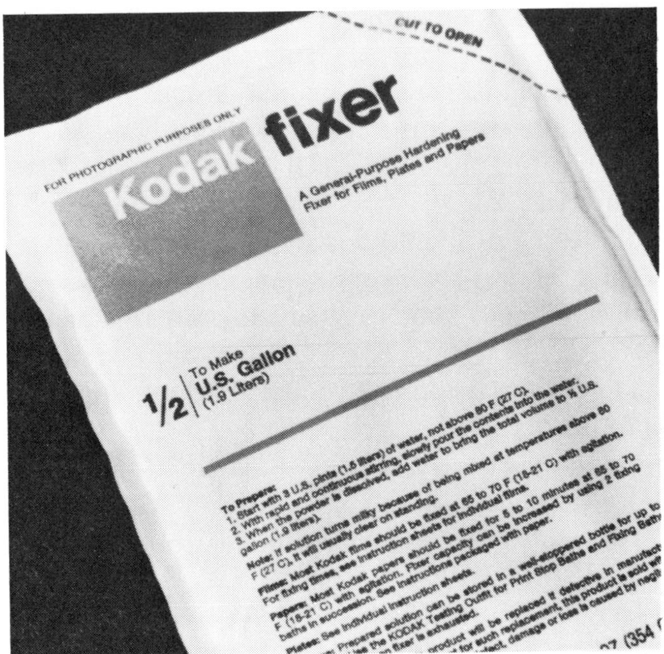

I recommend you start with Kodak Fixer for paper instead of the Rapid Fixer I like to use. It is slower working, but not so apt to bleach prints. Follow mixing instructions and use full-strength.

You've undoubtedly noted that you already have some of this stuff from when you got your film developing kit together. Although you already bought them for developing film, buy another 64-ounce bottle and another package of fixer for the prints. Do not attempt to use your film hypo for your prints. If you choose to use Kodak's Rapid Fixer for your prints, it must be mixed to only one half the strength used for film to avoid bleaching the prints.

GETTING THE SOLUTIONS READY

Put your trays in your kitchen sink or bathtub or other room which you can get dark. Spread some newspapers on top of what ever surface you are using so any spills will be soaked up. Developer makes awful brown stains and it also works like paint remover, so you want to keep it off of any painted or varnished surfaces. If you can use the bathroom and can keep the trays on a board laid across the bathtub, this works fine. Any spills then go down the drain and you can wash up easily afterward. Or, use the drainboard of the kitchen sink, taking great care to keep the developer away from any painted surfaces.

An alternative to the tray setup in a full-sized sink, is the Tray-Rak by Richard Mfg. Co. It stacks trays vertically to conserve space. Ideal for a bathroom or kitchen sink being used for print making. The equipment consists of a plastic coated wire frame in which the trays are held. Developer tray goes at the top, followed by the stop bath, with the fixer at the bottom. There is only provision for three trays so the hypo eliminator must be placed elsewhere. The eliminator cuts wash time and if your water bill is normally quite low, may not be of great interest to you. I do think it's wise to find space for it though because it helps to insure permanent prints when using non-RC paper.

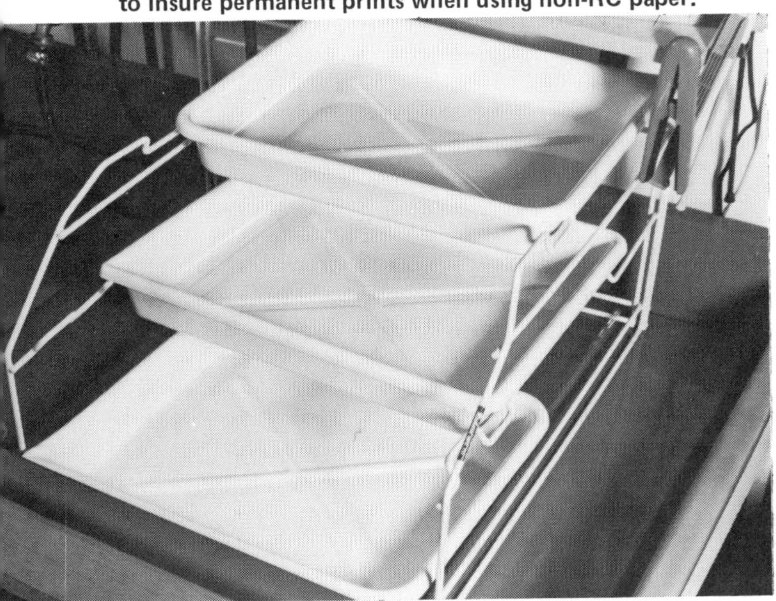

Before proofing is begun, the processing chemicals must be prepared. This shows the normal tray arrangement for making prints. This setup flows from right to left and the trays contain: developer; stop bath; fixer; hypo eliminator. The last item you can see here is my print washer. You won't need hypo eliminator when you use RC paper.

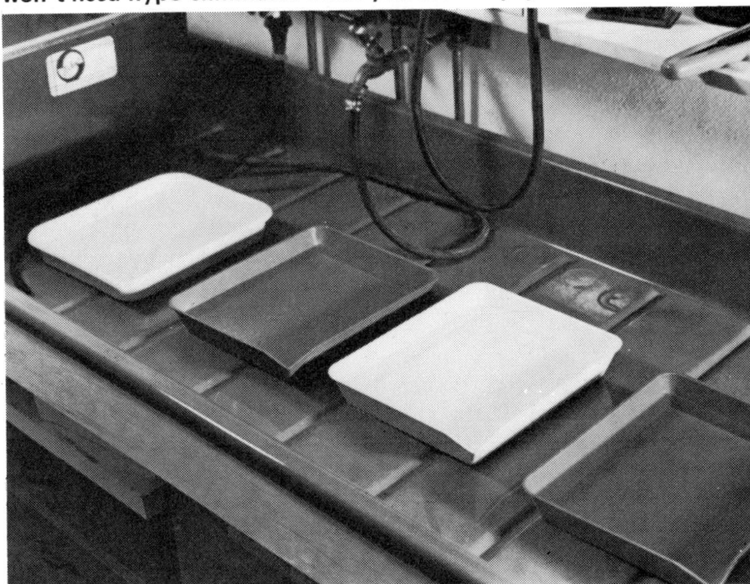

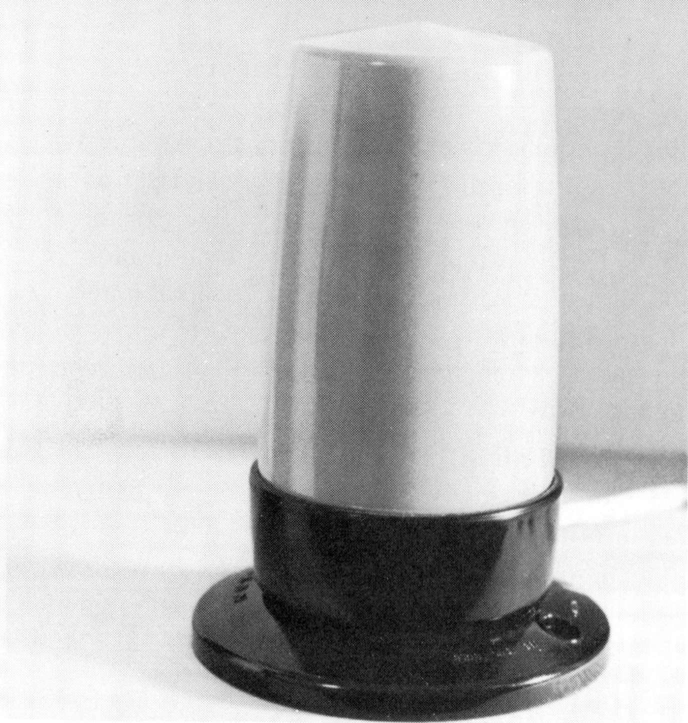

A safelight, such as this one made by Paterson, is necessary when working with print papers whether they are of the contact or enlarging variety. The light is inexpensive and may be set on a shelf or wall-mounted. It does not have an in-line switch and must be plugged in each time for use.

Sandmar Fireball Safelight costs about $10, lasts 2500 hours. It can be used in any lamp socket to provide a lot of *safe* light. Amber ones are for variable-contrast and graded enlarging and contact paper. Red one is used with ortho films.

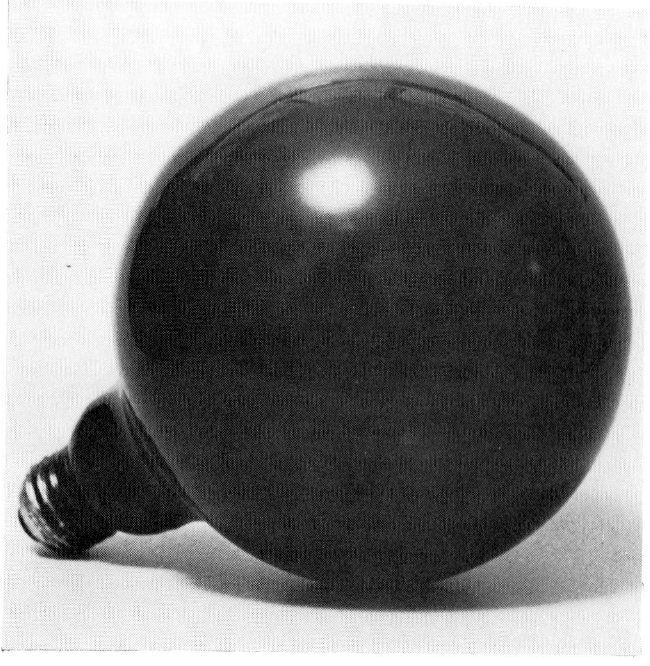

Developer—Mix the Dektol according to the directions on the package. This is your stock solution and it should be poured through the funnel into one of the brown bottles or your *air evac* bottle. Label it DEKTOL Stock Solution, Dilute 1:2. Add the date. Cool the solution in your refrigerator until it is approximately 65° to 75°F (18° to 24°C). Pour 8 ounces of this stock solution into a 32-ounce graduate. Add 16 ounces of water at the same temperature to the graduate and pour the resulting 24 ounces of print developer into the developer tray.

Stop Bath—Pour 1½ ounces of the 28% acetic acid into 32 ounces of water at 65° to 75°F (18° to 24°C) which you have placed in the stop bath tray.

Fixer—Mix the fixer and put it in a brown bottle. Label it FIXER and add the date. Cool it to 65° to 75°F (18° to 24°C) and place this 32 ounces of solution in the hypo tray.

Hypo Neutralizer—If you are using a hypo neutralizer, mix this and place it in another brown bottle. Label it NEUTRALIZER and date it. If you have an extra tray, it can be used for the hypo neutralizer. If not, you can use the neutralizer in one of the processing trays just before you wash the proofs. You won't need it with RC papers.

SAFELIGHT

Plug in the safelight and place it where it will be at least four feet away from your developer tray. It should be placed so it illuminates the developer tray.

CONTACT PRINTING METHODS

Although the three ways I will explain are all contact printing, I'll keep them separate to make it easier to understand what is going on.

Window-Glass or Contact-Proof Device Method—This requires the 8x10-inch piece of window glass—or larger—from the equipment list.

1. Cut the roll of negatives to fit an 8x10 piece of paper: Four to a strip with 2¼ square pix on 120; six to a strip with 35mm. If using proof device, clip the negatives onto the cover glass so the dull side will be down when you lower the glass and negs onto the paper.

2. Turn off room light, turn on safelight.

3. Open Kodabrome RC paper and take out one sheet. Use the scissors to cut the sheet in half, then in quarters. This gives you four pieces of

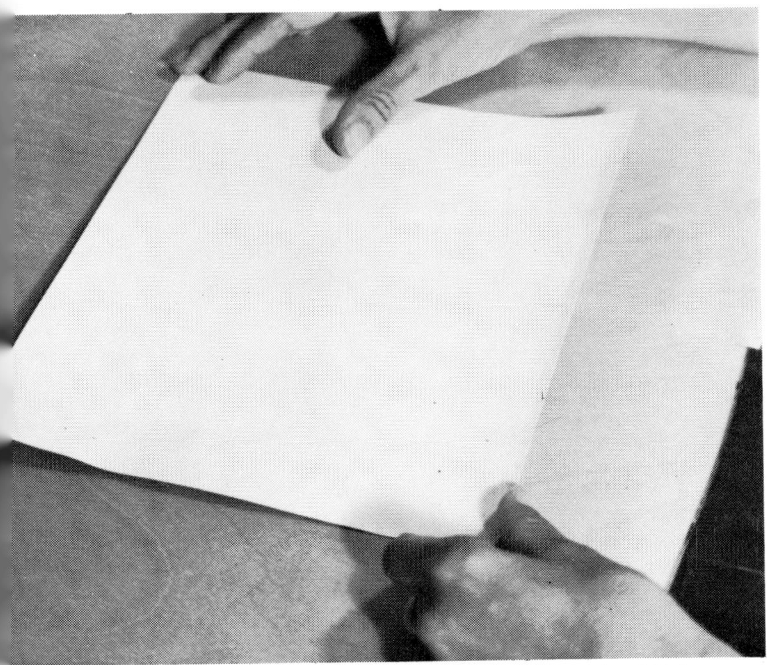

With the room light and enlarger light off and safelight on, place a sheet of enlarging paper in the marked area.

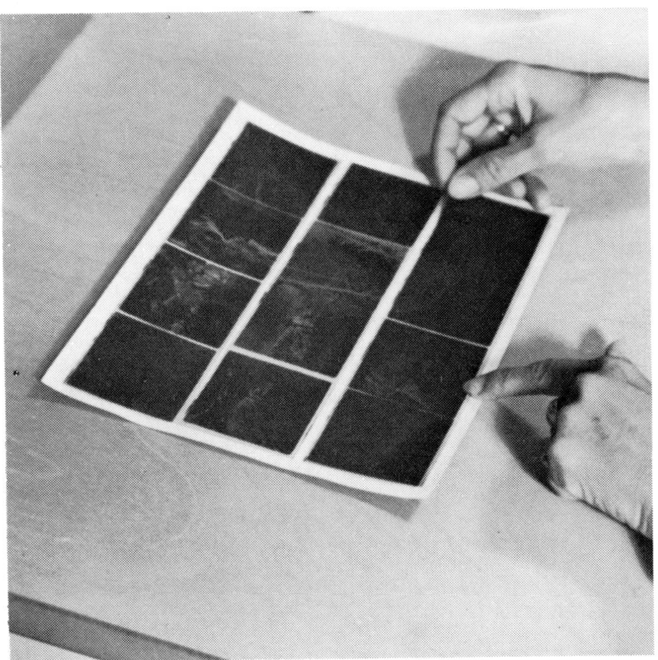

Place the cut negative strips on the paper, emulsion side down. Cut 120 film into three strips of four 2¼x2¼ negatives.

paper 4x5 inches. Return three of these to the envelope and put the envelope back into the outer package. The one you keep out is a test strip. Note that the paper package is light-tight and the maker ensures that it keeps the paper away from light by the use of flaps and by putting the open end of the second envelope inside of the closed end of the first one.

4. Lay 4x5 piece of paper on working surface, shiny side up.

5. Place two of the negative strips side-by-side dull side down, overlapping the paper.

6. Cover the negatives and paper with the window glass to ensure good contact of the negatives with the paper. Or, lower the proof device glass and negatives onto the paper.

Glass for contact printing—Get a piece of thick glass from a glass store. 11x14 inches is a good size because the extra weight of the glass helps to press the negatives firmly in contact with the paper. Have the glass people round the sharp corners and edges for you so you won't get cut as you handle it.

Cover the negative/paper sandwich with an 8x10 sheet of clear glass to hold the negatives in tight contact with the paper.

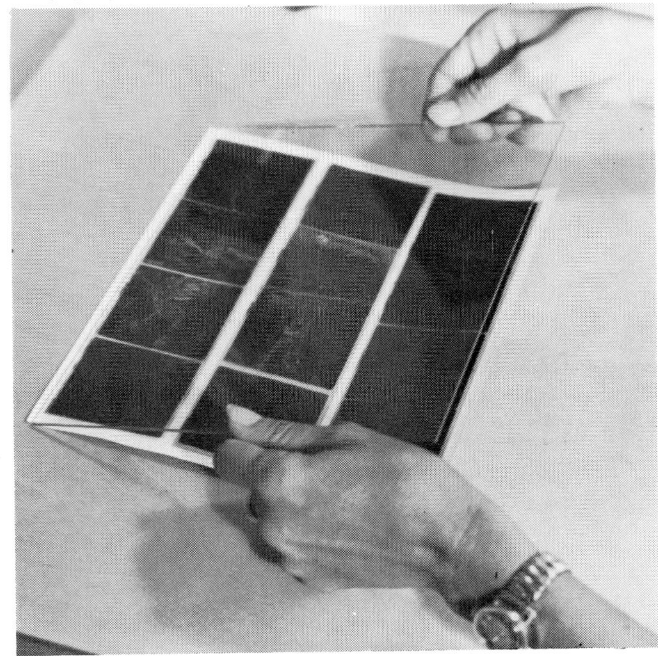

7. Expose the proof test strip by turning on a 15-watt frosted white bulb, approximately 4 feet from the glass/negative/paper sandwich for 4 seconds.

8. Remove glass and negatives or raise cover glass of proof device. Take out paper and put into tray of developer. Agitate the print in the tray by gently rocking the tray or by turning it over with the print tongs every few seconds. If you slide the edge of the paper under the surface of the developer it will usually go right in and be covered with the liquid without your hand getting wet. If your hand does get wet, wash it off in clean water and dry it thoroughly. Leave the test print in the developer for 1½ minutes.

9. Place paper in stop bath for 30 seconds by using developer tongs to lift the print out of the developer, then drop it in the stop bath without touching the tongs to the stop bath. Remember that the developer is alkaline and the stop

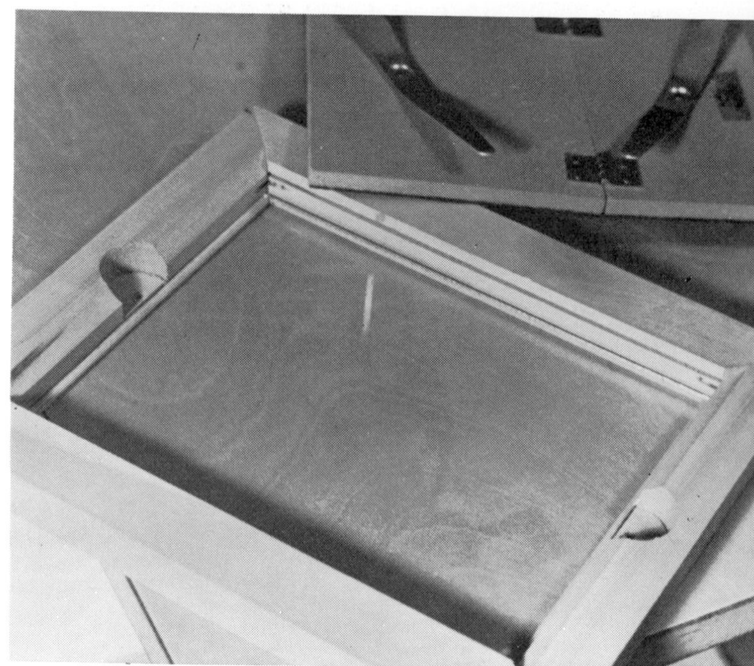

A proof frame such as this one by Premier can be of great help to hold negatives and paper when making contact sheets using the enlarger.

Keep those tongs where they belong—Developer is alkaline and stop bath and fixer are acid. You don't want to carry acid into the developer because it reduces the life of the developer. Keep the developer tongs in the developer and keep their tips above the liquid surface when you drop a developed print into the stop bath. When you use the stop bath tongs, keep them in the stop bath or the fixer. Both solutions are acid, so there's no problem with placing them on the edge of either tray. If you have stainless-steel tongs, these wash off and you never have to worry about which place you use them, but the warning applies: Once you start a printing session, keep the developer tongs only in the developer and keep the stop/fixer tongs only in those solutions. If you buy plastic tongs, always use the red ones for the developer and keep the black ones for the stop/fixer. If you buy bamboo tongs, mark the developer tongs so you will always use them only for developer. After a few sessions the developer tongs will be stained so dark you won't have any problem identifying them.

When using a contact-printing or proof frame such as this one, the negatives go in first, emulsion side facing up.

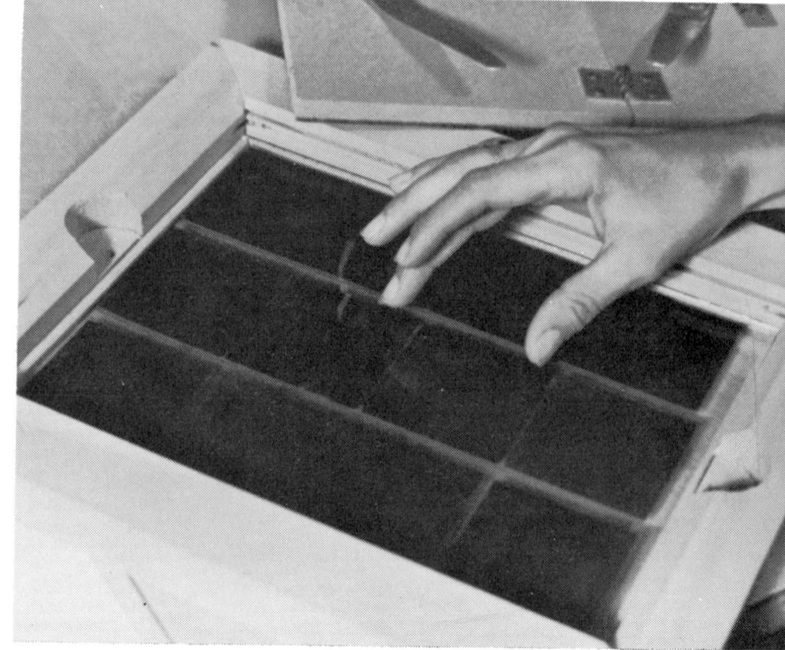

bath is acid. You don't want to reduce the alkalinity of the developer by carrying short stop or hypo into the developer with the tongs. Keep the developer tongs in the developer and the stop bath tongs in the stop bath or hypo. Don't mix 'em up, please!

10. After 30 seconds in the stop bath, put the print into the fixer. It won't hurt the print if you leave it longer in the stop bath, but don't turn on the light until the print has been in the fixer for at least a minute.

11. After a minute in the fixer, turn on the white light. If the print is too dark, go back to step 7 and expose another 4x5 piece of paper with the 15-watt frosted white bulb at 4 feet for 2 seconds. If it is too light, expose another 4x5 test strip for 6 seconds.

12. If it looked OK, continue to fix for another minute, then wash 4 minutes in running water and dry as described in the next chapter.

Contact-Printing or Proofing Frame Method—This method is accomplished exactly like the previous one except steps 1, 4 and 6 are slightly changed.

1. Cut the roll of negatives to fit an 8x10 piece of paper: Four to a strip with 2¼ square pix on 120; six to a strip with 35mm. Remove the back of the proofing frame. Lay the negatives onto the glass of the proofing frame dull side up.

4. Lay a 4x5 piece of paper onto the negatives shiny side down.

6. Close the back of the proofing frame, using the spring clips to secure it. Turn the frame so the glass faces the lamp you will be using to make the exposure.

Contact-Printer Method—Contact printers have become quite rare and you seldom see them anymore except at photo swap meets or in professional labs. Amateurs seldom use them because most pictures are made on roll film which must be enlarged. An enlarger can be used for proofing as I'll explain in the next section. Using a contact printer is accomplished exactly like the previous method with the proofing frame except you lay the negatives on the contact printer glass dull side up, then cover them with a 4x5 piece of paper shiny side down and close the platen or cover of the printer. When you close the cover, this may cause the white light inside the printer to turn on. Turning the printer off requires raising the platen or opening the

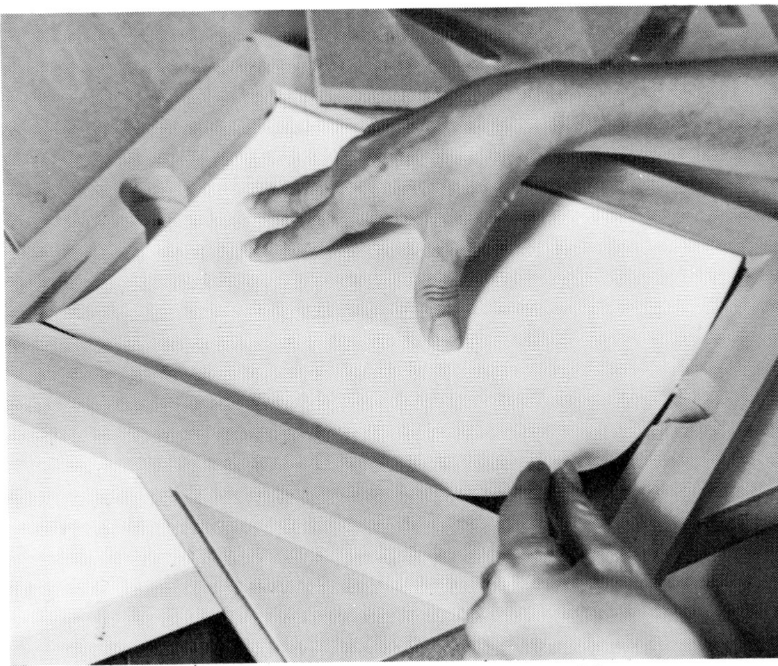

Next, place the enlarging paper on the negatives, emulsion side down.

Place the spring-held back on the frame ensuring complete contact between negatives and paper. Turn the frame over, place under the light you are using to expose your proofs.

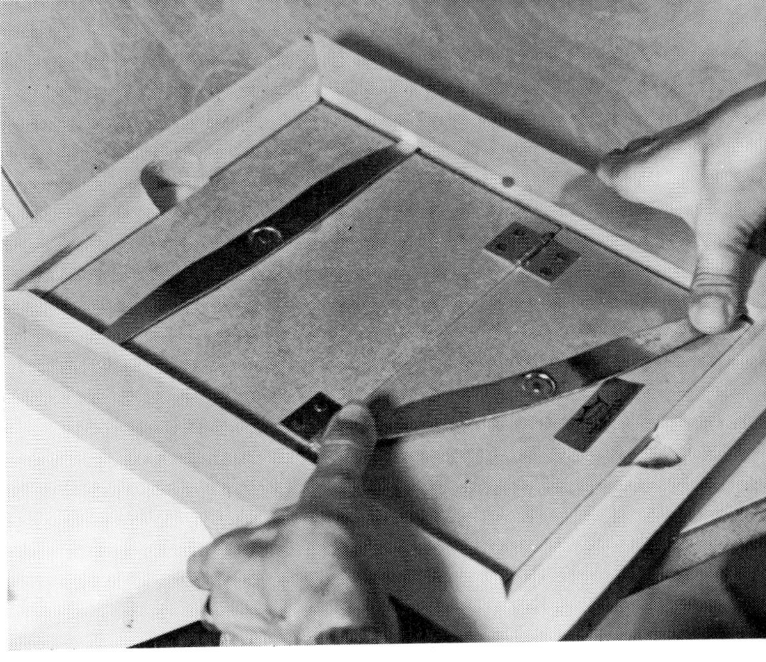

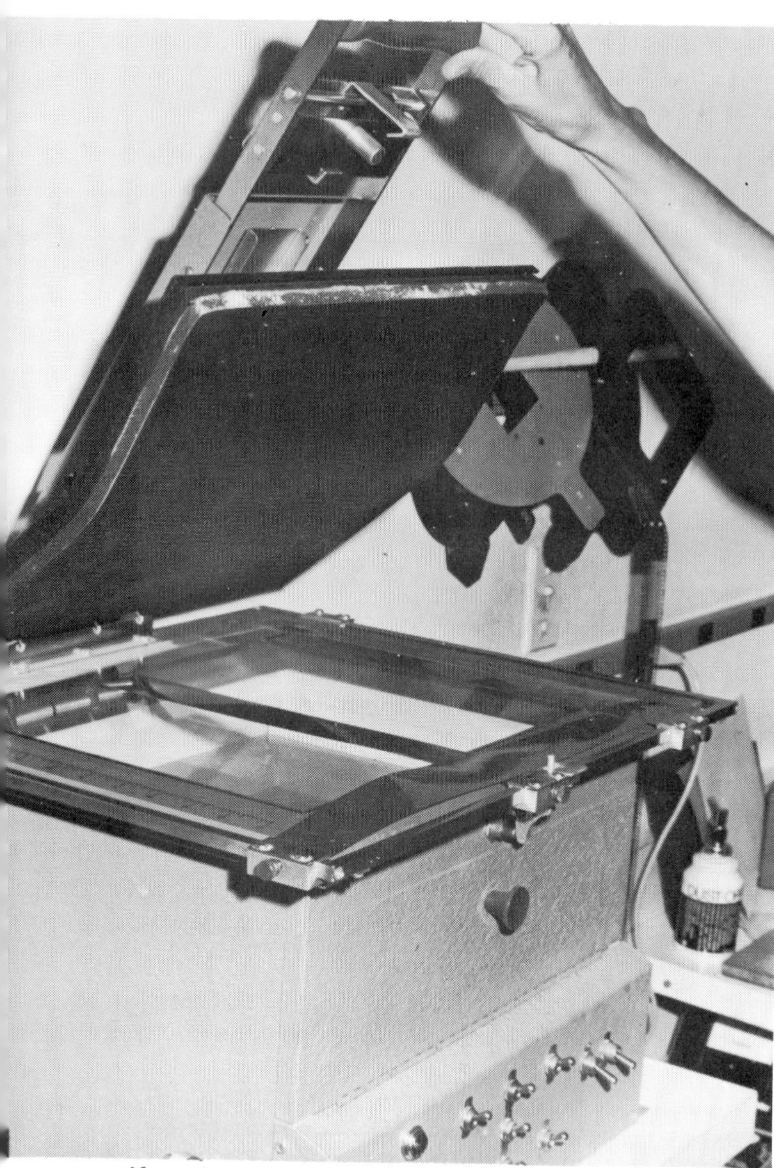

If you have a contact printer, making contact prints will be simple and quick. Switches control light to various areas of the printing surface.

cover. Some printers have a separate switch so you can close and lock the cover, then turn on the white light inside with a separate switch. No separate light source is required because it is built into the printer. I can't give you any idea of what exposure to try. You might start at five seconds and go up or down, depending on the appearance of your test print. If you run out of 4x5 test strips, cut some more as there's no sense wasting full sheets of paper just to find the correct exposure.

ENLARGER METHOD (for contact prints)

1. Adjust enlarger head height so the light covers an area an inch or so larger than 8x10 inches on the enlarger baseboard.

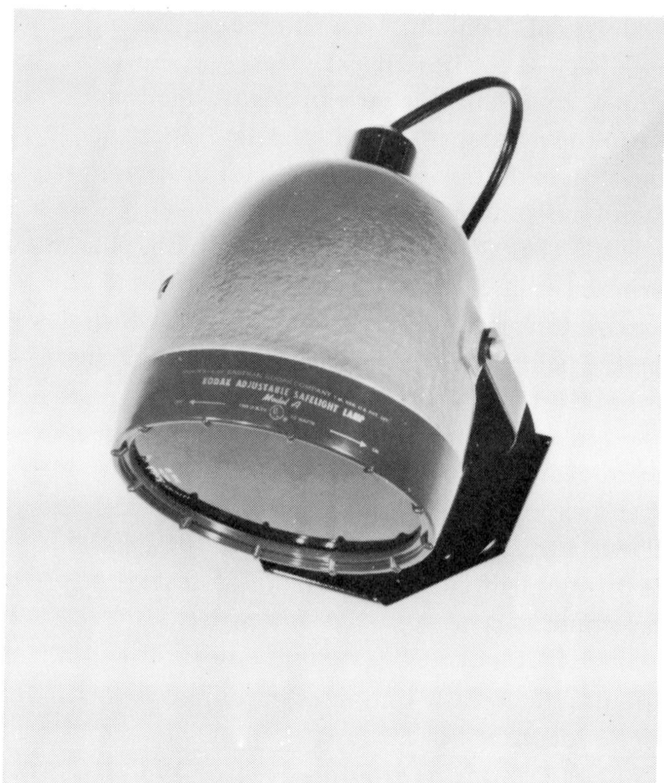

Kodak Adjustable Safelight Lamp Model A can be supported from wall or shelf. It takes a 5 1/2" filter and 15-watt bulb, neither of which is included. Your photo dealer can supply the proper filter to match your favorite paper type.

Kodabrome RC enlarging paper is what I recommend you use for proofing and enlarging. Resin-coated papers offer tremendous advantages for your darkroom activities.

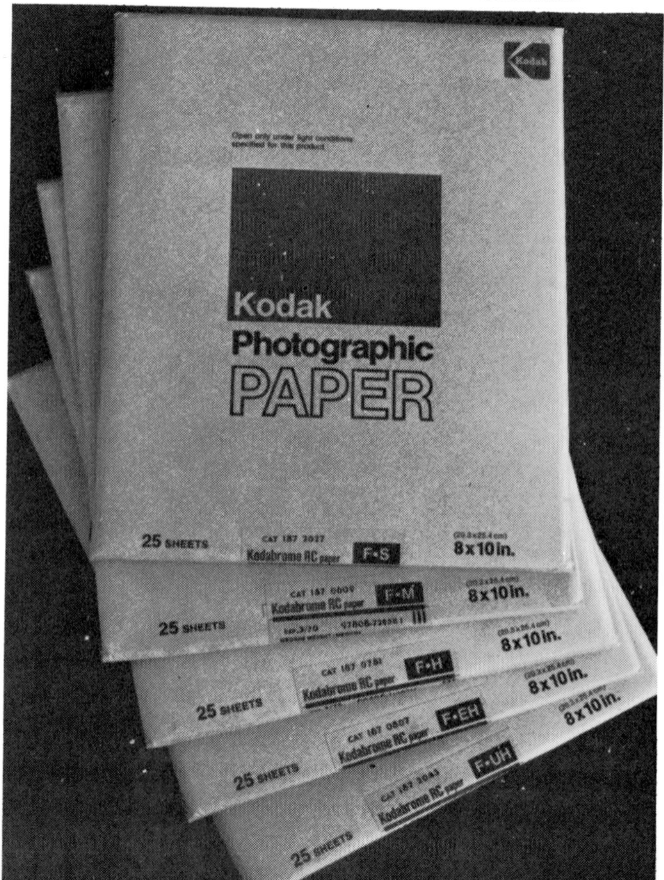

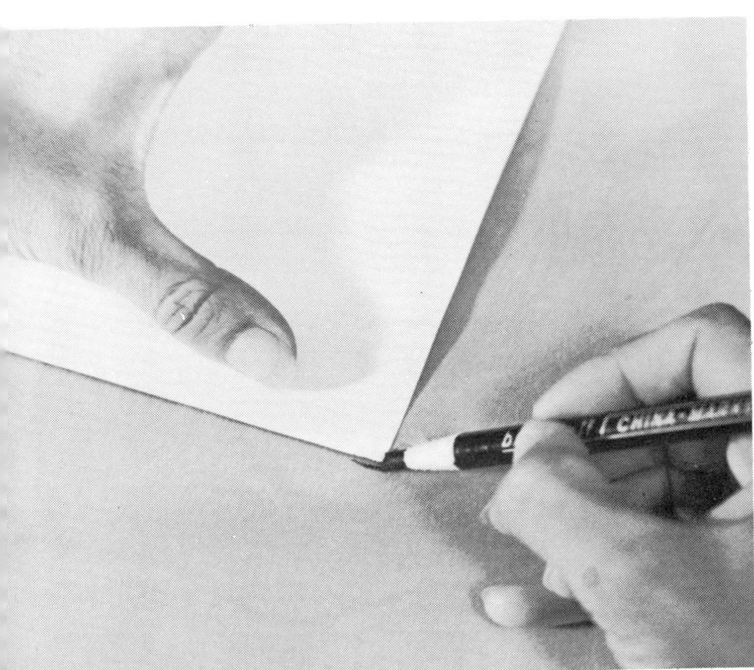

Using an 8x10 sheet of plain white paper in the light cone of the enlarger, make a grease pencil mark on the enlarger baseboard. This will give you a reference when placing the enlarging paper and negatives on the baseboard when the enlarger is switched off.

2. With a grease pencil or marking tape, mark the area covered by the light on the enlarger baseboard.

3. Cut the roll of negatives to fit an 8x10 sheet of paper: Four to a strip for 2¼ square pix on 120 film; six to a strip with 35mm. Tuck the negatives into the film clips if you are using a proofing device. The dull side must be down when you close the glass over the paper.

4. Turn room light off, enlarger light off and safelight on. Open Kodabrome RC paper and take out one sheet. Use the scissors to cut the sheet in half, then in quarters. This gives you four pieces of paper 4x5 inches. Return three of these to the envelope and put the envelope back into its outer package. The one you keep out is called a *test strip.* Note that the paper package is light-tight and the maker insures keeping the paper away from light by using flaps and by putting the flapped end of the second envelope inside the closed end of the first one.

5. Lay enlarging paper test strip shiny side up in the marked area.

6. Place two of the negative strips side by side on paper with the dull side down, or insert negs into clips of proofing device.

7. Cover negatives and paper with the sheet

If light leaks out of your enlarger, place a sheet of flat-black poster board or cloth over the wall behind your enlarger to avoid possible reflection of white light when the enlarger is turned on.

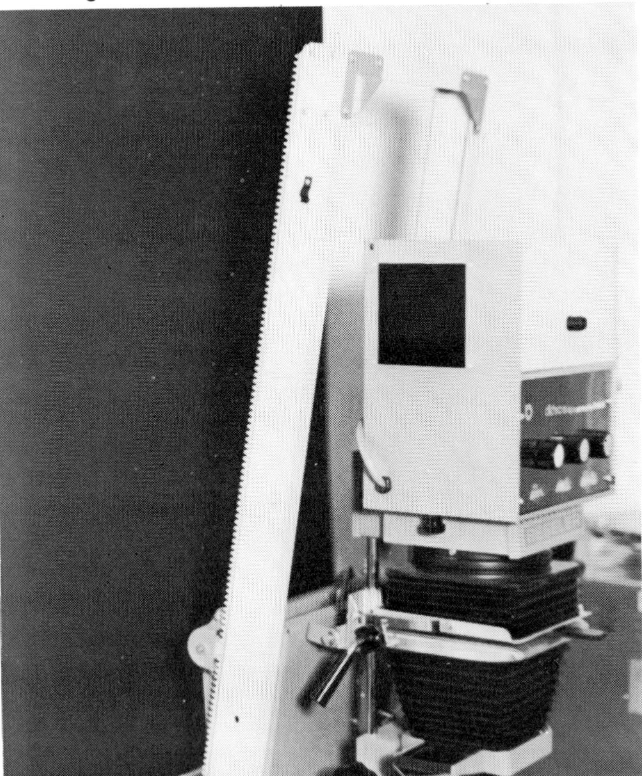

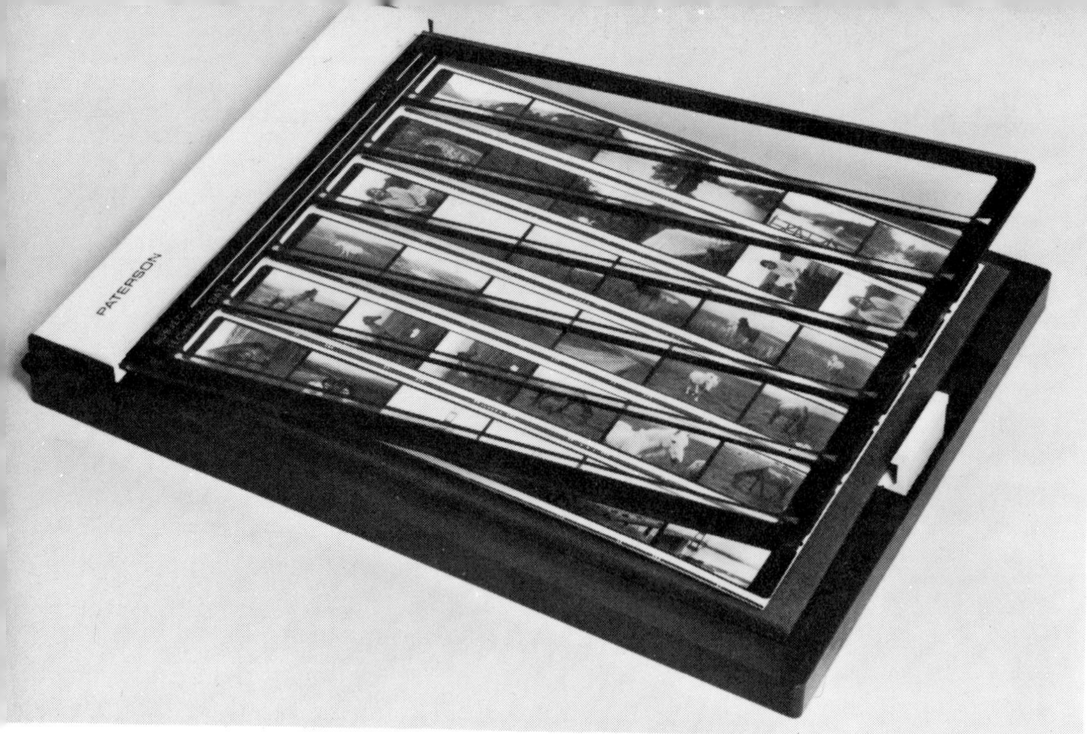

Paterson proofing device is offered in 35mm as shown here. Another unit handles 120 film. These hold the negatives in clips to make proofing an easy job.

of window glass to ensure good contact of the negatives with the paper, or lower glass with negatives onto paper if you are using a proofing device.

8. With enlarger lens diaphragm full open, turn on enlarger for one second.

9. Remove glass and negatives or open cover glass of proofing device. Put paper into tray of developer. Agitate print in tray by gently rocking tray or by turning print over with print tongs every few seconds. If you slide the paper under the surface of the developer it will usually go right in without your hand getting wet. If you wet your hand, wash it off in clean water and dry thoroughly. Develop test print for 1½ minutes.

10. Place paper in stop bath for 30 seconds by using developer tongs to lift the print out of the developer, then drop it into the stop bath without getting the tongs in the stop bath.

11. After 30 seconds in the stop bath, put the print into the fixer. It won't hurt the print if you leave it longer in the stop bath, but don't turn on the white light yet.

12. After a minute in the fixer, turn on the room light and judge the quality of your proof. If it is too dark go back to step 8 and expose another test strip with the lens aperture closed down two *f*-stops. If it is too light, expose another test strip three seconds instead of one. You may have to make several increases/decreases in exposure time to find the correct exposure. Once you have it, make a note of the time and aperture as you will be using your enlarger often for making proofs.

13. Once you have found the correct exposure, turn off room light, place a full 8x10 sheet of paper on the baseboard or in the proofing device, put all of the negatives from the roll onto the paper, lay the window glass on carefully or close the cover glass of the proofing device.

14. Turn on the enlarger for the exposure you found to be correct.

15. Remove glass or cover glass and place paper in developer for 1½ minutes, agitating the print in the tray as before.

16. Place print in stop bath for 30 seconds, then in fixer for one minute before turning on room light.

17. Turn on room light and check the quality of your proof sheet. It should be beautiful.

18. Return proof sheet to fixer for another minute, then wash for four minutes and lay the print on a towel to dry.

EXPOSING BY SUNLIGHT

A third method is faster, and eliminates the need to set up the darkroom. You must have a proofing frame and a material called *printing-out-paper,* sometimes known as proof paper. Kodak labels it "Studio Proof." It is sensitive to ultraviolet and you can handle it in normal room light. Negative strips are placed in the proof frame, dull side up—shiny side toward the glass. Cover the

Contact sheets are the best way to determine which negatives on each roll are worth printing. A contact print gives images the same size as the negative image. This sheet was made in a proofing device which provides title information to aid in filing.

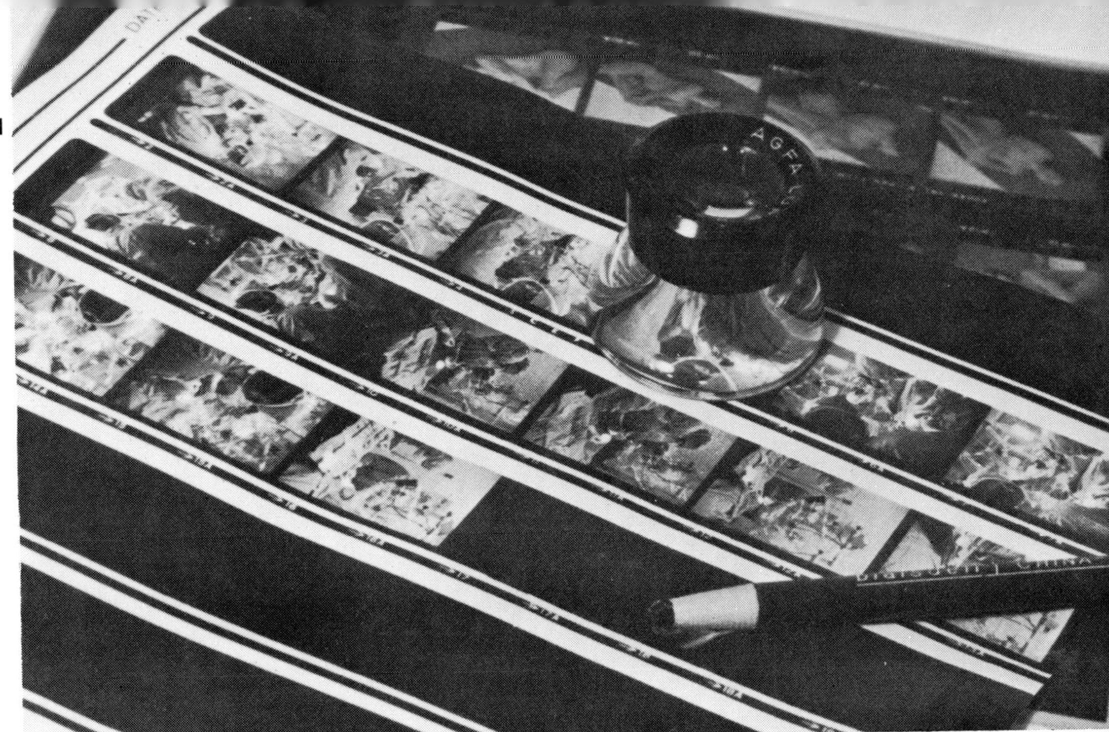

negatives with proof paper with the shiny side down toward the negatives, and lock the proof frame. The "sandwich" is held in direct sunlight until the paper appears dark purple and then taken inside and opened. Surprise! Nearly instant proofs.

The proofs are not permanent and will continue to darken with exposure to light. If you wish, you can soak the proofs in fixer for five minutes. Wash and dry as described in the next chapter and you will have made them permanent. If you do fix them, you'll notice they change to a tan sepia color, but don't be alarmed. After all, proofs are made only to determine which negatives you wish to enlarge. Don't concern yourself too much about top-notch quality. Decide beforehand if you are going to fix and keep the proofs made on printing-out-paper. With this paper the fixer will bleach the image a great deal, so give it considerably more exposure than you would normally. Images which appear to be about twice as dark as desirable will bleach out just about right when run through the fixer.

B&W PROOFS FROM COLOR NEGS

For convenience, time and economy, you can proof color negatives the same as black and white. With printing-out-paper or by the darkroom methods, the only difference will be that a longer exposure time is necessary. Proofs will appear a bit flat in contrast because, when printing on

If you have an enlarging timer such as this Time-O-Lite, set it at one second. A wrist watch with sweep-second hand or a mental count of "one-thousand-one" may be used if necessary. The lens aperture should be set at its widest opening.

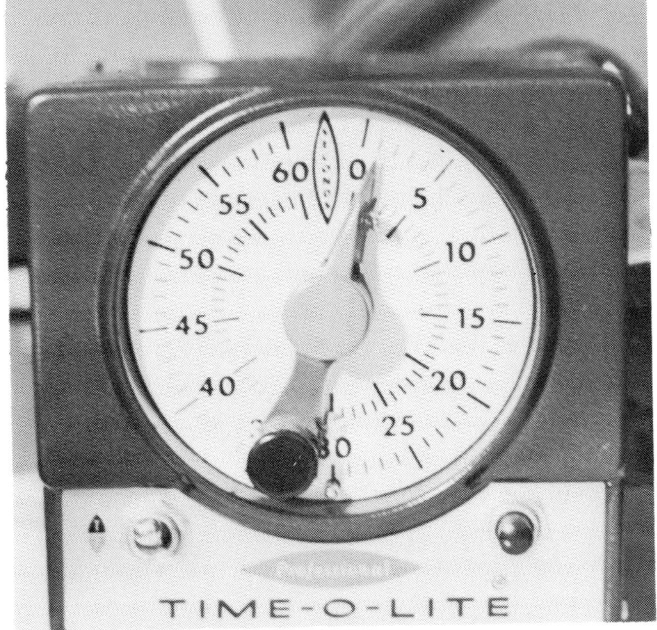

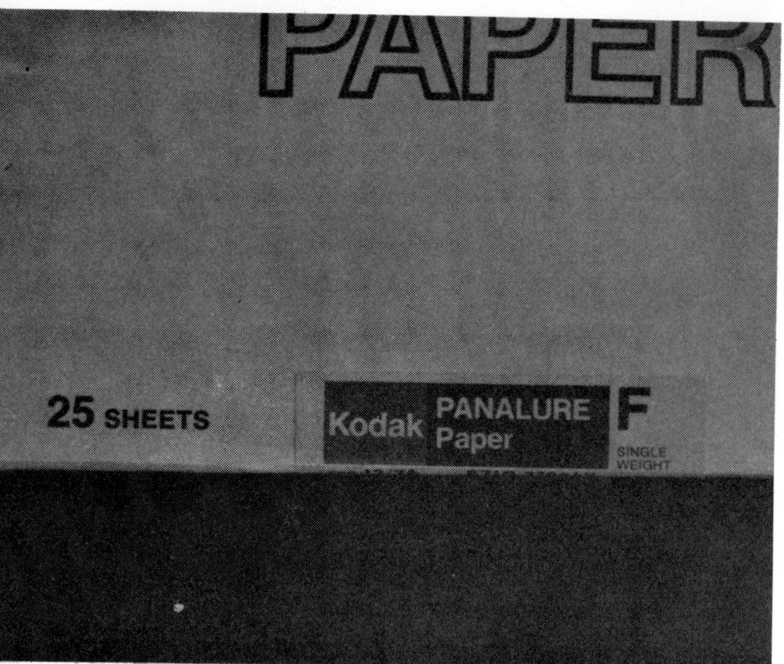

Kodak's Panalure paper lets you make black and white proofs of color negatives. It is a panchromatic paper so you get a good rendering of all of the color.

paper designed to be used with a safelight, the orange-colored base of color-negative film cuts the paper's sensitivity to white light. But, again, you only need proofs for file and reference information so quality is of less importance. By the way, making proofs is the only time I will let you get by with print quality less than the best!

If you want to get maximum print quality in your color-neg proofs, Kodak's Panalure paper is designed for making black and white prints from color negatives. This paper is sensitive to all colors of light and must be used in total darkness. You may, if you feel it necessary, use a No. 13—dark amber—safelight with this paper for a few seconds at a time, no closer to the paper than four feet. Expose the Panalure under the enlarger in the normal manner and process by time and temperature. With Dektol developing solution at 68°F (20°C) I recommend a developing time of 1½ minutes. Colder solutions take longer, warmer ones slightly less. A couple of small test strips may be worth the effort. After developing, Panalure is handled during the processing, washing and drying as any *standard* black-and-white paper. This means fixing for 10 minutes, then a one-minute water wash. Follow this with hypo neutralizer per instructions and finally wash in running water for at least 10 minutes. Dry as described on page 120.

FILING PROOFS AND NEGATIVES

Proof sheets are great for reference—they can be filed in a loose-leaf binder and index-numbered to the corresponding negatives. This eliminates the need to handle the negatives when searching out a particular frame for printing. The less negative handling, the better.

Negatives may be stored in a number of ways. The simplest is to use clear plastic holders with pockets such as Print File Negative Preservers, which hold an entire roll on one page. There is space marked at the top of the sheet for subject, date and file number. You can even put the negatives in the preservers, then make your proofs without having to handle the negs again. Although the sheet will not fit in the proof frame used for printing-out-paper, it can be used in a contact printer or under the enlarger with a piece of glass. It allows you to keep the negatives in nice, neat rows. The negative holders can also be filed in a loose-leaf binder for easy access.

Nega-File and Apeco make glassine negative envelopes to file individual strips of film. They are available in sizes for all roll and sheet film, along with file boxes for each envelope size. The boxes are well made and convenient for storage.

As for numbering to identify your negs and proofs, a simple way is to use roll and year. The proof sheet made from the first roll taken in 1975 would be numbered **1-75**. Seem simple? It is. When checking proofs for printable negatives, make notes such as **12-74-18**. The eighteenth frame on the twelfth roll shot in 1974. Naturally the negative sheets or envelopes are numbered to correspond.

If you are using color-negative film as well as black-and-white, use the same numbering system and add the letter "c" at the end: **1-75c**.

One more thought on filing. Don't throw away proofs and negatives you think are of no value at the moment. File them all. You'll be surprised at how often over the years you will look back through your file and see something you overlooked before. As you progress and mature photographically, your ideas and values will change, and a negative which seemed dull and uninteresting today may just fit your desires tomorrow. At the very least, it is a visual diary of your past photographic ability and progress.

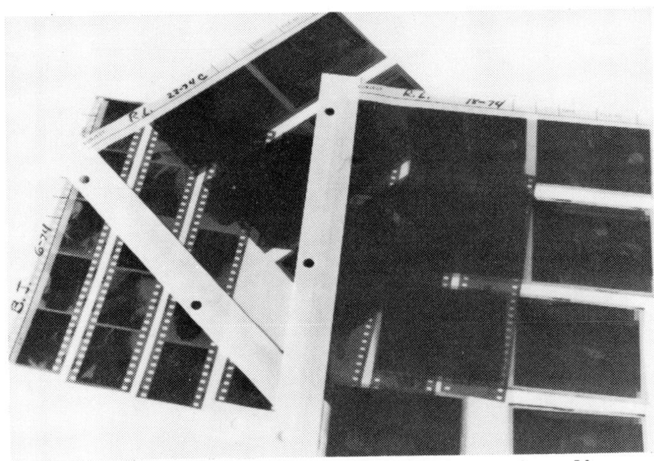

Clear-plastic sheets are excellent for filing negatives. Negatives are easily viewed and may be contact-printed using the glass-cover technique or with a contact printer, without having to remove them from the protective sheet.

The negative sheet with its contact sheet may be conveniently filed in a loose-leaf ring binder.

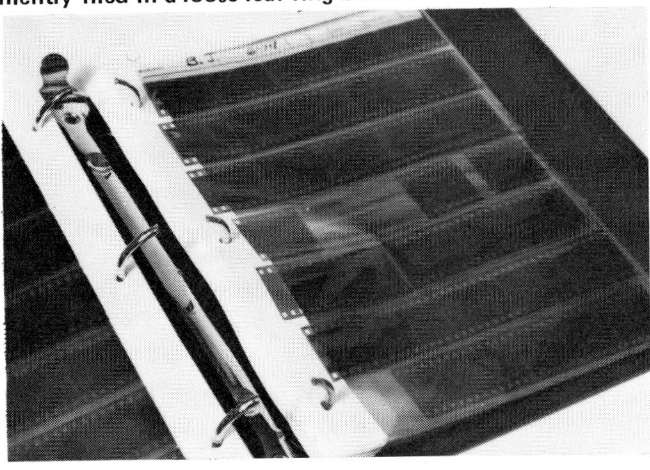

Glassine negative preservers hold single strips of film in any and all sizes. They may be filed and stored in anything from a commercially made wooden box, to—and probably more common—an old shoe box. DO NOT GET THESE ENVELOPES WET AS THEY WILL STICK TO THE FILM AND LEAVE A RESIDUE WHICH IS ALMOST IMPOSSIBLE TO REMOVE!

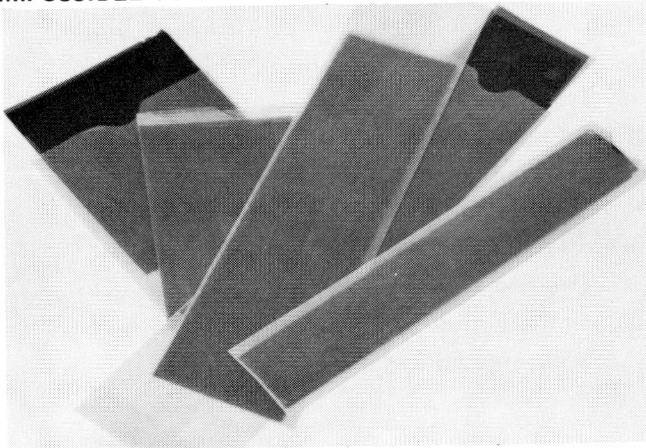

PRINT SELECTIVELY

Now your negatives are in their numbered, protective envelopes. Sit down, relax and study the proof sheets. Look closely at each and every frame, using a good magnifier such as an Agfa Lupe 8x. Be critical. At least two-thirds of them seem to have no reason for being at all, right? This is the time when you wonder what you had in mind when you made the camera exposures. This is how a proof-sheet saves you time and money.

It is disheartening to spend time in the darkroom making enlargements from every frame to find out that you really don't need or want them all. Save all negatives—remember tomorrow! But be selective about what you enlarge today. A picture which is obviously bad on the proof sheet will only be bigger, not better, in an enlargement. A basically bad picture is bad—no matter what size you make it. Learn from your errors and select only the negatives you really want enlarged.

This is a good time to determine roughly how you will crop the picture to improve its composition or visual effect. An unwanted tree or hand at the edge does not always mean the frame is of no value. The enlarging process allows you to use only the part of the negative you like.

For the world's simplest numbering system, read the text. This is the proof sheet for the seventh roll I shot in 1974.

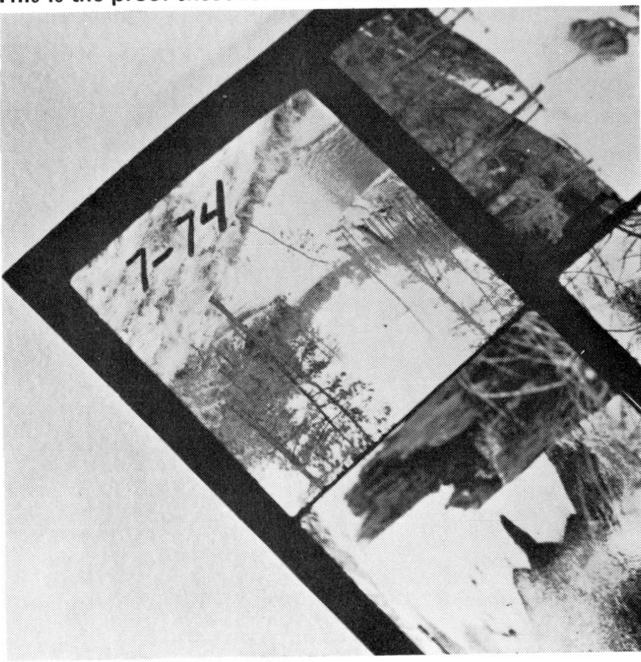

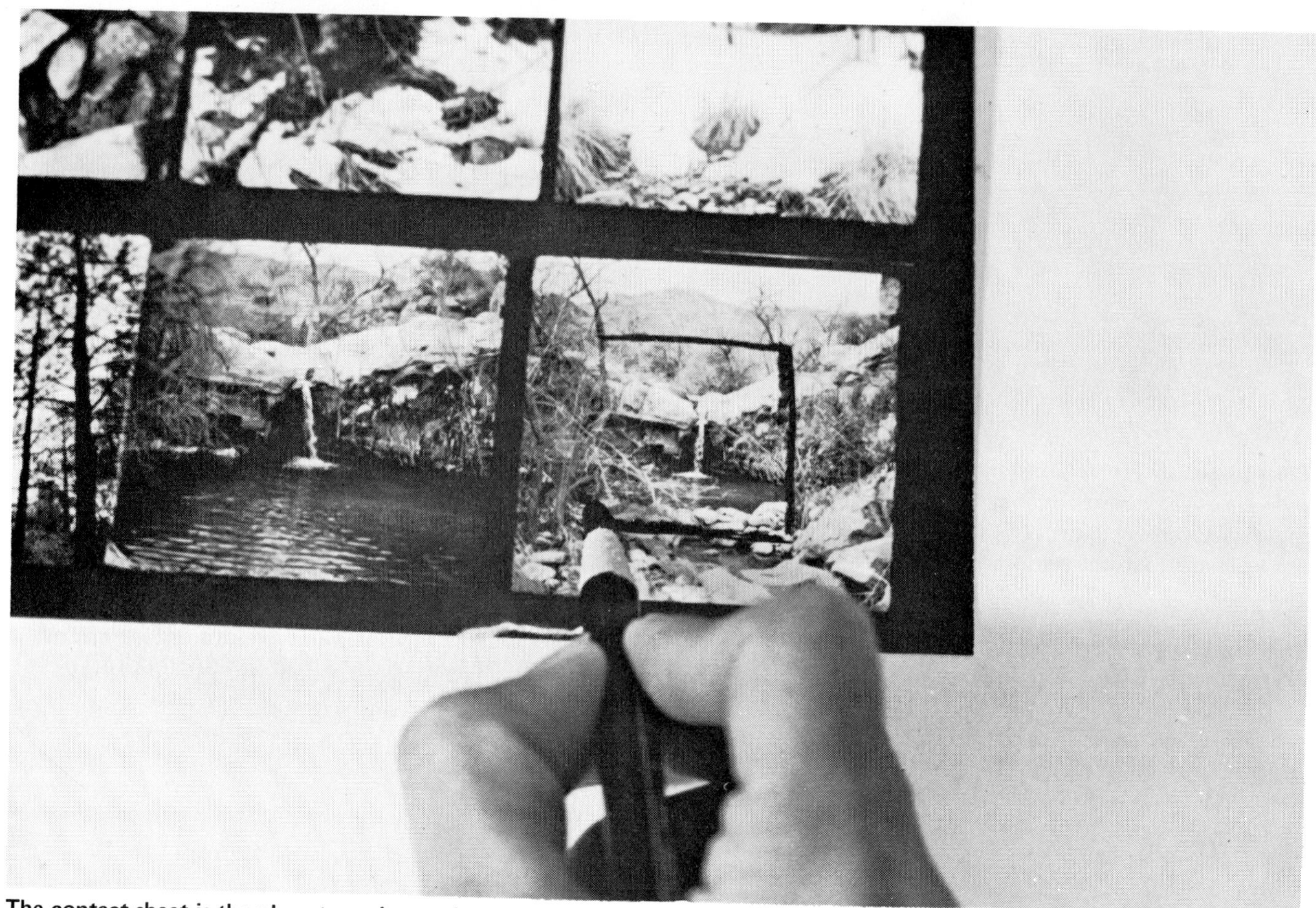

The contact sheet is the place to evaluate what you really have on film. Once you've determined which negatives you want to print, use a grease pencil to mark off the rough area you want to use. You don't have to use every millimeter of the exposed negative. This is where you start to refine the composition you created when you clicked the shutter.

THINK CLEAN

Now, regarding marks on the dry negatives, first determine the cause. If the film base—shiny side—is water-marked, streaks of dull grayish material will appear, running lengthwise down the film. This is caused by mineral deposits in the wash water and can be eliminated by using fresh, clean Photo-Flo prior to drying. If you still have an occasional water spot, clean the film when dry with Kodak Film Cleaner and cotton balls. Work very gently as the film will scratch if too much pressure is used. Make sure the film is free of dust before using the cleaner because this, too, will result in thin scratches which will need correction later.

If you find small dirt or dust particles dried into the emulsion, the film must be rewashed. When the film is thoroughly wet, very gently remove the offending material with a wet cotton ball if the grit has not already been removed by water action.

After the wash, soak for one minute in Photo-Flo, squeegee and hang to dry. Be sure the spot chosen for drying is free from dust-laden air.

If you have encountered dirt particles either in the camera or during the developing process, you may have film with very fine scratches. Scratches print as thin white lines and are extremely difficult to correct on the final enlargement. A bottle of Edwal No-Scratch will do wonders here. With the applicator brush, apply a thin even coating of the fluid on the side of the film which is scratched. Place the negative in the enlarger and print normally. The scratch will completely disappear when the negative is printed. Wipe off the fluid gently after the negative is printed and before you file it away.

The best way is to take extreme care to avoid dirt, scratches and spots through the entire procedure beginning with the camera.

Choosing Your Darkroom Equipment

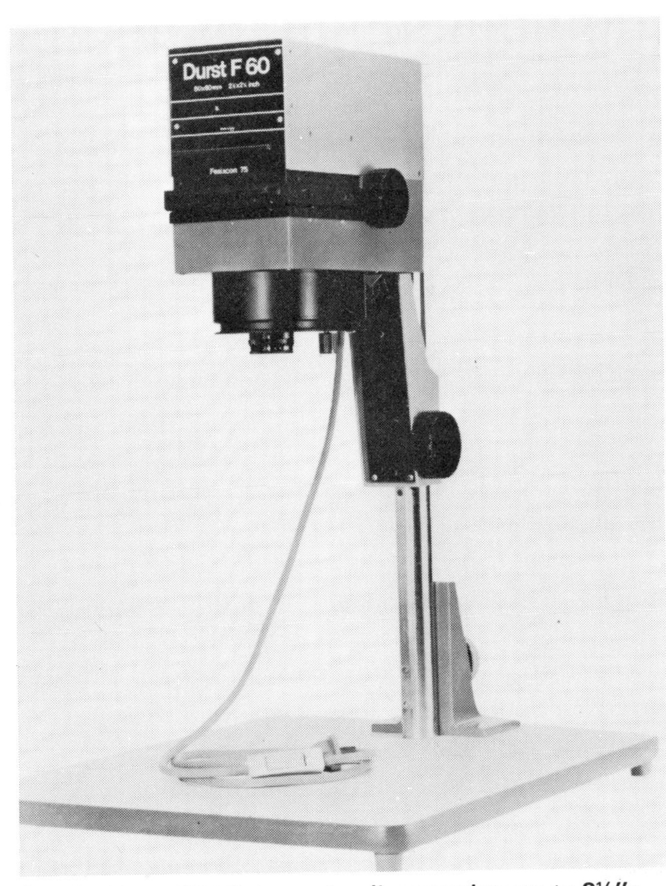

Popular Durst F60 Enlarger handles negatives up to 2¼"x 2¼", takes apart for storage. Switch is in power cord, or you can use a timer to turn it on and off.

Let's discuss the equipment necessary for printing photographs. Here's a list:

Enlarger
Washer
Dryer or blotter roll (not essential with RC paper)
Safe light
Print trays
Chemicals
Timer
Assorted little things

ENLARGER

Several good enlargers are available. In the U.S., Simmon Omega, Durst and Beseler are considered to be excellent choices. They handle negatives from sub-miniature through 5x7 inch. In general, 35mm models cannot handle larger negatives, enlargers for 2¼ square can handle that size and 35mm, and larger enlargers can handle any size from 35mm through the largest negative carrier which will fit into the enlarger. I use Beseler in my home lab and recommend the Model 23C which accommodates negatives from 8mm through 2½x3¼ inches without changing the condenser lenses in the enlarger. Even though you may now feel you'll be using 35mm exclusively, as your proficiency grows you may want to use the larger formats of 2¼ square or larger to gain the extra quality and convenience of larger negatives. You will probably advance to color printing and the 23C is designed to use an optional head with built-in color filters. If you want to do a lot of darkroom magic with litho films and negative sandwiches as discussed starting on page 97, you might even consider buying a 4x5 enlarger. These are also available with color heads with built-in color filters.

Less costly enlargers are available and—in general—you get what you pay for. The least expensive equipment will usually give you less than top-quality work and may not stand up well with the usual day-to-day use. I recommend buying the best equipment you can afford. It's foolish to put yourself deeply in debt for the sake of what is now a hobby. But, it is just as foolish to buy cheap equipment and suffer the anguish of producing inferior work. Photography should be fun and mentally rewarding, so get equipment which allows you to be at your creative best—within the limitations of your pocketbook. If you have to start with cheap equipment, do it! At least you'll be getting started—and you may be able to make enough money enlarging pictures for your friends so you'll soon be able to afford the good stuff.

If you can't afford the equipment you've decided is just what you must have, check your

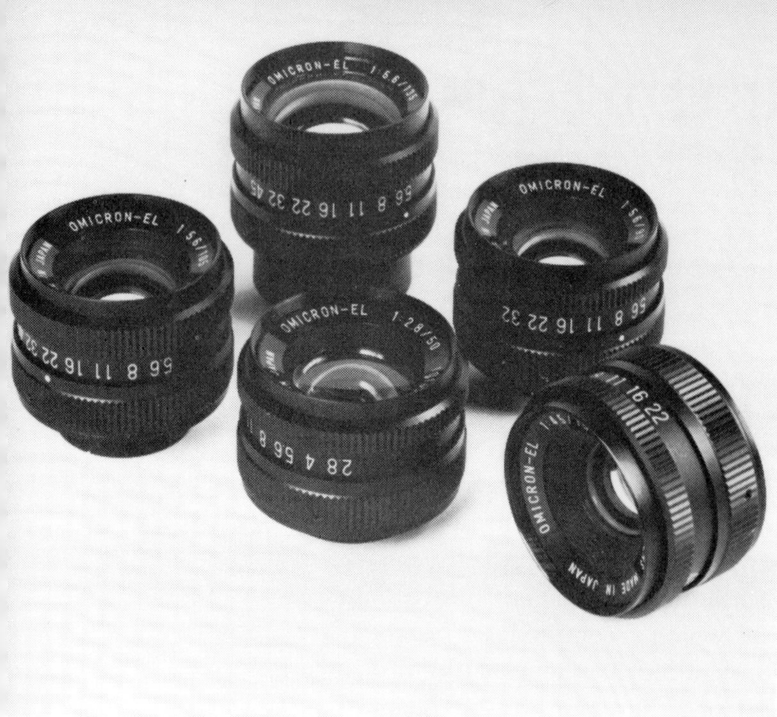

A sharp crisp negative printed through an inferior lens loses drastically in its translation to a printed image. Fine enlarging lenses such as these by Omega are among your most important investments. Be sure the lens focal length matches the negative size you are using.

If you have decided to purchase an enlarger and stick with 35mm or the instant-load film, the normal lens will have a focal length of 50mm. If you have gone one step farther and can handle the 120-size film, the lens necessary will have a focal length of 75mm. If you've gone really big time to 4x5, you'll need a 135mm lens.

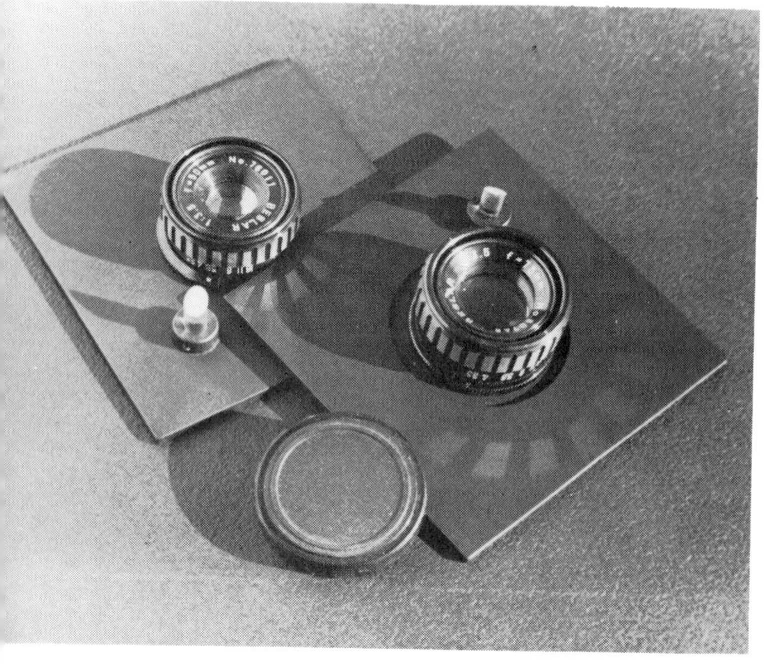

camera store to see what's available in used equipment. Let them know what you are looking for. Just the piece of equipment you are looking for may be traded in or disposed of by another photographer. Watch the classified ads in your newspaper and the bulletin boards at supermarkets, etc.

Should these avenues fail, consider enrolling in a night class at your local high school or community college or adult-education center. Take a photo course which allows lots of darkroom usage, assuming there are darkrooms in these facilities. Some areas have rental darkrooms which can get you through the period where you are saving up to buy equipment for your home darkroom.

ENLARGING LENSES

Enlarging lens focal lengths are related to negative size. The lens must be long enough to "cover" the negative. The usual rule of thumb is the focal length should be at least equal to the length of a diagonal drawn from one corner of the negative to the other.

Typical focal lengths are 50mm for 35mm film, 75mm for 2¼x2¼ and 90mm for 2¼x3¼ negatives. This is no place to look for bargain-basement tools, either. If your negative was exposed through a $200 camera lens, it makes little sense to print it through a $5 enlarging lens. From camera exposure to finished print, your quality peak is determined by your worst piece of glass.

If you work with several negative sizes you will probably start off with a lens of the correct focal length for the largest negative you intend to print. If you use 35mm and 2¼ square negatives, this will limit the size of print you will be able to make with the smaller negatives—at least by projecting the image onto paper at the enlarger's baseboard. Once you really get into darkroom work, you may end up with a lens for each negative size so you will be able to get the biggest possible prints on the enlarger baseboard from each.

Lens Mounting—When you buy a lens, make sure it can be mounted onto your enlarger. If there's any doubt, carry the lensboard or enlarger to the store with you. Make sure the lens will fit before you buy it. Sometimes, a lens may require a special flange or require cutting a larger hole in the lensboard to make it fit. If you don't have the tools or knowledge for doing this sort of work it will have to be done by a camera-repair place. Some enlargers—especially for 4x5 or larger negs—require special extension or recessed lens mounts to work with different focal-length lenses. Check the enlarger catalog for details on what is required for each of the lenses you plan to buy. Otherwise, you may find the lens fits the enlarger OK, but you can't focus the image onto your paper.

Lens Testing—Whether you are buying a lens for an enlarger or buying an enlarger already equipped with a lens, test that lens before any money changes hands. Or, get it in writing on the sales slip that the store will exchange the lens as many times as required to get a lens which is completely sharp from corner to corner. Have the clerk or store manager sign the sales slip. If they don't want to do this for you, then "be from Missouri" and insist they prove the lens' capabilities to you. I once bought one of the highly-touted—justly so!—El-Nikkor 50mm enlarging lenses. The first one I took home did not project a sharp image of the entire negative. A second one wasn't much better. The store only had those two so I had to go to another store—or else wait for another shipment—to get a third copy. The third time was the "charm." It tested perfectly and has worked fine ever since.

How do you test the lens for coverage? Expose a piece of film to the light and develop and fix it. Scratch horizontal, vertical and diagonal lines into the emulsion with a needle. I use a steel ruler to guide the needle as I make the scratches and try to do it fairly regularly with scratches about 1/16-inch apart. Be sure you scratch through the dark emulsion so you can see the scratches when you hold the negative to the light. Kodak offers black and white focus test negatives in the roll film sizes including one in 35mm which is glass mounted to ensure perfect flatness.

Place your test negative in the enlarger's negative carrier. Insert the carrier into the enlarger and cover the enlarger baseboard with white paper. Turn out the light and turn on the enlarger. Open the lens to its maximum opening and run the enlarger head to the top of the post where it gives you maximum enlargement. Focus the image, preferably with a focus-checking device, at the center of the image on the enlarger baseboard. Look at the lines very carefully. Check the corners of the projected image to see whether they are as sharp there as they are in the center. If they are fuzzy at the edges, check to make sure nothing is cocking the negative carrier and be sure the enlarger head is truly perpendicular to the enlarger baseboard. If these things check OK, reject the lens and try another one. Keep trying until you get one that gives you sharp lines in the center *and* all the way to every edge of the projected image. You won't be sorry you made this test—if you skip it you could find that you have to stop the lens way down to get the corners into sharp focus. That can be a pain when you are making large prints where the exposure times get very long and you'd like to be able to use the lens wide-open or nearly so.

An enlarger with glass-less negative carriers may allow the film to buckle or bow in the middle. The image can be sharp in the center and fuzzy at the edges and vice-versa. You've seen this when you've projected slides. Once they warm up, the center of the picture "pops" in or out of focus as the slide moves due to heat from the projection lamp. The enlarger lamphouse should be designed so the negative never gets hot enough to "pop" or move from the heat. To judge the lens' covering power fairly, I suggest you sandwich the negative between two pieces of glass when testing a lens. With a glass-less carrier you may have to stop the lens down to *f*-8 or *f*-11 to get a sharp overall image—from the center to the corners and edges. In this case you are improving depth of field *at the negative* by using smaller apertures, just as you would in taking a picture. You also greatly increase the exposure required to make a big print or a print from a section of the negative.

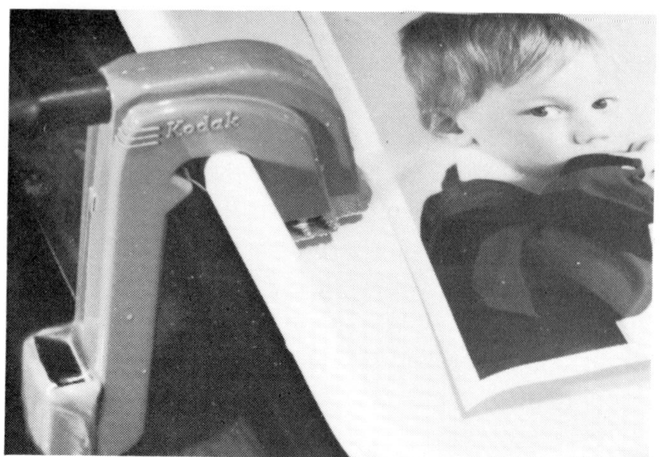

Kodak Tray Siphon is always useful because it converts any 11x14 or larger tray into an efficient print washer.

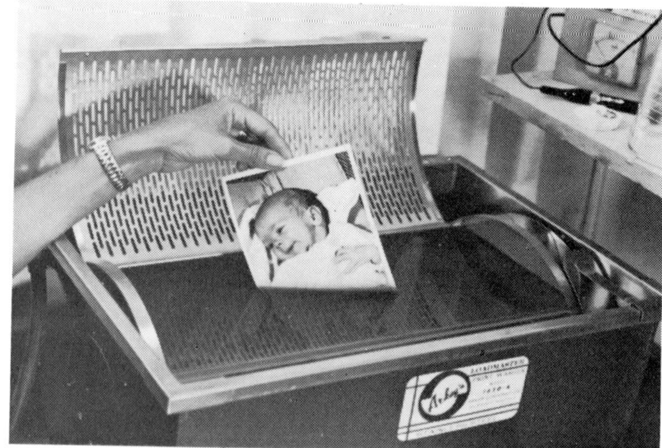

Depending on the type of paper you use, washing time may be from as little as 4 to more than 20 minutes, with single-weight papers.

PRINT WASHERS

Print washers range from tray siphons through dream-type goodies such as Arkay's 1620 Loadmaster. Prices run from under $10 to about $150. One of the most efficient methods of washing prints I have found, is the Kodak Automatic Tray Siphon. It is especially good if you should decide you want to make prints in larger sizes such as 16x20. Most moderately priced print washers will not handle prints larger than 11x14 easily. Regardless of the washing system you decide on, I recommend you also have this siphon. It fits easily into a drawer when not in use and will prove especially practical if you do not have a permanent darkroom set up. You can use it with any of your print trays, but a large deep tray is best. You might consider using a plastic cat-litter tray for print washing with a tray siphon. Although some are irregularly shaped, you will find some can accommodate prints up to about 11x14. You can buy litter trays in supermarkets, discount houses and pet stores. If your darkroom is not permanent and must be put away after each use, I vote for the tray siphon. It is inexpensive, handy and effective. Arkay drum washers are excellent for large quantities of prints, including 11x14's.

If you don't want to buy a tray siphon or print washer, put a wire rack, preferably Teflon or rubber-coated, in the bottom of your sink so the prints won't clog the drain. Or, just run water into a tray and dump the tray several times during the washing period. If you are using RC paper, the four-minute wash period allows you to use the least-expensive washing methods or equipment.

Regardless of what washer you choose, it will be more effective with the use of a hypo-neutralizer solution as a separate bath prior to washing. Hypo neutralizer removes sodium or ammonium thiosulfate from the fixed prints and allows a much shorter washing time. I'll tell you more about this when we get to chemicals. You don't really need it with RC papers.

Clean equipment is a must also. During days of high air humidity, chemicals have a tendency to "float" around the darkroom and settle on areas which may later contaminate unexposed or unprocessed material. This prototype print washer coated with dried-on hypo needs to be cleaned. I'll do it tomorrow.

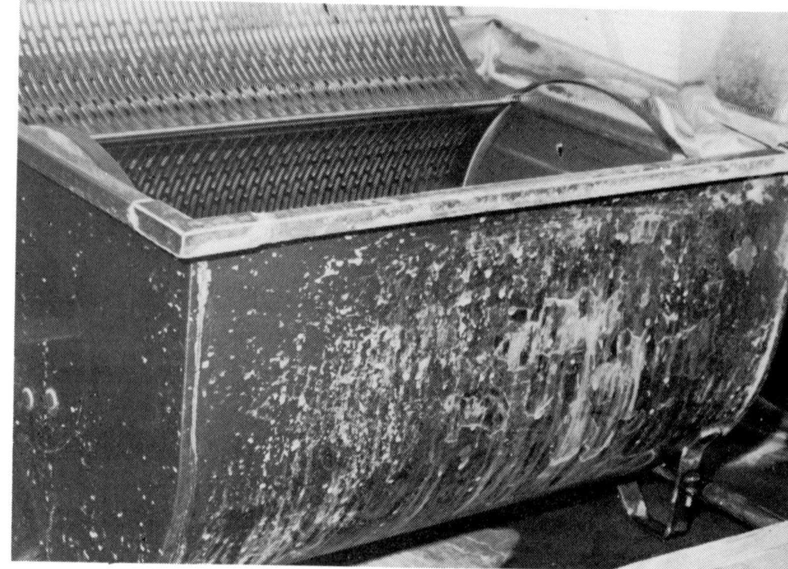

DRYERS

Amateur photographers used to start out not worrying about a heated dryer. But, by the time they had gotten serious about the hobby, a heated dryer started to become very important, especially if a lot of prints were being made. Drying prints sometimes took more time and energy than had been spent making the prints in the darkroom. A lot of people dropped out of the hobby because it was just too much trouble to finish the prints with appropriate washing and drying once they had been made. The availability of hypo neutralizer to cut the washing time helped, but the drying problem was still real.

Choosing which dryer to buy was usually decided by the amount of money available. A dryer often cost as much or more than a quality enlarger.

Now that resin-coated—RC—papers are widely available, you can standardize on these and never worry about getting a heated dryer. My recommendation is to use RC papers. Take advantage of their quick processing and fast drying and you'll wind up making more pictures and having more fun in the darkroom. You'll never have to scheme and dream of how to get enough money together to buy a heated dryer.

RC papers cost about the same as ordinary papers. And, because the RC papers take less chemicals, less water for washing and no electrical energy for drying, you might actually save money by using them.

Photographically-sensitive emulsion is about the same on all types of materials. It is a dispersion of silver particles in a gelatin layer on the base of the material. In the case of film, the base is clear. Printing papers have a similar emulsion coated onto one side of a sheet of paper and usually wind up with a positive image to be viewed by reflected light, uncommonly called a reflection print. You can also view it as a transparency by holding it in front of a very bright light.

Chemical reactions of developing and fixing, followed by removal of the chemicals by washing, are all based on the inherent quality of gelatin to allow water and water-based solutions to penetrate the emulsion and get at the silver crystals. As far as the thin layer of emulsion alone is concerned, processing liquids go in and out rather quickly—in fact surprisingly quickly.

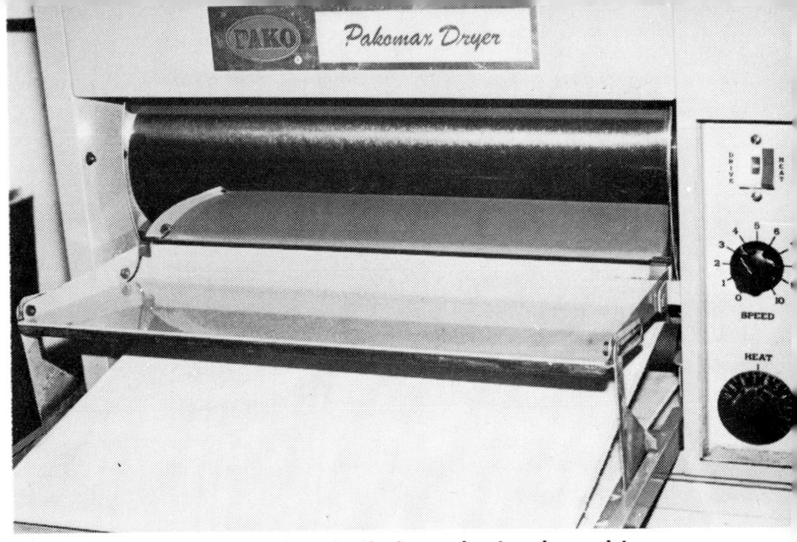

PAKO commercial-type electrically-heated print dryer dries glossy or matte prints in a hurry. This is a big-bucks item you won't need if you use RC paper exclusively.

Ordinary printing papers have emulsion coated on a paper stock much like this page except the surface behind the emulsion is usually treated with a whitening and smoothing agent to reflect light better. As you know, paper absorbs liquids too and this is the basic problem in washing and drying prints.

More hypo soaks into the thick paper backing of an ordinary printing paper than into the emulsion. Because the paper is thicker it is harder to wash the hypo out of it. If you don't get it all out, the print will later stain or change color. There are specially meticulous processing instructions you could follow to give your prints *archival* quality, meaning the image will last so long the print can be stored in archives to last nearly forever. Basically the trick is thorough fixing and washing.

As you can see, it's no help to get the paper backing all soaked up with chemicals and then have to spend a long time washing it—plus a long time drying it out again. With the advent of modern plastics, some unsung photographic hero invented waterproof paper. In my opinion this achievement can be ranked with tomatoes in cans and other benefits to humanity.

Before the photo emulsion is coated onto waterproof paper, both sides of the paper are covered with a thin layer of clear plastic similar

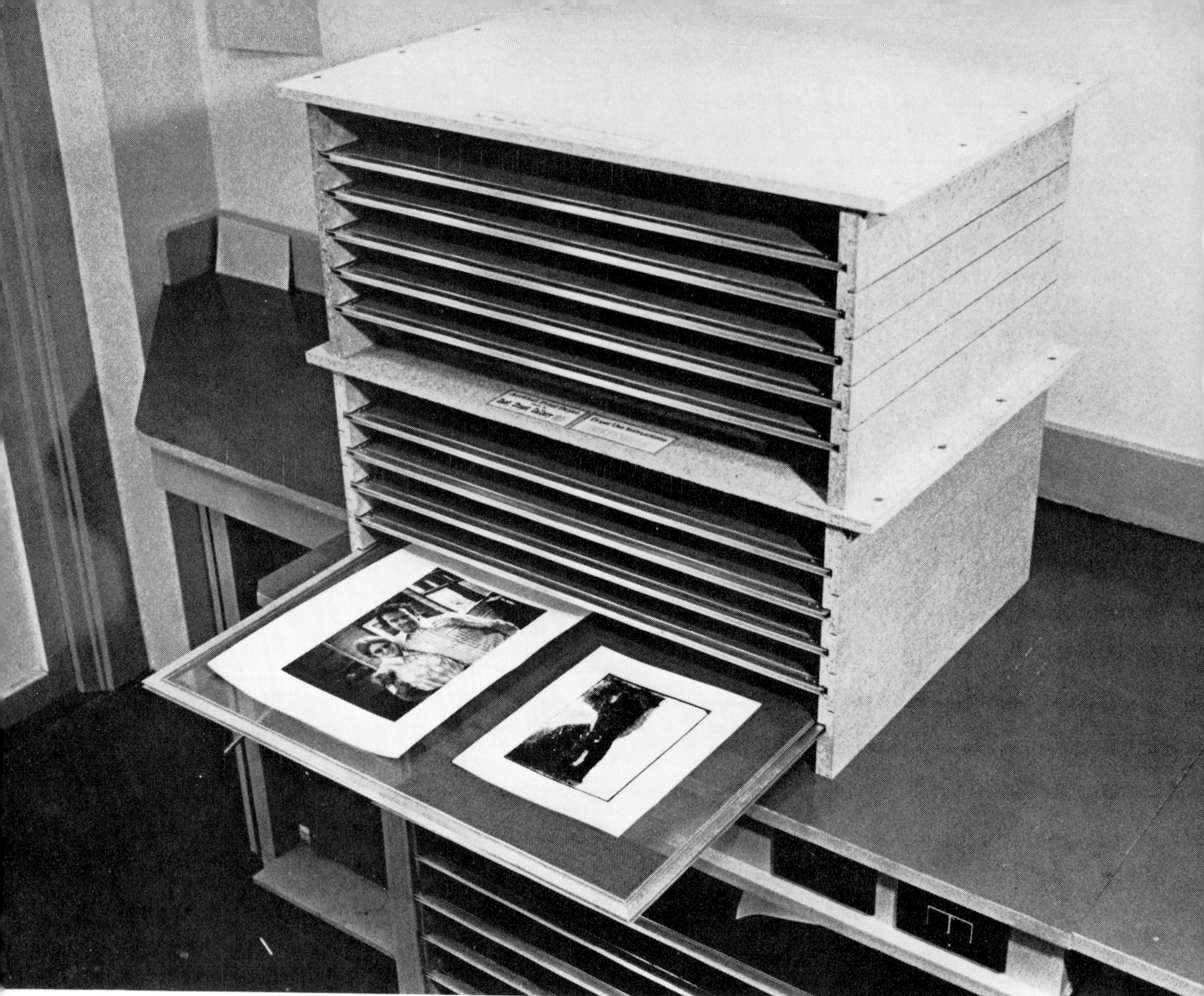

If you want to air dry prints, I recommend you make or buy a screen-type dryer like the one shown here. It is simple to use and requires no electricity to operate it.

to the baggy your sandwich is in. Inside, the paper stays dry and cozy to simplify your life in the darkroom. Only the cut edges are exposed to soak up chemicals into the paper base. Plastics of this type are called resins by chemists, so this paper is called *resin-coated,* or RC. Try it, you'll like it.

Prints on RC paper will usually dry in less than an hour by simply laying them face up on a flat surface. Faster drying is obtained—usually about 30 minutes in low humidity—and the prints will tend to dry flatter if you dry them face up on plastic screening stretched onto a frame. That way, the air can get at both sides of the print. I've taken a RC print outdoors on a warm day and waved it in the breeze. It was dry in about two minutes. Of course, I live in Arizona where the humidity is really low and that helps!

Don't dry RC glossy papers with the emulsion against a heated surface because the emulsion will stick to the heated surface and ruin your print.

Glossy Prints—Glossy RC papers can be air-dried by themselves to give a highly polished glossy appearance. Blow a little warm air on them with a hair dryer and they'll dry in a few minutes with an even better gloss. RC papers don't have to be dried against a smooth surface to get the glossed appearance. That's why I am recommending you start out using RC paper. I don't think you'll ever want to use any other kind.

A glossy print appears to have slightly greater contrast than a matte-surface print. Glossy prints are chosen when you want maximum detail to show. As a minor disadvantage, glossy prints also show the most grain from the negative. This is most apparent in overall gray areas, such as skies.

If you want your photographs reproduced in a newspaper, magazine or book, you may be requested to submit glossy prints. Anything else can be a matte surface. Ordinary—non-RC—papers with a glossy surface get a highly polished appearance by drying the smooth emulsion in firm and complete contact with a smooth surface—usually chromed metal. Non-RC glossy papers dry to a semi-matte surface if you don't dry the emulsion in contact with a smooth polished surface.

Matte-Surface Prints—These have a non-polished emulsion surface. The emulsion may show the texture of the paper base or its texture can be applied by calendaring rolls as the paper is made. Matte surfaces are most popular for portrait and scenic subjects. A non-reflective surface gives a less-commercial appearance than prints dried to a high gloss. Matte surfaces also tend to hide grain and soft-focus problems. You can dry matte-surface papers by any of the methods I'll tell you about: Blotter paper, plastic screens, platen dryers, and drum dryers. Matte papers are never dried by squeegeeing them against a polished surface. When dried on heated driers, the prints are placed with their backs against the polished, heated surface and the faces are held down by the cloth aprons. Kodak offers their Kodabrome and Polycontrast Rapid RC papers in a matte surface labeled N. These should be air-dried.

Color Prints—Most color printing paper is of the RC variety, which should be dried face up on plastic screens, or laid face up to dry on any flat surface.

Non-resin-coated color papers can be dried on plastic screens, in a blotter stack or roll, or on a flat or drum-type dryer. When attempting to gloss these non-RC papers it is important to use a drum dryer designed to gloss-dry *color* prints.

The general trend to RC papers is proceeding at such a rapid pace that it appears all color papers will be of that type within a very few years. My advice is not to buy a drum-type dryer for color. Use the RC papers and plastic screens. The money you save will make hundreds of additional prints for your personal pleasure!

WARNING: When using RC papers it is tough to tell which side is the emulsion and which side is the back. They should curl slightly toward the emulsion side. If you lightly drag your dry fingertip across the surface of the paper, your fingertip will tend to drag more on the emulsion side. Another trick is to bite gently at one corner of the paper. The emulsion side will usually stick to your tooth; the back side will not.

Plastic Screens On Frames—Whether you use RC or regular printing papers, plastic screen stretched onto a frame makes a fine print dryer. You just place the squeegeed RC-paper prints face up on the screen and they dry quicker than you would imagine—usually in 30 minutes to one hour. Ordinary paper b&w prints are dried face down on the screens to help reduce curling. Drying time is two to eight hours, depending on humidity. Prints may dry with some curling, but if you intend to mount the prints or have time to place them under weights for straightening or intend to use them in albums, getting really flat prints may not be important.

If you are making a lot of prints at a time, build several of the frames and a support box with rails or grooves to stack the frames in. Leave about an inch or two between each frame. A commercially made device of this sort is shown in one of the accompanying photos.

Blotting Paper—Blotting paper in books, sheets or rolls makes the least costly and slowest of the drying methods available to you. If you want matte-surface prints and don't mind waiting—and waiting—and waiting, you may be happy with blotting papers for drying. Getting dry prints may take overnight or several days, so you will be patient, won't you? Many people have used this method for years and would not consider changing. I'm so impatient there's no way you could get me to use it. Unless you use RC papers exclusively, I suggest you get a book or roll of blotting paper to use until you decide how deeply you want to get into darkroom work. It is an excellent drying arrangement to start with.

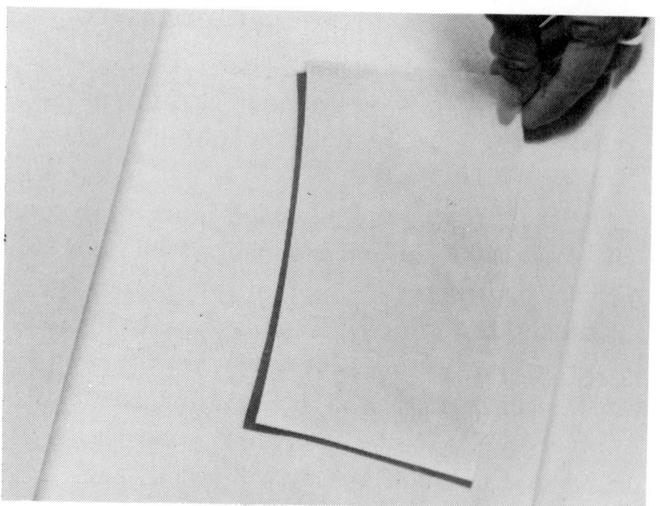

In lieu of purchasing an expensive heat dryer, use either a package of blotter sheets—

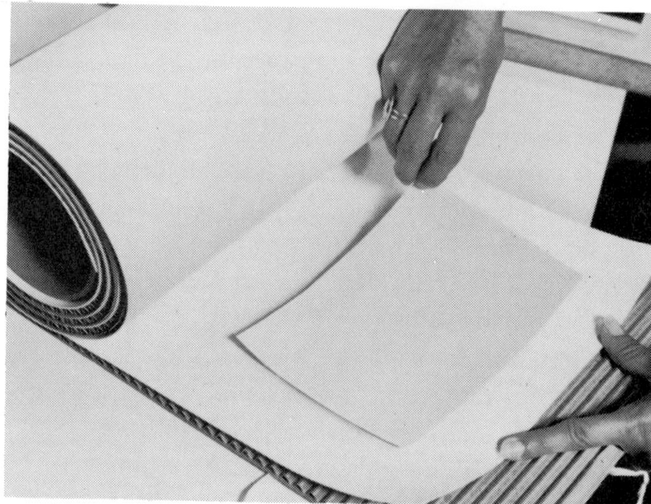

or a blotter roll. Both are made of heavy absorbent fiber material and keep prints fairly flat due to pressure. They are slower than heat equipment so try to evaluate your print volume you must have before you decide. It will take prints overnight or longer to dry in blotters.

Ferrotype Plates—If you want glossy prints and only glossy prints, these can be dried on chrome-plated brass or steel sheets called *ferrotype plates.* Although you won't need any artificial heat to dry the prints, these can be used on a platen-type heated dryer. I'll explain exactly how to dry glossy prints on ferrotype plates on page 120. This procedure is not required for glossy RC papers.

Platen-type Heated Dryer—If you plan to make only a few matte-surface prints at a time and are not content with the surfaces available on RC papers, then one of these dryers—either single- or double-platen—would be a good choice. These can also be used with ferrotype plates to dry glossy prints.

Drum-type Heated Dryer—These expensive units usually cost $200 or more. Both gas-fired and electric models are available. Glossy prints are easiest to dry against the chrome-plated drum of this type dryer. If you plan to make large quantities of prints on non-RC paper and want them to dry reasonably flat and ready for use—whether matte or glossy surface—buy a drum-type dryer IF you can afford it. But, before you make the

Drying time depends on the equipment you have available. A drum-type dryer is fastest and also the most expensive. You won't need to make this investment if you use RC papers.

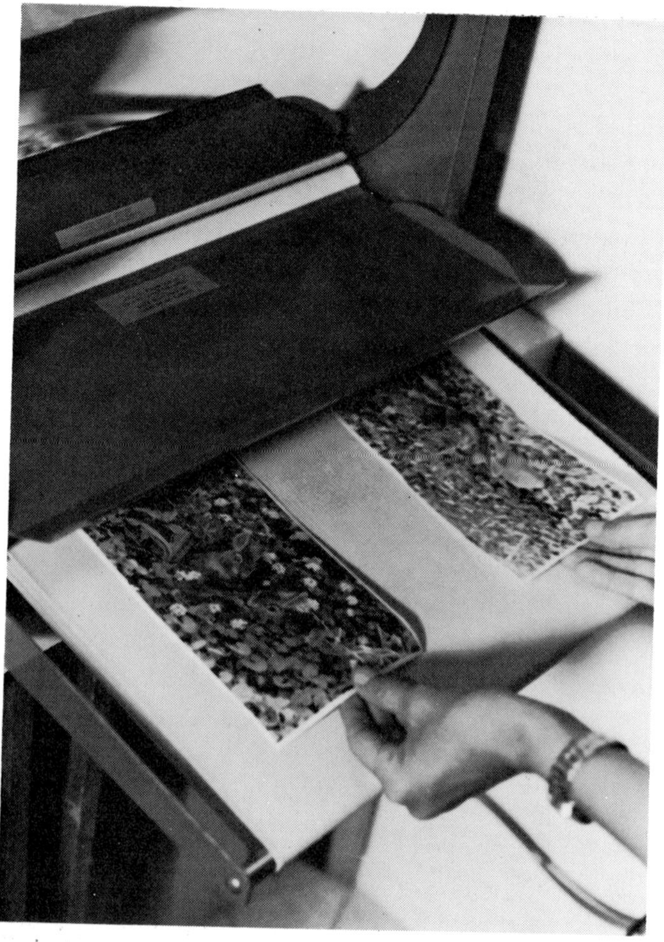

HEED INSTRUCTIONS WHEN USING RESIN-COATED PAPERS!

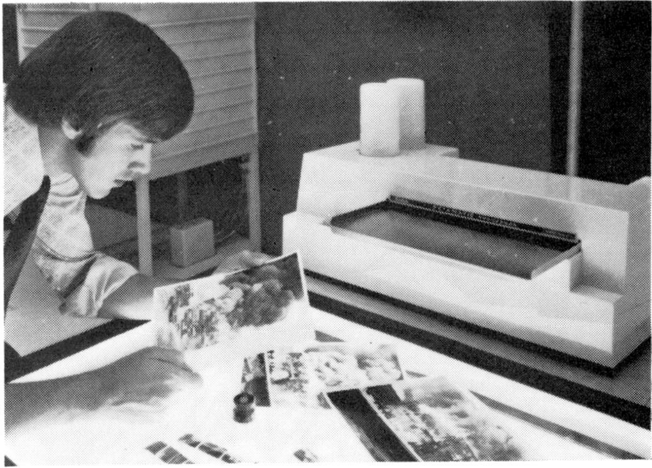

The device at right is a Kodak Ektamatic Processor. This is a stabilizer-processor. The Activator and Stabilizer are in the two bottles atop the machine. Rollers inside the unit apply very small amounts of the solutions to the prints so prints are limp-dry when they come out. Photo courtesy Eastman Kodak.

investment, consider how far ahead you'll be moneywise by using RC papers which typically dry in about 30 minutes to one hour when laid on plastic screens.

Stabilized Prints—I've left this discussion until the last of the drying information. Stabilizer processors are so expensive—often over $400—they are not often used by amateurs. Details on drying stabilized prints won't interest most readers.

A stabilizer processor is a machine which develops and fixes prints made on special stabilizer paper. This paper has the developer incorporated in the emulsion. It is exposed just like you would any other contact or enlarging paper. You develop it by inserting the paper into the processor. An activator solution makes the developer work, then the paper is put through a stabilizer to "fix" the image. Stabilized prints come out of the stabilizer-processor limp-dry and air-dry to a usable point in about 15 to 30 minutes. Stabilized prints must not be dried on the same screens or in the same blotter paper or on the same dryer as any of the other types of materials you are handling. The residue from stabilized prints will contaminate other prints because stabilized prints are not fixed and washed when they come out of the processor. They are still loaded with chemicals. If you fix and wash stabilized prints like your regular black-and-white prints, they can be dried on the same screens, blotters or heated dryers as any of the other prints. Stabilization processors are made by Agfa-Gaevert, Fisher, Ilford, Kodak, Spiratone and Supreme Photo Products. Your camera dealer can provide literature on these units. They are generally quite expensive.

PAPER SURFACES & WEIGHTS

While we are talking about prints, papers and such like, you might like to know that you can get all sorts of printing papers. Different surfaces ranging from glossy to dead-dull, fabric imitations, whites and off-whites, cream-colored, some with colder or warmer tones, colored paper bases and different paper-base thicknesses. Your camera shop has sample books you can look at to select the kind which strikes your fancy. Just keep in mind that only RC papers offer quick processing and easy drying. You are in for a lot of work when you choose any other kind.

Two thicknesses usually available at camera shops are called *single-weight* and *double-weight.* Weigh a piece of each and sure enough, one weighs about twice as much. The thicknesses are also approximately doubled from about seven thousandths of an inch for the single-weight, to about 15 thousandths for the double-weight. The practical difference is the single-weight feels rather flimsy. There is also an even flimsier paper called *light-weight.*

Kodak RC papers are supplied in a *medium-weight* which is a bit heavier than single-weight.

Single- or medium-weight costs less and I recommend it for learning, fooling around and making prints to be mounted on something. If you want prints that feel substantial in your hand, use double-weight. It takes longer to wash and longer to dry and it costs more, too. Because it's not available in RC, you may want to forget about it.

Photographic printing papers are supplied in cut sheets and in rolls. Rolls are typically used for making mural-size prints. You'll usually buy paper in standard-size sheets, such as 4x5, 5x7, 8x10, 11x14 and 16x20 inches. Slightly different sizes using metric dimensions may be supplied outside the United States.

Cut paper comes in envelopes and in card-board cartons, depending upon the quantity. U.S. papers are typically supplied in envelopes of 25 sheets, and in boxes of 100, 250 and 500 sheets.

Sheets are packed all the same way with the top sheet reversed so its emulsion does not contact the waxed surface of the envelope or the wrapping paper. The developer might not work correctly on that spot. This is seldom a problem, but I thought you'd like to know about it anyway. It's a good idea to invert the top sheet when repacking paper into its envelope or box.

Cutting Paper—Always make sure your hands are clean and dry before handling paper. It is best to stack two sheets together emulsion-to-emulsion when cutting several pieces to a special size.

Using Paper in the Darkroom—Keep a separate box for storing paper you know you'll be needing for a printing session. That way you avoid frequent rewrapping and handling, with the possible danger of exposing a lot of paper accidentally because you left it out of the box or envelope. Unless you are regularly using variable-contrast paper, be sure to mark the box with the paper type and grade. Special containers called *paper safes* are available. These close automatically after you remove a sheet of paper.

SAFELIGHT

A safelight lets you see and move about comfortably in the darkroom. It produces colored light which the printing material can't see or is insensitive to. A safelight is usually a low-wattage white lamp—usually 15 watts—covered by a filter. The normal filter for contact and very slow enlarging paper is an OA—green-yellow. High-speed enlarging papers require OC—light-amber. Kodak Panalure paper for producing black-and-white prints from color negatives calls for a No. 13—amber—as does Ektacolor RC. Kodalith and Kodagraph films require a No. 1A—light-red—safelight.

A safelight must be safe—meaning it doesn't expose the paper you are using—so test and see. With the light four feet away, lay a piece of unexposed printing paper on the enlarger baseboard, emulsion side up. Place several coins on the paper at various spots and wait two to three minutes. Develop normally and inspect to see if the shape of the coins appears on the paper. If not, your light is safe. If you can see where the coins were on the paper, you have a fogging problem. To correct it, use a smaller bulb in the light, or move it farther away from your work area. Also, double-check to make sure you are using the safelight filter specified on the information sheet packed with the printing material you are using. An unsafe safelight will create a low-level fog on the print and keep you from obtaining good clear highlights.

Filters do fade over the years, so test periodically to make sure you are not fogging your prints.

PRINT TRAYS

You should have trays in several sizes so you won't have to use more solution than is necessary when you are making small prints—and so you'll have plenty of room to manipulate and agitate the prints. Use trays one size larger than the prints you are making. An 11x14 tray is for 8x10 prints and an 8x10 tray is for 5x7 prints. You'll need at least three trays of each size you decide to have. One for developer, a second for short stop and the third for fixer. *Short stop* is what old hands call the stop bath. You will not be allowed to use the term until next week.

I recommend that your fixer tray be two sizes larger than the print size and perhaps deeper than your other trays. This is because prints will accumulate here as you go along. It is also a good idea to have an extra tray available for hypo-neutralizer use prior to washing. The kitty litter trays I suggested for print washing also work well for hypo and hypo neutralizer. Also, you might consider using Rubbermaid Dishpans. The 12½x 14½x5½ inch size is perfect for hypo, hypo neutralizer and washing.

Tray-size recommendations begin to make less sense when you get up to prints in the 11x14 and 16x20 size. Then the sheer cost and size of the trays versus the few times you use them may indicate that you will use trays of the same size as the prints and put up with the minor inconvenience of having to be more careful in handling the prints. If you are going to make 16x20 and larger prints, consider getting or making large trays. Making murals is discussed in the Special Techniques chapter.

Label the trays and use the same chemical in the same tray each time. This helps to eliminate the possibility of chemical contamination in case you get sloppy about the clean-up procedures at the end of the printing session. Dymo tape makes good tray labels which will stay on trays for quite awhile.

Stainless steel trays last forever but they are expensive. While enamel is less expensive, it will chip sooner or later. Then they rust and you end up with rust stains on your prints. Various plastic types are least costly, quite serviceable and readily available. I say you should make plastic trays your first choice, with the rubber or plastic dishpans for hypo and washing. This is a logical way to get fully equipped at lowest cost.

CHEMICALS

The most widely used all-purpose developers for printing are Kodak's Dektol and Ektaflo Type 1. Dektol is supplied in powder form. When mixed with water it makes a concentrated *stock solution* to be diluted one part Dektol to two parts water—1:2—for use. Store the Dektol stock solution in a Falcon *air evac* container to give it the longest possible shelf life. If your printing sessions are infrequent, buy Dektol in a carton of six packets, each to make 8 fluid ounces of working solution. With these you mix exactly what you need and don't worry about the stock solution oxidizing before you print again.

Ektaflo Type 1 is supplied as a liquid in a handy one-gallon Cubitainer with pouring tube. This stock solution is diluted one part Ektaflo with nine parts water—1:9—for use.

Cost figures on these two developers are about the same. The Cubitainer design gives Ektaflo a longer shelf life than Dektol stored in ordinary bottles. As with all developer solutions, oxidation from contact with air shortens working and shelf life. Because the Ektaflo developer is in a plastic bag inside the cardboard container, air is effectively kept out.

When preparing a working solution, make sure the stock solution is clear in color. As it becomes exhausted from oxidation it will turn dark-brown. If this happens, discard the stock solution and mix fresh developer.

Normal developing time with either Dektol or Ektaflo is 1½ to 2 minutes. Ektaflo is a bit slower in producing the first faint image than

Tray cleaning—Developer trays get a dark stain in them which can be removed by putting your leftover stop bath in them overnight, then washing the tray.

My favorite print developer is Ektaflo, Type 1. The collapsible plastic liner keeps air out so the developer doesn't oxidize.

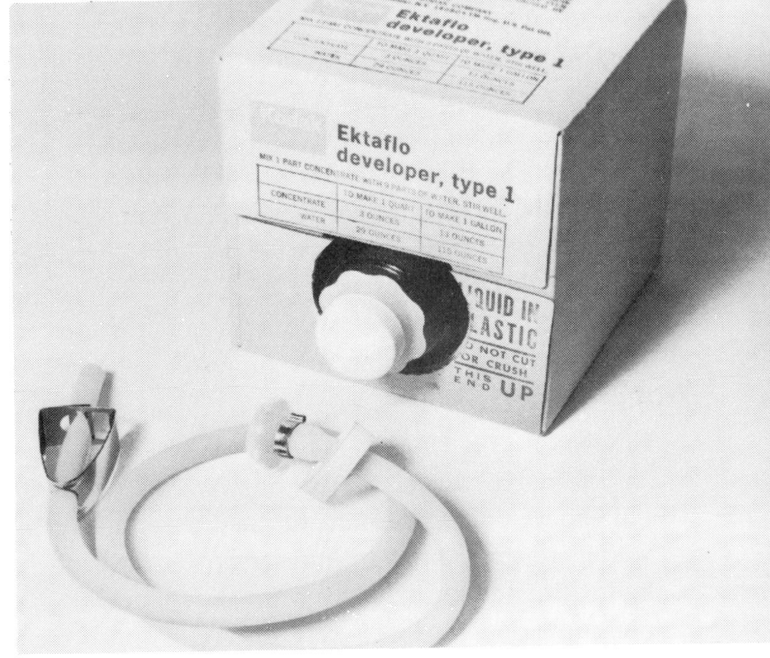

Dektol. Both developers give neutral or cold tones on cold-tone papers.

After you have the mechanics of printing down pat with glossy paper, you may want to try other paper surfaces, perhaps with warm tones. Glossy papers nearly always give cold tones. For warm-toned papers consider using Kodak Selectol developer and developing the prints for 1½ minutes. Or, use Ektaflo developer, Type 2, and develop the prints for 2 minutes. These developing times are for working solutions at 68°F (20°C). Paper colors or tones are built into the paper—but you have to use the matching developers to insure getting the warmer tones.

As of 1975, no warm-tone RC papers were available, although these papers can be toned to get a somewhat warmer appearance.

STOP BATH

To make a working solution, dilute 1¾ ounces of 28% acetic acid with 32 ounces of water, just as you did to make a solution to stop development of negatives. Mix it correctly: Too weak will be slow to halt developer action and exhaust itself quickly; too strong produces gas bubbles in the print emulsion which end up as tiny white pin-points on the finished print.

Kodak has three "indicator" stop baths. They are yellow when freshly mixed and turn blue or purple when they are exhausted. When they appear dark under the safelight you know it's time to mix a fresh batch. Kodak Indicator Stop Bath comes in 16-ounce and 1-gallon bottles of concentrated solution which is diluted for use. Kodak Ektaflo Stop Bath comes in a one-gallon Cubitainer. Dilute it 1:31 for use. Either of these two baths will process 80-8x10 prints in a gallon of working solution. The third option is Kodak's Universal Stop Bath, a carton of six packets. Each makes 8 ounces of working solution—adequate to process a mere 2-8x10 prints.

WARNING: Don't mix indicator stop baths too strong because they tend to stain prints yellow if you do.

FIXING BATH

Fixing bath, called *fixer* or *hypo,* dissolves the undeveloped silver salts in the print emulsion which—to this point—are still sensitive to white light. Hypo desensitizes the print. Keep its temperature at 65-70°F (18-21°C).

When you put the print into the hypo, then turn on the white light to check its quality, you'll be in a hurry to turn off the light and concentrate on making the next print. You tend to forget about your "finished" print lying there soaking hypo into its paper backing. There are recommended fixing times for prints and you should observe them. You are only trying to fix the silver in the thin layer of emulsion. There's no reason to leave the print soaking beyond the recommended time because this causes hypo and silver compounds to be trapped in the paper backing so it is difficult to get complete washing. If the print is not completely washed, your prints may end up stained and non-permanent months or even years later.

With fresh fixer and especially with rapid fixer—even if it doesn't happen to be freshly mixed—when you leave the print in for an overly long time you may find your prints bleach out, taking on a washed-out appearance because the fixer has "reduced" the silver image. This is especially true with warm-toned papers.

Fixing RC Papers—As you might suspect, RC papers require very short fixing times. Two minutes is Kodak's recommendation for Kodabrome RC or Polycontrast RC papers. Any longer time allows fixer to penetrate the cut edges of the paper so it is hard to wash out.

Fixer Types—Fixer comes in powdered form such as Kodak Fixer. It is mixed with water to make the working acid hardening hypo solution. You immerse ordinary prints in it for 10 minutes for complete fixing. RC papers require only two minutes! Liquid-concentrate fixers include Kodak Ektaflo Fixer and Kodak Rapid Fixer. Ektaflo Fixer is diluted 1:7 with water for use. Ordinary prints should stay in the working solution for 10 minutes, RC papers for two minutes. My own favorite is Kodak Rapid Fixer which you dilute with water according to the directions on the bottle, then add a liquid hardener according to directions supplied with the two bottles. Rapid Fixer does the job on ordinary prints in just six minutes and you should not ever leave prints in it for longer than 10 minutes. When you are using Rapid Fixer you have to pull the prints out before the magical 10 minutes have elapsed or you can expect bleached prints and prints which are terribly hard to wash completely. RC papers should be fixed for not more than two minutes.

Single-Bath Fixing—Here you use fixer in a single tray. This method takes the least space, so it is most often used in the home darkroom or temporary darkroom you've set up in the kitchen or bathroom. When you use this method, keep track of the number of prints you have made and discard the fixer after using it to fix 100-8x10 prints or an equivalent area in one gallon of fixer. It is easy to mark usage on the bottle label after a printing session, so do it. Follow the recommendations on the fixer label as to how long you leave the prints in the hypo.

Two-Bath Fixing—This method is not used for RC papers because they are fixed so fast there's no need to be moving them from one tray to another. With ordinary prints you can use two trays of hypo. Prints are placed in the first tray or *bath* for three minutes. This removes most of the undeveloped silver salts. Drain the print for five seconds and place it in the second fixing tray for another three minutes, then put the print in the wash water. Large quantities of silver build up in the first fixing bath, slowing the fixing process. The second bath remains relatively fresh and free from stain-causing material. After 200-8x10 prints or the equivalent area per gallon of fixer, dump the first bath and replace it with the second bath. Mix a fresh second bath to assure uniform fixing for print after print.

Checking Fixer Action—How do you know whether the fixer is still working after you have run a large number of prints through it—especially when you forgot to keep track? You can worry about this a little, remembering that your prints may stain if they are not completely fixed and if the exhausted fixer has filled your prints with silver thiosulfate compounds which may not come out with washing.

Buy Kodak's Testing Outfit for Print Stop Baths and Fixing Baths. Or you can make a tester which will last longer by diluting Kodak Rapid Selenium Toner 1:9 with water.

After you have completely fixed the print, leaving it in the fixer for the recommended period, squeegee the paper and place a drop of the solution on a white border. Blot off the solution after three minutes. Any remaining coloration other than a just-visible cream tint indicates excessive silver compounds in the fixer and it should be discarded. When the hypo is really exhausted, the stain will be dark brown. If you don't want to risk a good print, make the test on the edge of a test strip or a piece of unexposed photographic paper which you have left in the fixer for the recommended time.

By now you are getting the idea that it takes quite a few solutions to get serious about doing it in the dark. You are right, but you can count the number of prints processed through the solutions and eliminate the need to spend money for some of the items I've been telling you about.

Agitate the Prints in the Fixer—Frequent moving of the prints so they don't stick together is essential to get good fixing. Be careful when moving interleaved RC prints because the sharp corner of one print can damage the surface of any other RC print it contacts.

HYPO NEUTRALIZER (not for RC papers)

This is one solution you can skip if you are using RC papers.

Regardless of whether you choose a single- or two-bath fixing method with regular or rapid fixer, you should use a hypo neutralizer before washing ordinary (non-RC) prints.

This type of solution saves water and cuts your time in the darkroom. I prefer B.P.I. No. 30. A 10-minute soak in the working solution—with periodic agitation—cuts washing time to 15 minutes. This is a considerable saving in time and water over the one-hour period typically recommended for prints.

The concentrated B.P.I. solution from the bottle is diluted 1:10 with water to make the working solution. B.P.I. claims a capacity of 1,250 single-weight 8x10 prints per quart of concentrate, so don't worry about it losing strength during an evening's printing session.

Using hypo neutralizer means an extra tray in the sink or in your line up of trays, but it is well worth it. Short of a two- or three-hour wash, hypo neutralizer is the best way to make sure your prints are completely washed so they won't stain or fade due to chemical residue in the paper.

Kodak calls their neutralizer a Hypo Clearing Agent. It allows completely washing films and single-weight papers in only 10 minutes. If you slosh the prints through a plain-water prerinse prior to placing them in the working solution, one gallon of working solution will clear hypo from 200-8x10 prints or an equivalent area. Prints

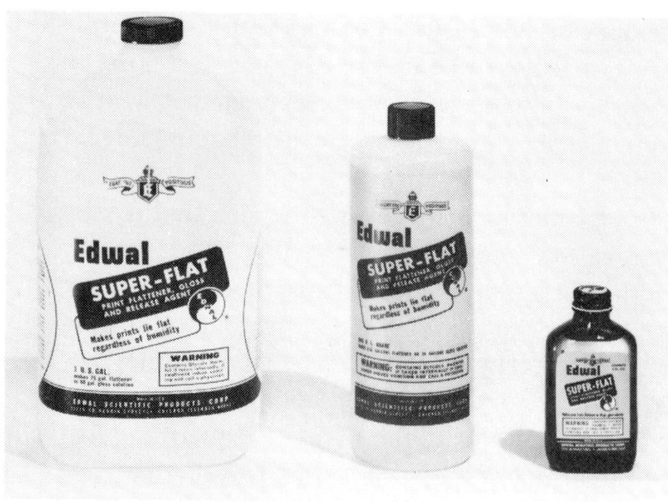

You can use Edwal Super-Flat to eliminate curl *and* promote high gloss in the dried print. Super-Flat comes in three sizes of liquid concentrate.

remain in the solution two minutes for single-weight; three minutes for double-weight.

GLOSSING SOLUTION (not for RC papers)

The only other chemical you may need will depend on the dryer you have and whether you want prints matte or glossed. If you want a matte finish or if you are using a double-weight matte-type paper, you won't need it at all. You also don't need it with RC papers.

If you have a dryer with chromed-metal plates or a chromed drum, it is a good idea to use a *glossing* solution. Edwal Chemicals makes one called *Super-Flat*, which also helps reduce print curling in addition to promoting high gloss.

After washing, glossy prints should be soaked in this solution for one minute. Then place them face down on a sheet of window glass, smooth plastic or the back of a clean tray and remove excess fluid by wiping across the back of the print with a print squeegee. A new automobile windshield-wiper blade makes an excellent squeegee for this job. The glossy print is then ready to go on the dryer, face—emulsion side—toward the drum. Or you can squeegee and roller the print onto the chromed-metal ferrotype place, emulsion side against the chrome.

Run this solution through a funnel with a strainer before a batch of prints is put in. Otherwise, dust and lint particles in the solution will adhere to the face of the print and cause small marks in the gloss.

WORDS ABOUT THE TIMER

It is as important to observe the clock for print making as it is for film processing. All steps should be timed from developer through the glossing solution.

When you put a print into the developer you should be watching a sweep-second hand on a clock or watch. As you progress in doing darkroom work you may come to use the timer less for print developing and rely more on your personal preference for print tone. Be careful if you start doing this because full-term development guarantees solid blacks and the best possible gray scale in your prints if they have been exposed correctly on the right grade of paper.

It is very important to follow the recommended times for fixer, hypo neutralizer and washing because these directly affect the permanence and even the quality of the images on your prints.

ASSORTED ITEMS

Under assorted items are such things as clean towels. Dry hands are a must. Wet fingers on film or paper invariably leave unwanted marks. Moisture from a chemical solution can leave marks which are irreparable. **Always wash and dry your hands thoroughly before handling sensitive materials!**

Have and use a sponge to mop up all wet spills on work areas. A clean work area greatly cuts down the chances of contamination to materials and equipment.

It's handy to have a dodging set consisting of several pieces of dark-amber plastic, cut into a range of sizes and shapes, and a metal rod to hold them. I'll cover their use in more detail later. This set is used to hold back light on selected areas of the enlarged image which would otherwise print too dark or void of detail. With practice, you can dodge a print just by using your hand and fingers, but there will be times when your hand makes too large a shadow for the small area you want held back. At these times, the dodging kit can be of real service.

Other accessories should include an enlarging

focusing aid for checking image sharpness at the easel, and a camel-hair brush to whisk dust off negatives. The best brush for this purpose is one called Staticmaster which has a built-in pulonium strip to capture dust as it is brushed off. A can of compressed Freon gas sold as Dust-Off, is handy for blowing off dust particles from negatives. A bottle of Edwal's No-Scratch can cover up small scratches on film as may be caused by careless handling of the negatives or by dirt in the camera.

Print tongs are a valuable aid which allow you to keep your hands out of the processing solutions. This eliminates the need for constant hand washing and getting dry towels. I recommend plastic tongs or rubber-tipped wood ones because metal tends to rust and have an abrasive effect on the print surface. Label the tongs for use with specific solutions and use the same ones in the same chemical every time to avoid the danger of solution contamination. This is very important when using wooden tongs as they do soak up the solution.

Some of the things you bought for film processing will be used for the print process. Your plastic funnel with strainer, plastic stirring rod and thermometer are all things you can use for both film and print processing.

A paper trimmer is nice to have in the darkroom as it allows you to buy large paper sizes and trim them to make several small prints from one sheet of paper. It also helps trim prints when they are mounted on a stiff support.

ENLARGING TIMER

An enlarging timer is a desirable—but not an essential—accessory for your darkroom. You can time exposures by watching a sweep-second hand on a clock or watch—or even by counting to yourself. There's usually a switch on the enlarger cord so you can turn it on or off. You can get accurate and repeatable exposures by watching a clock, but it is harder—but not impossible—to do all of the dodging and burning in when the on/off cycle of the enlarger is not automated with a timer. A timer is also especially helpful when you are making a lot of prints of the same negative.

If you buy an enlarging timer, there are several kinds. Some are simple wind-up clockwork or electric-clock mechanisms which you have to set each time you want to make an exposure, then

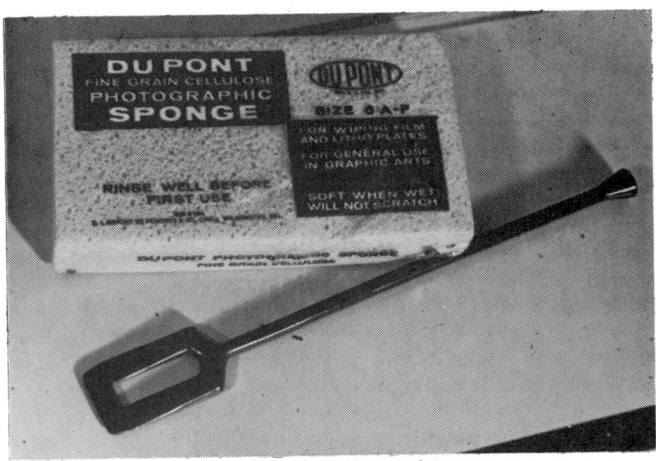

Soft photographic sponge may be used to remove excess moisture from processed roll film. One should always be handy to wipe up spills from any work area. DO NOT USE A MOP-UP SPONGE ON FILM! A stirring rod is a great aid in all chemical mixing situations.

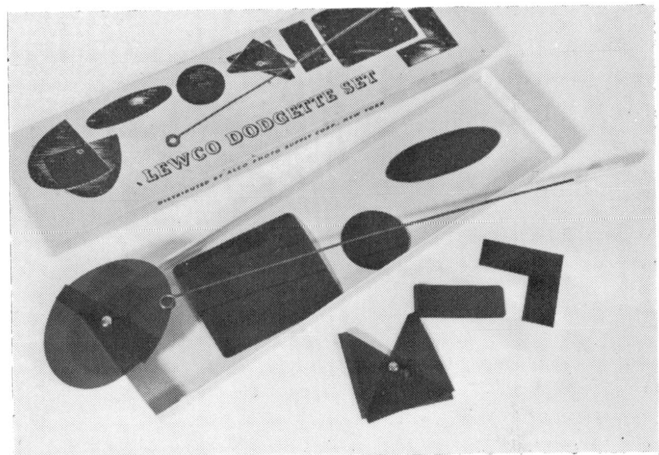

Store-bought dodging set used to hold back light during print exposure to hold shadow-area detail.

Homemade dodging set consists of a bent piece of coat hanger and shapes cut from black poster board. The board is held in place by masking tape and special shapes may be cut with ease to fit the need.

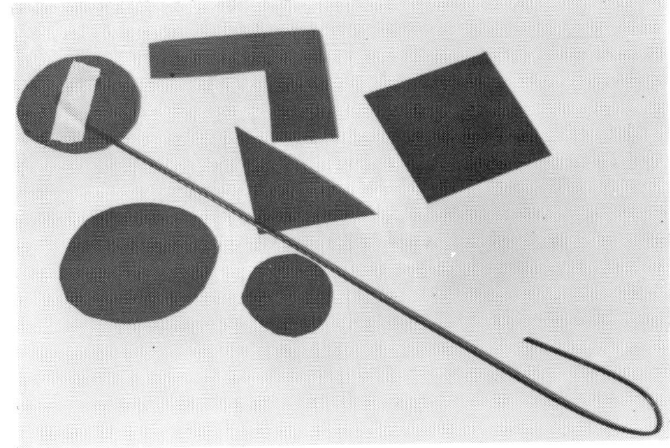

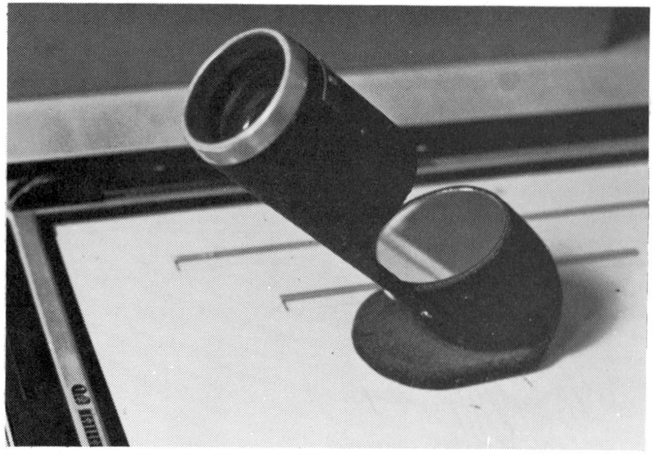

Magnasight enlarging magnifier enlarges the projected image so you may focus under the enlarger with ease. Several manufacturers offer similar ones.

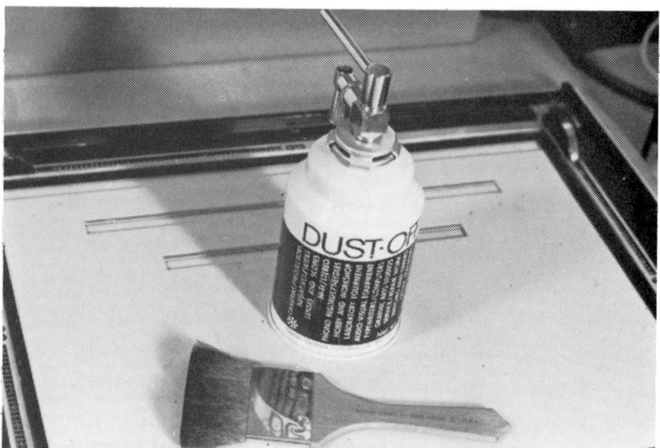

Clean negatives are a must for enlarging. A good camel-hair brush and a can of Dust-Off are the best way to get dust off of negatives.

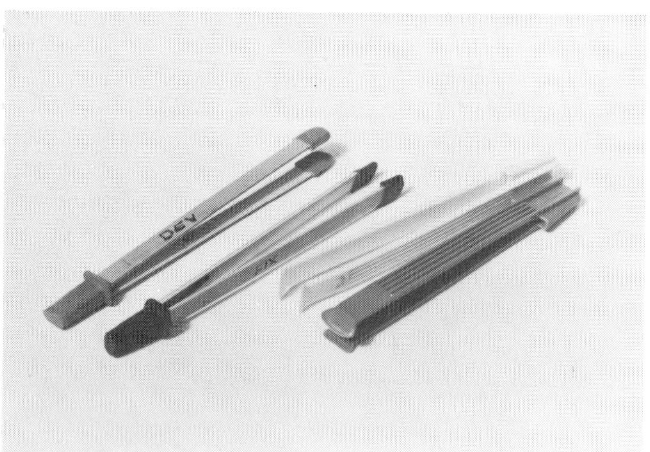

Many photo enthusiasts find they are allergic to a variety of darkroom chemicals. Most notably, those usually found in developer solutions. Print tongs such as these allow you to keep your hands dry and free from irritation.

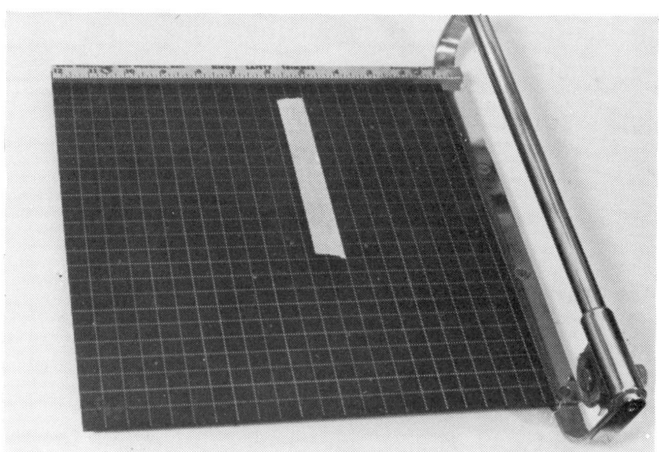

Always a useful item, the paper trimmer can help eliminate the problem of having to store several sizes of paper. Buy only the largest size you expect to use and cut it for anything smaller which may come along. This one is by Nikor Products.

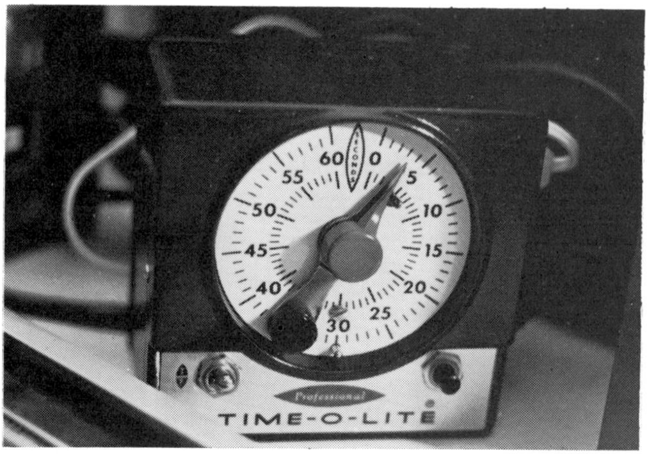

If reproducibility is necessary in your printing, buy a good enlarging timer if you can afford one. It's bad news to have an unwound wrist watch run down during a long print exposure.

start them running. These include a switch to turn the enlarger on and off, and a power cord to plug into the wall outlet. An outlet on the timer is used for the enlarger power cord. Resetting the time for each exposure doesn't sound like a handicap until you have to work with one of these for awhile. When you realize a single test print requires setting the timer four or five times, you may want to watch the clock until you can afford one of the timers which resets itself to the selected exposure.

Some of the best timers are made by Time-O-Lite, Omega, Heathkit, Honeywell-Wein and Unitimer. These timers also have a switch so you can turn the enlarging lamp on for focusing the negative image on the easel. You'll want one of these when you get deeply involved in darkroom work, but *you don't have to have one when you start out.*

EASELS

Standard Sizes—Non-adjustable types come in standard sizes such as 4x5, 5x7, 8x10, 11x14. The border or margin is built into the easel and you get the same width border whether that's what you want or not. You may find the non-adjustable easels are so light that you have to tape them down to the enlarger baseboard to prevent their moving around as you insert the paper. It's also possible to mount them on a weighted board so they'll be harder to move accidentally.

Adjustable Easels—These let you vary the print size. You can make standard sizes—*and* you can make custom sizes. Borders can be from about 1/8-inch width to as wide as you like. There is less of a storage problem when using an adjustable easel, but they are more expensive than buying one or two non-adjustable ones. In the long run, an adjustable easel is a good item to plan on having in your darkroom equipment line up.

Borderless Easels—These give you prints without borders. If you know you are going to mount the prints, you get more usable print area without borders. You get 5% more image area by eliminating a ¼-inch-wide border from an 8x10 print.

Some borderless easels use vacuum to hold the paper against the easel. I prefer this type because it lets me make odd-size prints. There's no need to use a standard size piece of paper and later cut it to the desired size.

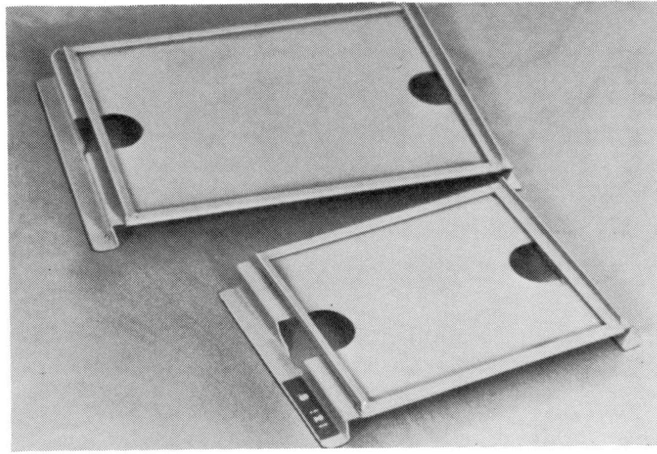

Fixed-size easel by Speed-Ez-El. Inexpensive and handy. Comes in wallet size through 16x20. They are a bit light and you may want to tape them to your enlarger baseboard when you get the picture composed.

Saunders Omega adjustable enlarging easel for prints 4x5 through 11x14. Relatively expensive but versatile and a life-long investment.

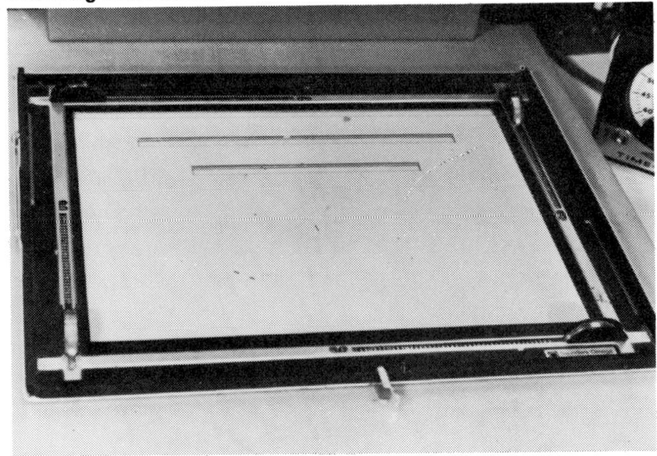

MISCELLANEOUS STUFF & JUNK

The items I've listed will serve to outfit a very workable darkroom. You will accumulate a lot of other items to make developing and printing easier or more interesting. You'll see the need for these as you gain experience and new preferences—perhaps preferences different from those I have placed before you. When in doubt, stick to good name brands of equipment and think four or five times before you buy some plastic gee-gaw that may have limited usefulness. If you don't buy it you won't have to store it or throw it away someday. The money you save can buy a lot of film to take more photos so you'll get better at what you're doing.

How To Print

Assuming you have gathered the equipment you need and have a roll of negatives to enlarge, here's where the fun begins!

Let's repeat the equipment list from Chapter 4 and make an addition:

Enlarger
Washer
Dryer or blotter roll (not essential with RC paper)
Safelight
Print trays
Chemicals
Timer
Assorted little things
Kodabrome RC medium contrast 8x10 enlarging paper

SET UP

First, get your darkroom area ready for printing. Set up the trays in a logical sequence. Put the developer tray at the opposite end of the sink or drainboard from the washer or last hypo-tray. My darkroom is set up so I make prints right to left. The washer is at the extreme left end of the sink. You may have to use a card table covered with oil cloth or newspapers because your sinks may not accommodate more than one or two trays. I've seen home darkroom setups with a plank spanning the length of the bathtub. Trays were set on the plank. The bathtub caught any solution spills. It worked fine except the user had to bend over or get down on her knees to see what was going on in the trays. Regardless of how it is set up, do it the same way each time. Also remember that you will find it considerably more convenient to make 8x10 prints in 11x14 trays.

If your darkroom climate is comfortable—between 60° and 80°F (16°–27°C)—then the processing chemicals will be usable for printing. They can be poured right from the bottle—mixed with tap water at the same temperature if they need to be diluted—and used at that temperature.

Temperatures for printing solutions are not so critical as for film processing, but try to keep them as near 68°F (20°C) as is convenient. Cool solutions by floating a plastic bag of ice cubes in the tray for a few minutes. A steel developing tank of hot water placed in the tray will rapidly raise the solution temperature.

Trays may be set up to process right to left as seen here or left to right if you prefer. However you do it, be consistent each printing session. It's always best to work toward the print washer if you have one.

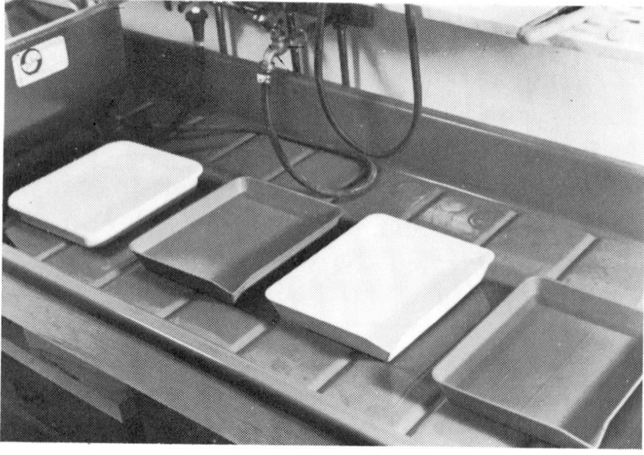

Printing solutions kept in a region of 68° to 72°F (20° to 23°C) provide comfortable working times. Higher temperatures cause developers to work too rapidly, producing streaking patterns. Too cold makes for flat prints extremely low in contrast.

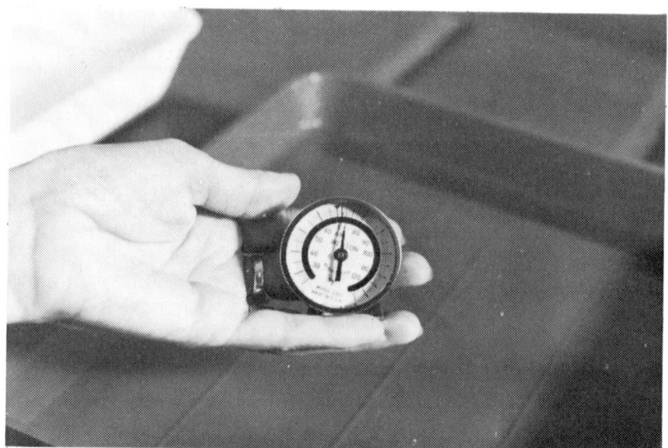

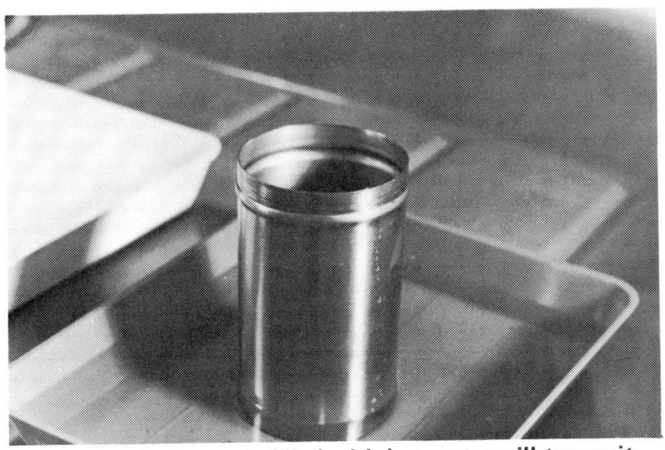

A steel developing tank filled with hot water will transmit a great deal of heat. Watch that the temperature doesn't rise too quickly and get the solution warmer than you wanted.

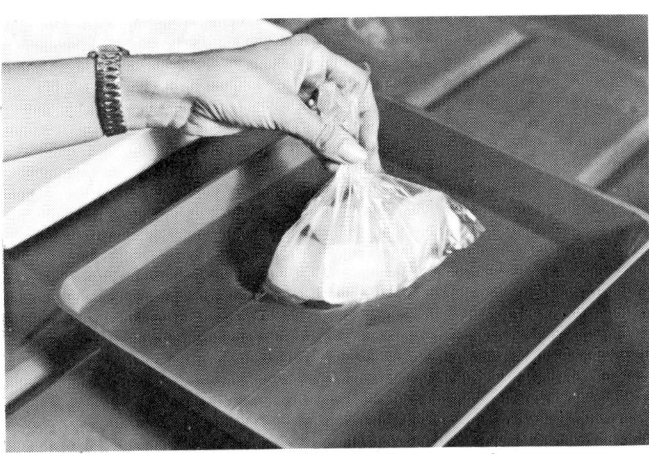

A plastic bag of ice cubes will quickly lower the temperature of processing solutions. Do not put cubes directly in the solution or you'll be diluting the working solution.

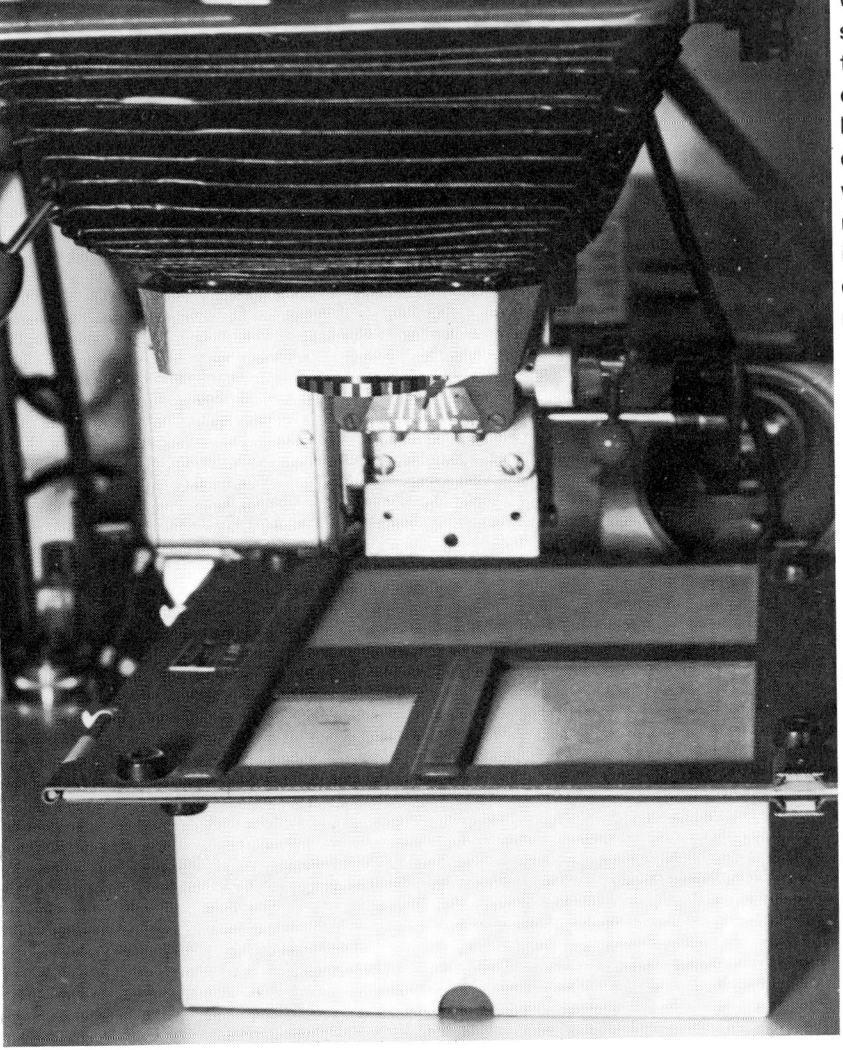

When you want to make a print which is same size or smaller than your negative, you may find that the enlarger head won't go low enough toward the easel. Solve the problem by raising the easel toward the lens. When the enlarger bellows is at near full extension, you will notice that the focus adjustment changes not the focus, but the image size. The focus is adjusted by raising or lowering the entire enlarger head. Some playing around will be necessary, but don't give up, it'll work.

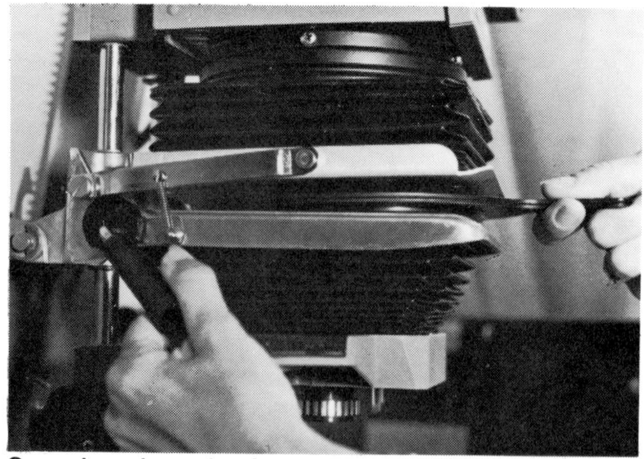

Open the enlarger head to accept the negative carrier by operating the lever at the negative stage.

After the negative carrier is in place, close the negative stage securely by returning the lever to its original position.

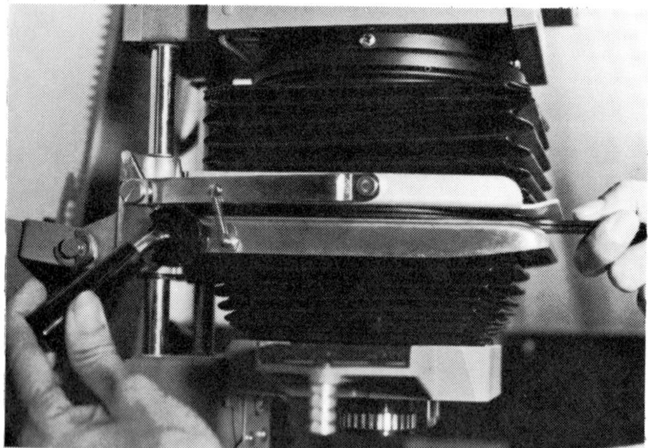

This knob, located at the support girder, controls the elevation of the enlarger head. The higher the head, the larger the image projected. Just like a flashlight; the farther away, the more area covered and with less brightness as well.

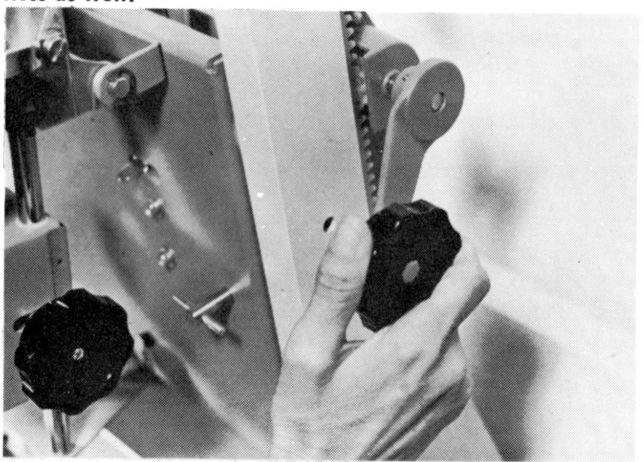

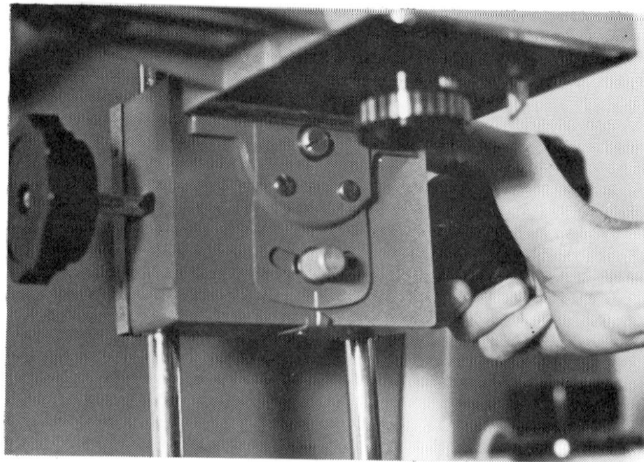

Focus knobs at lens-board level are used to adjust focus of the image on the easel. Focus should operate smoothly yet be tight enough not to drift once set. Line under round screw aligns lensboard with easel.

Aperature ring on lens to adjust lens diaphragm and amount of light projected from lamp house to easel.

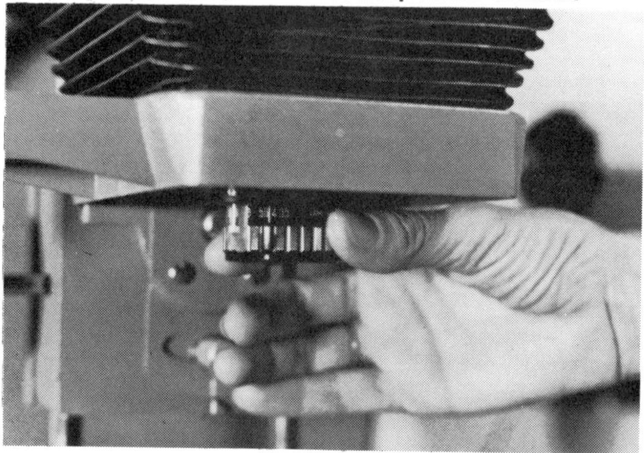

This little sliding drawer houses a red filter which may be inserted above the lens. This allows you to project an image from the negative while the enlarging paper is still in the easel. This can be helpful when making multiple exposures on the same sheet of paper.

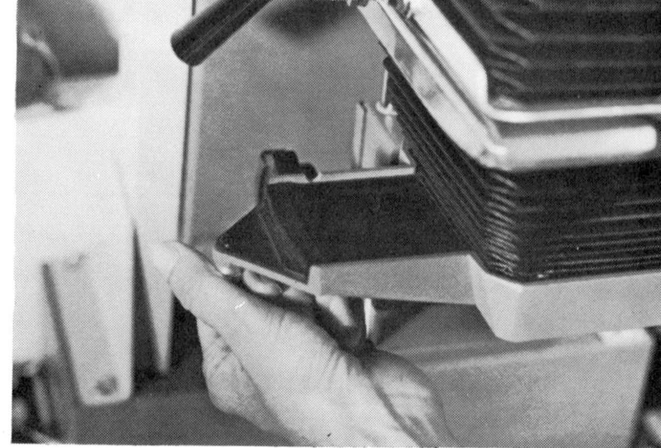

Omega enlargers are available with standard and extra-long girders. Tall models are for making really big prints. These B-22 and B-22-XL models are for 35mm and 2 1/4-inch square negatives.

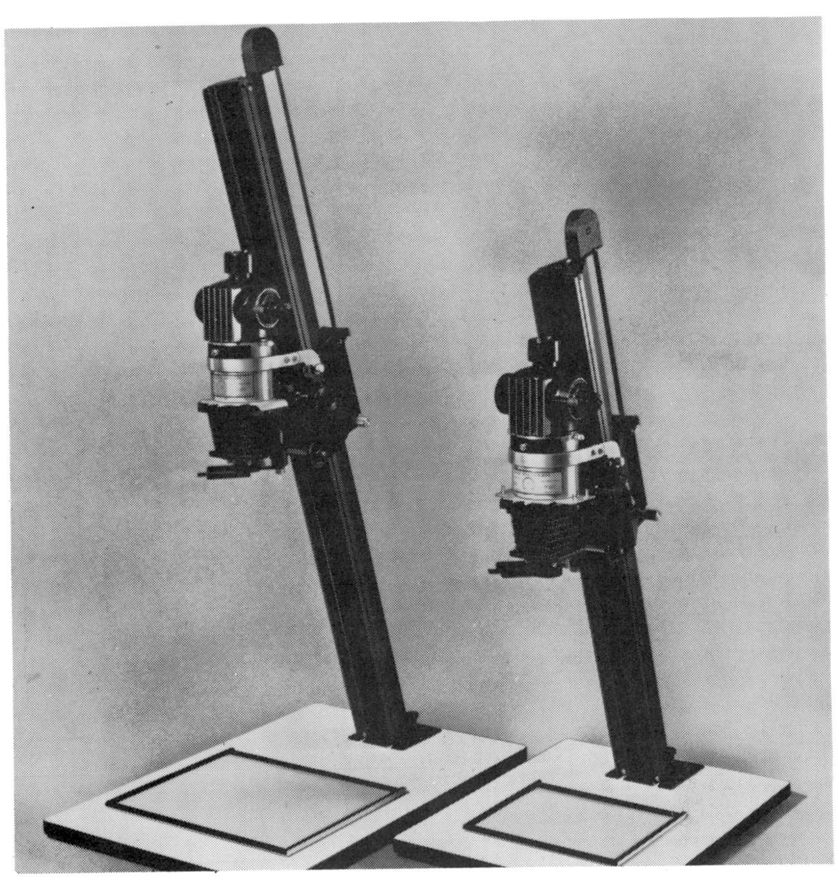

These are Super Chromega Dichroic 4x5 D2 and D2-XL enlargers. Timer and voltage control units are on baseboard. Easel at right is for making borderless prints.

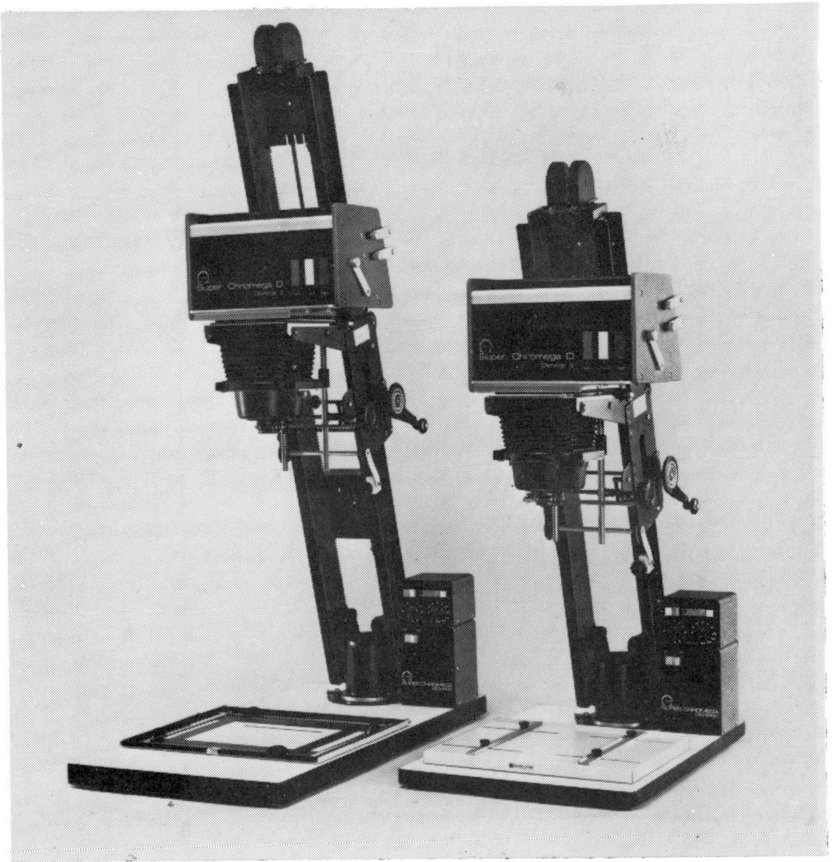

CLEAN THE NEG

With the trays set up, it's time to get out the negatives. Holding the negative *always by the edges,* inspect carefully for dust. Whether you see any or not, always go over the negatives very gently on both sides with a soft camel-hair brush or Staticmaster brush. If you have a can of Dust Off, a squirt or two of the compressed air will help also. Insert the negative in the negative carrier. If it is a glass-type carrier, be sure all glass surfaces are spotlessly clean. Check the negative for dust again. Get rid of any dust you see.

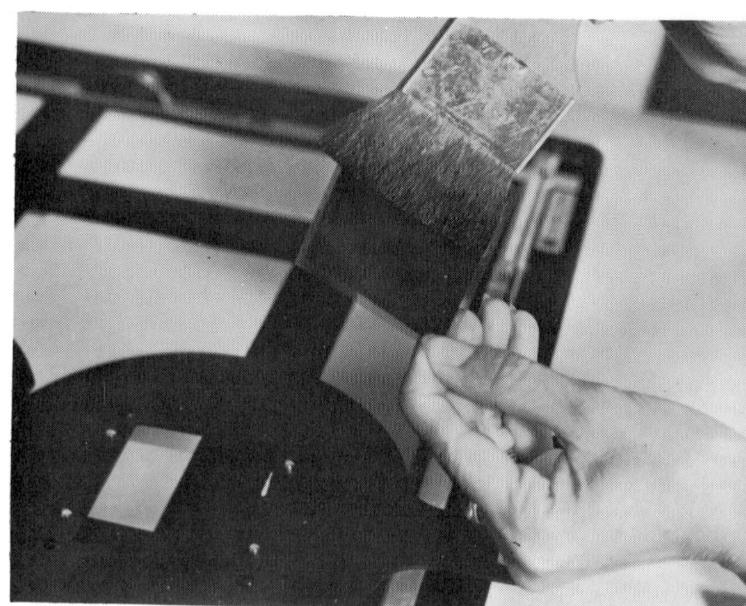

ALWAYS handle the negative by the EDGES! Clean BOTH sides with a soft camel hair brush.

Clean up your enlarger—Having a good clean negative is not enough if your enlarger is not just as clean. Your household vacuum cleaner is just the ticket here. Remove the condenser head and the lensboard and with the hose attachment used to clean little nooks and crannies—the long slender thing—vacuum the entire enlarger assembly. With a firm tap of your finger on the outside of the bellows, dislodge all dust and clean inside. This is important because it's the dust and dirt inside the bellows which leap onto the negative when the negative carrier is placed in the enlarger. If this happens, all effort spent in cleaning the negative was wasted.

While you have the vacuum out, use the brush attachment to clean all working areas of the darkroom completely, including enlarger baseboard, dryer areas and a really important spot—around the paper trimmer. The trimmer produces great quantities of fine paper particles which will "float" through the air to cause many dust-spot problems. Before reassembling the enlarger, wipe the condensers and the lensboard clean with a SLIGHTLY damp soft cloth and vacuum the area inside the housing above the condensers and around the lamp.

It's a good idea to keep this housekeeping on a once a month schedule. This is true whether you use the darkroom during that month or not. In fact, more dust will probably accumulate when your equipment is not in use.

A can of compressed air (Dust-Off) is a big help in removing stubborn lint or small hairs from the negative.

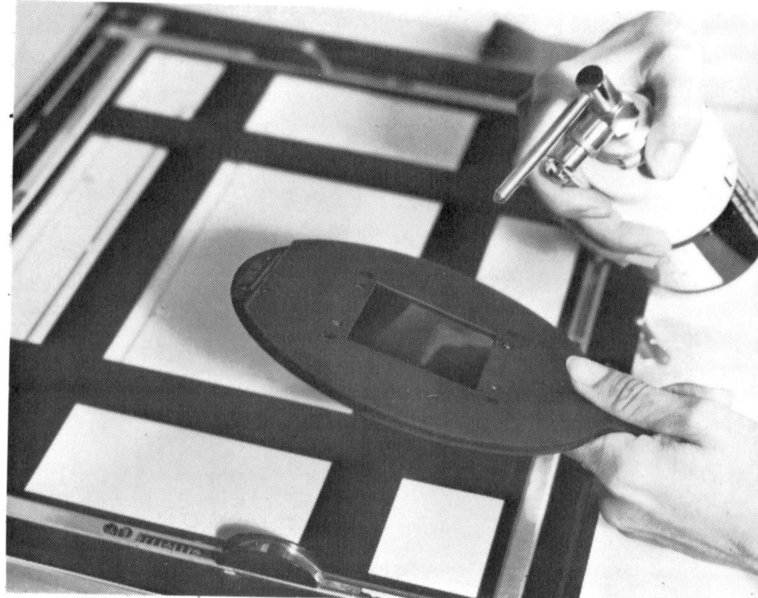

Look at your negatives positively—You may want to find a particular frame on a strip of negatives and wonder how it will look before you've had time to make contact proofs. If your negatives are a bit on the thin side, you can hold the negatives dull side up so the rays from a light strike the emulsion at a slant. Tilt the film back and forth and you will find an angle where the negatives appear to be positive, especially if you have a black background under the negatives.

MAKE A TEST PRINT

Insert the carrier into the enlarger with the negative's emulsion side down. The emulsion is not as shiny as the base. Make a test print, following these steps:

1. Turn off the white light and turn on the safelight. Many darkrooms are set up for printing so the safelight is always on. This can make it harder to focus the image on the easel. Some timers are arranged with an outlet for the safelight so it is automatically turned off when the enlarger is turned on. You'll decide which way works best for you after a few printing sessions.

2. Turn on the enlarger and raise the enlarger head so the negative image you want fills an 8x10

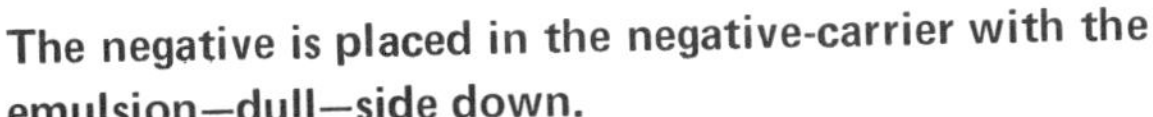

The negative is placed in the negative-carrier with the emulsion—dull—side down.

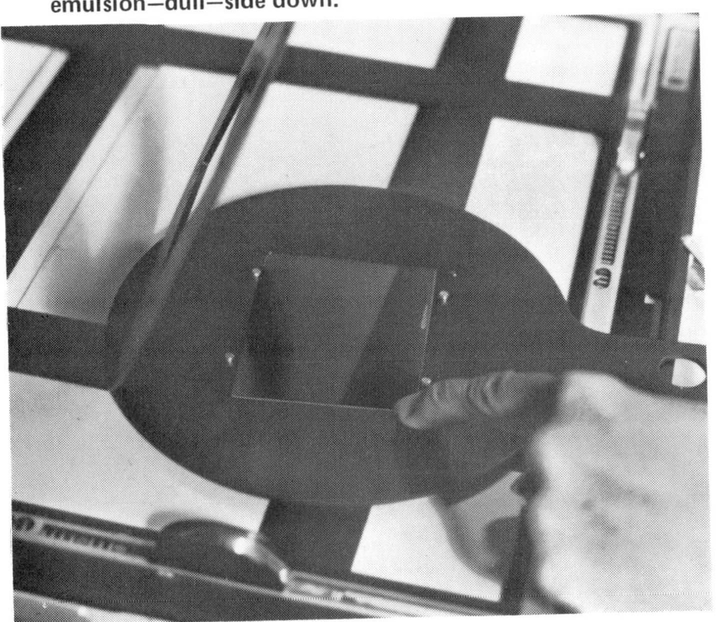

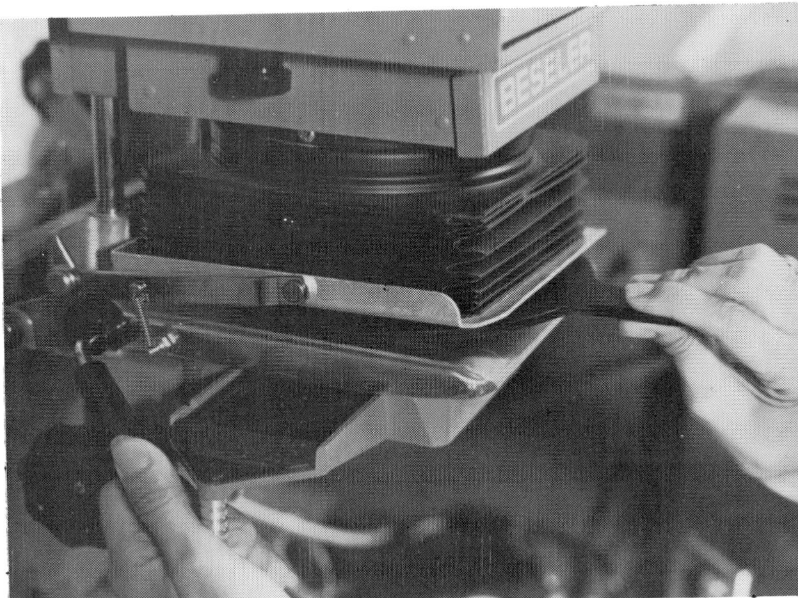

Make sure the condenser head is fully closed over the negative-carrier so the film is held flat for sharp prints.

Always use a focusing aid to ensure critical focus on the easel.

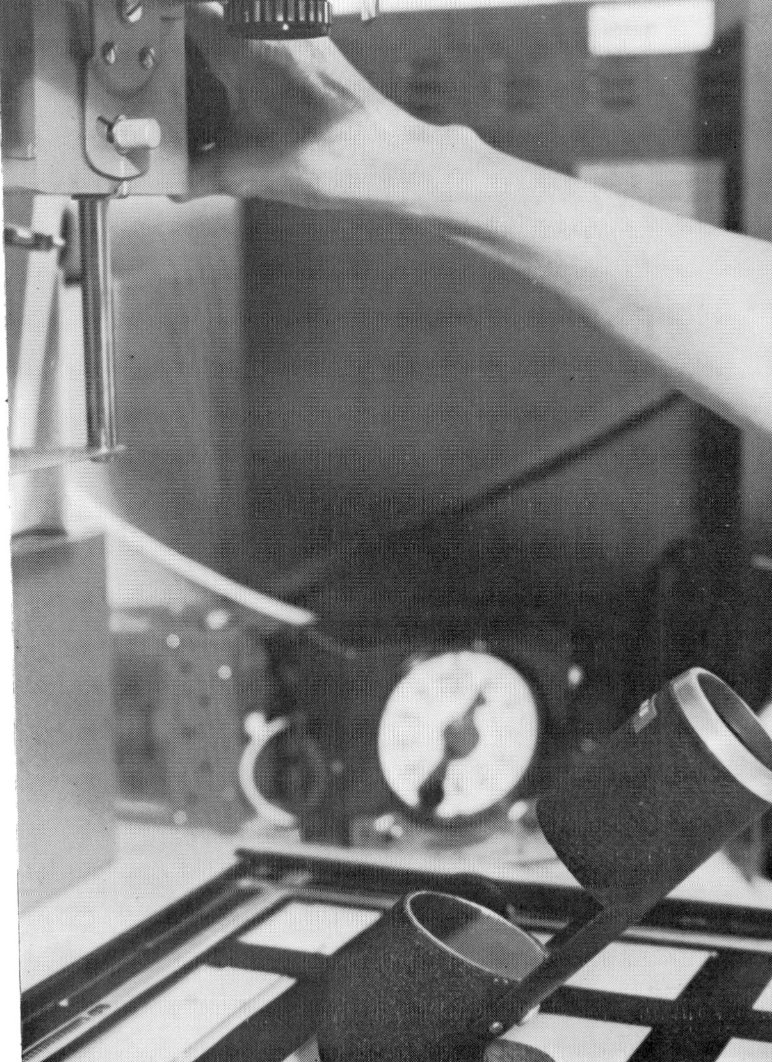

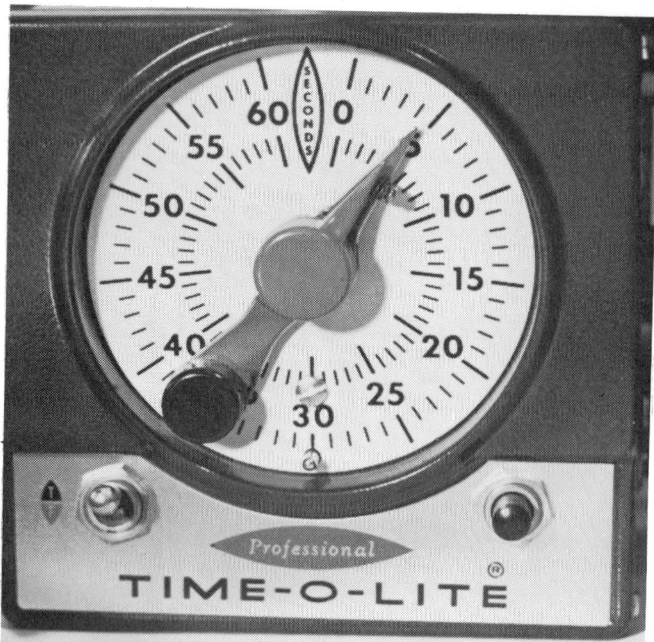

Set your enlarging timer to 5 seconds to make the test strip. Expose for 5 seconds, move the cardboard cover and expose again for 5 seconds. Try to make your test strip to give varying exposures in the most important area of your print.

easel. A piece of enlarging paper should be in the easel.

3. Focus the image on the easel. Use a focusing aid if you have one. These magnify the grain structure so you can focus critically. Turn off enlarger and take the piece of paper out of the easel. This is a dummy sheet used only for focusing, so save it. Mark it on the back and/or front so it doesn't get mixed up with your unexposed paper.

4. Turn on the white light, set your lens-aperture ring on the enlarger to *f*-11. If you have an enlarging timer, set it to five seconds.

5. Turn the white light off, remove an 8x10 sheet of paper from its box or envelope and secure it in the easel. CLOSE THE PAPER BOX OR ENVELOPE. Put the flap end of the inner envelope into the outer one so the flap is opposite the opening of the second envelope.

6. With an 8x10 or larger piece of heavy cardboard, cover three-quarters of the printing paper and turn the enlarger on for five seconds.

7. Move the cardboard so one-half of the paper is covered and expose for another five seconds. Don't move the easel or paper as you move the cardboard. If your easel tends to slide around on the enlarger baseboard, put a rubber mat under it or tape it to the baseboard.

This is what you see when you look through the magnifier. The large image is easier to focus than looking at the photo projected onto the easel.

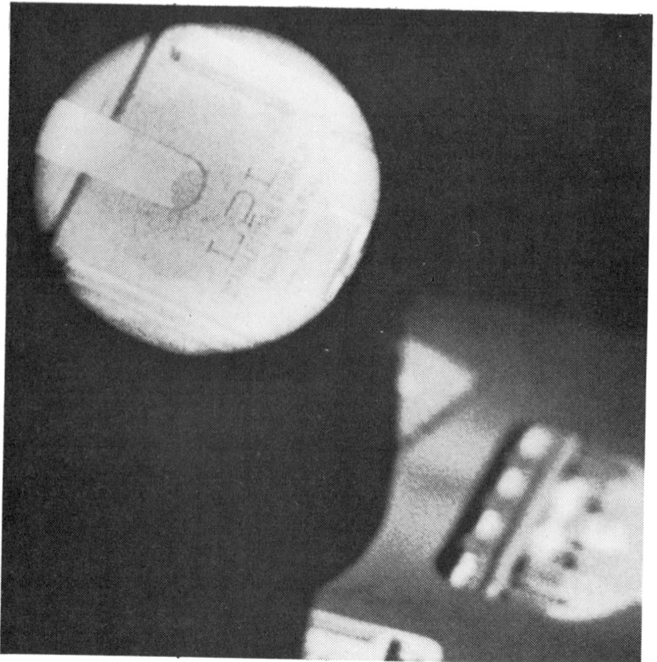

CHECK TO SEE THAT THE PAPER BOX IS CLOSED TIGHTLY BEFORE TURNING ON THE WHITE LIGHT! The penalty for this comes straight out of your pocketbook!

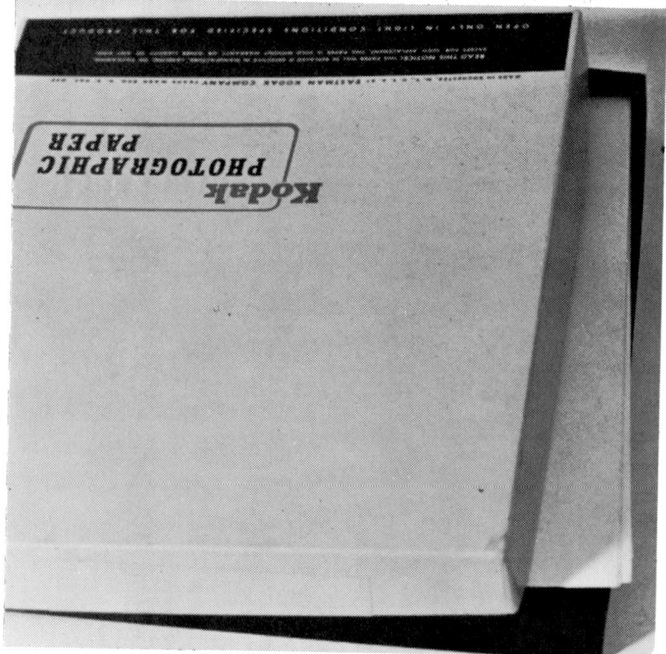

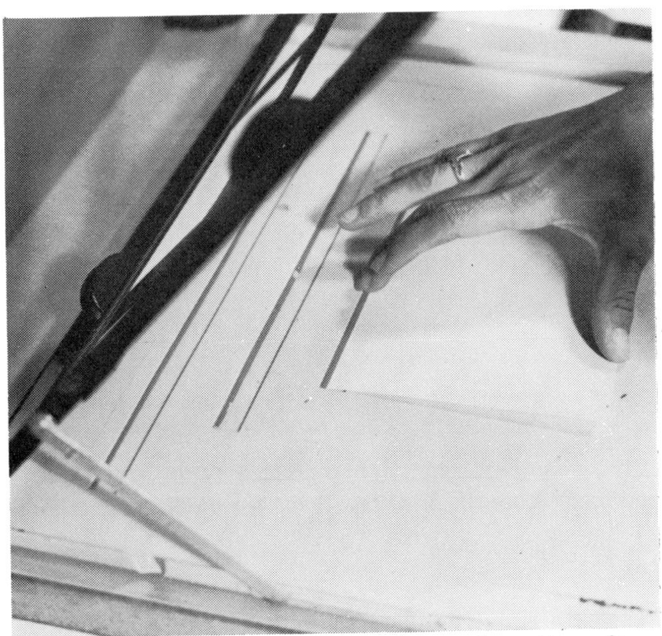
Place the enlarging paper in the easel securely so it won't move during the exposures.

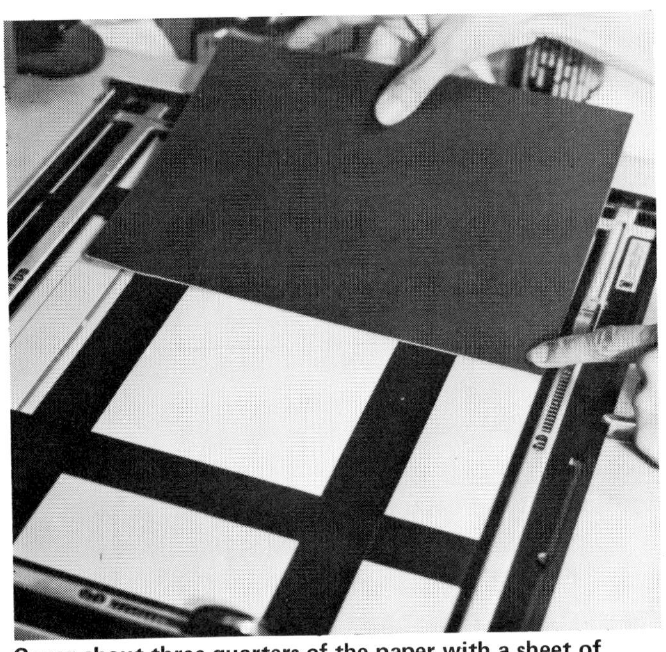
Cover about three-quarters of the paper with a sheet of black cardboard and expose for 5 seconds.

After each 5-second exposure, move the cardboard another quarter of the paper length for an additional 5-second exposure until the entire sheet has been uncovered.

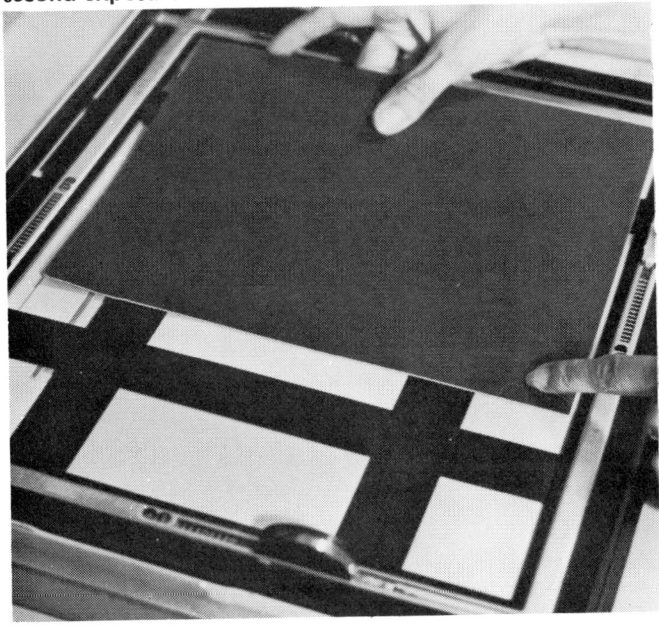

1/Place the exposed paper in the developer tray face down.

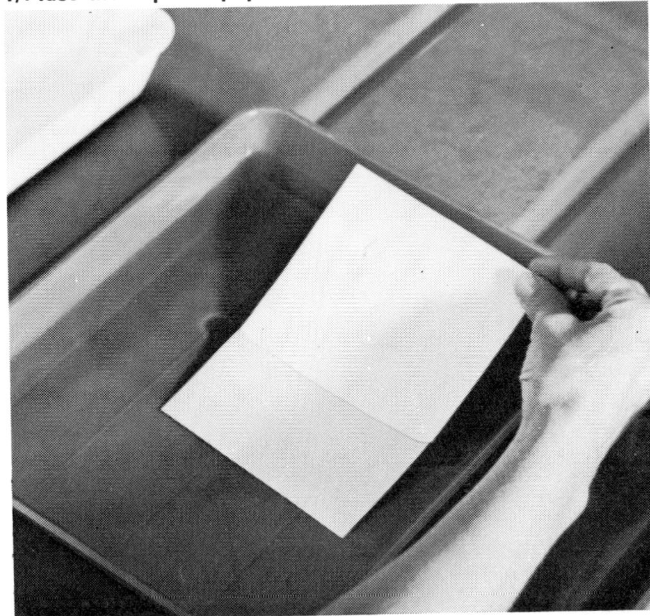

8. Cover only one-quarter of the paper and expose for another five seconds.

9. Remove the cardboard from the paper completely and expose for another five seconds.

You now have exposures of 5, 10, 15 and 20 seconds on the paper.

10. With the white light still out and safelight on, place the exposed paper into the tray of developer, face down. The paper should remain face down for at least the first 30 seconds of the 1½ minute developing time.

Constantly agitate the print in the developer by turning it over and moving the tray in a rocking motion for the total development time.

11. At the end of 1½ minutes, remove the paper from the developer; holding it above the tray to drain for five seconds.

12. Then place it into the stop bath for 30 seconds but don't let the developer print tongs touch the stop bath.

13. Remove the print from the stop bath, allow to drain for five seconds.

14. Place it in the fixer tray and agitate for one minute.

15. Turn on the white light and look at your test print—test strip. The first thing you will notice

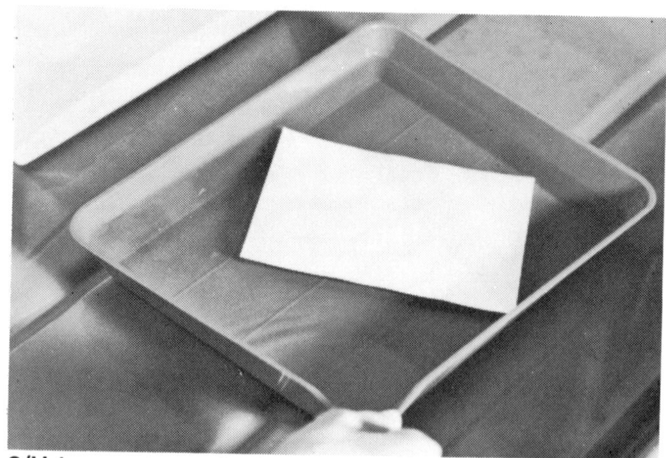

3/Using constant agitation by tipping the tray gently back and forth, leave the print face down for the first 30 seconds.

4/Turn the print face up and continue agitation for the remainder of the total 1½ minute developing time.

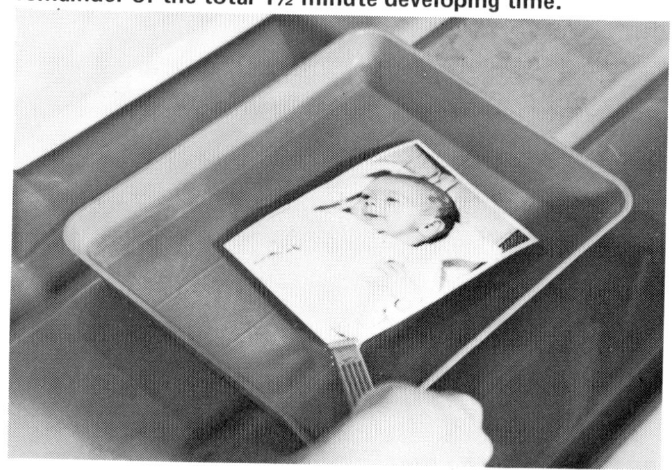

2/Quickly and gently cover the paper with solution by using your print tongs to dunk the paper under the developer surface.

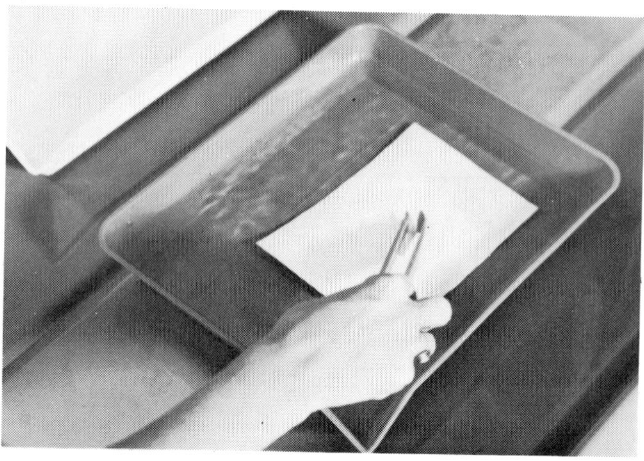

5/Using the print tongs, remove the print from the developer and drain excess solution for 5 seconds, then . . .

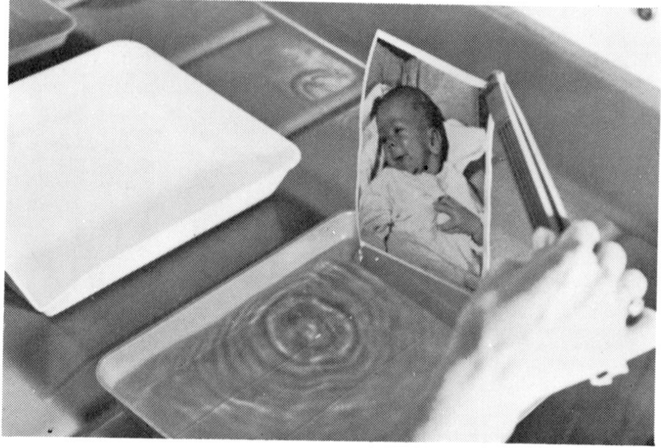

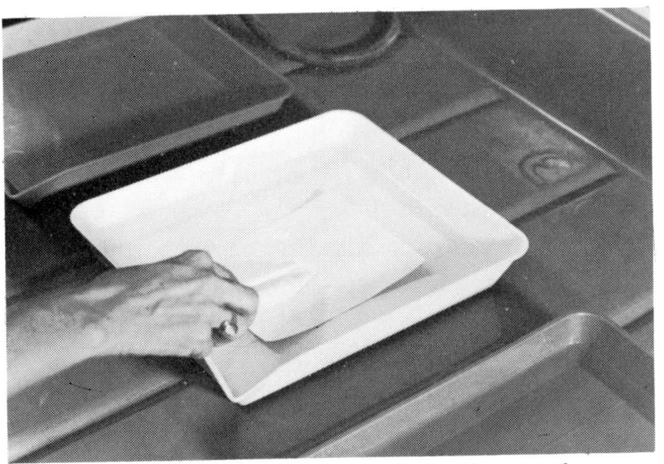

6/ . . . place the print in the stop bath for 30 seconds.

7/At the end of the stop bath, drain for 5 seconds and . . .

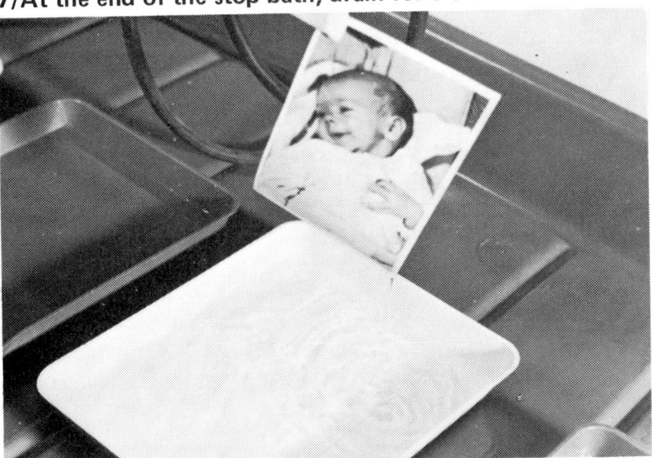

8/ . . . place the print in the fixer and agitate constantly for one minute.

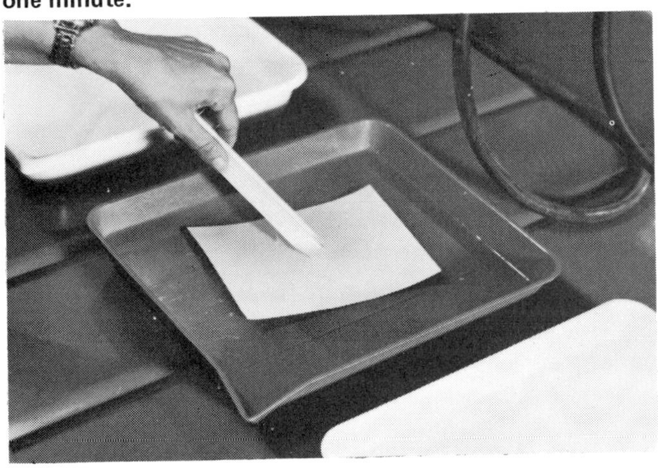

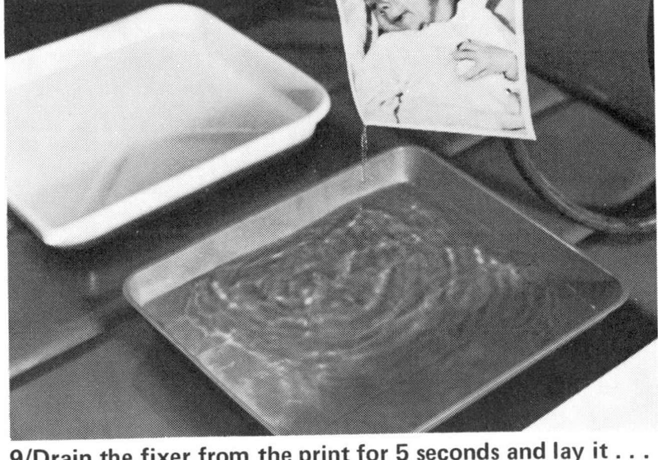

9/Drain the fixer from the print for 5 seconds and lay it . . .

10/ . . . on the back of an extra tray for evaluation under white room light. Don't try to determine contrast and tone with the print in solution as it will appear too dark under the safelight and too light when viewed under white room light. After evaluation return the print to the fixer for the balance of fixing period.

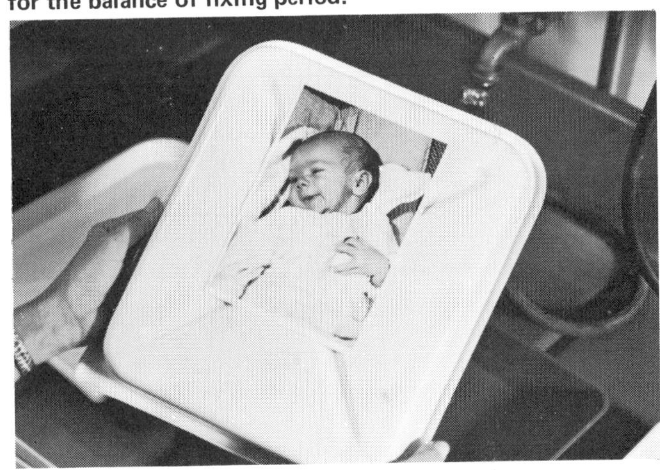

11/The final solution before washing is the hypo neutralizer. A saver of both time and water if you are using non-RC papers. You don't need it with RC papers.

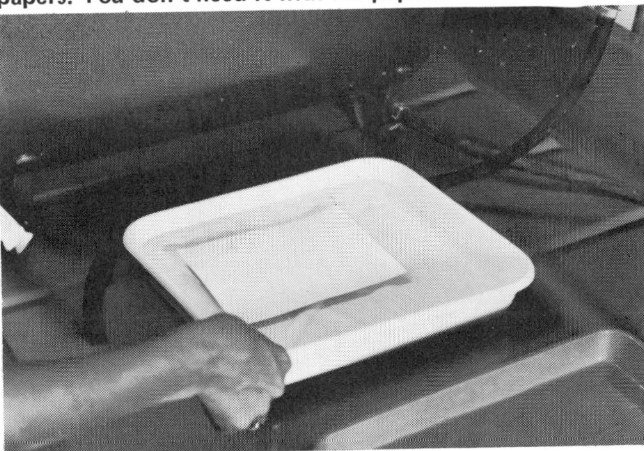

is that you are either in the ballpark with at least one of the exposures, or you are definitely wrong. If the 5-second exposure is much too dark, then repeat the above steps with the enlarger lens set at *f*-16. If the 20-second exposure is too light, repeat the above steps with the enlarging lens set at *f*-8.

Hopefully, your initial try gave you the correct exposure somewhere between 5 and 20 seconds. Now you must determine which exposure—5, 10, 15 or 20 seconds—is the best. An exposure somewhere in-between may give you the best print. You can usually visualize this as you check the test print.

If you can't imagine which exposure will give you the print quality you want, make another test print in a range of exposures you think will be close. To save paper, use only ¼ of a sheet of paper this time. If the 5-second exposure was too light and the 10-second one too dark, make a test print with exposure steps of 6, 7, 8 and 9 seconds. Expose for 6 seconds, then move the card one step and expose for another second. Don't uncover the last step because it already has the 6-second minimum exposure you need.

PRINT AT SELECTED EXPOSURE

Decide on the exposure you prefer and set your enlarging or developing timer to that exposure —or remember the exposure so you can watch a sweep-second hand. Turn off the white light, remove sheet of printing paper from the box and secure it in the easel. Now start the timer or turn on the enlarger and make your exposure just as before. Remove paper from easel, place emulsion side down on hard surface and record exposure data on back of print toward outer edge using No. 1 pencil. Don't press too hard with the pencil or you'll mar the emulsion.

Place sheet in developer tray and continue procedures as for the test strip.

When you get the print in the fixer, leave it there for two minutes, then take it out and turn on the light to evaluate it. If it's a "keeper," wash the print in running water for four minutes, then dry it by squeegeeing off the excess water carefully and placing the print face up on a towel. These fixing and washing instructions apply only to RC paper. If you are using ordinary non-RC paper you will have to go the much longer route of fixing for 10 minutes, then rinsing the print in water for a minute, then hypo neutralizer for the

Mark all information concerning filters and manipulation data on the back of the print before exposing. This ensures that you can repeat successes or avoid further errors. Use a soft pencil, don't press hard and write with the paper on a hard surface.

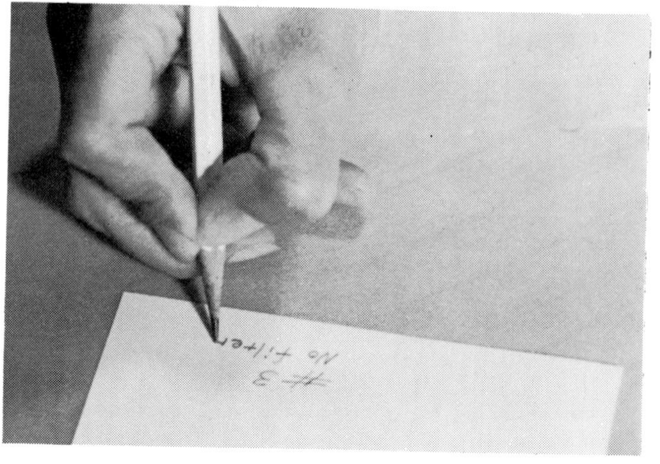

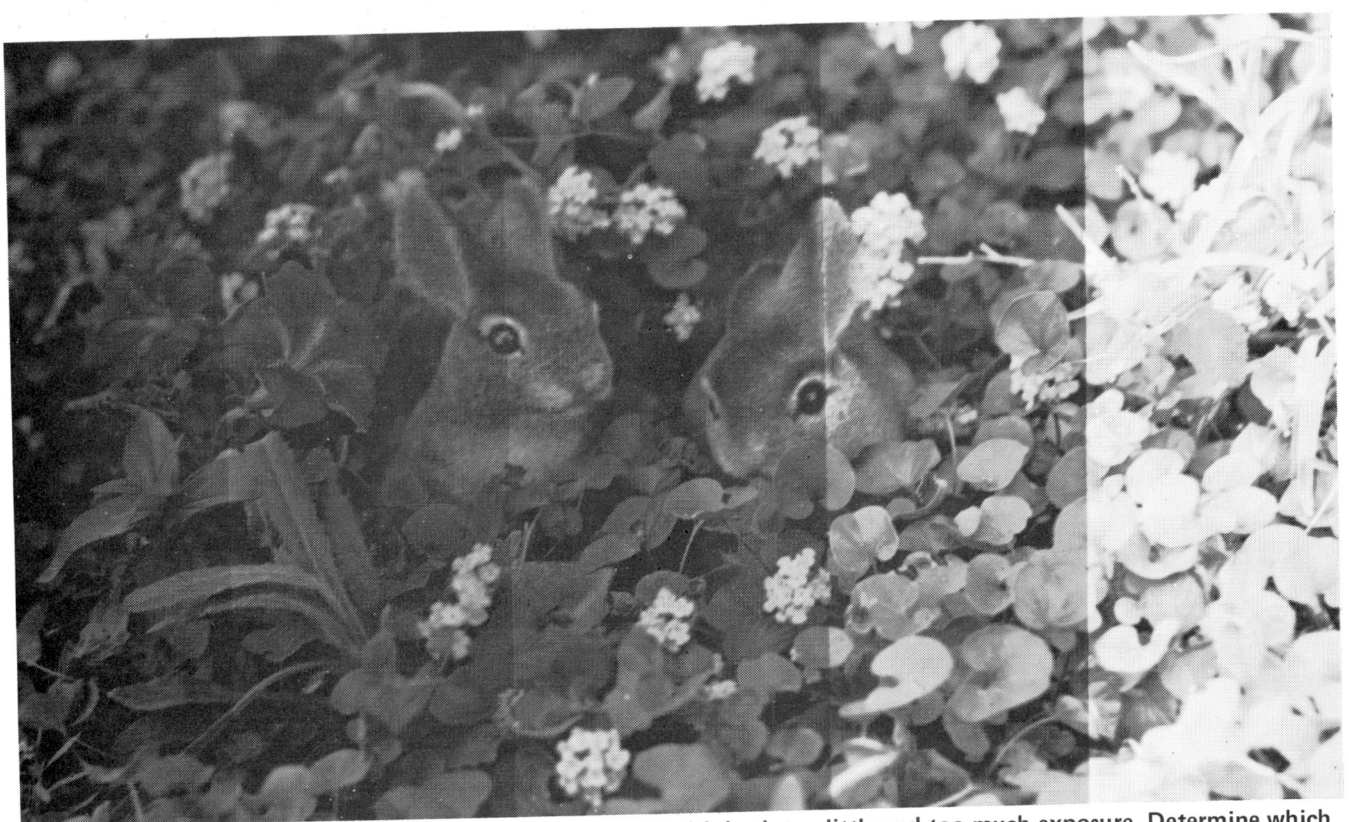

The test strip should look something like this showing areas with both too little and too much exposure. Determine which exposure gives the most pleasing contrast and detail.

Place a new sheet of enlarging paper in the easel and expose for the time you felt was the best, and . . .

. . . you should have just the print you saw in your mind when you made the camera exposure.

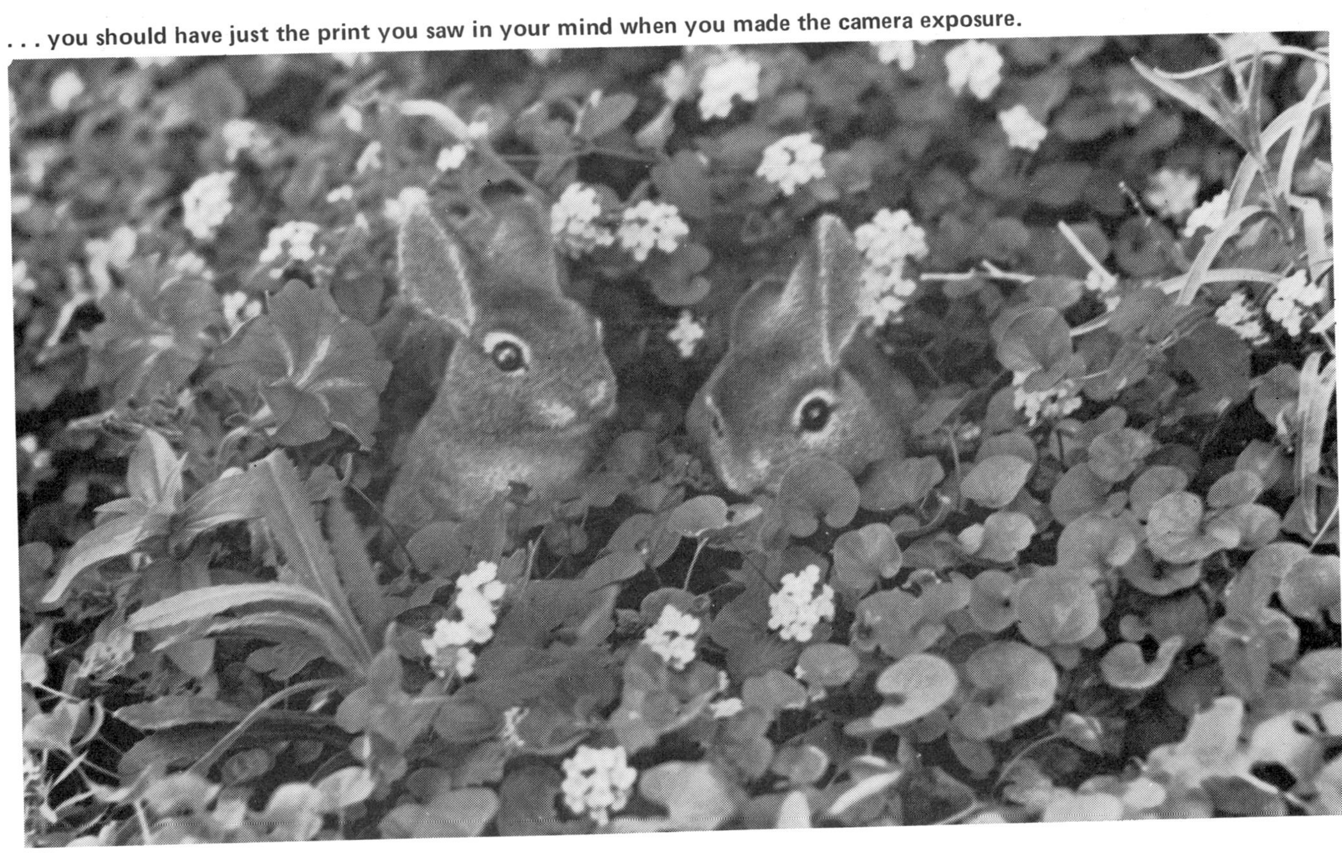

recommended time shown in the instructions, then washing for at least 10 mintues or longer before drying.

JUDGING PRINT QUALITY

Experienced darkroom technicians judge print quality and contrast under white light. You do, too. It's easy to be fooled when viewing the print by safelight, because it appears darker than it will under white light. Always take the time to view a fixed print by white light before deciding you are completely happy with it and moving on to the next negative. It can be very discouraging to think you have a hypo tray full of beautiful prints, then turn the white light on to find they should all have been a little darker.

Remove the fixed print and lay it on the back of a white print tray for viewing. Don't try to judge the photograph when it is under solution. The print actually looks a bit lighter than it will when it finally dries. This difference between the wet and dry print appearance is not usually very important, but you should be aware that dry prints are a little darker than wet ones.

Each print should be exposed, processed and evaluated as if it were the only print you were going to make. The only time more than one print should be run through the developing process at one time is when you make several identical prints from the same negative and have already evaluated a test strip from that negative. Then several prints can be exposed and run through the developing process at the same time.

If you have done everything right to this point, you should have a print that pretty well pleases you and has good rich blacks and clear, sparkling highlights. If they are not quite so, don't be discouraged. If the *overall* exposure on the print is about what you had in mind, then examine it closely and see if there are any small details that disappoint you. You may have shadow areas that have gone quite black and have lost some details that you thought were important. Or at the other extreme it may have highlights which lack detail you would like to see. You've looked at the negative and know these details are there. This brings us to a discussion of the two simplest and most widely used methods of correcting print flaws.

CONTRAST

The next problem is whether or not you are pleased with the overall contrast of the print. Overall contrast is the visual difference between the brightest area and the darkest area. Are the areas which should be dark black a dark muddy gray instead? Highlight areas should be clear, crisp and white. Do they have an overall grayish appearance? If so, you have a contrast problem.

A minor bit of term defining is needed here. Technically, the visual or measured difference between the brightest and darkest areas of a print is called *contrast range.* The same idea is implied by the expression *overall contrast.*

Contrast—not overall or range—is the visual difference between adjacent parts of a scene as they appear on film. Which only means that middle tones of gray have contrast because they are different shades or densities and therefore contrast is not limited only to the extreme light and extreme dark areas.

However most photographers use *contrast* to mean a combination of both ideas. If a print doesn't have enough contrast there is not enough overall separation between light and dark, and also there is not enough visual separation between middle tones of gray—such as a cat sleeping in a chair.

As you will see, if you make adjustments to improve overall contrast you also help the middle tones, so the precise technical interpretation doesn't have much pratical impact on what you do.

CONTRAST CONTROL

Contrast can be changed by several different methods.

Paper Grade—Enlarging papers and contact-printing papers come in grade numbers 0 through 6 and in paper-grade names *soft, medium, hard, extra-hard, and ultra-hard.*

Name grades were adopted by Kodak in 1974 and I expect most makers will use these to replace number grades as they nearly all follow whatever the leader does. Kodak RC papers come in *soft, medium, hard, extra-hard* and *ultra-hard,* approximately equivalent to grades 1 through 5.

Grade 2 or medium paper is *normal* and is used with *normal* negatives. Normal negatives have good dense highlights and clear shadow areas and all the grays in between. A grade 1 paper is called a *soft* paper and is used for printing negatives with large, fairly dense, blocked-up areas as well as large areas of very, very low density. Grade 1 paper will reduce the contrast of the negative, as it appears on the print.

Hard papers numbered 3, 4 and 5 or *hard, extra-hard* and *ultra-hard* are used for printing very flat, low-contrast negatives. Grade 5 *(ultra-hard)* produces extreme contrast and is the hardest paper available from some sources, usually on special order. If you choose to use graded papers, then grades 1, 2 and 3, *soft, medium* and *hard* should get you through practically any printing problem.

Some paper manufacturers furnish grade 0, which is extremely flat and an extremely contrasty grade 6. Don't get into the habit of using these extreme grades. While they are fine for experimentation, if your negatives do not print consistently well on grades 1, 2 or 3, it's time to go back to camera exposure and film processing, to see where you are creating your own problems. You may need to use different ASA ratings for your film to get the results you want. Kodak, in their Kodak Darkroom Dataguide, publishes a table on paper speeds. These speeds are from ANSI Standard PH2.2-1966 and are approximate relative exposures for the papers listed. Kodak Polycontrast paper used without a filter has a speed of 160 while Polycontrast Rapid has an unfiltered speed of 320. The higher number indicates the "rapid" paper is twice as fast as the former and would require one whole *f*-stop less exposure to produce the same density print from the same negative printed. The following are speed ratings for some commonly available papers:

Paper	Contrast grade	Paper speed
Kodabromide	1	500
	2	320
	3	200
	4	160
	5	125
Kodabrome RC	Soft	400
	Medium	400
	Hard	400
	Extra-hard	200
	Ultra-hard	200
Polycontrast	No filter	160
	1 filter	100
	2 filter	125
	3 filter	100
	4 filter	50
Polycontrast Rapid/ Rapid RC	No filter	320
	1 filter	250
	2 filter	250
	3 filter	160
	4 filter	64/50 (RC)

In general, the higher the contrast grade or contrast filter, the more exposure is required. Read the data sheet packed with each package of paper. Knowing how an unfamiliar paper is speed-rated compared to your standard type and grade, can save a lot of waste. A handy print exposure dial in the Kodak Darkroom Dataguide is worth the price of the guide. Consider this my recommendation to buy one.

Processing—Contrast can be changed to a limited degree such as one-half paper grade, up or down, without changing to a different grade paper. If you desire slightly more contrast, cut the exposure back about 5 percent and then overdevelop the print by about 50 percent. On the other hand, if you want to cut contrast just slightly, try overexposing by about 5 percent and pulling the print from the developer after about one minute.

Care must be taken here to be sure the print or developer is agitated. An overexposed print which is not agitated in the developer will have muddy-gray swirls in the shadow areas.

Although this variation of exposure and development time can be of great help to give you that extra edge you look for, *it is limited.* No more than one-half paper grade up or down should be attempted.

If this technique still leaves your print short of the desired contrast, change to a different paper grade.

Variable-Contrast Paper—It's easy to get carried away with graded papers and find you have a darkroom full of many boxes of different grades and surfaces, most of which you use only rarely. As you become more experienced in photographic technique from the camera through the enlarger, you should find the great majority of your negatives will print on the same grade of paper.

This six-print series shows some of the differences and effects which occur when prints are incorrectly exposed or developed.

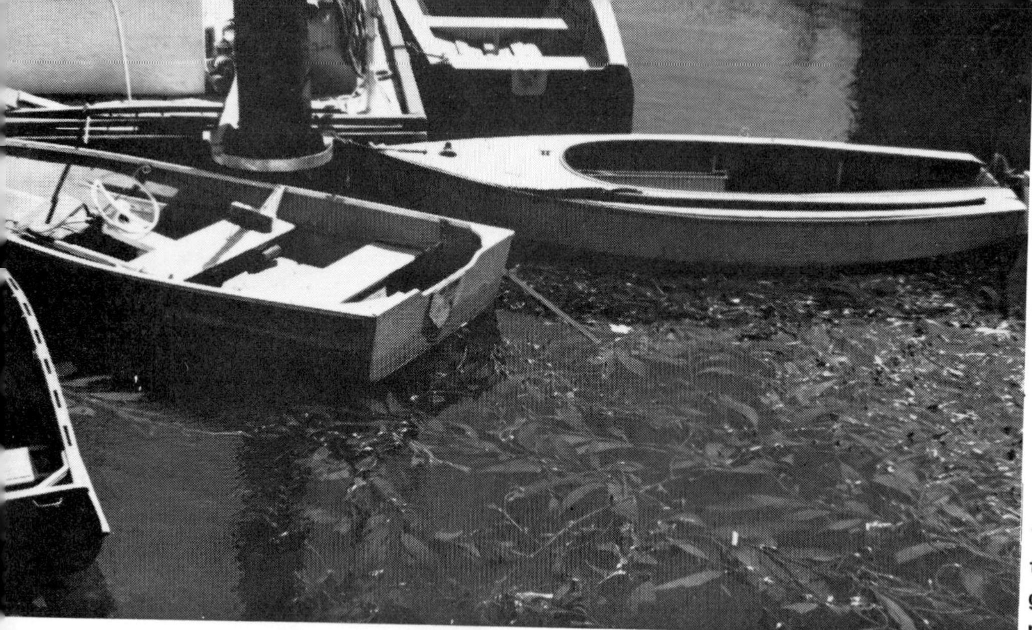

1/Correct exposure, developed for specified time. Result: Pleasing overall appearance with good shadow detail, definite blacks, good middle tones and some detail in the highlights.

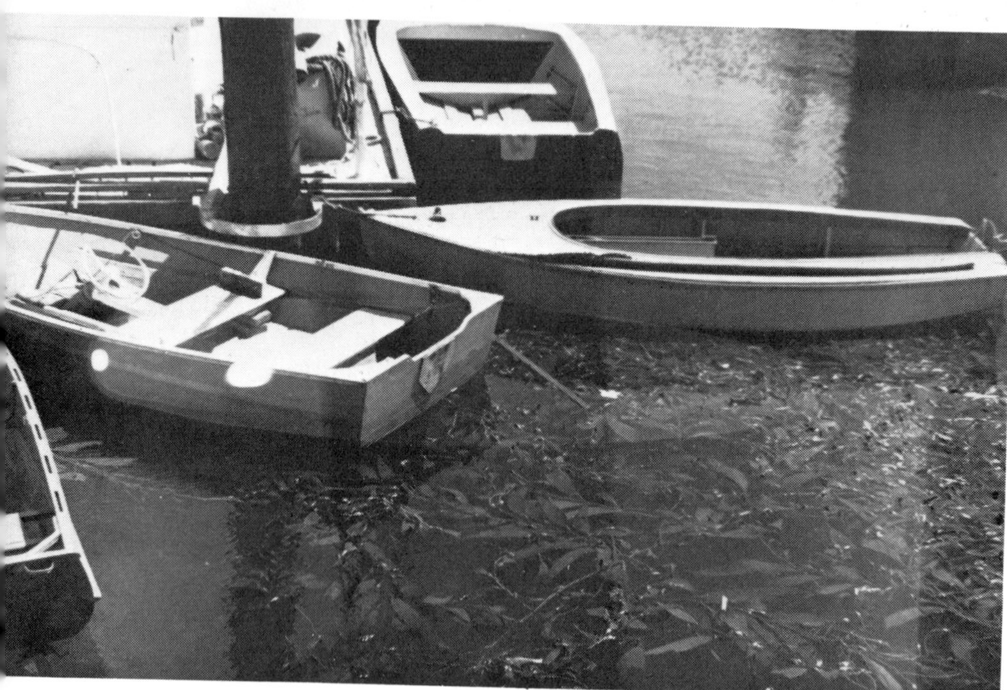

2/Correct exposure, print not agitated in the developer. Result: Uneven development, streaking.

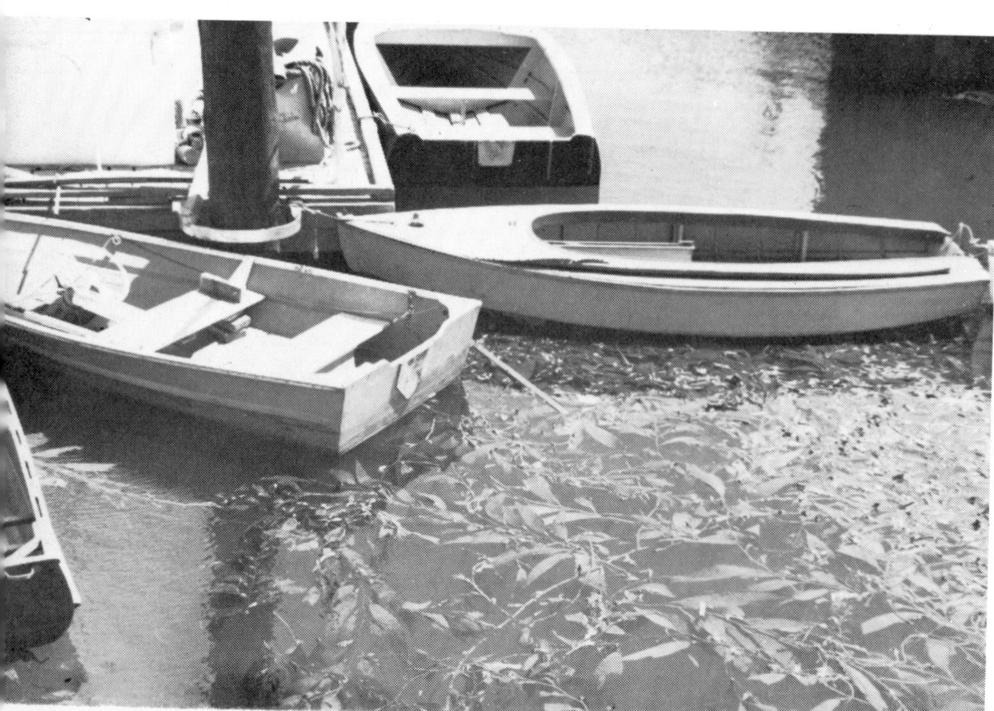

3/Correct exposure, wrong paper contrast (too soft). Result: Flat appearance.

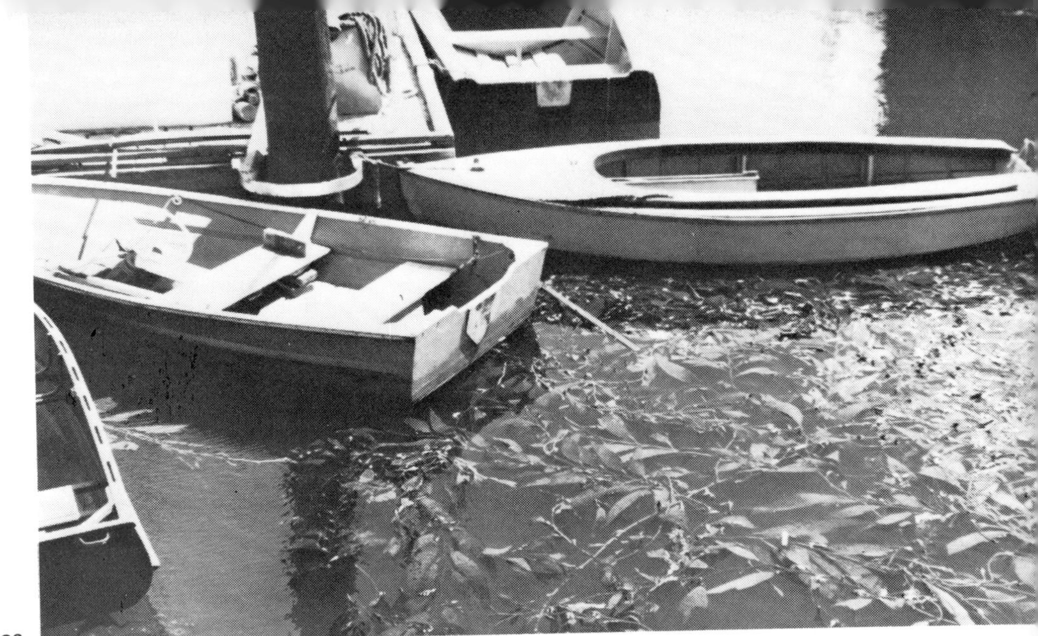

4/Under-exposed, under-developed. Result: High contrast with little detail. A print on too-high-contrast paper has a similar appearance.

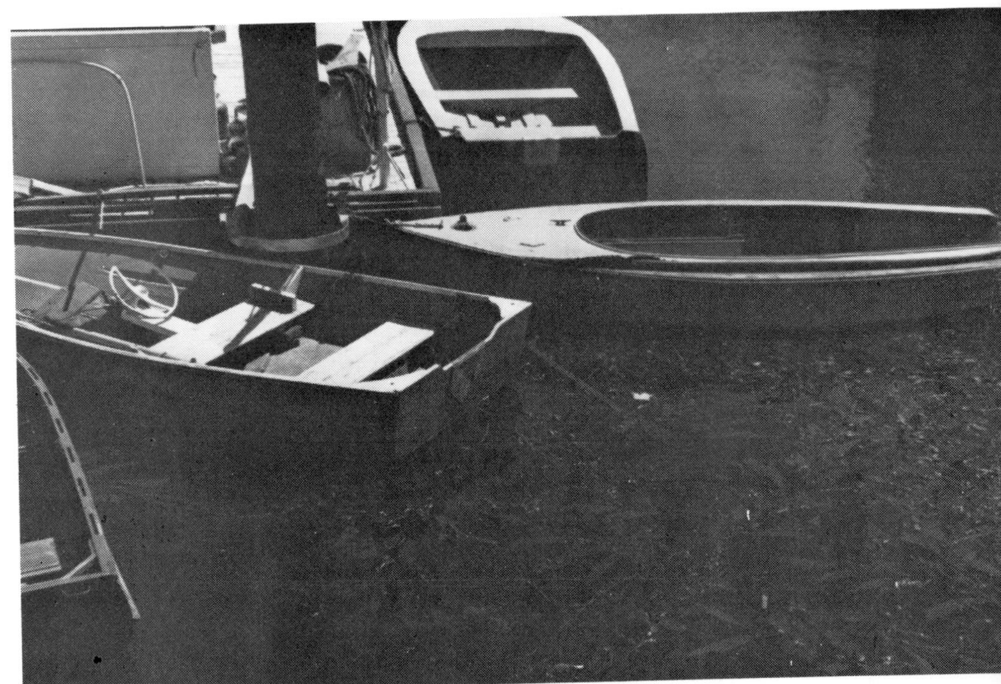

5/Over-exposed, under-developed. Print pulled before development was complete. Result: Muddy print with some streaking. Little detail in shadows. Shadows quite black. Highlights greyed.

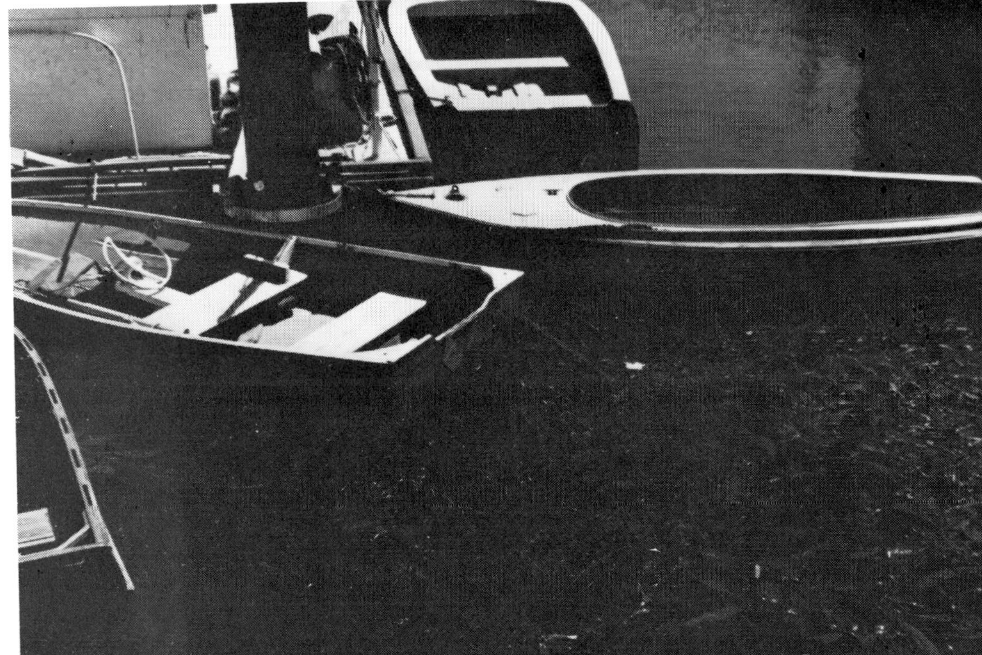

6/Correct exposure, over-developed. Result: Added detail in highlights, reduced detail in middle tones and shadows. Print takes on an ominous "dark" appearance.

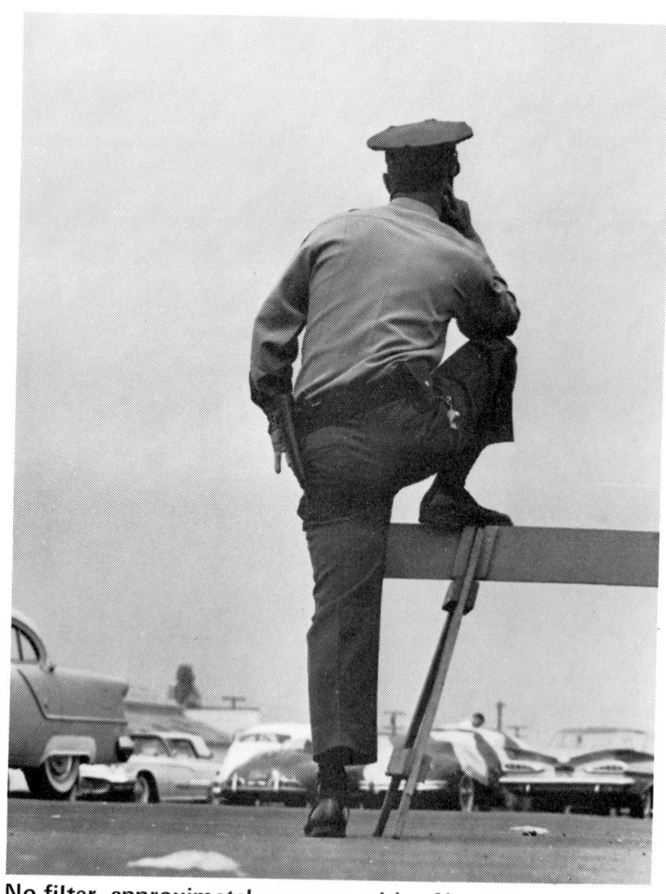

No filter, approximately same as with a No. 2 filter.

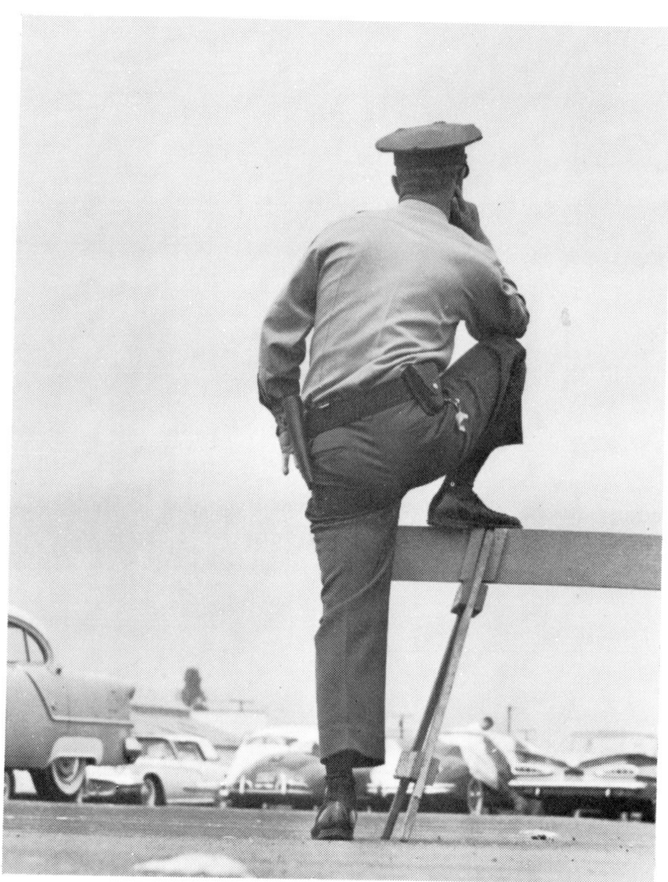

Contrast change using Kodak Polycontrast F and filters No. 1,

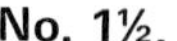

No. 1½,

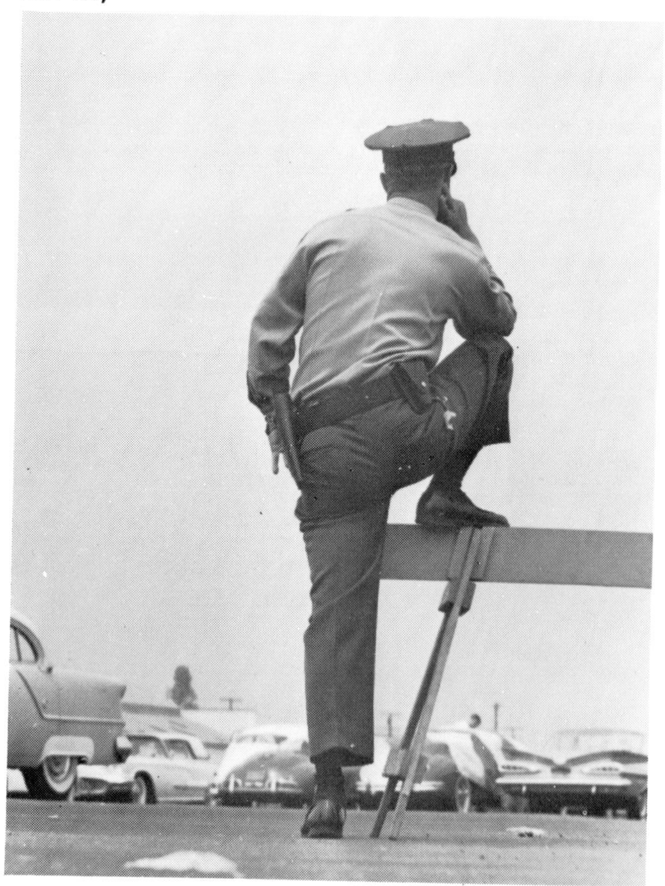

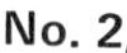

No. 2,

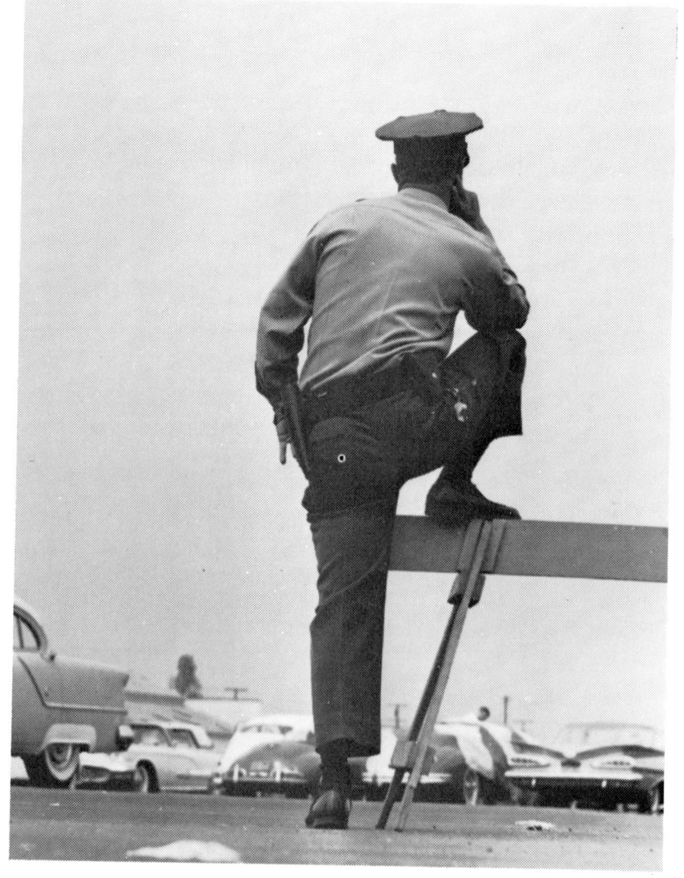

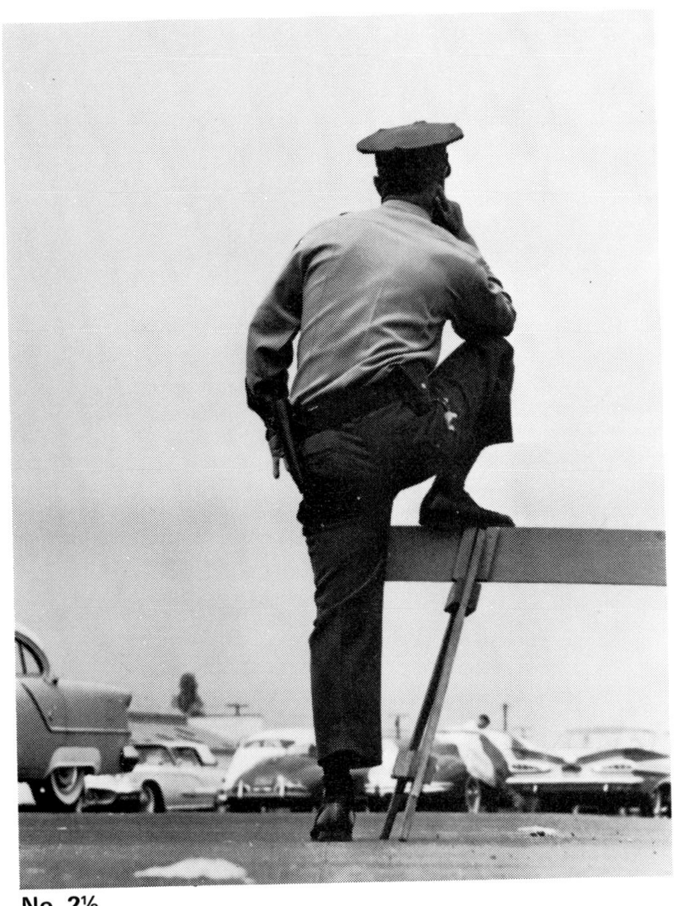

No. 2½

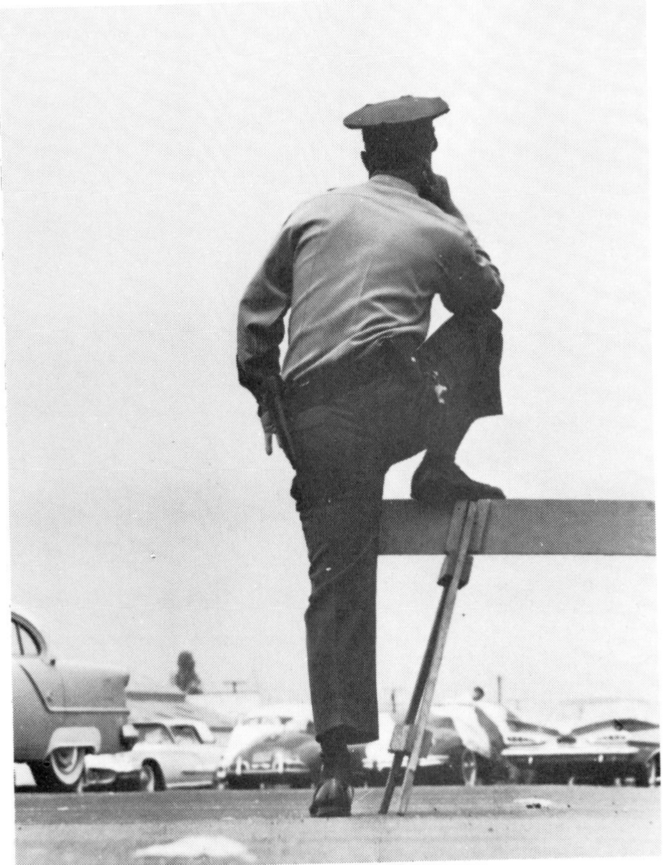

No. 3,

No. 3½

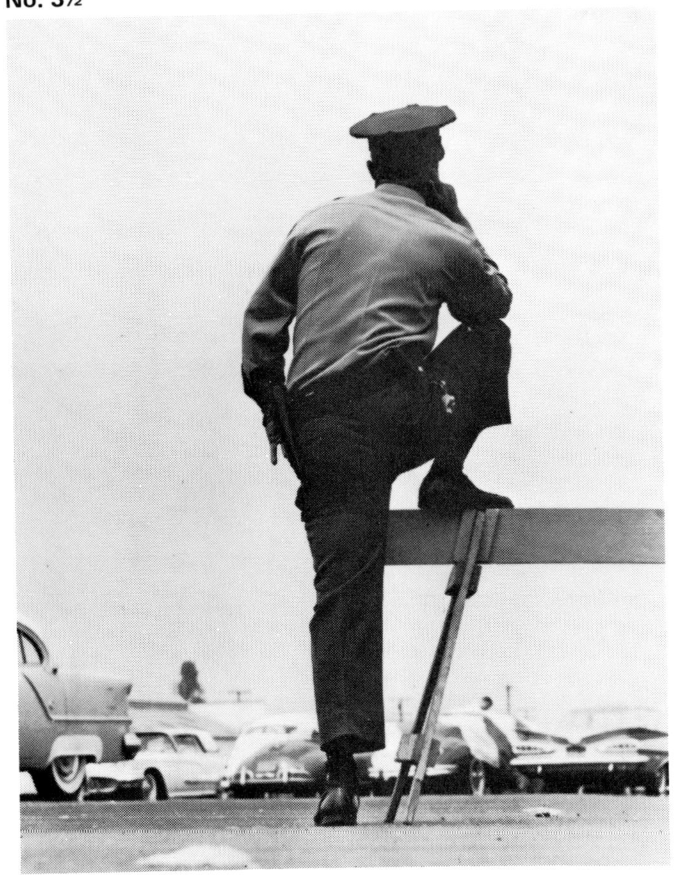

and No. 4.

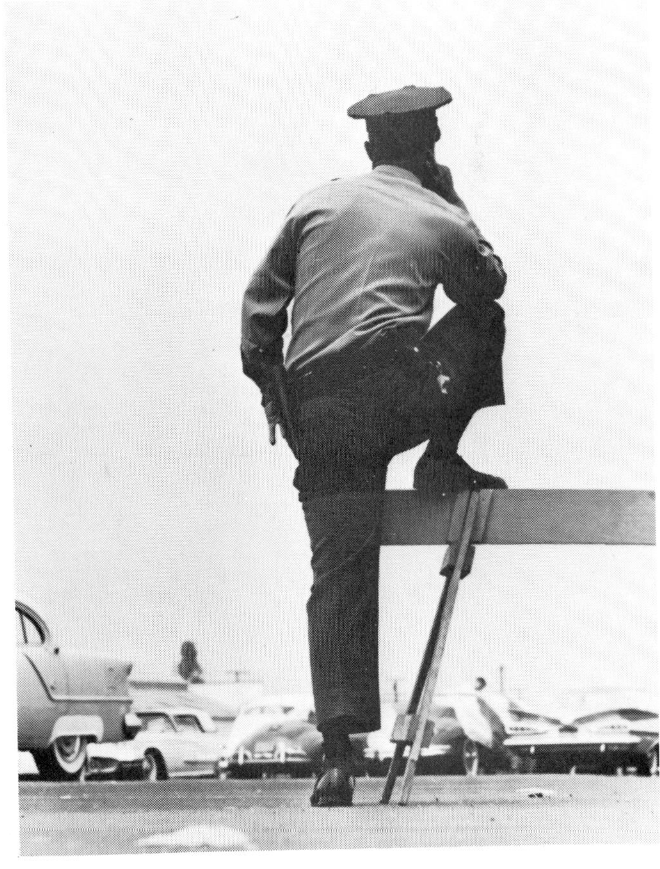

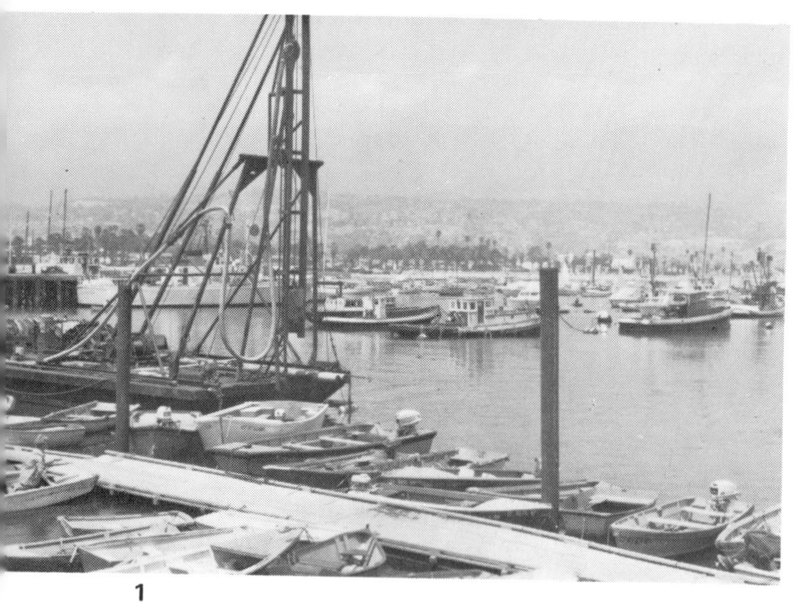

1

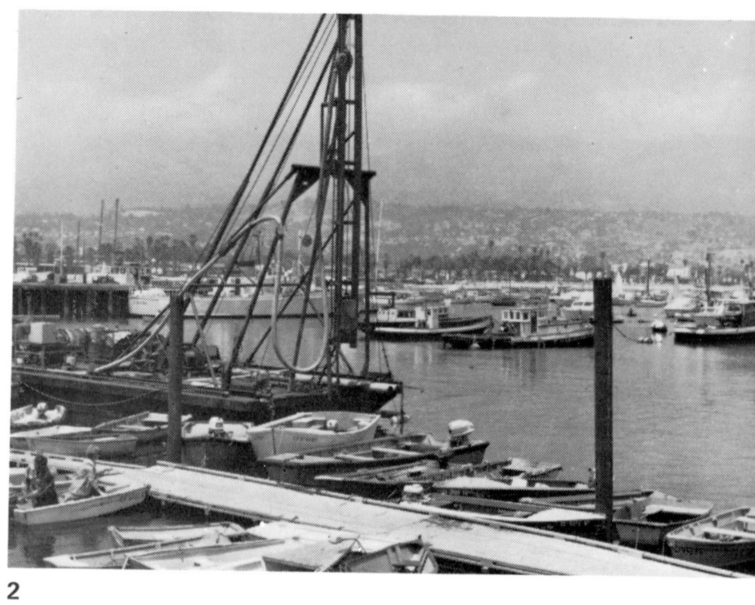

2

3

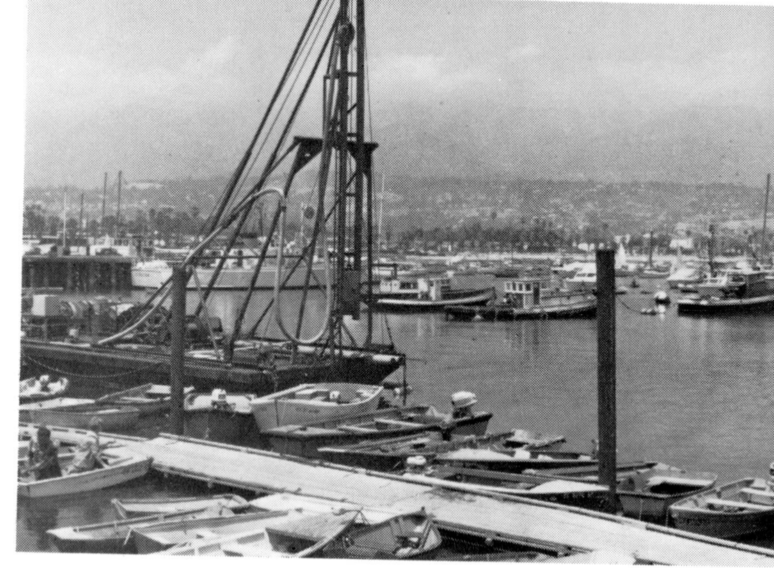

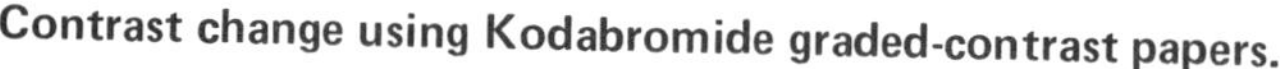

Contrast change using Kodabromide graded-contrast papers.

4

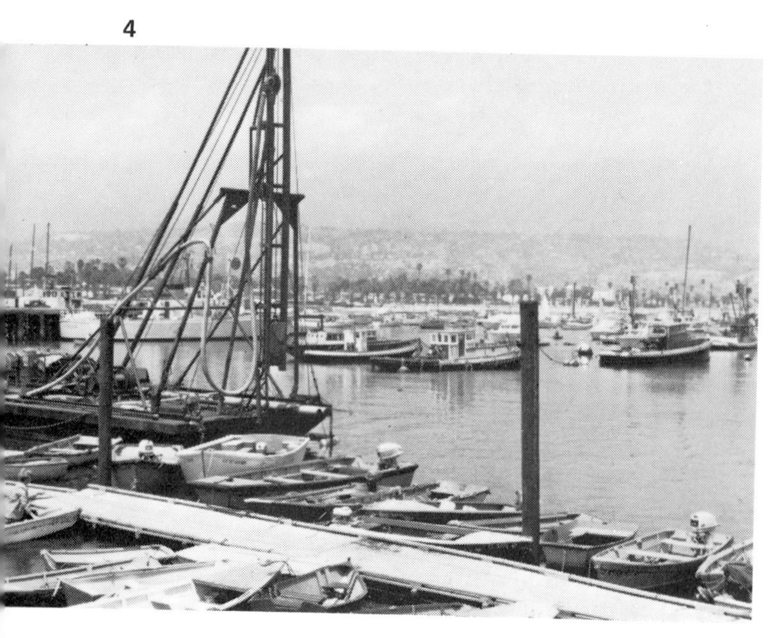

5

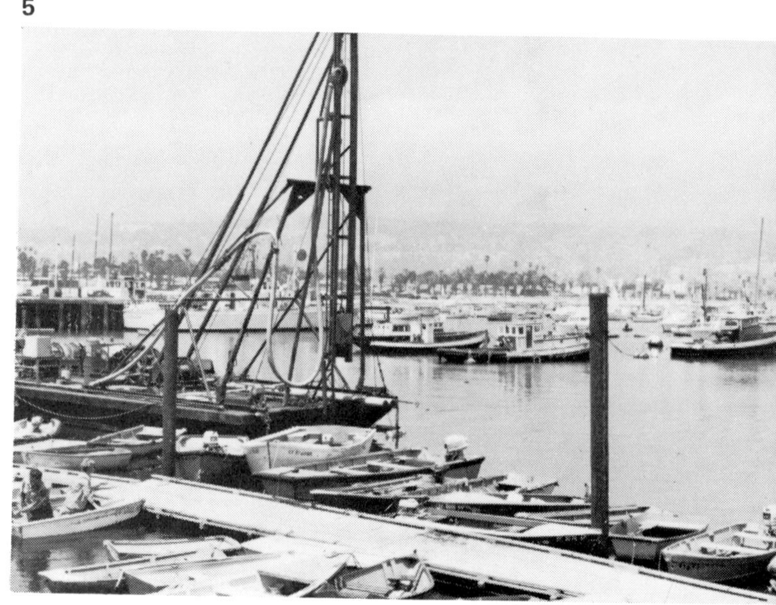

Contrast comparison with Kodabrome RC papers, courtesy Eastman Kodak Company. You can use different grades of paper (or filters with Polycontrast papers) to create effects available no other way.

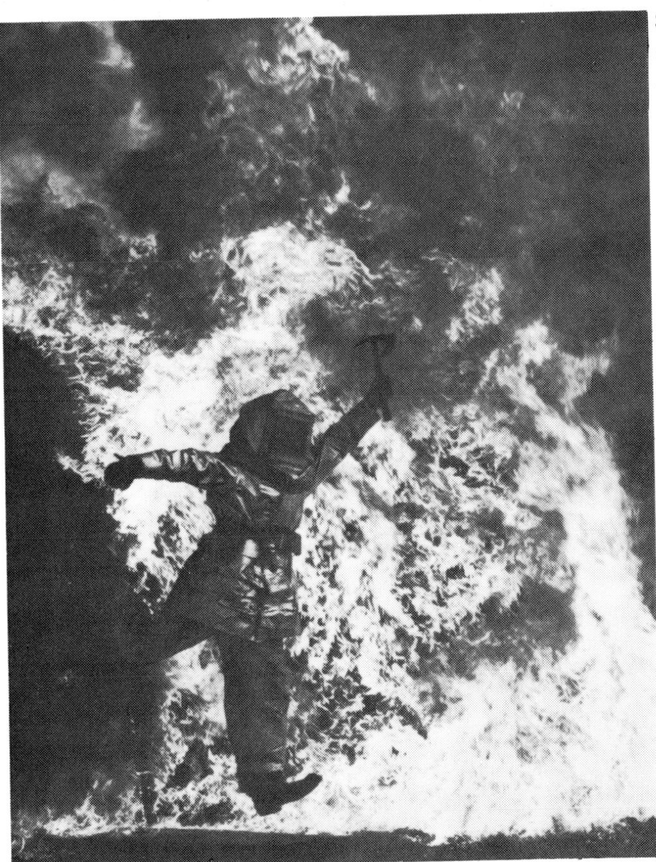

SOFT—with this negative, have good detail in flames, fire-suit, fire-ax is visible. Face plate is easy to see as a separate element of head covering.

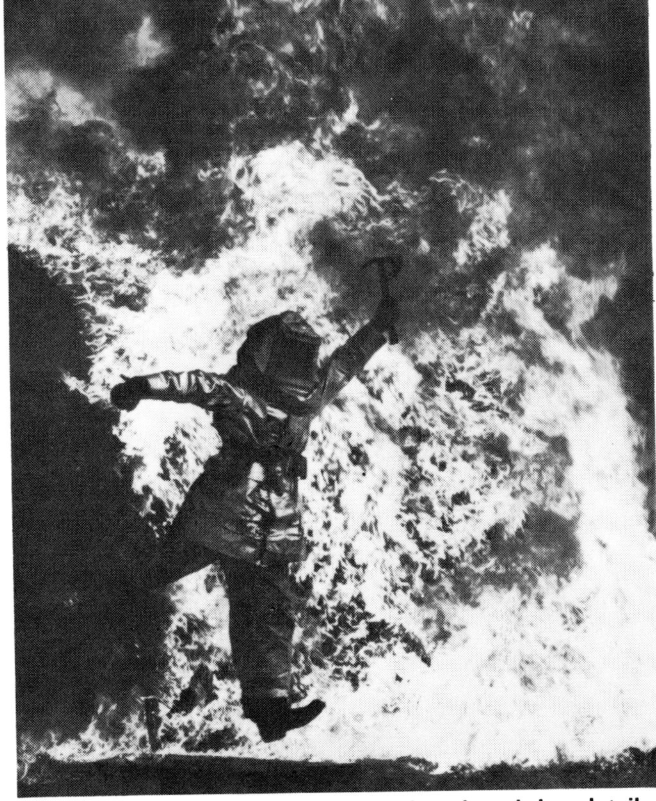

HARD—you can still see the fire-ax, but there is less detail in flames. Highlights on suit are whiter than in print on soft paper.

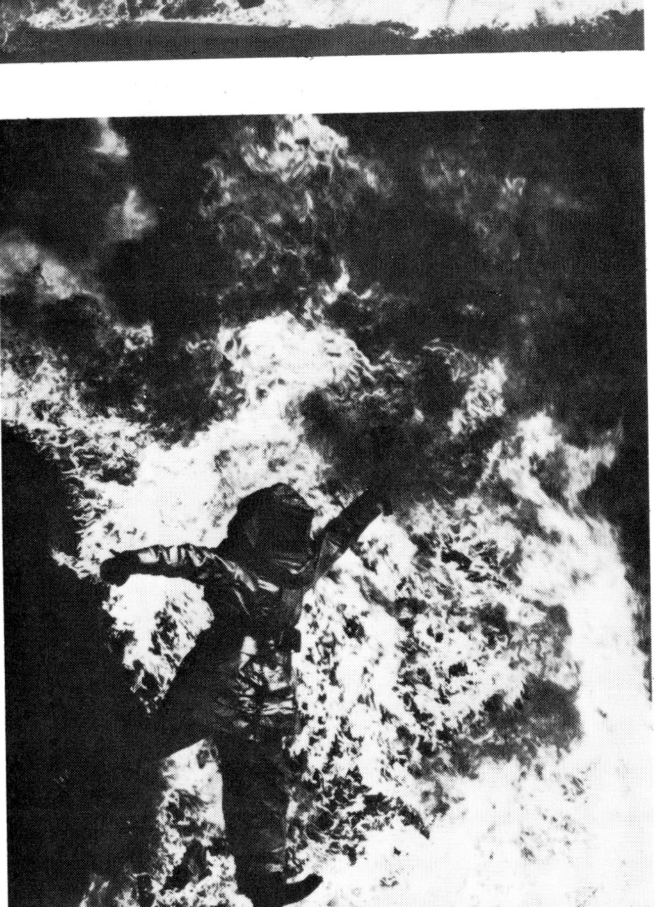

ULTRA-HARD—approaches a line print. Everything is pretty much black-and-white. Fire-ax has disappeared, head covering has lost all detail.

It makes no difference whether the grade is 1, 2 or 3, soft, medium or hard.

This being the case, it makes little sense to go to the expense of having several grades of paper which are rarely used. A simple solution is quite popular today—use *variable-contrast* paper, called VC, with a set of variable-contrast filters. While these add a chunk of expense, they pay for themselves in the long run. As of 1979, a set of Kodak Polycontrast—PC—filters cost about $41. VC paper comes in one type which is sensitive to several colors of light. VC paper contrast is changed by using filters to change the color of the printing light. The filter is used under the enlarging lens or in the filter drawer if your enlarger has one. By use of the proper filters, *one* paper allows you to achieve the equivalent of graded papers, although with less range of grades.

Variable-contrast papers have two emulsions on the same paper base. One is blue-sensitive and is a high-contrast emulsion; the other is green-sensitive and has low-contrast. By printing through filters, you select the contrast you want by allowing a particular color of light to reach the paper.

Filters which are bluish to a varying degree affect the blue-sensitive high-contrast part of the emulsions. Yellow filters affect the green-sensitive emulsion. Yellow is the combination of red and green light but the emulsion is not sensitive to red and is affected only by the green component of yellow.

Readily available VC papers are Ilford Ilfospeed Multigrade and Kodak Polycontrast Rapid II RC. Various surfaces are available in medium weight. Both are RC papers available in glossy and matte surfaces. This gives you the double advantage of VC and RC in a single paper. This is a hard combination to beat! Each manufacturer makes a set of filters to be used with its paper. Ilfospeed Multigrade filters cost about $40 and are marked in steps from 1 through 7. Polycontrast filters are numbered from 1 through 4, in half steps. Both of these papers, when used without filters, are roughly equivalent to a number 2 normal or medium paper.

With the Ilfospeed Multigrade filters, beginning with number 3 and going to number 1, contrast decreases. Filters 4 through 7 are used with flat negatives to increase contrast.

With Kodak Polycontrast filters, numbers 1, 1½ and 2 are the softening filters; 2½ through 4 increase contrast.

VC papers are sensitive to different colors of light. So if you use a standard Kodak OA filter, you should switch to a different filter when using them. Ilford recommends an Ilford S No. 902 filter when using Ilfospeed Multigrade. Kodak recommends their Wratten OC filter for use with Polycontrast. Safelight filters are relatively inexpensive and take only a few seconds to change.

I think VC papers are the answer to the problem of extra expense and darkroom space to stockpile graded papers. With VC papers and filters, with slight contrast control from varying exposure and development time, you should be able to print every negative you have. If you are serious about darkroom work, also buy one package each of grade 0 and grade 6 and you'll be *totally* prepared for every printing need.

Variable-contrast papers such as Kodak Polycontrast used with the appropriate filters eliminate the need for several boxes of graded papers. Polycontrast is also available in RC (resin-coated) form.

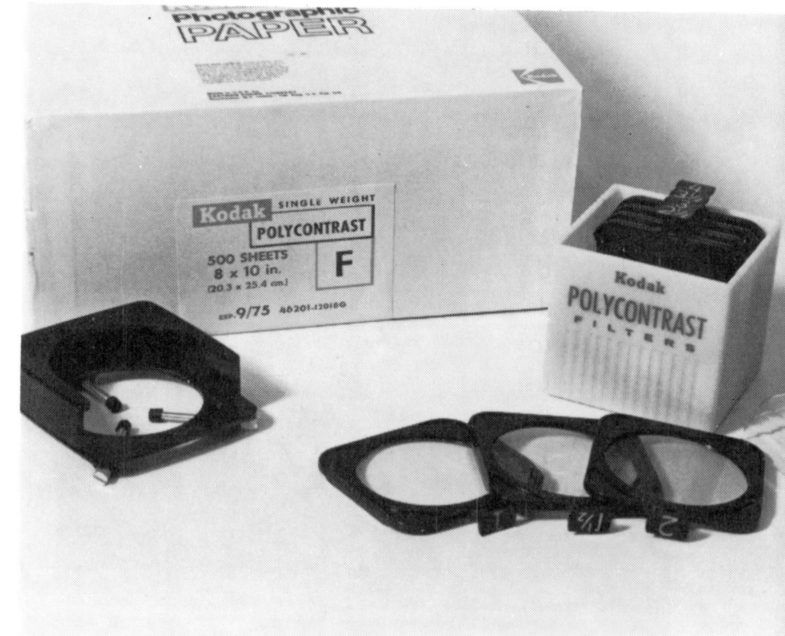

HINTS AND TIPS

When you made your first test strip, I asked you to use an entire 8x10 sheet of paper. That was because it was your first print and I wanted you to see the changes due to exposure. As you become more accustomed to using your equipment and working under the safelight, you will gradually be able to see and visually judge approximate exposures. It's a good idea, when working with a new negative, to tear or cut a full sheet of paper into one-inch wide strips. One of these strips laid across the easel and exposed for what you think will be the correct time can work very well as your test strip. If you have misjudged and your exposure is off greatly one way or the other, you have only wasted a small piece of sensitive material.

Take a minute or so to study the projected image on the easel, after you have cropped and focused. Try to pick out problem areas that will need dodging or burning-in, and use these manipulations on your first print following the test strip. Or, make further test strips to check your ideas about what the dodging and burning-in times might be.

Keep a soft pencil near your easel and make notes on the back of the print following exposure and before development. Record exposure time, lens-aperture setting, paper grade and any information necessary concerning print manipulation or process variations. Be sure the paper is on a hard surface when you make notes. If you put the paper on top of another sheet or some soft material or write very hard, an indentation will be quite visible on the emulsion side. Pencil marks will not come off during processing and will remind you exactly how you made that print. I suggest keeping the marks near the edge in the area of the print border.

An increase or decrease of 2 or 3 seconds in exposure time can be very apparent in the final print. Without notes for reference, it is difficult to recall which slight exposure changes or manipulations gave you that perfect print out of the several you made.

Write it on the back—A soft pencil such as a No. 1, or a *Stabilo* or an A. W. Faber *Castell Magicus* can be used to make notes on the back of your enlarging paper—if you write gently and stay toward the edge. *Stabilo* and *Magicus* pencils will write on the plastic-coating of RC papers. You can note what you did about exposure, dodging, burning-in, grade of paper and type. When you get ready to make another print of the same kind, just pop the original one in the easel and set the enlarger for an identical image. Put a piece of paper in the easel and expose for the same time. If you nearly always use the same f-stop, you can omit that from the notes. Only include it if you used something different from your usual f-8 or whatever.

Customizing your proof sheets—Occasionally one or more frames will be so overexposed or underexposed that they do not print well with the single exposure used to make your proof sheet. The remedy is simple. Cut a piece of paper about the same size as the affected frame/s. Put this piece under the frame/s you want to show with better quality. Re-expose, giving more exposure if the negatives are dense, less exposure for thin negatives. If you like, the piece of paper can be a different contrast grade or exposed through a different VC filter (in which case you may have to alter the exposure time to accommodate the different paper/filter). Process the small print just as you did the large one. When the prints are dry, trim the paper to include the frames you want to replace, then rubber-cement or dry-mount the small piece in place. Professionals use this trick all the time because it allows them to show their clients proof sheets which look as if all of the exposures were just about perfect.

COMMON PROCESSING PROBLEMS AND THEIR SOLUTIONS

Problem	Cause	Cure
Yellow stains	Excess development	Use recommended times.
	Improper fixing	Agitate in fixer.
	Exhausted fixer	Use fresh fixer.
	Insufficient washing	Constant water flow following hypo-neutralizer bath.
	Stop bath too strong	Check and remix, following instructions.
Fog	Exposed to white light	Keep paper in box and away from enlarging source.
	Unsafe safelight	Check for proper filter or faded filter.
	Prolonged development	Use recommended times.
	Exhausted developer	Use fresh solutions.
	Wrong paper storage	Store in cool, dry place.
White spots	Developer or hypo on paper	Keep hands and work area dry.
	Air bubbles in developer	Constant agitation.
Dark spots	Air bubbles in fixing	Agitate one minute before turning on white light.
White hairline marks	Scratches on negative	Apply Edwal No-Scratch to negative.
Dark hairline marks	Rough handling of paper before development	Handle carefully, check edges of easel for rough spots. Remove from dry prints by rubbing with cloth dipped in methylated spirit —denatured alcohol—and household ammonia in equal parts. Rewash and dry the print after doing this.
Blisters	Stop bath too strong	Increase water in bath.
	Temperature difference of solutions	Keep all solutions as close to wash water temperature as possible.
Contrast excessive	Wrong paper grade	Use lower grade or VC filter.
	Underexposure/ overdevelopment	Increase exposure and maintain normal development time.
Flat gray lacking "snap"	Paper fogged	See Fog.
	Enlarger lens dirty	Lens cleaner and tissue.
	Exhausted developer	Use fresh solution.
	Overexposure/ underdevelopment	Decrease exposure and maintain normal development.
	Wrong paper grade	Use higher grade or VC filter.
Fading	Exhausted fixer	Use fresh solution.
	Insufficient wash	Constant water flow following hypo-neutralizer bath.

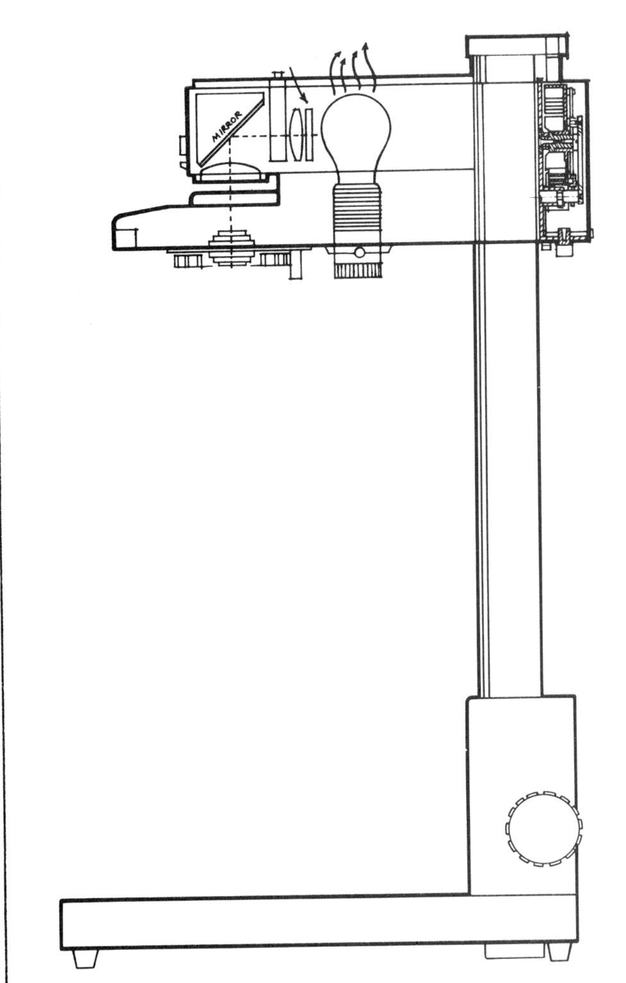

Most enlargers position the lamp above the negative, which can cause cooling problems. This Durst A300 Autofocus has its lamp at one side with a mirror to reflect light through the negative. This keeps heat away from the negative. "Autofocus" enlargers automatically focus the lens as you change image size by moving the enlarger up and down.

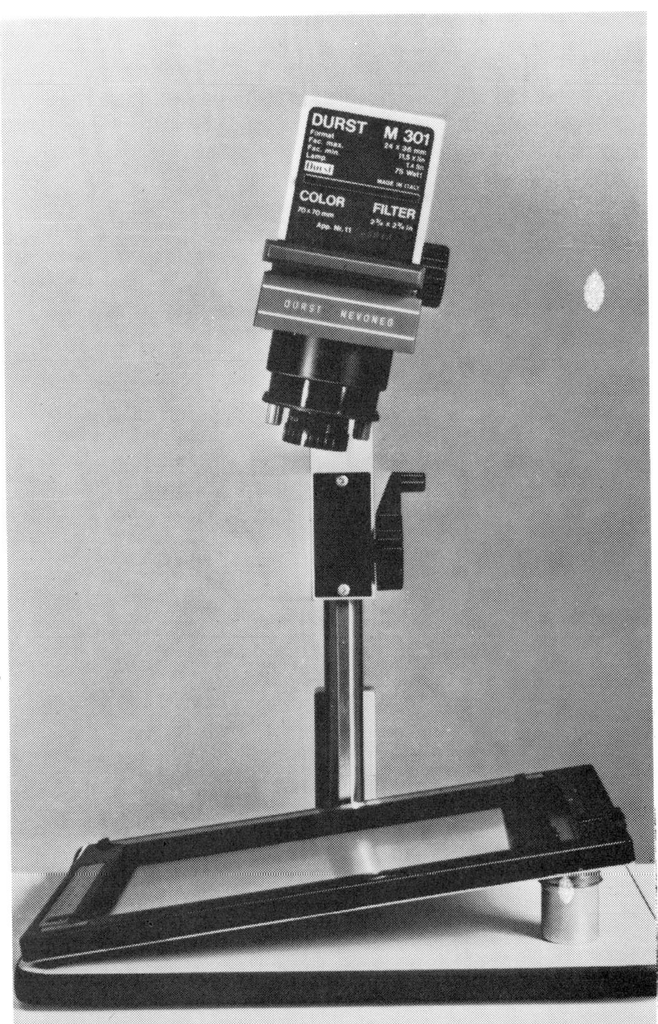

Distortion control—to introduce or correct distortion—can be done by tilting the easel, the negative, and the lens board. This Durst enlarger is being used with the negative and the easel both tilted to introduce distortion. Such controls are especially useful for correcting architectural perspective where you had to tilt the camera to "get it all in." You will have to stop down the lens to get added depth of field to keep the picture sharp all over. Try focusing on the center, then check the edges of the image with your focusing aid.

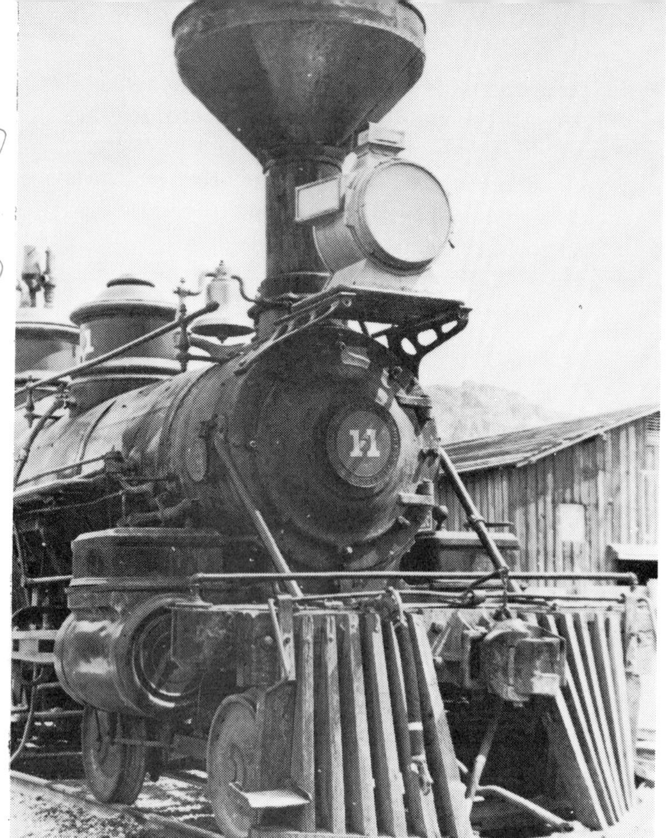

I exposed for the dark metal on the engine. The overexposed light areas washed-out in a "straight" print.

After a "straight" exposure, I burned-in lower corners with four times the initial exposure to show detail in the light and dark portions.

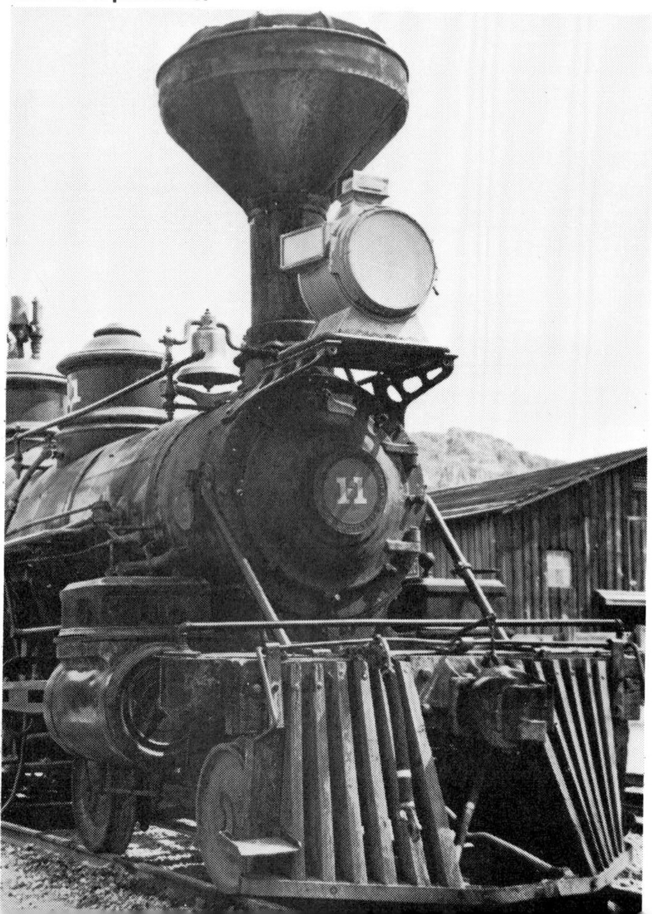

DODGING & BURNING-IN

Dodging is holding back exposure in a selected area of the print to keep that area from printing too dark. *Burning-in* is giving increased exposure to a selected area to make that area darker, or to cause details to print in a high-light area. Burning-in is often used to darken a sky or to eliminate a distracting bright spot.

I mentioned the handy dodging kit in the last chapter. It has several pieces of dark-amber plastic cut into various sizes and shapes. If an area of your print lacks detail because it is too dark, look through your dodging kit for a shape approximating that of the area you wish to hold back. If the area you wish to give less exposure runs relatively straight across one side of the print, then dodging can be done very effectively with a piece of cardboard or with your hand. If circular, use a circular dodging tool.

Before you try dodging on your next print, practice a little. Turn off the light and turn on the enlarger. Using your dodging tool or your hand, cover the area you want to have less exposure, making sure you cover only the area you want to be lighter on the next print.

When dodging, you must move the tool or dodger in a circular motion at all times to avoid definite lines which would make it obvious the print had been manipulated. You don't want to dodge during the whole exposure; that gives no image at all in that dark place. If 10 seconds gave an acceptable print except for the too-dark area, try dodging that area for two to three seconds.

Overdone dodging is very obvious and distracting on the print. Dodging can be tricky when exposure time is short. If the exposure you used was five seconds at *f*-11, it may be difficult to dodge the way you like for one second. You can obtain the same print exposure by exposing for 10 seconds with the lens aperture at *f*-16, which is twice the time at half the aperture. This gives you more time for the dodging process.

Dodging should never be noticeable on the final print. Considerable practice is required to develop good technique. You can't just read about it—you have to do it!

If there is a light area on the print where you want detail but none shows because of lack of exposure, it may be corrected with the burning-in

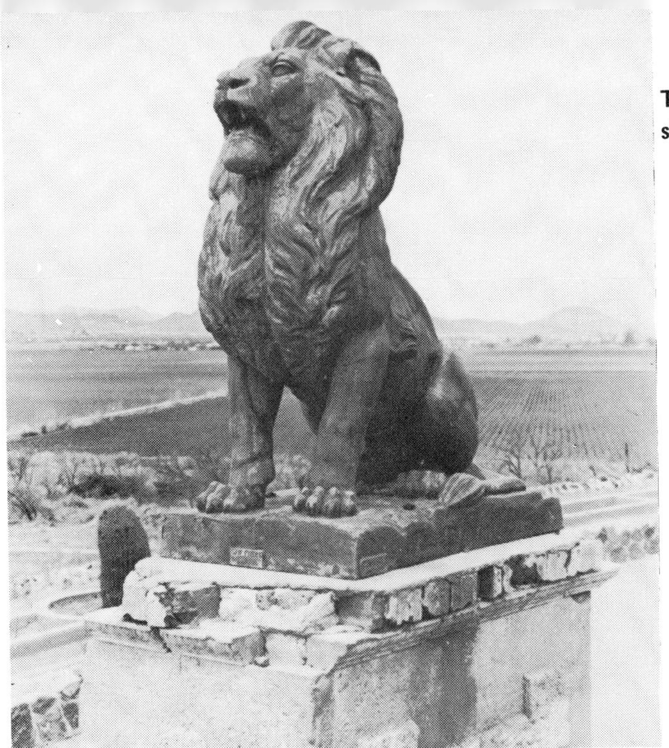

This print shows a great difference in overall density and should be manipulated some way for proper balance.

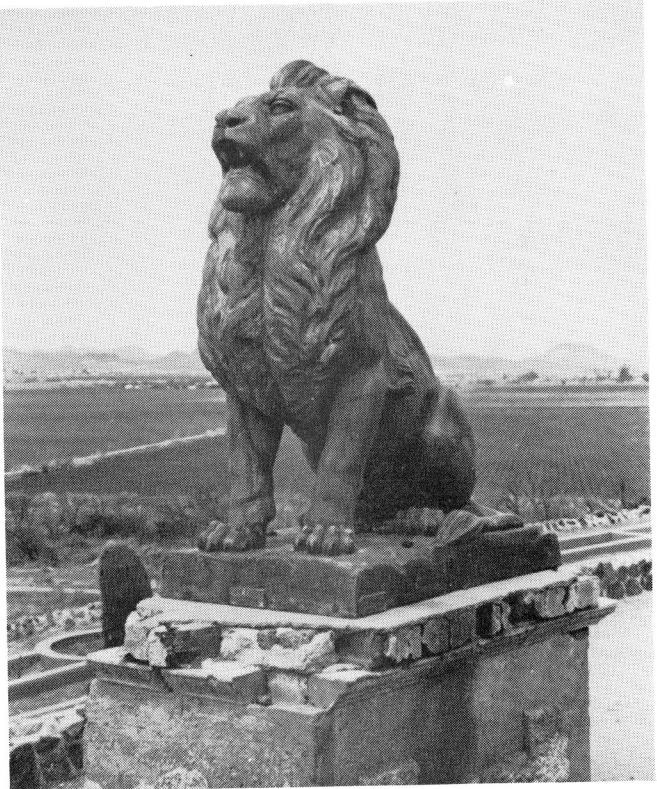

Although the print could be handled by "dodging" or "burning-in," I increased the overall exposure.
During the exposure, part of the center area was dodged to keep it from going too dark. It was held back for approximately two-thirds the total exposure.
When dodging, remember . . .

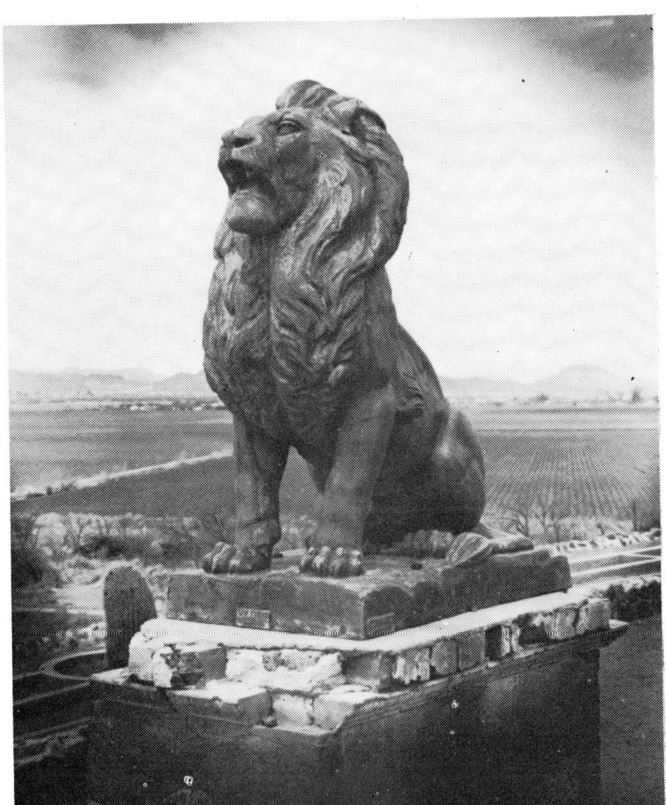

. . . keep the dodging tool moving.

process. This can sometimes be done by using the edge of a cardboard or your hand. If the area needing increased exposure is in the center of the print, you won't be able to use the edge of cardboard or your hand. Take a piece of 8x10 inch or larger cardboard and cut out a hole about two inches in diameter near the center.

Now, let's practice the burning-in technique. With white light off and enlarger on, hold the cardboard under the lens so the area you want to make darker is projected through the hole in the cardboard and onto the easel. Keep the cardboard moving constantly in a circular motion to avoid sharp lines from the burning-in tool.

Burning-in may require *considerably* more exposure than the correct exposure for the rest of the print. A two-inch hole may be too large, so make pieces of cardboard with various hole sizes and keep them near your enlarger.

To make a print using both the dodging and burning-in techniques:

1. Turn off the white light.

2. Remove a sheet of paper from the box and close the box securely. Secure the sheet of paper in the easel.

3. Pick up the dodging instrument and have it ready.

4. If you have one, start the enlarger timer and, after your exposure has run about three-quarters of its course, hold the dodging instrument in the light path so it blocks the light over the area you wish to hold back. Remember to keep the dodging instrument in motion at all times. Let the timer turn the enlarger off, or count seconds to yourself so you can turn the enlarger off. A foot-switch on the enlarger circuit is handy when you are using your hands for dodging. If you don't have a timer or foot switch to turn off the enlarger when the burning-in or dodging is finished, just raise the burning-in cardboard or dodging tool to cover the enlarger lens. Then you can use your other hand to turn off the switch.

5. Put down the dodging instrument and pick up the cardboard with the center cut out for burning-in. Hold the cardboard beneath the enlarging lens so the cutout is in the approximate area you wish to have more exposure. Activate the enlarger timer or turn on the enlarger and

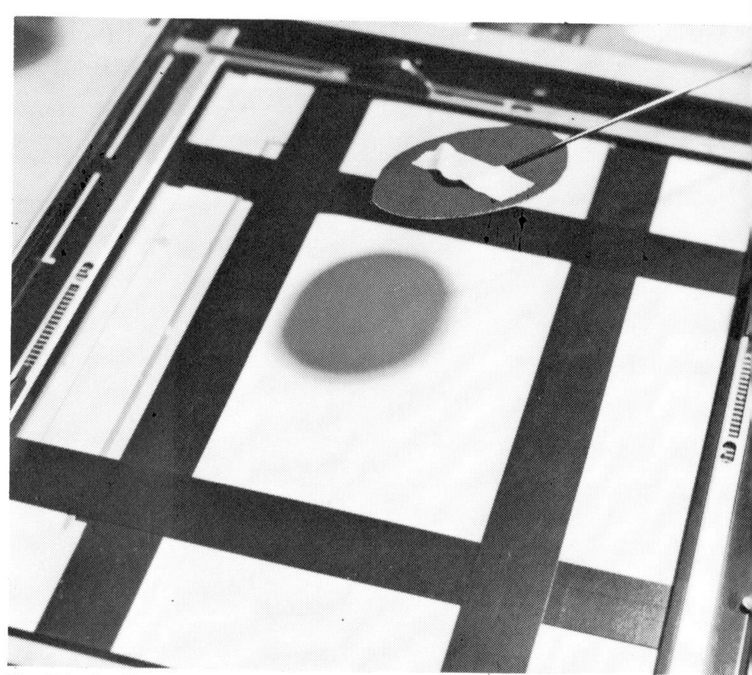

To "dodge" is to hold back exposure in a selected area. It may be done with almost anything which will create a shadow where you want it. Use a home-made dodger like this, or . . .

. . . with a little practice, you may find that your hand gives you a greater variety of shapes to cover irregular areas.

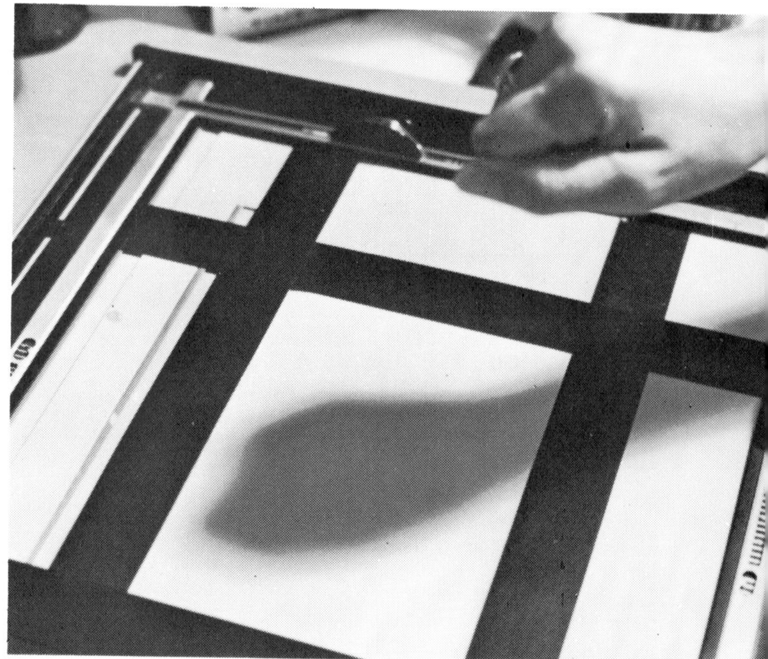

check quickly to see that the area to be darker is being projected through the hole in the cardboard. Keep the cardboard moving in a circular motion until the desired additional exposure is made.

6. Remove the paper from the easel, develop, stop and fix normally. Be sure the paper box is closed, turn on the white light and evaluate.

There should be a considerable difference now between this print and your original print. If the areas you manipulated are still not completely to your liking, make another print and vary the dodging and burning-in times until you are satisfied. Beginners often forget to move the dodging and burning-in tools during exposure. This results in sharp edges showing obvious manipulation. This is corrected only by experience. It is well worth your time and effort to practice because you will find most negatives can be improved by some manipulation.

Every now and then you will run into the problem where a negative will have a small area so dense that no amount of burning-in can get it to darken the way you'd like it. These spots can be awfully bothersome and unattractive, and if there is some way to eliminate them, you should. Well, there is! Look around in a dresser drawer and dig out that old penlight operated by a couple of AA 1.5-volt batteries. If you've lost it, get another. They are inexpensive and very handy. Make a cylinder of heavy black construction paper and tape it around the penlight so the paper sticks out about two inches past the bulb. The light can now be used to expose areas of the print very selectively.

After you have determined what area you wish to knock down in brightness, make a normally exposed print. With the paper still in the easel, slide the red filter built into your enlarger, in above the lens. Turn the enlarger lamp on and you have a fairly dim red image projected. This light will not affect the paper and you are now able to pick out the offending spot. Get the penlight with paper cone in position and flash the spot for a couple seconds. This will take a bit of practice but is a real snap when you get the hang of it.

You may also use this new found tool during print development. Expose and develop the print normally. When the development is complete,

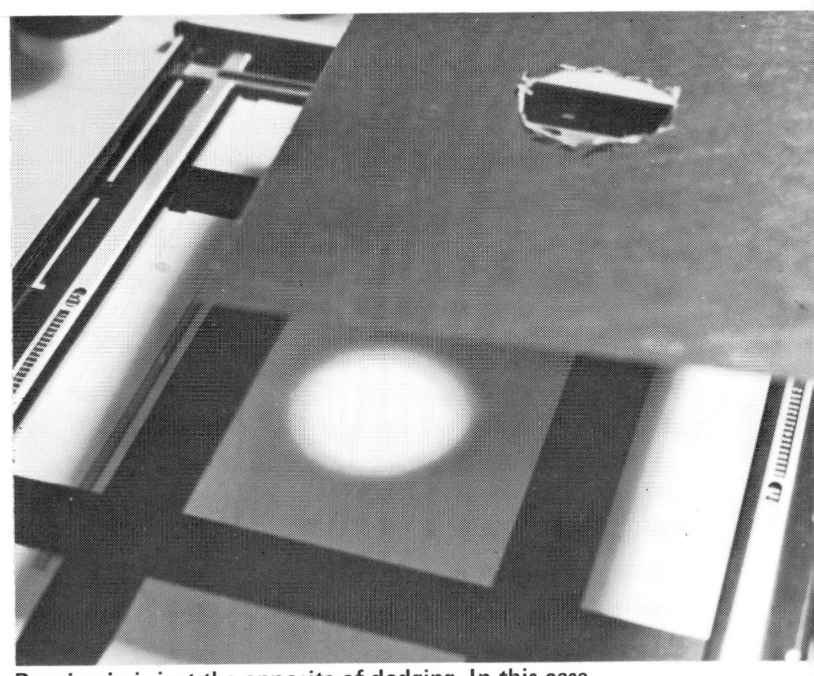

Burning-in is just the opposite of dodging. In this case, you are giving extra exposure to particular areas to preserve detail lost due to overexposure when doing your camera work.

Simple burning-in device—Cut or tear a hole into a piece of chipboard (cardboard). Then do the same to another piece. Now you can hold the two pieces together in whatever way you wish so you end up with an opening of approximately the shape you want. You can do this with squares, triangles, ovals, teardrops and circles. If you offset each of these slightly, you might be able to get all of them onto one piece and duplicate them on another piece. Then you merely move the cardboard so the holes make your shape and burn-in to your heart's content. Saves a lot of fussy hole cutting and a lot of time when you are really turning out the prints.

remove the paper from the solution and expose the desired spot with the penlight. This may be somewhat easier than exposing on the easel, because you can watch the spot darken and when you are satisfied, stop the action by placing the paper into the stop bath.

To go first class, check your local electronics supplier or Edmund Scientific about a variety of fibre optic tubes available at low cost today. These can give you a very small spot for "zapping out" tiny unwanted highlights which you feel are distracting from the main subject in your photo. Most put out low light levels and are extremely easy to manipulate. This item, as will the adapted penlight, will allow you to "nose" around the darkroom for dropped items without danger to light-sensitive materials.

Another method of darkening areas of the print which appear washed-out and too light, is with the use of stock developer. This is developer which is not diluted with water as normally used for printing. The stock solution is naturally quite strong and should be used with care. Or a working solution of developer may be warmed to about 100 degrees in a separate container and used for the same purpose. Either stock developer or warmed solution may be applied with a cotton ball to the area you wish to darken. Either solution will accelerate developing action in the areas to which it is applied, but prolonged use over the same spot may cause a gray cast—localized chemical fog—to appear. Remember you only want a slightly darker area, not a gray and muddy one.

A couple other methods of achieving about the same results are to lift the print from the developer and hold the offending area between the palm of one hand and the fingers of the other, or to hold the print close to your mouth and exhale. The heat from your body or breath will gradually warm the developer on the print surface and cause greater developer action. These techniques may be repeated several times until the light area has darkened to your satisfaction. Just be careful to stop before the spot turns gray.

Popular Durst F60 Enlarger handles negatives up to 2¼" x 2¼", takes apart for storage. Switch is in power cord, or you can use a timer to turn it on and off. Enlargers which come apart for storage in small spaces are very helpful when you have to put everything away after every printing session.

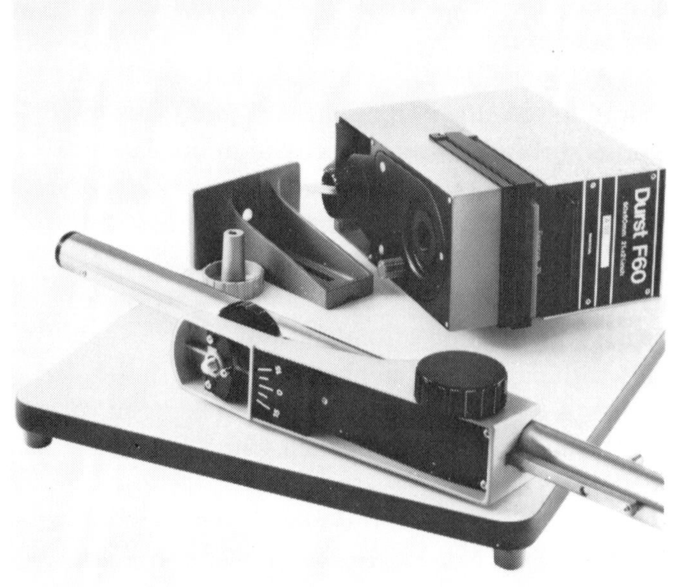

Count those seconds yourself—You expose quite accurately without a clock or timer. Just use the old technique of saying to yourself, "One-thousand-one, one-thousand-two, one-thousand-three," etc. Practice it a few times while watching a clock and you'll get an idea of how fast you must say the words to yourself to be accurate.

Special Techniques

Here are some special techniques you can use in the darkroom on cold winter nights. They work on hot summer nights, too! Most are quite easy but some get a bit difficult. They all can be fun and give you the opportunity to express your creative talent. They can also be of great help in adding interest to rather ordinary and lifeless negatives. These techniques require some practice and experimentation so don't be afraid to try a different approach if you see a possibility.

PHOTOGRAMS

Photograms are extremely simple to make and they can be very interesting and artistic. This process does not require a negative or any film material. You simply place small objects with interesting outlines on the enlarging paper and expose with the enlarger. This produces a silhouette image of the objects used. Opaque objects produce white patterns on a deep-black background; translucent objects make fascinating shadowy images.

Raise the enlarger head to cover the entire easel with light. Use any size negative carrier, but *no* negative. With the white light off and safelight on, put a small piece of paper on the easel for use as a test strip. Place the objects to be silhouetted on top of the paper and expose with the enlarger. Process the test strip normally and evaluate for contrast. The background should be a deep, full black. Determine exposure from the test strip and repeat the process using a full sheet of paper.

You may want to experiment with paper contrasts. I used No. 2 paper for the accompanying photo, but No. 6 might be better for translucent objects such as leaves, dried grass, seed pods, etc.

Try several object arrangements until you feel you have a pleasing composition. Nearly anything will work to make photograms so let your imagination run free!

For a variation, use a negative to project an image on the easel while you have the objects there too.

Photograms are simple, fun and effective. Choose a few items of any type, place them on the paper in the easel . . .

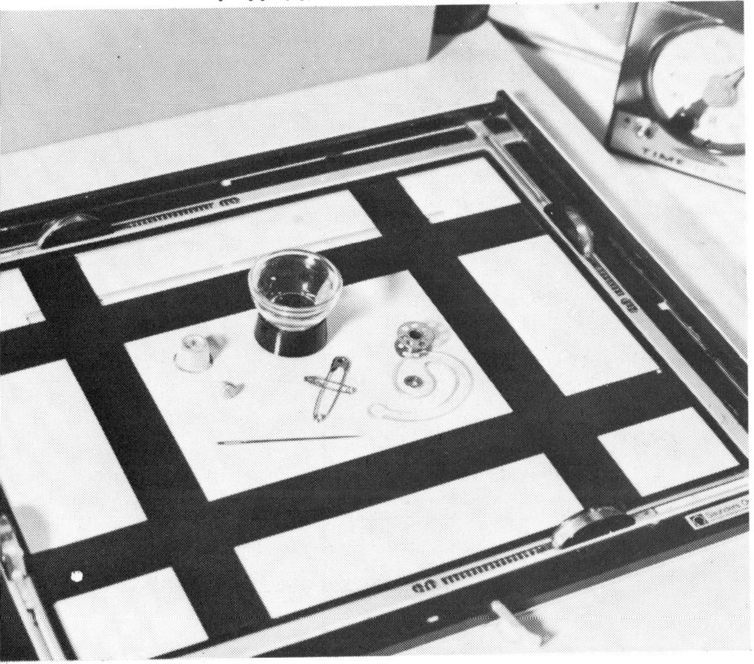

. . . and expose for a high-contrast abstract print. This technique works with any material with an interesting design or shape. Try some fern leaves.

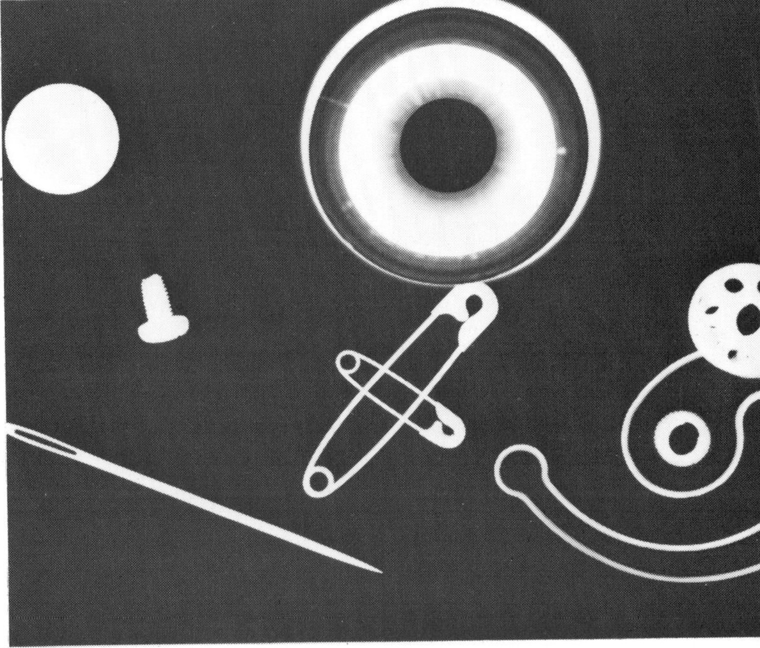

DIFFUSION

Diffusion "breaks up" the projected image, tending to soften sharp edges. It can be very pleasant on some portraits and scenic photographs. Many older people are pleased when their pictures are diffused just enough to soften age lines. Scenic views take on a nice flowing appearance.

This effect can be created through the use of soft-focus attachments on the camera, but one doesn't always know what's desired until proofs are made. And if you do it in the camera, you've lost the sharp image forever.

Diffusion can be caused by anything that tends to scatter light and it's interesting to note that only light can be scattered. That is, you can't scatter darkness because there isn't anything to scatter.

The effect of diffusion therefore is different on a negative than on a print.

Camera-lens diffusers spread the highlight image areas into the shadows. Diffusion during the enlarging process spreads the light which will make shadows on the print into the highlight areas, so care must be taken to avoid excess diffusing because it will give gray and muddy prints.

About a quarter of the total printing exposure time will usually give you all the diffusion you want. In any event, don't diffuse for more than 50 percent of the total time. Remember you only wish to soften the image—not totally degrade it.

Diffusion gives a pleasing, soft effect and also reduces contrast and minimizes grain.

Diffusion attachments for enlarger lenses are available but you can use cellophane which has been crumpled, then smoothed out again. You can use a piece of nylon or silk stocking, or a piece of fine-mesh window screen. All work equally well. Cellophane can be taped over a hole in a piece of cardboard. Stocking material is commonly stretched in an embroidery hoop frame.

Another diffusion trick is to smear petroleum jelly on a piece of glass and hold this under the lens for part of the exposure time to give a diffused effect with a light, airy feeling to it. I'll tell you more about this as a specialized form of vignetting just a few pages later in this chapter.

The negative is printed as usual with the diffusing material held in motion beneath the enlarger

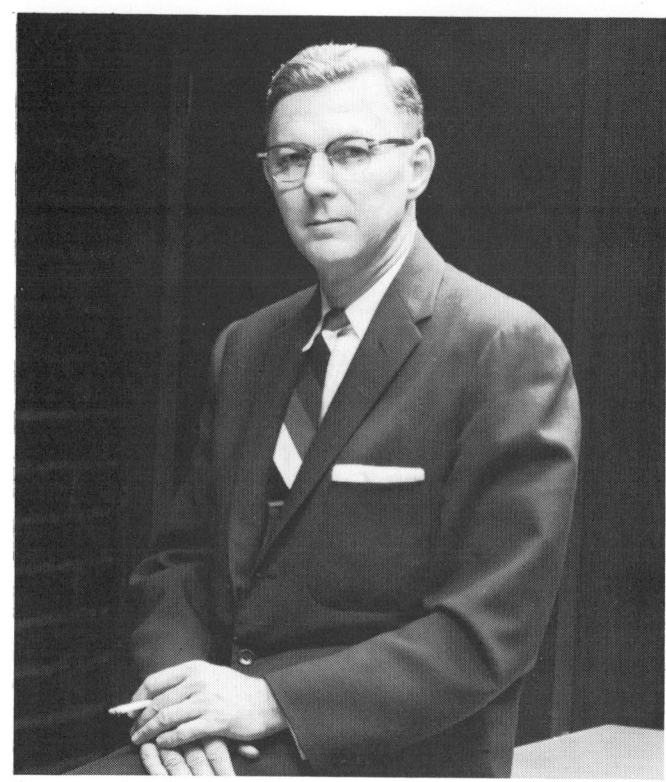

An example of a straight print made from a sharp negative.

The same negative printed using a piece of silk stocking to soften the image.

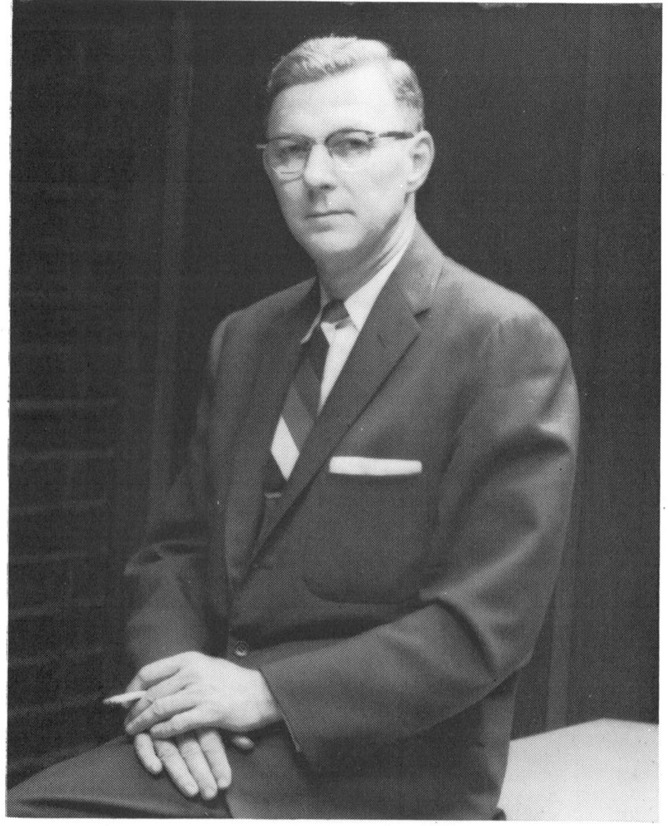

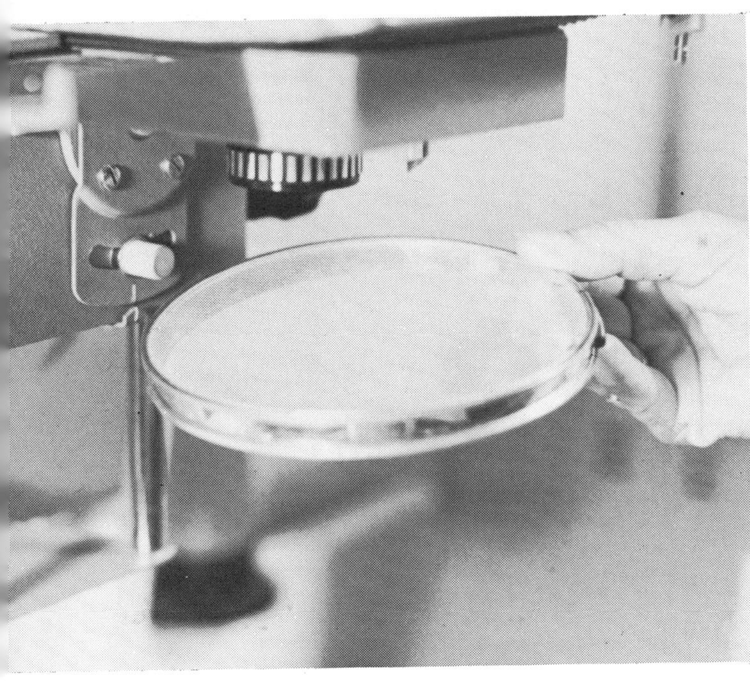

lens for up to half the total exposure time. The time of diffusion depends on the subject matter and the amount of softness desired. Experience is the best teacher.

Anything placed in the light path during exposure reduces the amount of light reaching the printing paper. Therefore, increase total exposure slightly to keep the print quality you are after. You'll probably find softness of the image is quite pleasing in a somewhat lighter-than-normal print.

It's a good way to please your Aunt Mabel if you're concerned about her will.

TEXTURE SCREENS

Texture screens are somewhat like diffusers because they also "break up" the image. They do it by adding a visible pattern to the picture—rather than just softening the image.

Contact Texture Screens—These can be purchased in many sizes and patterns such as a fine-wire mesh, or one giving the appearance of canvas. These are placed in contact with and on top of the printing paper during exposure. Household items can also be used effectively for this purpose. Window

To diffuse or soften the image projected onto the paper, try a piece of silk stocking in an embroidery hoop for part of the exposure, keeping it moving. Or use a piece of cellophane—crumpled and straightened out or a sheet of glass coated with petroleum jelly, for about 50% of the total exposure time. More than 50% produces a too soft and mushy image. Whichever material you choose, KEEP IT IN MOTION DURING THE TIME IT IS BETWEEN THE LENS AND THE PAPER!

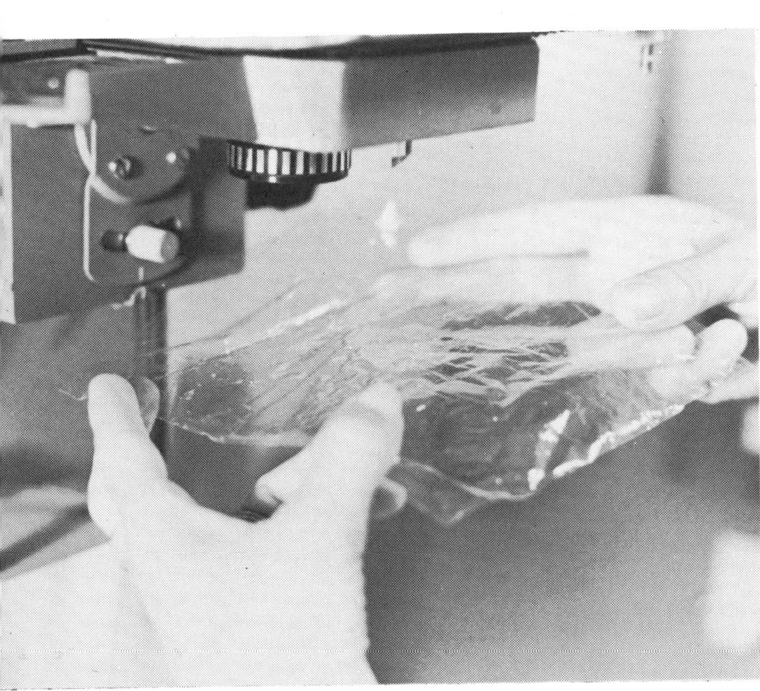

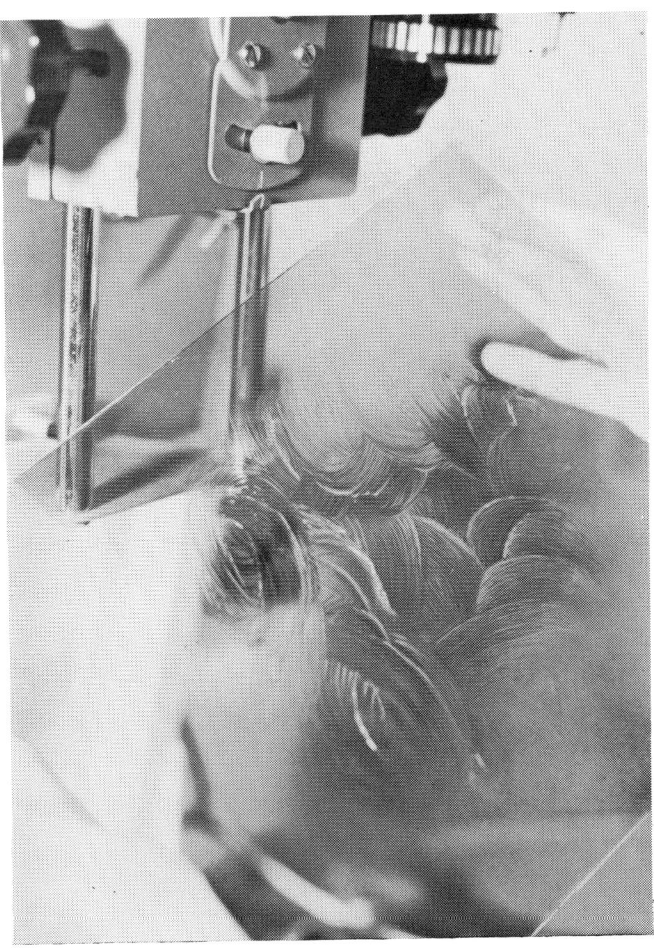

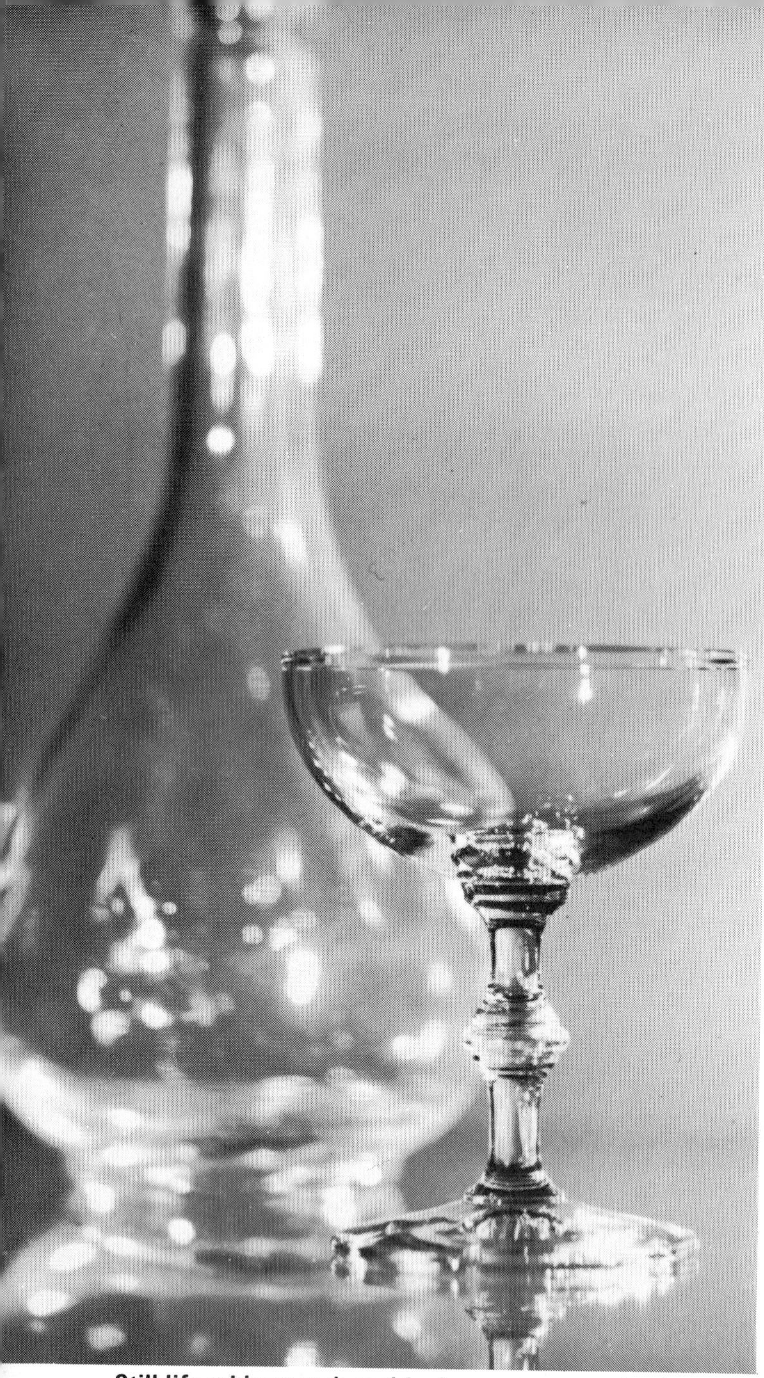

Still-life subjects such as this glass arrangement lend themselves very well to texture-screen effects.

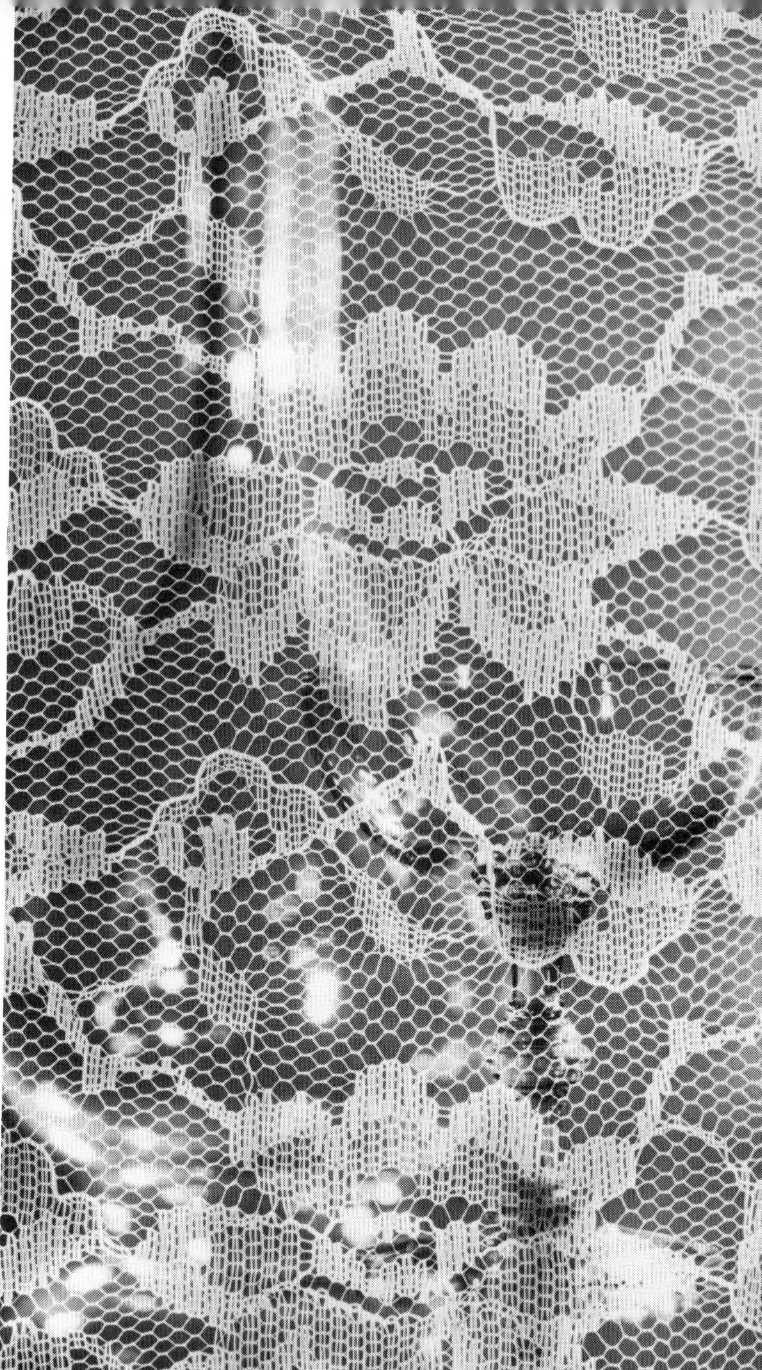

In place of a commercially produced texture screen, you may wish to try any household item with a definite pattern—such as a lady's scarf or a lace table cloth.

screen, fancy lace or paper material and coarse-woven fabrics, for example. Nearly anything which has a strong texture and will transmit light can be interesting.

Contact texture screens can be used for all or part of the total enlarger exposure, depending on the contrast and effect desired, when using contact screens. It's important to secure the paper, perhaps even fastening it to the easel with masking tape to insure the paper won't move when you remove the texture screen. You may also want to tape the easel to the enlarger baseboard to prevent its moving.

Projection Screens—These achieve the same result, but are sandwiched with the negative in the enlarger. With this type screen, the greater the image magnification, the coarser the pattern. You leave the screen with the negative for the *total* exposure. You can make your own texture screens by photographing strongly-textured subjects such as wood, groups of leaves or rock patterns onto high-contrast film. These will come out as line patterns if you use Kodak High-Contrast Copy film. It's available in 4x5 and in 36-exposure rolls of 35mm. Process in Dektol or D-19 developer, stop bath, fix and wash as usual.

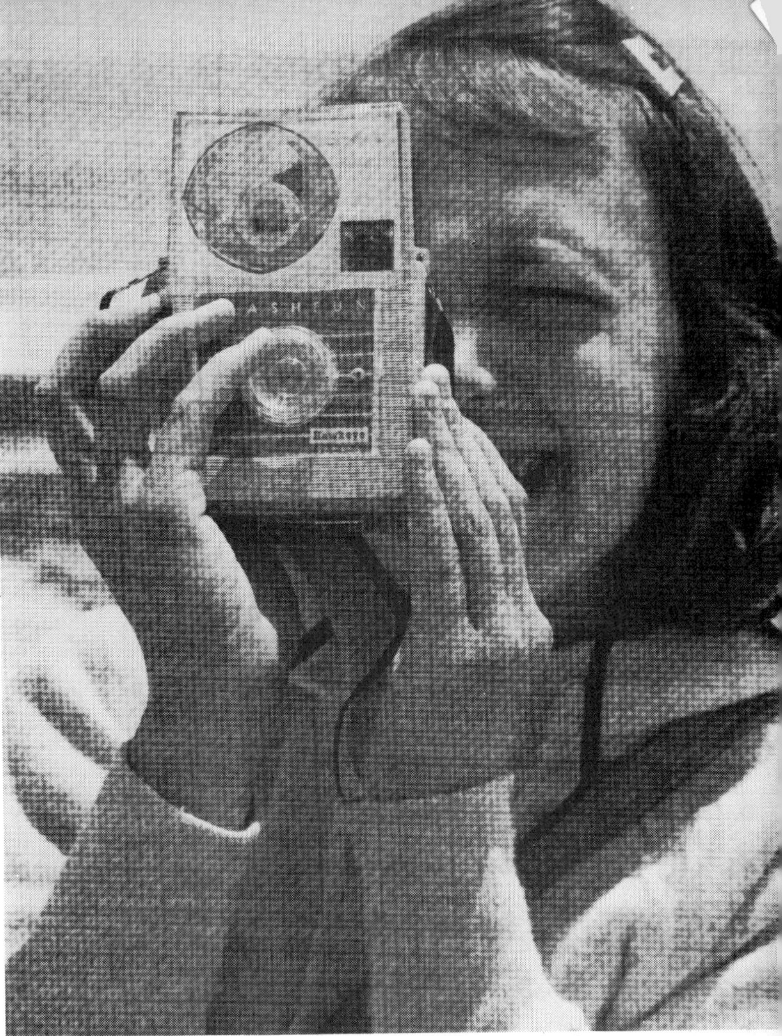

"Linen" texture screen is very popular. A lot of people seem to like the "cloth" look it gives to their photos.

"Brush-stroke" texture screen is especially useful with outdoor scenes. It gives them a somewhat-painted look. If you've always wanted to "paint" nature scenes this lets you do it with your camera.

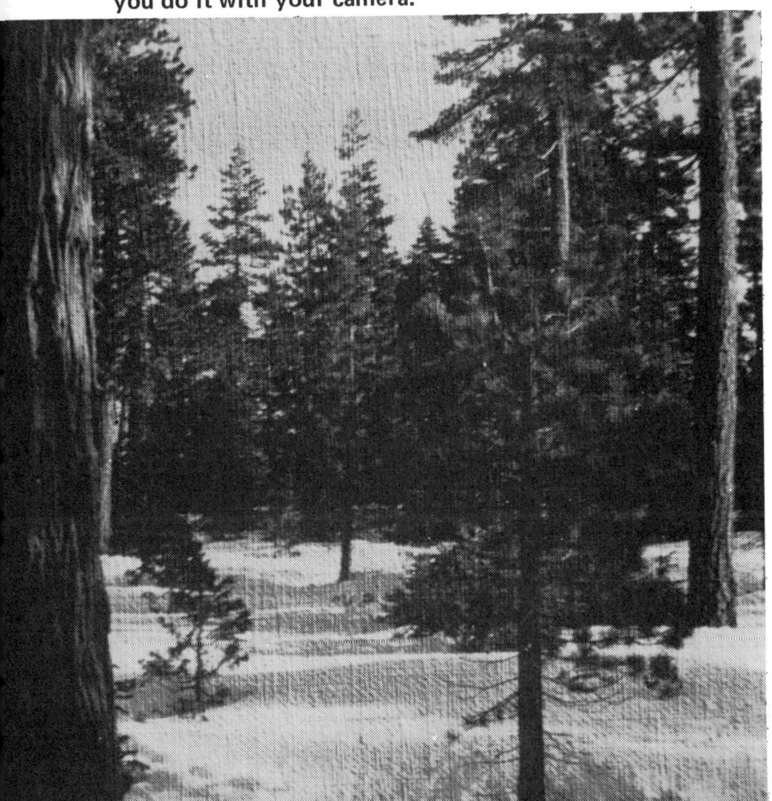

"Grain" texture screen gives a far more grainy appearance than you'd be able to achieve if you purposely processed film for highest grain. Any texture screen tends to soften lines and hide blemishes.

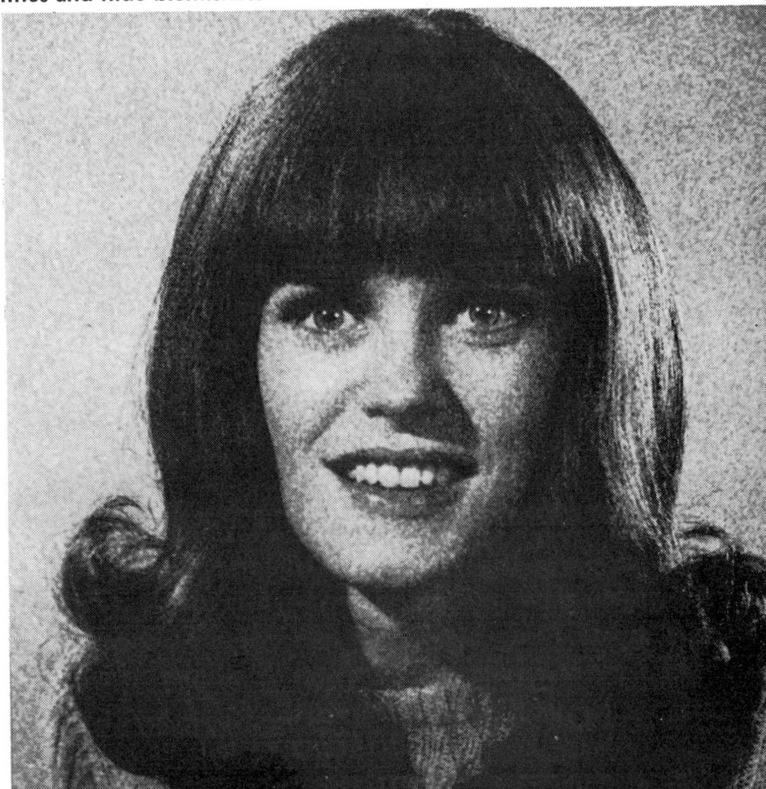

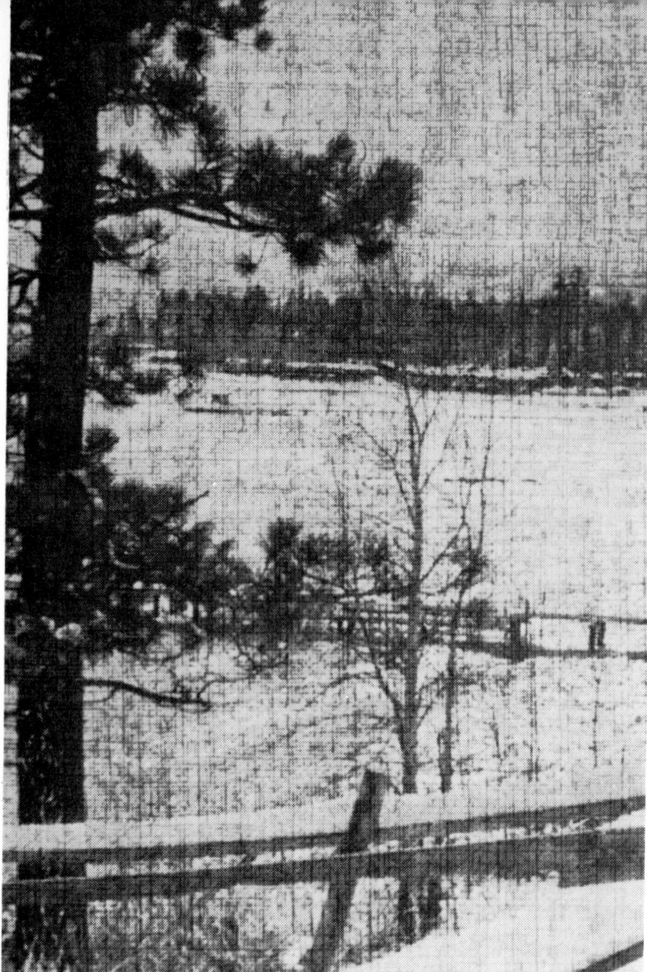

This tapa-cloth effect is especially pleasing with landscapes and also with some portraits.

How to Use Projection Screens—Texture screens are usually available in three types:

The first type is for sandwiching with color slides to give desired texture effect when projecting the slide.

The second type is for sandwiching with color or black-and-white slides. The texture film is placed on top of the negative with both films emulsion side down. This is tough to do because both sides seem equally shiny in darkroom light—or even daylight—so you have to hope a little here. Hold the two films together between two pieces of cardboard to avoid fingerprints. Tape both films together on the exposed edge, making a hinge of the two films. Do not tape the image area. This method allows you to clean the films before printing and keeps them flat and in contact with each other while being printed. You may want to use a glass-type negative carrier if one is available. This ensures the texture film will be held close to the negative and held perfectly flat.

The third type is for making big black-and-white enlargements from a portion of the negative, while keeping the texture to a minimum.

This screen is darker with more contrast to be used by the superimposure method. Superimpose the texture by first exposing your picture negative on the paper. Then with a second exposure expose the texture negative over the first exposure before developing the print. The texture negative will require about five stops less exposure than your picture negative's exposure. By super-imposing with these screens you have unlimited control of the desired texture and the 35mm or 2¼ x 2¼ size screens can be used with any size negative.

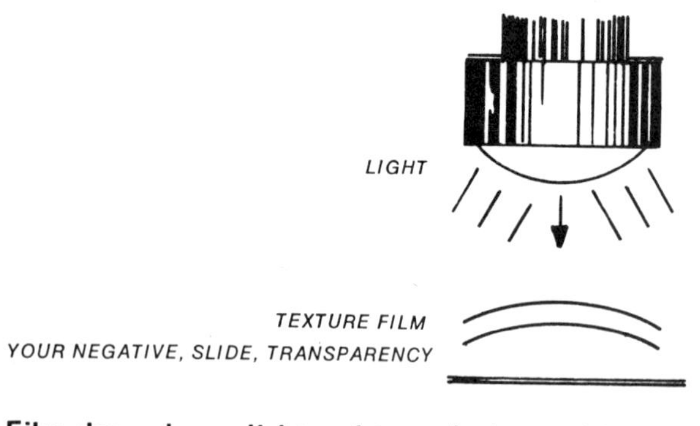

Film always has a slight curl towards the emulsion side. So put your film texture screen film together with the negative film the way they fit on each other, piggyback. The film holder will then flatten both together so that they will both be in focus.

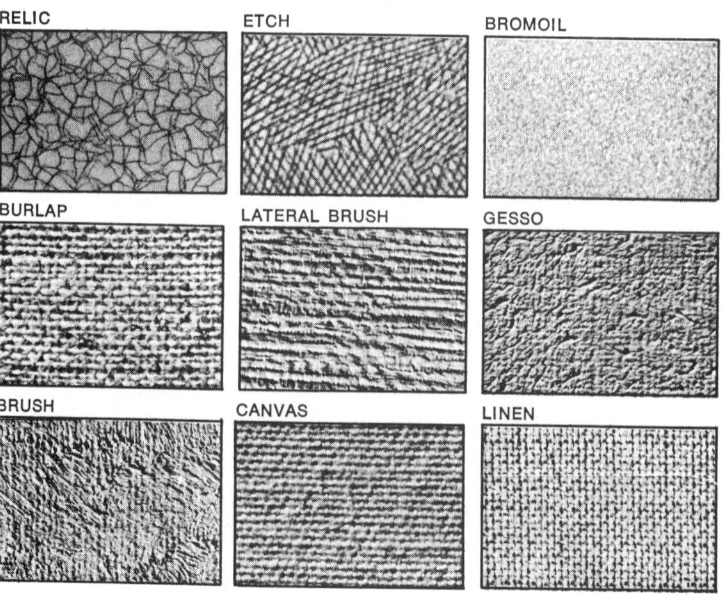

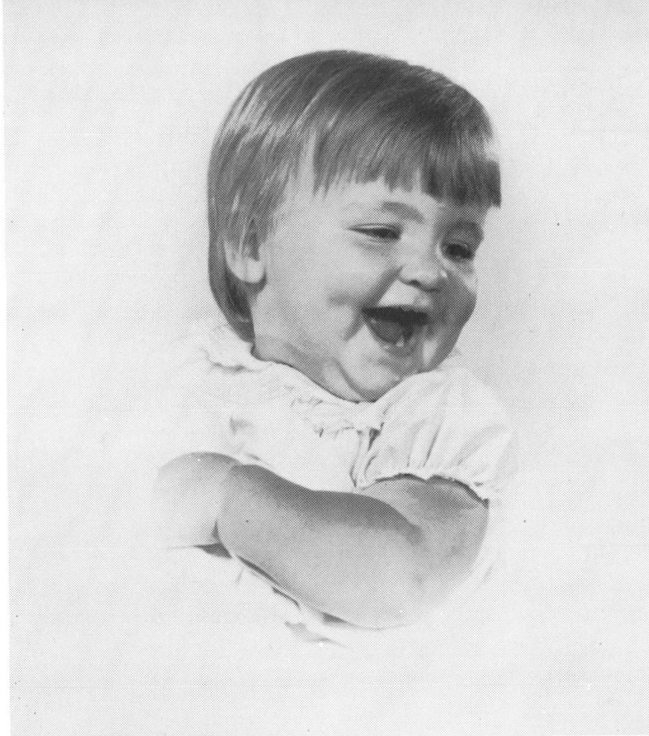

Vignettes, either white . . .

. . . or black border, give a little something extra to a portrait print.

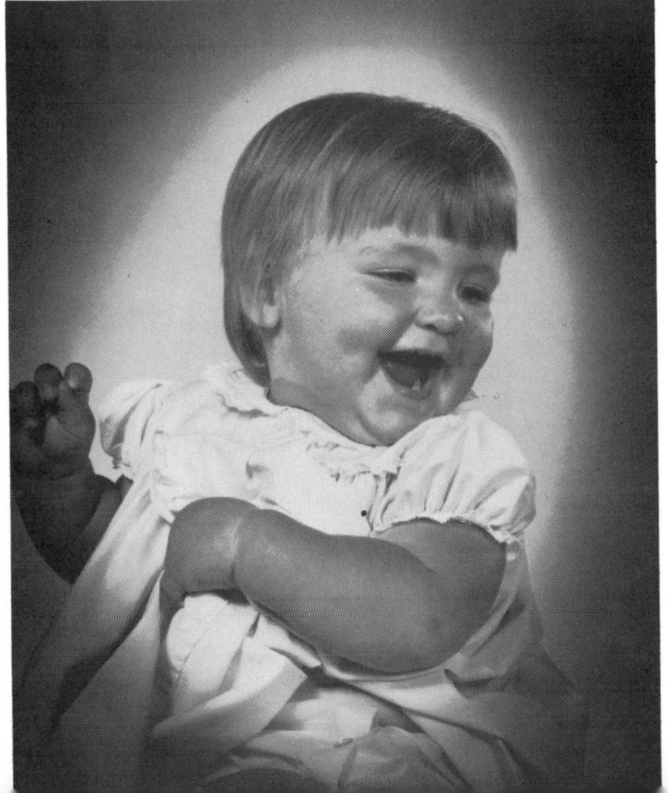

VIGNETTES

A *vignette* is a printed-in frame or border around the point of interest in a photograph. Vignetting is generally used for portrait prints. It can be either black or white, depending on whether you dodge or burn-in.

To create a white vignette, simply cut an oval, round or other-shaped hole in a sheet of cardboard and hold it beneath the enlarger lens during exposure. Only the area projected through the opening will print. The surrounding area will remain white because it is not exposed.

To print a black-border vignette, make a normal exposure of the negative. Then—using a piece of cardboard of the desired shape as a dodging tool—make another exposure while shielding the subject of interest. It should take at least four times the normal exposure to darken the vignetted area sufficiently. Keep the dodger in motion so the darkened area will have soft feathery edges. If you're in doubt as to the amount of time required to get the desired degree of darkening in the background, make a test strip.

Vignetting not only adds interest to a portrait by giving the subject greater impact on the viewer, it can effectively eliminate distracting objects not necessary in the scene. This practice has been used for many years and it is still popular among portraitists.

PETROLEUM JELLY ON GLASS

An interesting effect is produced by printing through a clear sheet of glass smeared lightly with petroleum jelly. Only the center portion of the glass is left untouched, so the main point of interest is sharp and distinct. The grease can be "feathered-in" at the edges of the clear opening.

This technique is akin to vignetting except the area surrounding the subject looks like you are looking through soft clouds. Petroleum jelly diffuses and distorts the image and gives a light airy effect. It can be especially nice for photographs of young girls or children.

The amount of light fall-off and image distortion depends on the thickness and pattern of the goop. Keep the glass moving in a circular pattern as you make the exposure. You can vary the effect by exposing for part of the time through the "jelly glass" and part of the time without it. Petroleum jelly can be smeared over all of the glass and the glass held under the lens for part of the exposure time if you are seeking an overall diffused effect.

GRAIN

Although a great deal of time and effort is normally spent to hold visible grain patterns to a minimum for sharpness and contrast, excess grain can be an attractive asset to some photographs. Pictures taken in very low-light levels become quite forceful and moody when a great amount of grain is introduced.

Large grain can be obtained in several ways. You can use an ultra-high-speed film such as Kodak Royal X Pan or Agfa Isopan Record. High grain is produced by overexposing and overdeveloping film. Use a non-fine-grain developer such as Kodak Versatol. Increase exposure one *f*-stop and add 50% to developing time. Overall print quality will be decreased but the effect can be pleasing.

One of the most effective ways to increase grain is to make a very big enlargement of a very small section of the negative. When trying to produce large grain, it is best to begin with camera exposure, so choose film, exposure developer and image size with the final result in mind. Contact and projection texture screens can also be used for grainy effects with any negative.

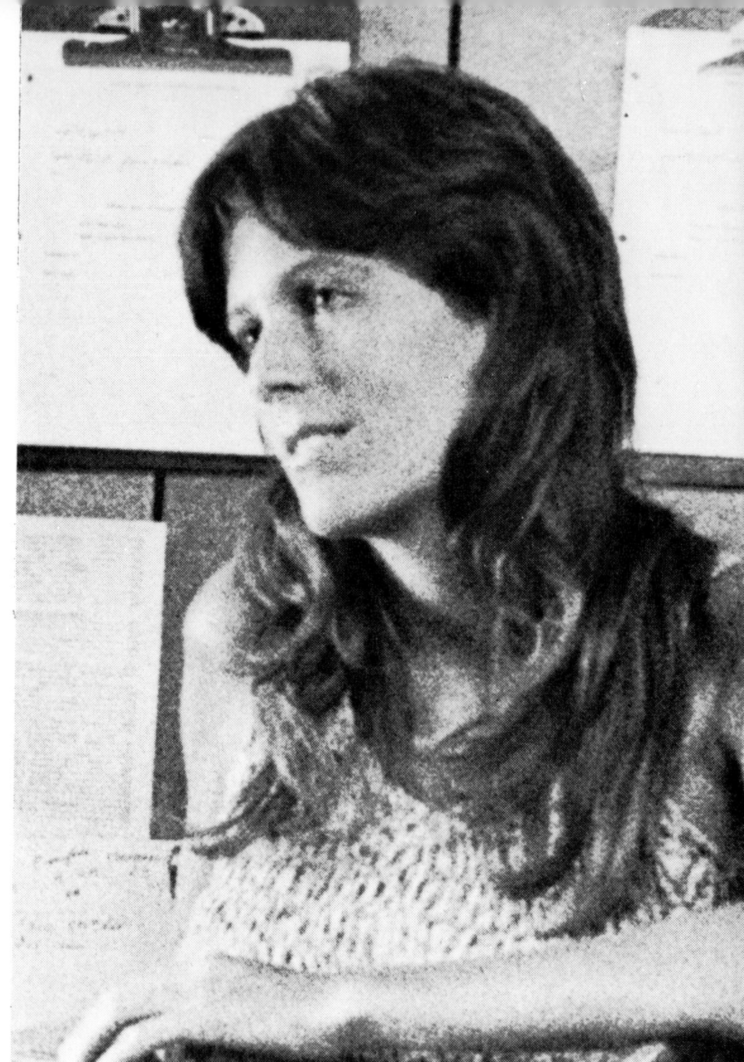

Grain can produce a nice casual feeling in a candid portrait. In this case, grain was produced by exposing 35mm Kodak Recording Film at a speed rating of 1600, then processing in Kodak DK-50.

A straight print . . .

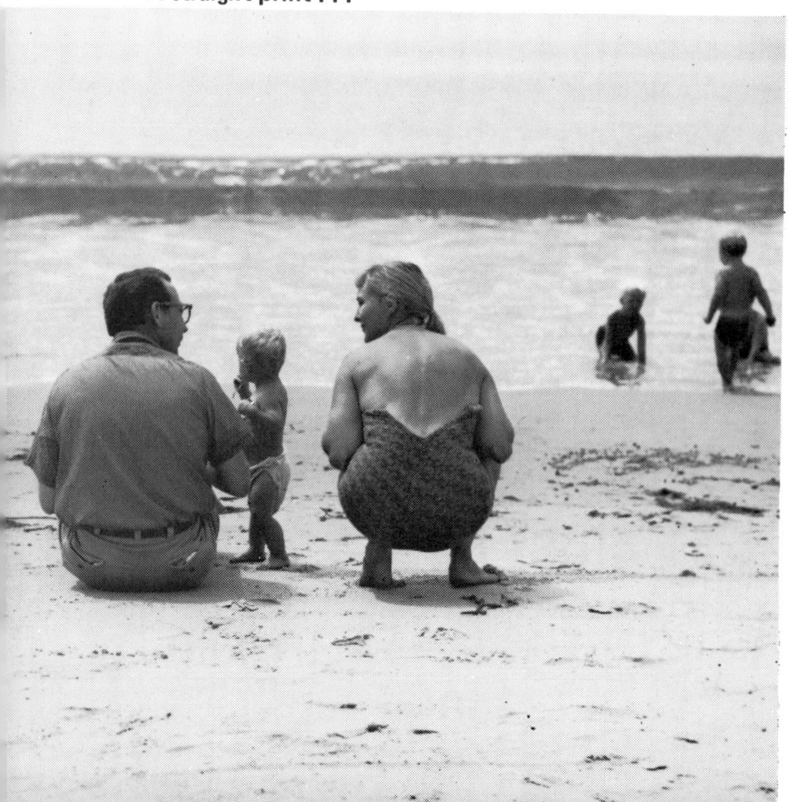

. . . and the softening effect caused by printing through a sheet of glass coated with petroleum jelly.

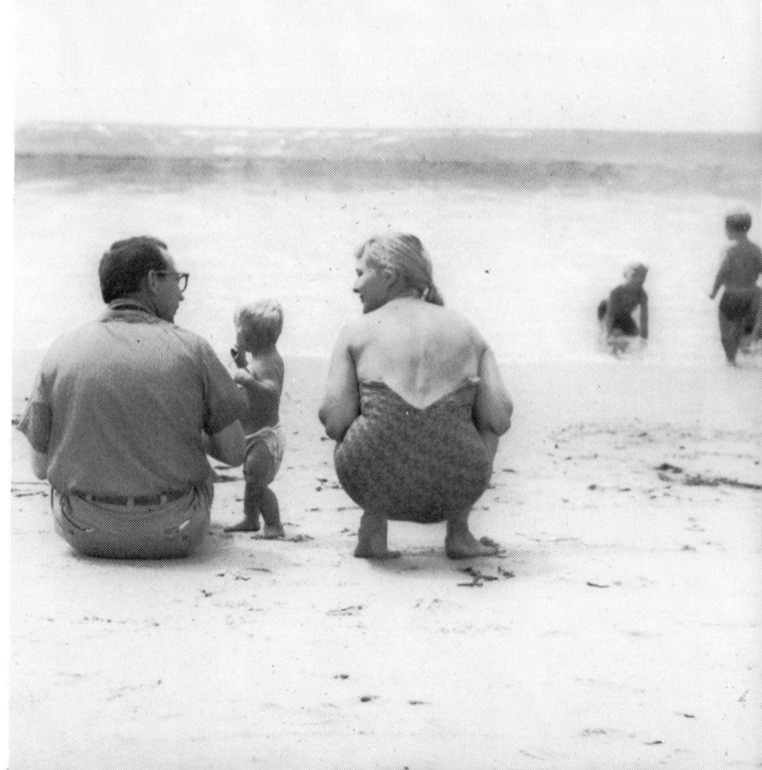

REDUCING TO LINE COPY

Here's a popular trick. Print a normal negative to produce only solid blacks and whites. No gray tones should appear in the print. In the printing industry, this is called *line copy* because it is comparable to black lines on white paper. Subjects with strong patterns lend themselves well to this technique.

Although reducing to line can be accomplished by printing onto 35mm film such as Kodak High Contrast Copy Film, it is easier to use film in a larger format, especially if you have an enlarger which will accept larger negatives. DuPont Ortho Litho 4x5 Film is excellent for this purpose. Kodak Kodalith works equally well. If your enlarger won't handle negatives this large, merely crop the image to the maximum size usable when making the camera or enlarger exposure. Incidentally, this is a good reason to consider starting out with a 4x5 enlarger if you can afford it.

Place the negative into the enlarger and focus the image to the desired size on the easel. This size will be 4x5 or smaller, because the result must ultimately end up in the negative holder of your enlarger. Set the enlarger timer to one second and the lens aperture to *f*-16. Ortho films may be used under red safelight at a four-foot distance. Place a sheet of litho film in the easel on top of a piece of black paper the same size. The paper is necessary because copy film is extremely thin. Light transmitted through the film to the light-colored easel base will reflect back to cause a double image if you don't use the black paper.

Develop the film in your regular working print developer for 45 to 60 seconds with constant agitation. Place film in stop bath for 30 seconds and in fixer until the cloudiness—anti-halation backing—disappears. Examine in white light.

You now have a positive image on a transparent base—called a *diapositive*—with considerable contrast. Areas to be white should appear clear and clean. If these areas are somewhat gray, you've overexposed. Make another positive with a lens aperture of *f*-22. Even though the contrast has been increased at this point, you will still notice some tones of gray between highlights and shadows. If you have any problem getting the exposure right, resort to the test-strip procedure to work it out. Wash and dry the positive as with

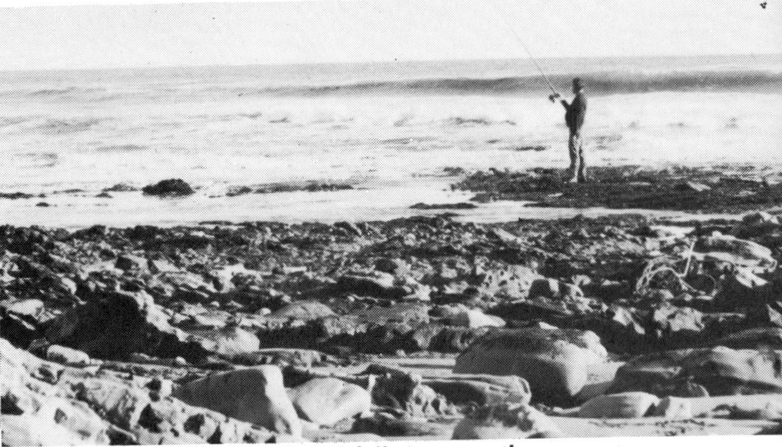

A normally exposed and printed full-tone negative.

The normal negative exposed onto a high-contrast line-copy film produces a high-contrast film positive which may be printed to produce a line-negative print.

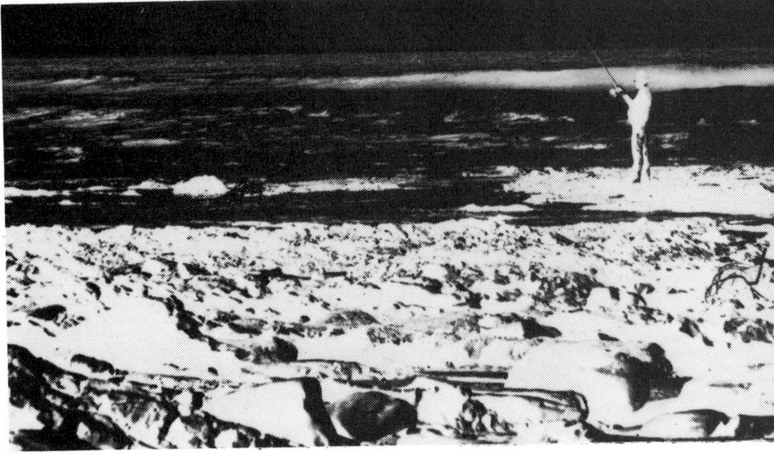

Going one step further, and exposing through the line-film positive onto another sheet of high-contrast line film, produces a line negative which then prints as a line-positive print. Now we've lost the fisherman's head because the wave turned from gray to black. Compare with top photo.

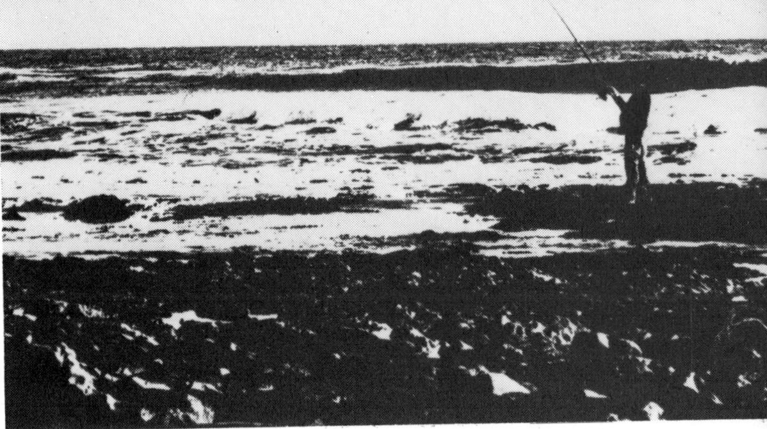

any other film. It dries quickly because it is so thin.

When the film is dry, place it in the enlarger, trimming if necessary for fit. Repeat the process used to produce the first diapositive image, thus obtaining another negative with even higher contrast. If all has gone well, you have a negative without gray middle tones which will produce a print of only pure black-and-white. Printing it on a grade 3 or 4 paper—or grade 6 if you have it—will help.

If the middle tones have not been completely eliminated, you can continue the negative-to-positive process on high-contrast film until you are satisfied. You can also get rid of middle tones in negative by using opaque to paint them out. Use a brush with water and Kodak Opaque. It is a dark-red material which adheres to either side of the film. Opaque is usually applied to the base side of the film while the negative is illuminated by a light-box, but you can hold it against a window and use daylight illumination. If you goof and get opaque on a clear part of the negative you can wipe it off with a moistened cotton swab.

If you wish, stop at a positive step and use this to produce a negative high-contrast image on the print. Pictorial scenes printed this way go well with contemporary decor.

You can also use these line negatives and positives to make diazo prints which I'll tell you about later. Line negs can also be reticulated, which is our next item of darkroom tomfoolery.

Prints made from line negs/positives can be toned. And, you can get interesting effects by carefully applying bright colors with Magic-Marker type pens or transparent water colors. The different light reflectivity of anything you apply to the print can be masked by spraying the final job with glossy or matte Krylon acrylic spray.

BAS-RELIEF

This technique produces a print with a feeling of depth. It can be done with any subject matter, but a simple uncluttered scene or portrait with good contrast is usually most pleasing. Place the negative in contact with, and above, unexposed film of the same type, emulsion-to-emulsion. This sandwich is covered with a sheet of glass to ensure good contact between negative and film and placed on the enlarger baseboard. With the enlarger lens

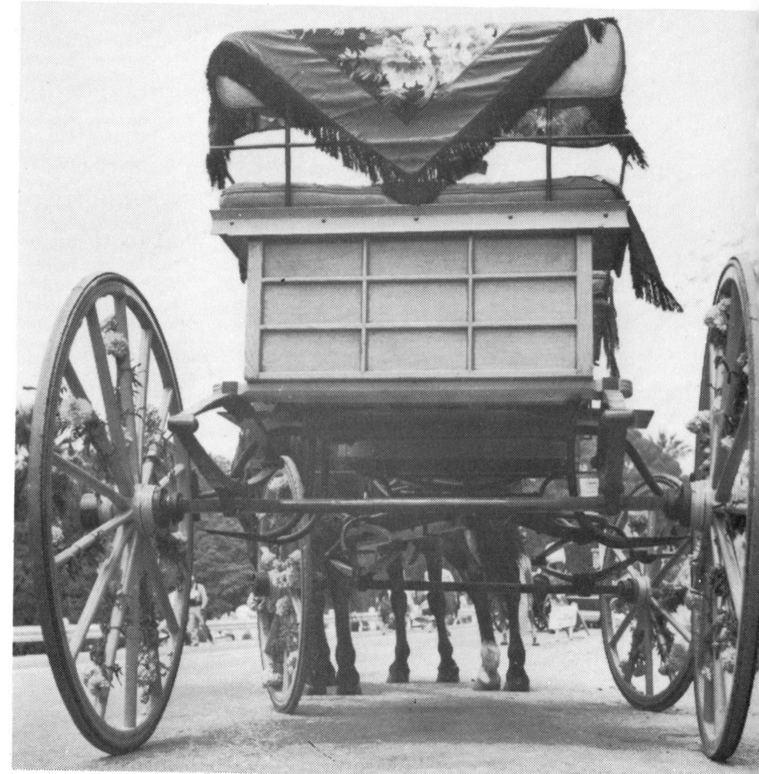

A straight print from a normally exposed continuous-tone negative.

One problem you may have when making high-contrast film positives is that of gathering dust which prints as black spots as in this illustration. A fine brush and Kodak Opaque will fill in the clear spots on the negative so they don't print.

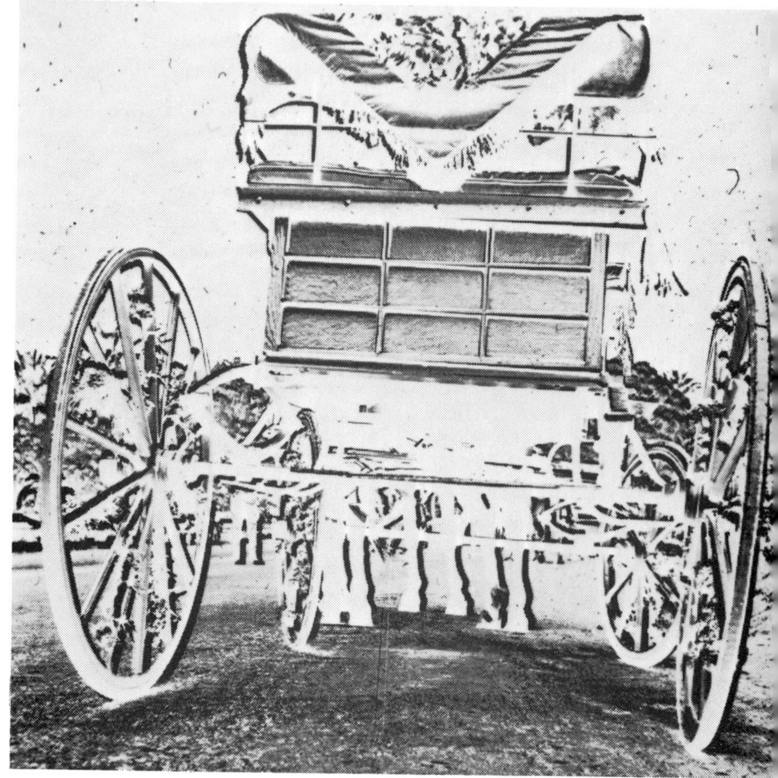

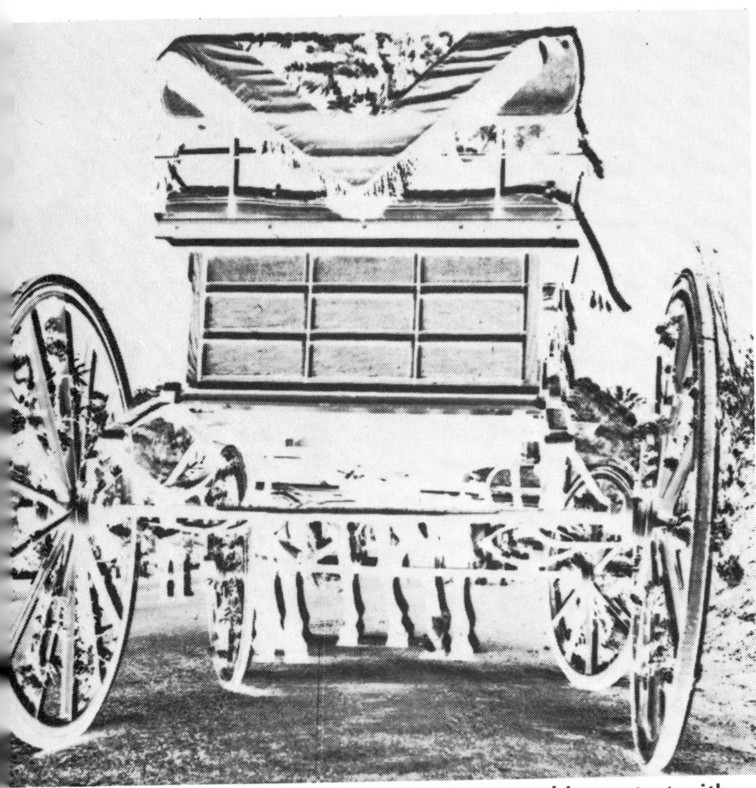

Bas-relief—the normal negative is exposed in contact with a high-contrast line material to produce a line-film positive. The film positive is then placed in contact with the normal negative and moved slightly out of register. The film "sandwich" is then printed normally.

Pseudo-reticulation: Today's films are very hard to reticulate as described. Here a sheet of clear glass gathered condensation from steaming water, then it was inverted and placed dry side over paper during exposure. This closely resembles reticulation effects.

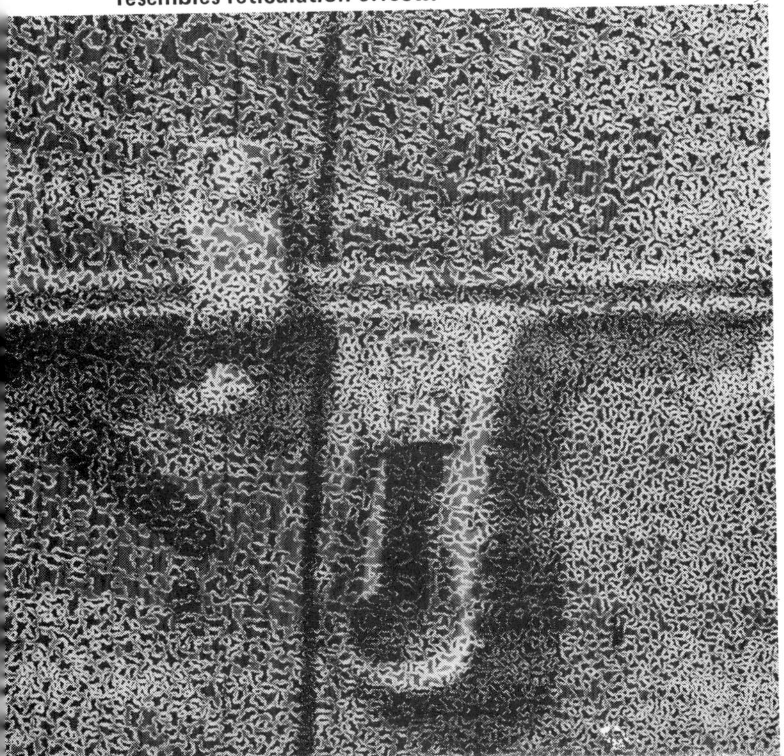

closed as far as possible, make several one-second exposures covering portions of the film with opaque cardboard in the usual test-strip manner. Process the newly exposed film, using the standard procedure for developing film.

Evaluate the result and determine the exposure to get a diapositive with the same relative density as the negative. With another piece of film, expose for the correct exposure determined in the test, process, wash and dry.

Now place the diapositive, emulsion side up, on a sheet of glass. Cover with the negative, emulsion down. Hold the set toward the light and move the images slightly out of register. Put the film pair down on the glass and tape together. Place the film sandwich in the enlarger and print as usual, using a high-contrast-grade paper. It may be necessary to use a glass-type negative carrier to keep the two pieces in contact.

Appearance of depth depends on the extent your images are out of register; too much destroys the effect completely. This is very attractive on simple scenes in light tones.

RETICULATION

This is tricky, so take care. Unlike the other techniques I've discussed, reticulation permanently changes the character of the negative. Make a copy negative if you intend to try this on a favorite photograph.

The object is to crinkle the film emulsion to produce a textured pattern on the print. Steps are as follows:

1. Process negative film normally except use a hypo without hardener added. I use Kodak Rapid Fixer without adding any hardener.
2. Wash.
3. Dip negative in hot water 125°F (52°C)—not boiling—until the emulsion becomes slightly soft, usually about 30 to 45 seconds. You'll see the emulsion swell. It gets a jellied thick look. When you see that starting, get the negative out of the warm water and—
4. Transfer negative to chilled water, 33° to 45°F (1° to 3°C), until emulsion cools.
5. Repeat steps 3 and 4 until emulsion has desired crinkle effect.
6. Fix negative normally in standard hypo with hardener, wash and dry.

Reticulation patterns will vary from small

tight lines to large distinct patches. Your own taste and luck will determine the final texture.

One more word of warning: Do not use water which is too hot or the emulsion will loosen from its film base and wind up as a soft ball of gelatin in the bottom of the tank. This can happen at the recommended temperature if you don't pay attention. Get the neg into chilled water the instant you see the swelling starting. Practice on old negs to get it right. Again, don't ever use original favorite negatives, even after you've learned this process. *Results are not repeatable with any degree of accuracy.*

Note—Today's films are extremely difficult to reticulate on purpose. The thinner emulsion layer does not want to pry itself away from its bond with the base material, and for all usual photographic purposes, that is good! You may find that you have to use temperature extremes not necessary a few years ago. If you find some old film which has been kept under reasonably good conditions, try it. Because you are going to try to damage the emulsion on a controlled basis, the image quality can be of less importance. Lantern-slide plates known as Kodak Projection Plates, are glass plates coated with a film emulsion. Their relatively thick emulsion will reticulate with ease. Don't let the water get too hot as there is a great chance that the emulsion will slide off the glass.

To expose the lantern-slide plate, mark an area 3 1/4 by 4 inches on the enlarging easel and with a negative in the enlarger, set the enlarger so the projected image fills the area marked. Close the lens aperture to the minimum setting and set the timer to 1 second. A red safelight may be used with the lantern-slide plate during the entire process. Place a sheet of black paper over the marked area and cover with the glass plate. Because the base material on lantern-slide plate is glass, the projected image may travel completely through to the easel and reflect back to form a double image in the emulsion. The black paper eliminates this problem. The emulsion side of the plate is completely covered with gelatin, while the base side is covered to about 1/8 inch from one end. Make sure the emulsion side is face up on the easel.

Expose the plate with the enlarger for one second and develop in your regular paper developer for 30 seconds. Place the plate in the stop bath for 15 seconds and then into fixer until all signs of milkiness disappear. View the positive image formed by transmitted light and determine correctness of exposure. If the image is too light, repeat the process, this time allowing an enlarger exposure of 2 seconds. When you have the exposure you like, wash the plate in running water for 10 minutes and begin the reticulation process. When done, you will have a positive image which may be projected in the enlarger to give you a reticulated negative image. Or, you can use the positive to make another negative on film or another glass plate. I think you'll like it and it's well worth a try.

MULTIPLE IMAGES

Producing several images on the same sheet of print paper can be done by placing two negatives together in the enlarger, by making separate exposures from different negatives, by making several exposures from the same negative onto different areas of the paper, or by using a multiple-image supplementary lens on the enlarger lens or on the camera lens when you make the original exposure. A contrasty paper such as **3, 4, 5** or **6** or equivalent is required to keep distinct images.

When printing two negatives simultaneously, it is only necessary to arrange the images in the composition you prefer, make a test strip and print. The exposure time may be considerably longer than you might expect.

To print more than one image through separate exposures, you have to figure how much exposure should be given each time you print. Some guesswork or trial-and-error is usually involved, depending on the nature of the separate images and amount of overlap.

When the overlapping images are all about the same contrast, here is a good first approximation: For two separate image exposures, each should be 1/2 of the total exposure. For three separate exposures, each should be 1/3 of the total. Determine the correct total exposure by making a test strip with one of the negatives. For example if your test indicates a total exposure of 15 seconds and you are printing three different overlapping images separately, give each one 5 seconds exposure.

If the images do not overlap and all have light backgrounds on the final print, each is exposing the background area of the other images and not much light will be on the paper from those backgrounds. Therefore each individual exposure must fully expose that portion of the paper and give total time to each. If the backgrounds are not light, you have to fiddle with it and maybe you can't do it at all.

To begin, put the first negative in the enlarger and project onto a sheet of plain white paper. Using a pencil, rough out the subject outline.

Remove the plain paper and make an exposure on printing paper. Turn the exposed paper over and mark the top with pencil. Replace the exposed paper in its light-proof box. Place the next negative to be printed in the enlarger, insert the plain paper with the penciled outline of the first image in the easel and determine desired composition using the pencil marks as a guide. If you want to print a third negative on the same paper, make another pencil outline now.

Replace the print paper in the easel, making sure the top is properly oriented, and expose. Repeat these steps until you have made all exposures and then process the print normally.

A personal note: Two different negatives are *enough!* Unless the images are very simple or show distinct separation more makes it nearly impossible to mentally sort out when viewing the print.

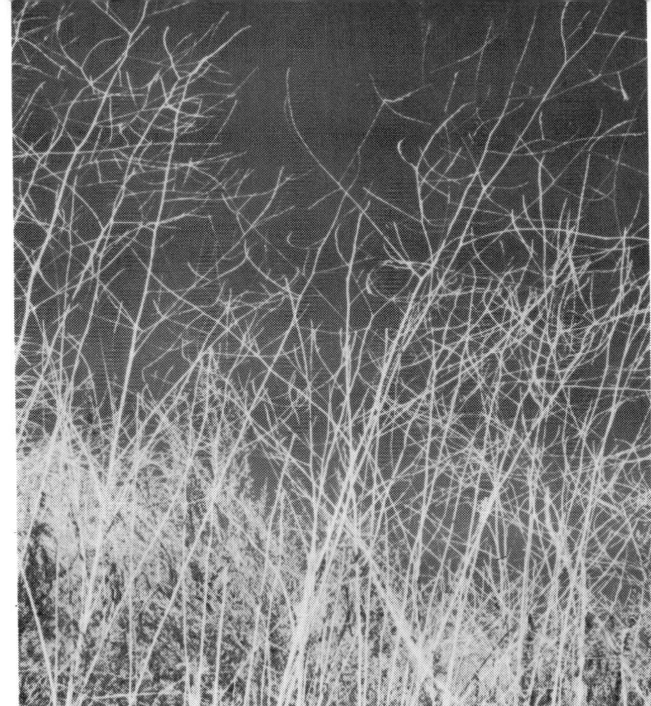

Negatives of grass, leaves, rocks, water or clouds are always nice to have available in your file.

A picture with some interesting lines but a rather dull background.

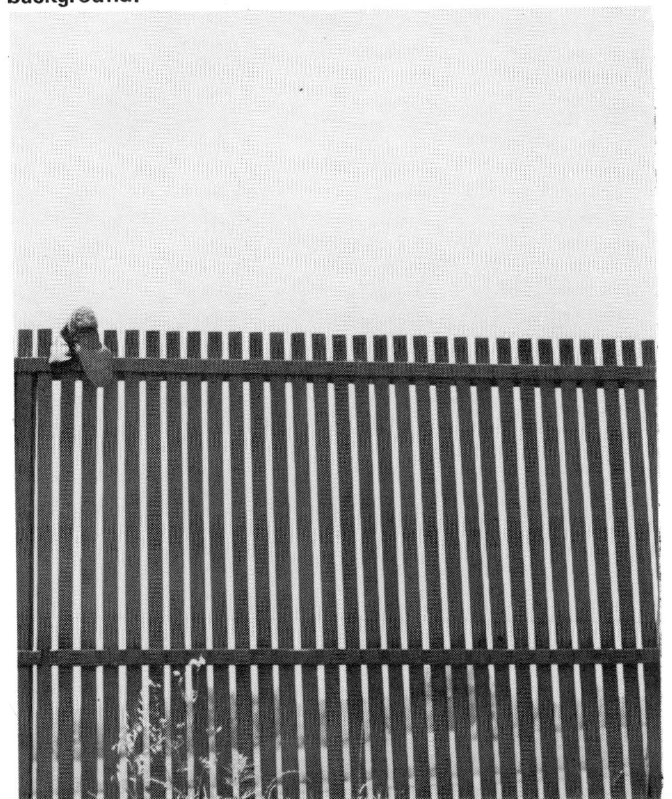

The two printed together make for a more interesting design.

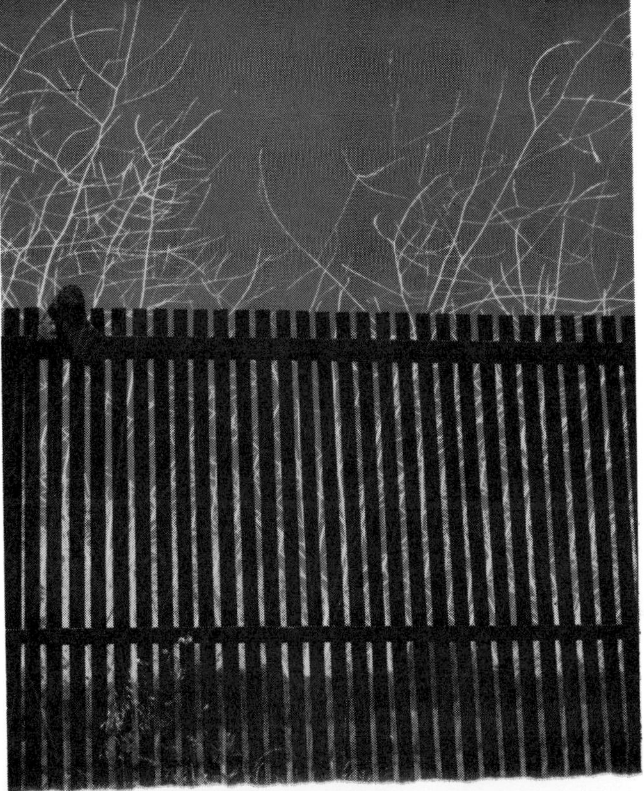

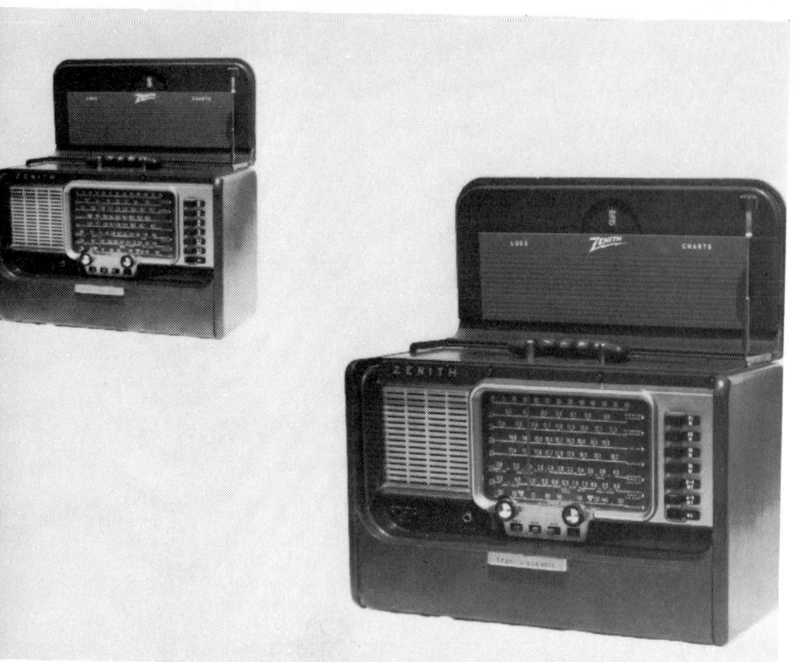

An example of multiple printing from a single negative.

Printing several images from the same negative is accomplished the same way, except the negative is left in the enlarger and separation is produced by relocating the easel following each exposure. Exposure for each image is determined as for printing with multiple negatives.

There are a lot of variables in these techniques, all determined by the amount and type of material on the negatives. Pleasing results require considerable experimentation, so don't hold back. You might want to try multiple images where different magnification is used on some or all of the images.

SOLARIZATION

Solarization is the partial reversing of the image on film or print by action of light on the partially developed material. When negative film is solarized, highlight areas are not affected. Shadows reverse to white and little change occurs in the middle tones. This resultant image prints with black outlines around each subject.

Subject matter should be rather contrasty for best results. Film should be processed to about three-fourths total time, removed from the developer and gently squeegeed to remove most moisture. Expose the film to a standard OA safelight for five to ten seconds at a distance of four feet. Return the film to the developer and complete processing to normal times.

Prints solarized during development appear almost completely reversed, that is, black highlights and white shadows. Solarization is difficult to achieve, requires much experimentation and I consider it to be totally unpredictable.

Prints are more difficult to solarize because the action is quite rapid. Develop the exposed paper completely, then transfer it to a tray of clear water. Wait until the water stops moving. Flash the print with a low-wattage white bulb—15 to 25 watts—at a distance of four feet. Switch the white light on and off as quickly as possible. Remember, they don't call you lightning fingers for nothing! A good exposure source is a safelight without a filter.

Now add one or two ounces of straight stock-solution developer to the water and agitate until desired effect is obtained. This will probably take three or four minutes.

It's fun if you hit it—good luck!

Relatively high-contrast subjects such as this make ideal subjects for negative solarization.

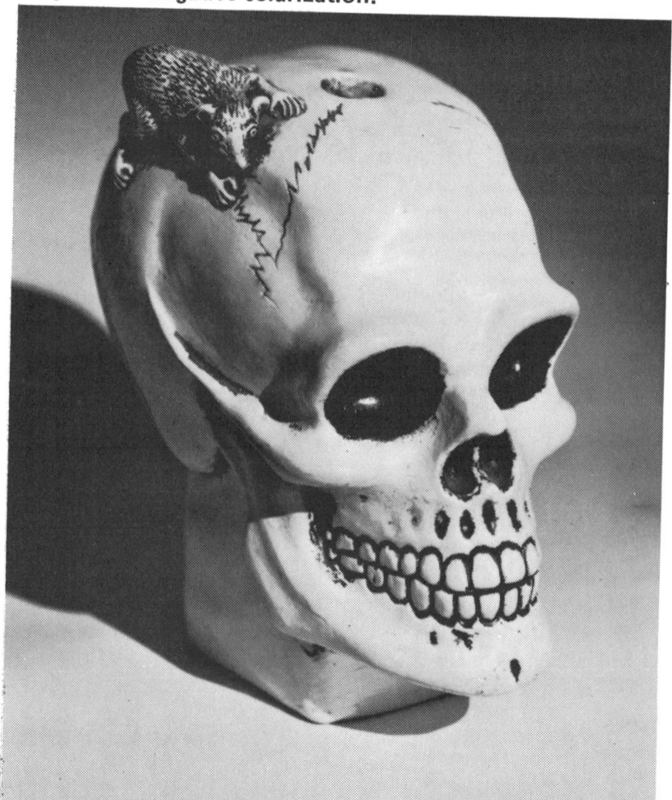

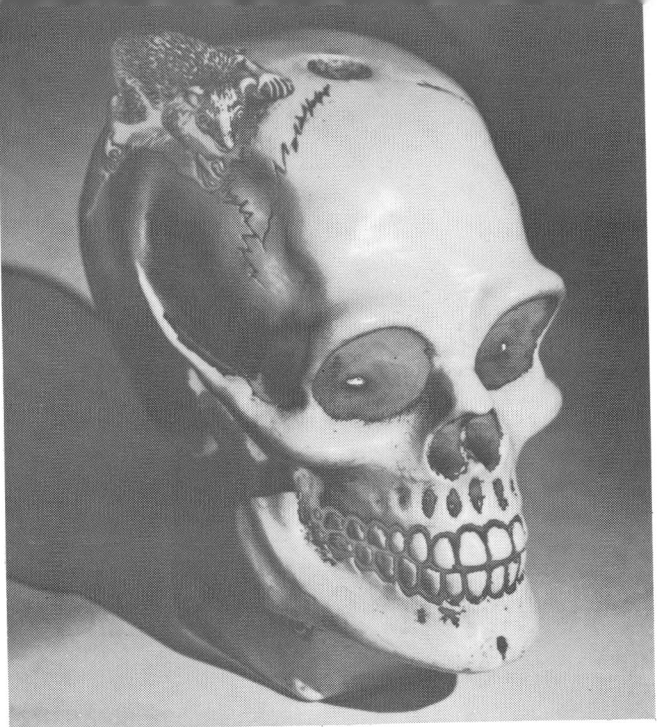

A print from a partially solarized negative. The neg was exposed to an OA safelight for five seconds when developing was three-quarters complete.

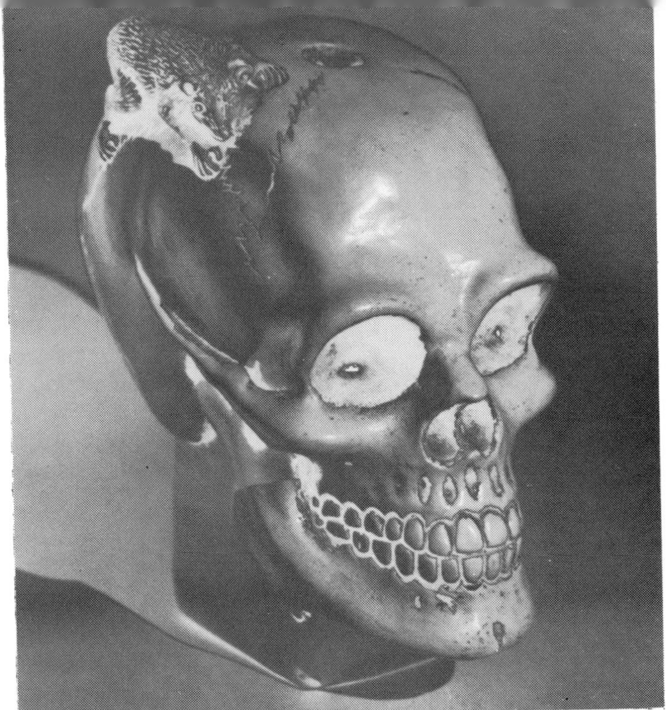

Full solarization with a 10-second safelight exposure when developing was 50% complete.

A straight print from a normal negative and . . .

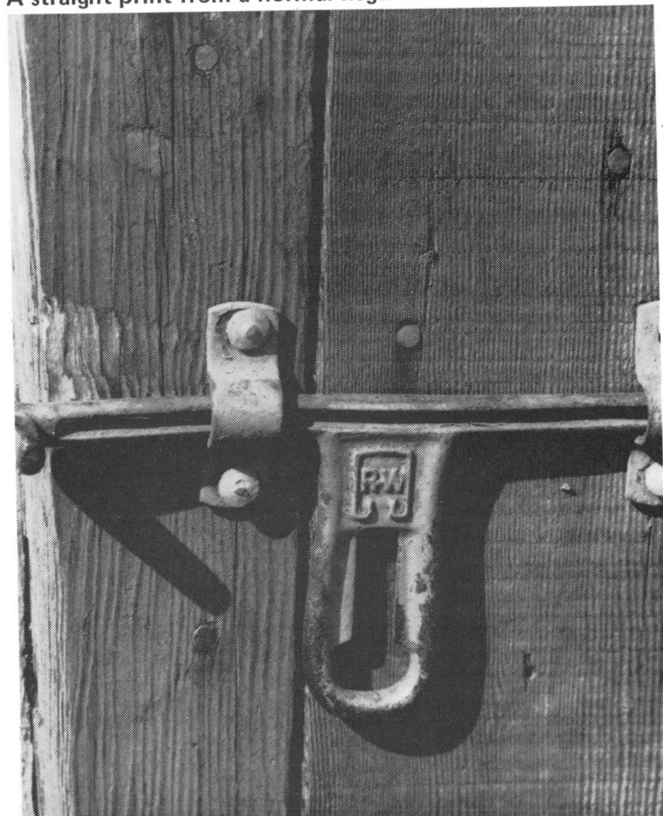

. . . a partially solarized print. It was exposed to a white light flash after the image was fully developed. Print solarization requires a great deal of experimentation and can produce a great variety of effects which you will find nearly impossible to duplicate one print to another.

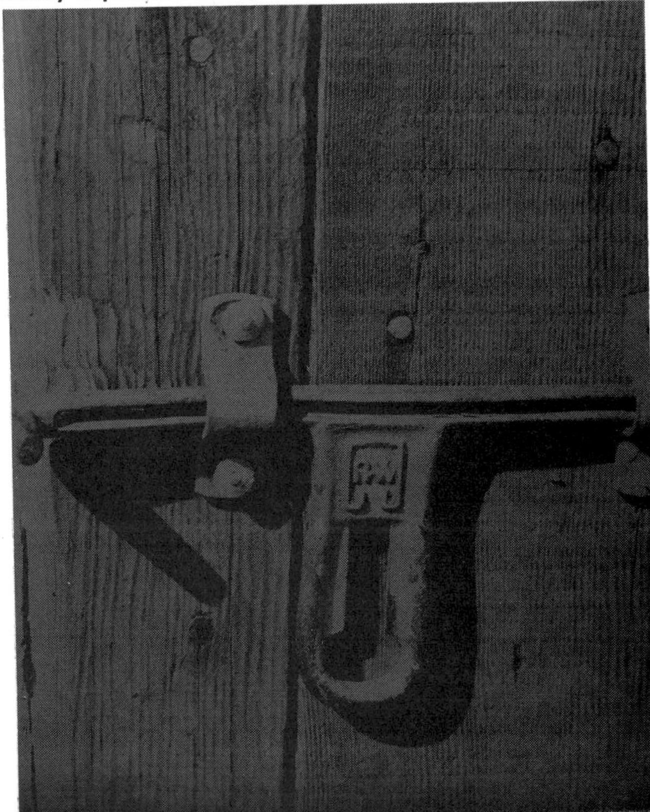

TONERS

A toner chemically converts the paper's black or gray silver image into an overall colored image: Blue-black, brown-black, yellow-brown or red-brown. This may do wonders for a photo which falls just short of the mood you had in mind when you shot the picture. The colored image is permanent if you take care in processing the print initially and follow instructions for the subsequent toning.

In fact, toning is part of the process used to achieve the utmost print permanence, called *archival processing,* so staining and fading will not occur from sulfur-bearing compounds in the air, the paper base or the wash water itself. Permanence is achieved because the silver image is converted to or covered by other metals or inorganic compounds such as silver sulfide.

Paper tone—either warm or cold—affects the end result. Cold-tone papers will not tone in most single-solution toners. You may not be able to tell they were ever even near a toning solution! Toners which do not work with fast cold-tone enlarging papers include Kodak's Brown, Rapid-Selenium and Poly toners.

Consult the paper-maker's literature to determine which papers are regarded as cold-tone or warm-tone. Pick warm-tone papers for the easiest and usually the best toning results. Some glossy surface papers, especially Polycontrast, may not tone well, leaving a mottled appearance.

To get any degree of brown toning with a cold-tone paper you have to use a two-step bleach/redevelop sepia toner such as Kodak's or Johnson's (available from General Photographic Supply). First bleach the print until the image is a pale tan, then wash the print to get rid of the yellow color from the bleach. Next the print should be put in the redeveloper until all parts of the image turn sepia. Follow this with another water rinse per directions and then put the print into a print-hardening solution for two to five minutes. Make this from one part Kodak Liquid Hardener and 13 parts water.

Before buying Kodak's Sepia Toner, be warned: The redeveloper is sodium sulfide. Every chemistry student's nostrils have been assailed by the rotten-egg odor this gives off. Use it outside or in a super-well-ventilated area—or buy the odorless Johnson kind.

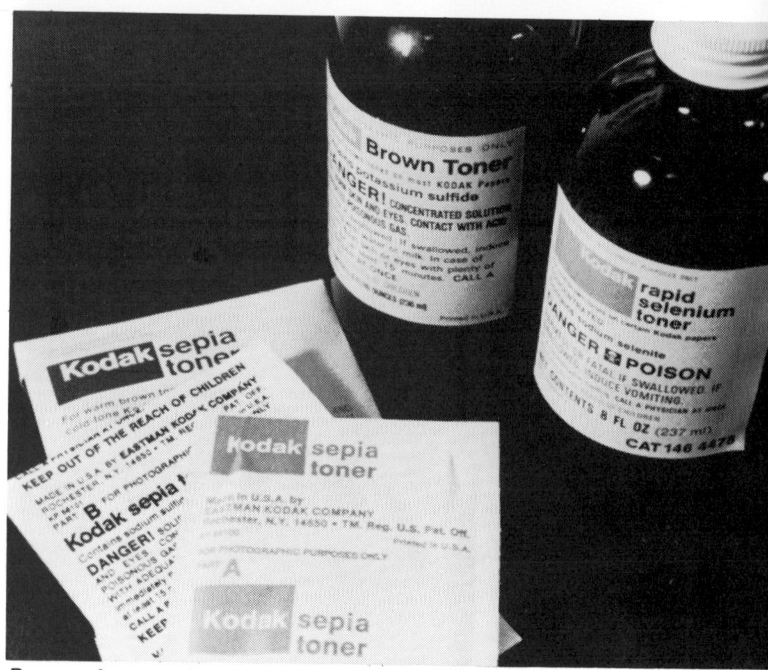

Prepared toners from Kodak. Sepia in powder form, selenium and brown in liquid. These materials are POISON so handle with care and use in a well ventilated area only.

Warm-tone papers are easiest to tone and they tone just fine with single-solution toners such as Kodak's Brown, Rapid-Selenium, Poly and Blue Toners. Kodak Brown Toner has an awful rotten-egg smell, so use it outside or in a well-ventilated area.

Kodak's Blue Toner is a gold toner which gives your warm-tone prints a navy-blue hue in a single solution. Put sepia-toned prints into the blue toner and you'll get red color from cold-tone paper and orange color from warm-tone paper.

Use toners in a well-ventilated area and keep your hands out of them. Use only plastic or glass trays or enamel trays completely free of cracks and chips. Toners contacting metal may react to stain the print severely.

Prints to be toned should usually be printed slightly darker than normal and development should be carried to the maximum recommended time—neither more nor less. Some density is lost in the toning process because the toning fades the silver image as it is changed to a different type of silver compound or covered with some other metal or inorganic material. Light prints show little if any toning effect, partially because the toning is fading them even lighter. The depth of toning achieved depends on a lot of factors such as type of paper and its age and condition, how you develop it, print density and the type of toner used. The temperature at which the toning is done also affects what you get in the end. Each toner comes with instructions on how to use it, including temperature, need for hardening the print afterward, etc.

The print should be fully developed and not "pulled" from the developer because the toner needs the complete silver image to work on in the process.

It is imperative that the print be completely fixed and thoroughly washed before using most toners. Any fixer in the emulsion or print backing may cause the toner to stain in irregular patches, giving an awful appearance you probably wouldn't like. Toners primarily affect the middle tones and highlights in the initial stages, so tone until the shadows begin to show definite coloring.

Your local photo dealer will have paper samples from various manufacturers and a number of these samples will be toned. These will give you an idea of what a particular paper/toner combination may give you. Toning can add a great deal to a print but a bad print toned is still only a bad print with an added overall color. Choose the subject matter well. Try to match the tone ot the mood of the photograph. I like toners used with landscapes or old things such as buildings, rocks, trees or old people whose faces show great character. These subjects are especially nice when printed on a strongly textured print paper like Kodak Ektalure X and sepia toned to a warm-brown color.

Experimentation is the key here as it is with all special effects. A few nicely toned prints hanging on your wall will show off your creative thinking and desire to do more than the average photographer.

More information on toners is available from any of the manufacturers. Kodak has two publications of interest: Pamphlet G-23, *The ABC's of Toning;* and the Kodak Professional Data Book J-1, *Processing Chemicals and Formulas.* You can probably find these in the technical data racks of your favorite camera store.

There are other ways to get overall color into your black-and-white prints, including the color-base papers mentioned in the accompanying sidebar. Also, you can get red, yellow, blue, green and sepia toning dyes from Edwal Scientific Products. FR has some dye-coupler toners. Either of these types of toners may not have the permanence of the others I have discussed.

THE DIAZOTYPE

Commonly known as *diazo,* only a few years ago this process was known only to makers of blueprints and a few experimental types. Today, it is in broad use by educators, especially in the scientific fields to produce teaching materials as well as the home photo enthusiast who has read the wealth of information circulating through the monthly photographic publications. It's an interesting process because the material is completely grain-free. To those who are ecology-minded, it has absolutely no silver in the emulsion. Rather, diazo is a light-sensitive diazo anhydride combined with a slightly acid compound, coated on a base of film, paper or cloth. You can usually buy diazo material at drafting-supply or blueprint-supply stores.

Luminos Pastel Paper—is a single weight, matte paper with a normal bromide emulsion. It is available in 100 sheets 8x10 inch packed in four 25 sheet packages of blue, green, red and yellow. Each sheet has been treated to produce an overall tint in its particular color. The tint affects the highlights as well as the shadow areas. It is exposed and processed the same as any normal contrast bromide printing paper. Makes some really interesting prints for poster type work. The red, blue and green are strong colors—yellow is pretty weak and not too desirable. It is distributed by Luminos Photo Corp., Yonkers, NY 10705.

Two more interesting things about diazo materials are that it is exposed to strong ultraviolet light and the image is produced by "development" in ammonia vapor. There are so many things you can do creatively with this material, that I can't possibly list anywhere near all of them, so I'll give you the rundown on how to produce your first diazotype, a couple of suggestions and let you go from there.

The first step is to choose an interesting negative of fairly high contrast.

Using the technique for REDUCING TO LINE COPY, make a high-contrast film positive. You may stop at this point with the line work and proceed to the next step if you wish, but I recommend you continue further and make a line negative from this positive . . . expecially for this first time.

The next step is to place the line positive—or negative—in a proof frame in contact with the diazo material, base of film to emulsion of diazo. Put the neg or positive against the glass. The diazo material is extremely slow in its response to light, so this procedure may be carried out in room light.

Take the proof frame outside and expose the film/diazo sandwich to direct sunlight for one to two minutes. This will take some experimentation and depends on the weather, time of day and time of year.

Now the magic part. Take the gallon salad dressing jar you got from your local dining establishment and have been mixing chemicals in since you started this book, and pour in about one inch of household ammonia. Be kind to yourself and do this in a WELL VENTILATED AREA. In the bottom of the jar, drop in a piece of hard wood so it rises above the level of the ammonia and will act as a support for the diazo film.

Place the diazo film in the jar, on the support and close the lid. Within three to four minutes, an image will have formed in the color you have chosen. This is a finished image. You don't have to fix it or wash it or dry it. Use it!

You now have an image in color line which has color in the areas the light did not strike and clear where it didn't. The ultraviolet destroyed the diazo it struck.

So far pretty good. Now, what do you do with it. Well, try mounting it against a background paper in a contrasting color. Make two more in different colors and put them together slightly off-register. Put it in register with the line positive. Copy any of the combinations onto slide or negative film in color. OK? Take it from there. Have a ball!

MURALS

Murals are very large prints in sizes 30x40 inches up to those which cover the whole wall. The problem with making prints of this size is obviously the space needed to expose and process the print material. Things have changed. Let's start out with exposure. Nothing really new here, but here's how. You must be able to project a negative image to size you want. Beseler enlargers have the capability of tipping the head so that it projects at a 90 degree angle. Omega offers a horizontal projection attachment. If your equipment is of another brand, loosen the bolts which hold the elevating girders to the baseboard and turn the whole assembly so the baseboard points to the rear of the enlarger head. PLACE A HEAVY WEIGHT ON THE BASEBOARD TO PREVENT THE ENTIRE ENLARGER FROM TIPPING OVER! You will now be able to project to floor level. Place a stiff sheet of Masonite or plywood on the surface to be projected on, attach to wall if necessary, place negative in the enlarger, compose and focus. So far, a little effort but nothing tricky, right? Now, before the exposure, let's discuss the processing.

Here's the new part: The Maxwell Mural Tank made by Maxwell Photo-Mural Tanks, 999 E. Valley Blvd. No. 6, Alhambra, California 91801. This item eliminates the need for large trays, sinks and washers. The paper is gently rolled after exposure, inserted in the tank and processed. Washing is carried out in the bathtub. Now, back to the print exposure.

Start as usual with a test strip. Remember that exposures will be longer for giant prints than for the sizes you are accustomed to making. Big prints may take several *minutes* to expose. Use double-face masking tape to adhere the paper to the "easel." When your test strip is exposed, it must be processed in the Maxwell tank so that you may accurately judge the density and con-

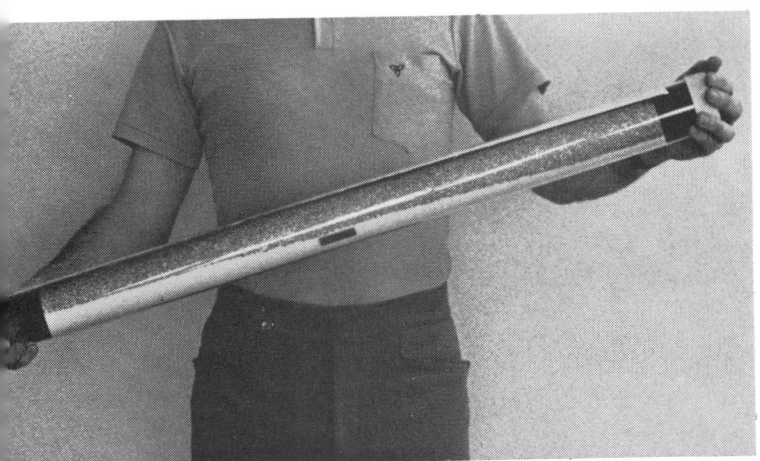

The Maxwell Photo Mural Tank allows you to make large prints, including mural size, without the expense of additional trays in extra large sizes. Oversize trays are high cost items which also create storage problems. The Maxwell tank enables you to produce large prints even while working in a kitchen or bathroom style darkroom.

trast the finished print will have. You will notice at this point that the print seems somewhat flat and lacking in contrast. Because of this, you may wish to pick an exposure slightly greater than you usually desire. Here's a summary of the processing steps recommended by the Maxwell:

Kodak Photo-Flo—working solution	32 ounces
Kodak Dektol developer diluted 1:4	32 ounces
Kodak Fixer	32 ounces
Stop bath	32 ounces
Hypo neutralizer—working solution	32 ounces

These solution quantities will not fill the tank completely, but don't be concerned. Steady, gentle agitation of the tank will accomplish processing easily.

Here is the processing procedure:

1. Determine exposure by test strips. Process in diluted developer and note required time of development. This will vary with individual techniques and preferences, but 4 minutes is average.

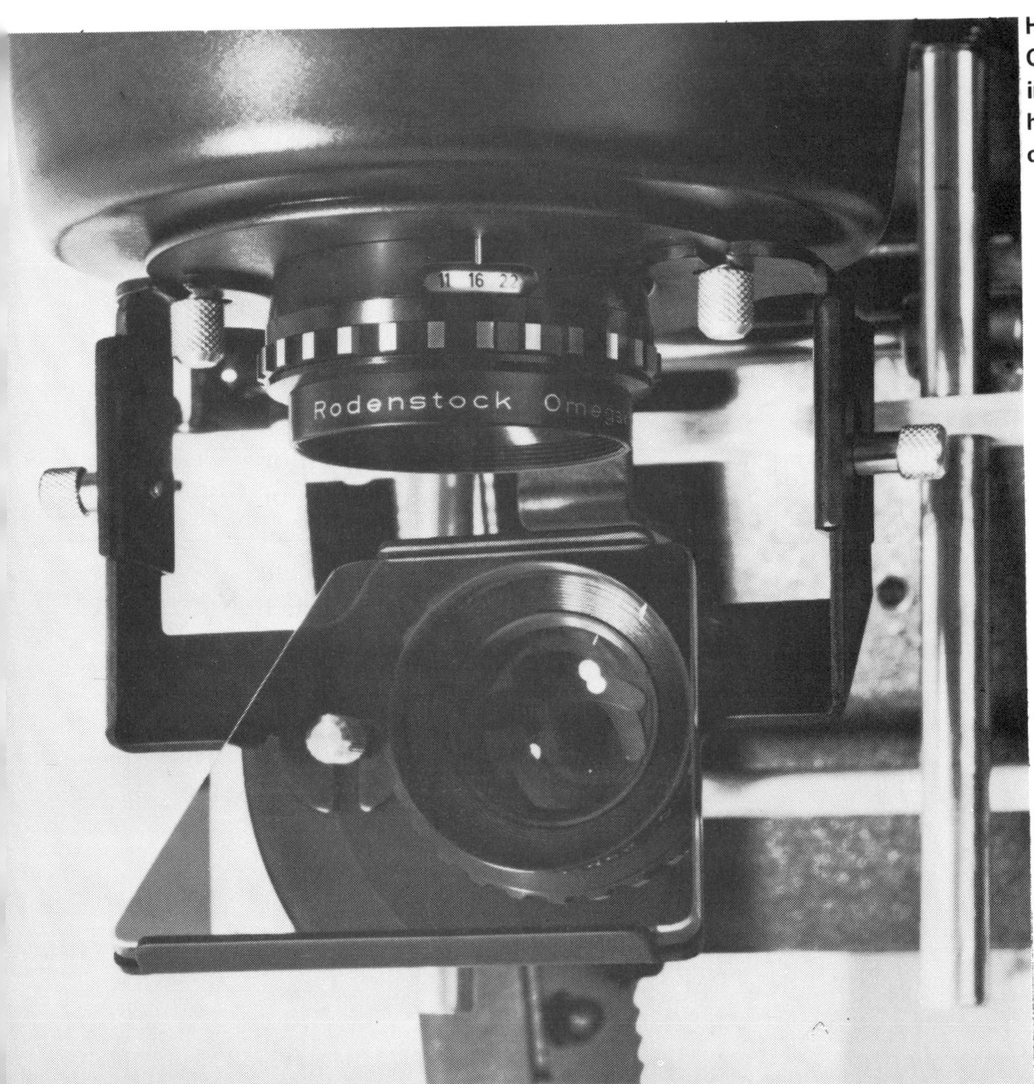

Horizontal projection attachment for Omega enlargers allows you to project an image onto a wall for oversize prints. Lamp house remains in its normal vertical orientation.

2. Expose the print.

3. Cover half the emulsion side of the print with the mesh liner. *Bend the print in half so that the emulsion side faces inward toward the liner.* Don't crease the emulsion. Prints 20x30 or less do not require bending.

Roll the doubled print into a cylinder, starting at the bent edge. Be careful not to crease this edge.

4. Slide the rolled paper and liner into the tank.

5. Pour about 32 ounces of Kodak Photo-Flo solution into the tank. Use concentration recommended by Kodak.

6. Holding the tank horizontally by the end caps, roll it continuously in the hands and rock it from side to side. This basic operation is performed at each subsequent step.

7. Soak for at least 2 minutes and return the Photo-Flo to its container.

8. Pour in the developer and repeat step **6** for the length of time determined by the test strip.

9. Pour out the developer and pour in a stop bath. Repeat step **6**. In this and all subsequent operations use the solutions for the length of time recommended by the suppliers.

10. Pour out the stop bath and pour in a hypo fixer-hardener. Repeat step **6.**

11. Pour out the hypo fixer-hardener and pour in a hypo neutralizer. Repeat step **6.**

12. Remove print from tank and wash in a bathtub. Wash as recommended by hypo neutralizer supplier.

Kodak makes Kodak Mural Paper in large rolls which you may cut to the size you desire. They also make large rolls of Polycontrast and Kodabromide if you prefer these papers. Exposures will vary from paper to paper but the processing remains the same. Mural-size prints can be very impressive in your home or office and are well worth the effort.

Mounting a mural is a bit different than mounting an 8x10 or 11x14. The support must be rigid such as Masonite or other fiberboard. The print is mounted wet and should be done following the wash process . . . or else you rewet it if it has dried. The print should be slightly larger than the board used as a mount and trimmed later for precise fit. A piece of paper such as brown butcher paper is cut to the size of the mural print to be mounted to the back of the print support to keep the support from bowing when the mural print dries and shrinks. I prefer to use a fixed, washed sheet of unexposed mural paper on the back of the support so that pressure from shrinkage is equal on both sides. Elmer's or Wilhold Glue diluted five parts glue to one part water is applied to the support with a paint roller or wide paint brush. Apply the glue evenly and thinly and position the backing paper. Use a print roller or squeegee to flatten the paper and remove air bubbles. Repeat the procedure on the other side using the mural print. Remove any of the glue from the face of the print now while it's still wet. Trim the excess paper with a razor blade or X-acto knife so that it is flush with the mount support and set the whole package aside to dry. It's a simple procedure, but take your time.

Murals—When you want to make large prints and don't want the hassel of making big trays, consider a Maxwell Photo-Mural Tank. Kodak paper comes in 30-, 40-, and 54-inch-wide rolls 30-, 100-, and 250-feet long. You just cut off the length you need and expose it with your enlarger—which you may have to swivel so it projects onto the floor or the wall. The paper gets rolled and placed in the tank for processing. Then you mount the finished print and hang it where your friends will be amazed.

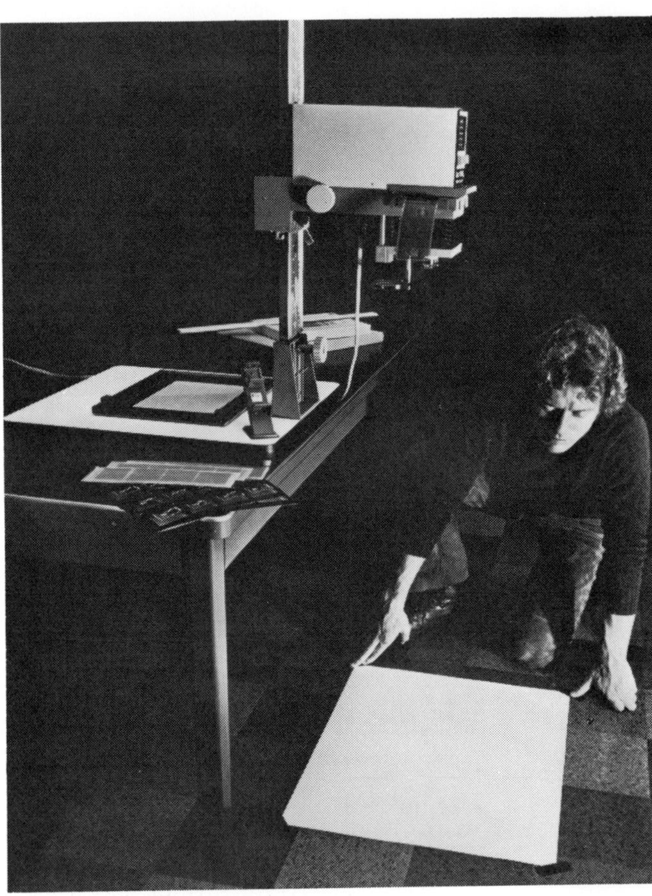

Here a Durst enlarger has been pivoted on its support column to allow projection onto the floor. Tape is being used to hold the paper in position and to ensure the paper stays flat. Clamp the baseboard or weight it so it can't tip when you do this.

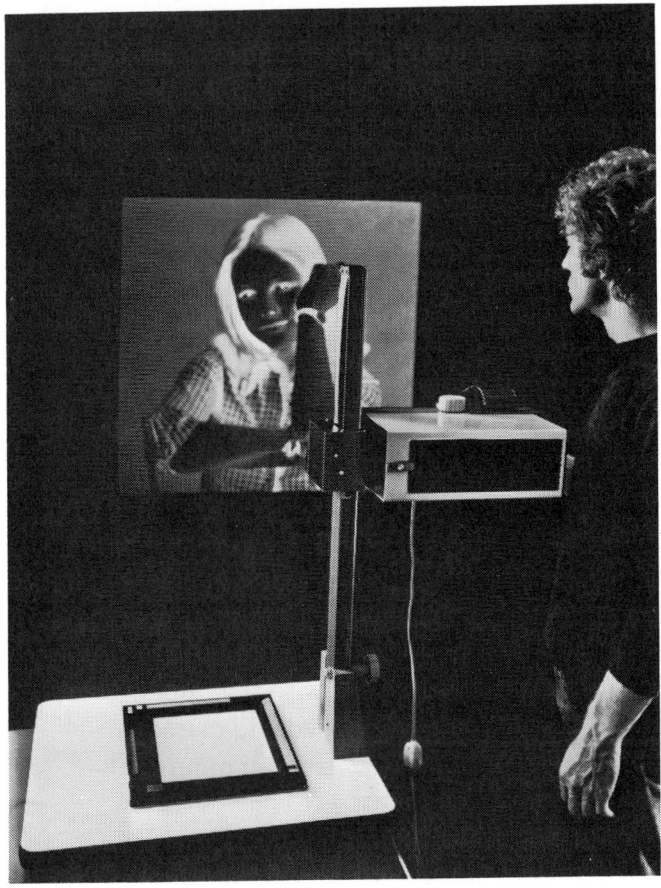

Some enlarger housings can be twisted for horizontal projection. This Durst enlarger is being used to project an image onto the wall. Make sure there is enough weight on the baseboard to avoid any possibility of tipping the enlarger onto the floor, or, clamp the baseboard to the table, if you prefer.

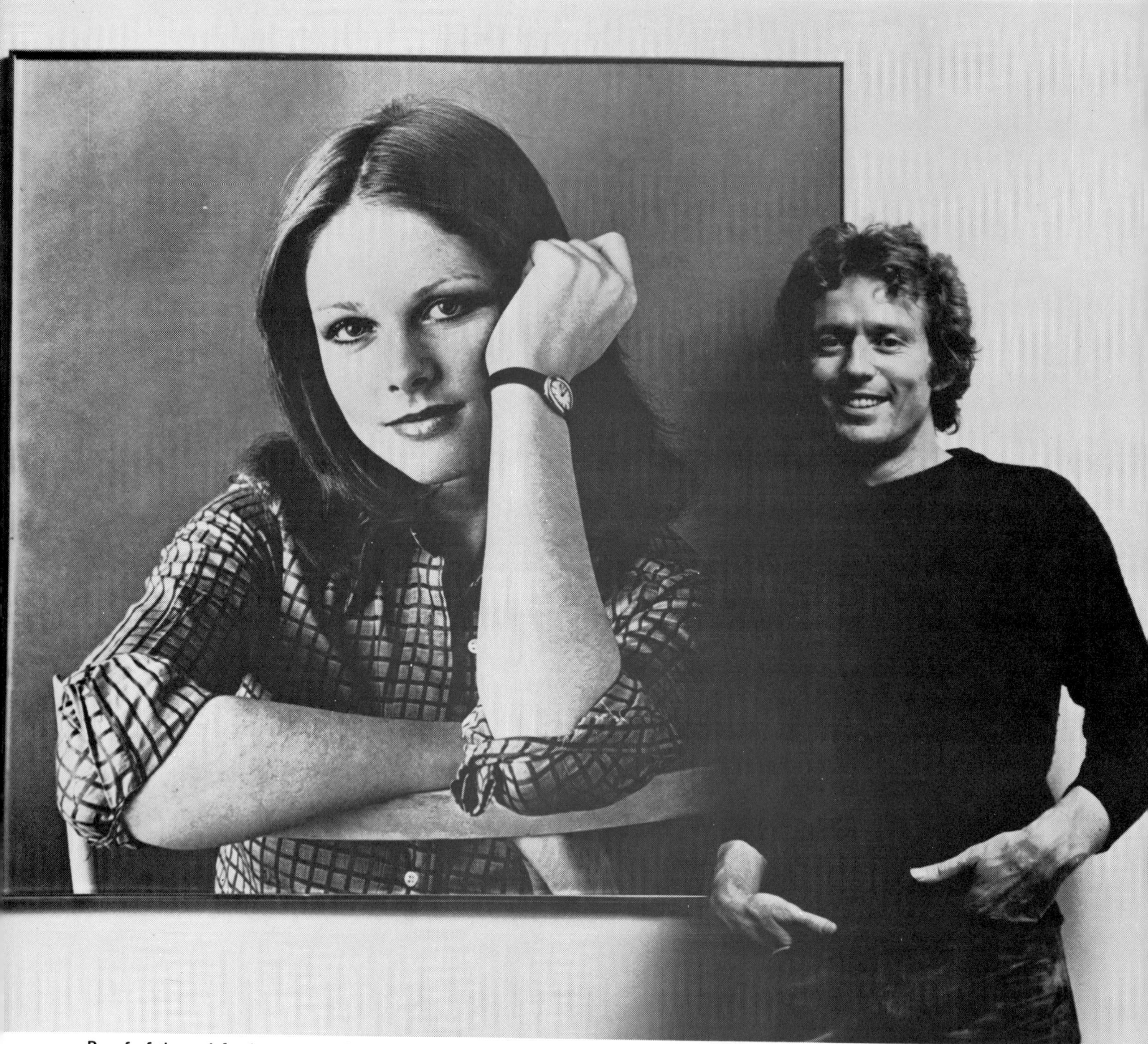

Proof of the satisfaction you get from making prints is being able to show off big ones. These make ideal decorations for your home or office—and great gifts for friends. Photography is satisfying fun.

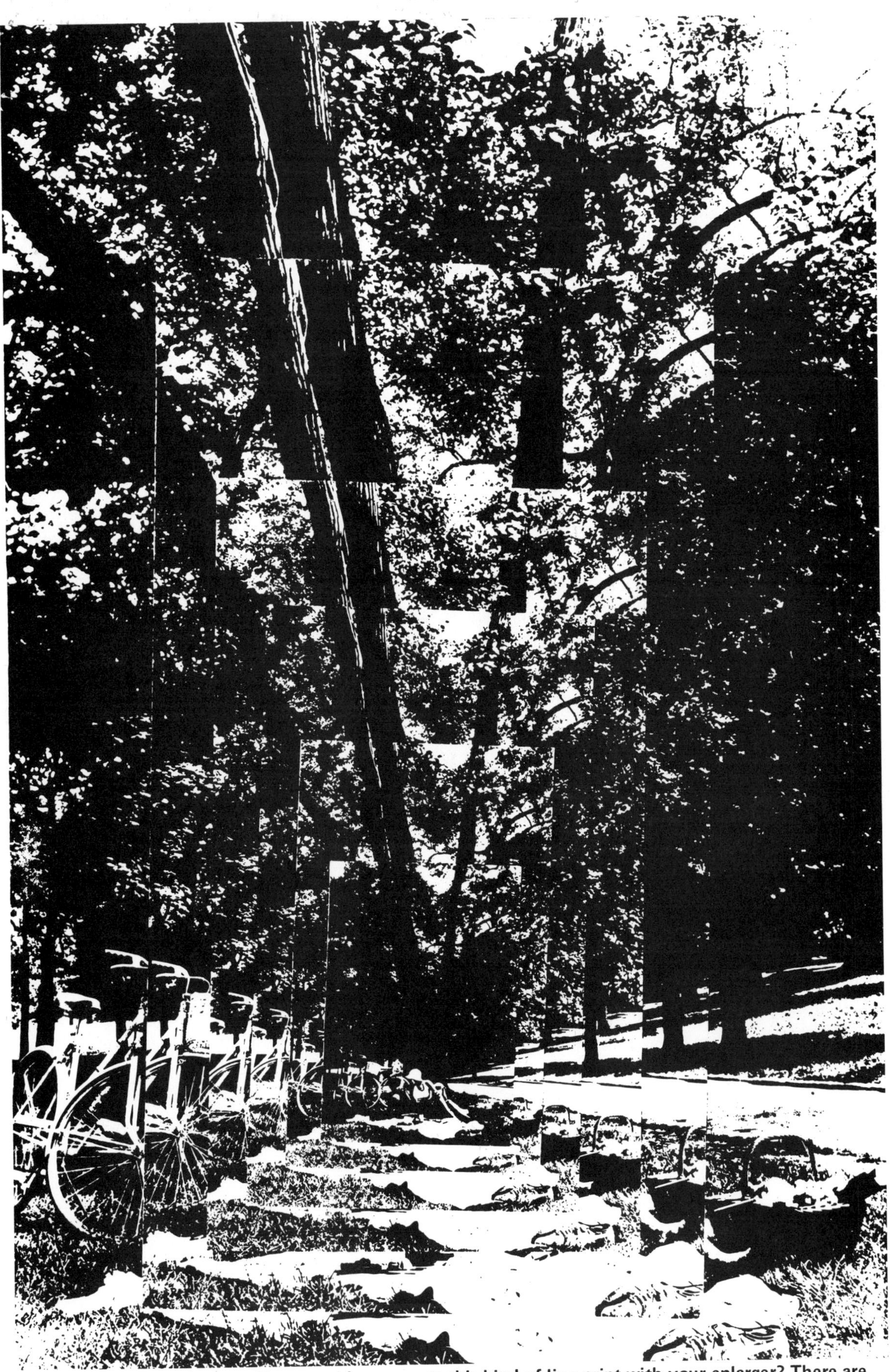

More darkroom tom-foolery. How would you create this kind of line print with your enlarger? There are six different magnifications and exposures on this print, supplied by the Durst folks.

Drying, Spotting, Retouching & Mounting

One of the most important parts of the photographic process is print finishing. The most heroic efforts in the darkroom can go for nothing if the end result is below par due to print finishing. Here we're concerned with drying, mounting and spotting. I also want to touch on negative retouching because it does have an effect on the beauty of the finished product.

PRINT DRYING

I talked a lot about this in the equipment chapter. Even so, there is still more I need to tell you.

Drying prints can be done several ways. They can be air-dried, blotter-dried, or glossed—hot or cold. Air and blotter methods produce a matte or semi-matte finish on ordinary non-RC papers, depending on the surface finish of the print material used. RC glossy papers air-dry to a perfect glossy surface.

Double-weight portrait-type papers dry with a matte finish and may not be glossed. Papers with an F (glossy) surface are intended to be glossed, but may be air or blotter-dried to a semi-matte finish with a nice soft appearance. F is Kodak's designation for glossy-surface paper. Other manufacturers use other letters.

Wooden frames covered with high-quality muslin or plastic-window-screen material provide an excellent means for air-drying. The prints are removed from the wash water and laid on a sheet of glass where they are squeegeed to remove excess water. They are then placed face down on the screens in a dry, dust-free place. Put them face up if you are using RC or color papers. Depending on room temperature and humidity, ordinary papers will dry in two to eight hours; RC papers in 30 minutes to one hour.

Blotting material comes in rolls or sheets in book form. It is made of heavy lint- and chemical-free absorbent paper. Washed prints are squeegeed on a smooth surface to remove excess water, then placed with the emulsion against the blotter paper in the roll or book and set aside to dry. Because air can't circulate around the prints, drying is slower with this method. Non-RC prints dried by air or blotter have a matte finish. They tend to wrinkle along the edges so they don't lie flat. Placing the dried prints under several heavy books or weights will usually correct this fault. They can also be flattened in a dry-mounting press.

Cold glossing non-RC prints requires either a polished-chrome metal sheet or stainless steel, or a sheet of plate glass. Most people who use the cold-gloss principle prefer glass because it is less susceptible to scratch damage than polished chrome or stainless steel. Glass is also easier to clean and less expensive. NOTE: Don't be tempted to use one of your windows as it could break when you apply pressure to the prints with a print roller.

The technique involves soaking the washed print in a glossing solution as described on page 64. One or two minutes of soaking is plenty. Wipe the face of the glossing sheet with water to remove dirt and apply a layer of glossing solution to the clean surface. Remove the prints from the glossing solution and lay them face down on the sheet, side-by-side. Using firm but not hard pressure, squeegee the back of the prints to remove moisture. A thin towel placed between your print roller and the back of the prints will soak up moisture and help keep the prints from tearing as you go over them with the print roller. The emulsion has to contact the smooth surface *completely* or there will be dull spots on the glossy surface when the print dries. Stand the glass or ferrotype plate in a location with little or no air flow and allow the prints to dry. This usually takes several hours. Dry prints will either fall off of the plates or you can peel them off very carefully, revealing a beautiful high gloss.

Drying with heat is fastest and costs the most. If you are drying non-RC glossy prints, a heated dryer creates more problems than any of the other methods.

Flat and drum-type dryers discussed in the darkroom equipment section are both efficient.

You soak the prints in a glossing solution as detailed in the previous cold-glossing discussion. If you are using a flat-type dryer, you squeegee the prints onto ferrotype plates, then place these on the dryer and stretch the apron over the plate to hold it in place. If your ferrotype plate is still warm from drying a previous batch of prints, cool it off before attempting to squeegee more prints in place. Prints slide around on a hot ferrotype plate instead of staying in one place as you squeegee them.

With the drum-type dryer, prints removed from the glossing solution are allowed to drain for a few seconds, then placed on the apron, face toward the drying surface. Built-in rollers squeegee the prints against the polished surface. Prints will dry in 5 to 15 minutes, depending on the amount of heat on the drying surface and motor speed.

Several problems can arise when using heated drying surfaces to dry glossy prints. They will occasionally stick if the dryer surface is dirty, if the heat is set too low or the drum speed is too fast. In that case, slow the drum speed and wait for the prints to make another revolution.

When prints stick to a dirty or scummy surface, great care must be taken to remove them. Do not scrape them off with a sharp instrument! That destroys the print and also causes serious damage to the polished drying surface. Polished chrome or stainless steel is highly susceptible to scratches. Once the surface is scratched, any print glossed in contact with the scratch will bear its imprint.

Stuck prints must be soaked off using a photographic sponge or soft cloth full of water. Let the dryer or ferrotype plate cool off before you attempt this. Don't expect the print to come off intact. Some emulsion will usually stick. Once the prints are soaked off, clean the drying surface using warm water and a soft cloth to apply a coat of cake-type Bon Ami cleanser. When it dries, remove the residue with a soft polishing cloth.

Another problem in using drum-type equipment is uneven drying, caused by a too-low heat setting or a too-fast drum speed. As the print begins to clear the apron the leading edge may be dry and have a high gloss but due to improper settings, the print has not yet had time to dry completely and part of the print remains stuck to the drying surface. When this happens, the print will free itself from the drum in sections and there will be definite creasemarks where the separate areas finally dry. This gives a very unpleasant appearance on the print surface. When this happens, the print should be soaked again in glossing solution and redried at a higher heat setting and/or a slower drum speed. Don't get heavy-handed when increasing the temperature setting. Uneven drying which appears as small round spots with a dull appearance can be caused by too much heat. When the print touches the drying surface and makes a sizzling sound, you are boiling the water, producing bubbles between the print surface and glossing surface which will cause uneven drying.

At times you may find your prints have an "orange-peel" appearance on the gloss. This is also caused by too little heat or too high a drum speed. This appearance is corrected by redrying in the same manner as above.

Dirt particles on the drying surface cause small indentations on the face of the print. This can only be avoided by always making sure the polished surface is completely free of foreign material. Chances are, these indentations on a print cannot be eliminated because they are physical impressions in the emulsion.

Irregular unglossed areas are very seldom found on prints dried with drum-type equipment. Flat, single or double-surface dryers will at times produce patchy spots with a dull-matte appearance. This is caused by poor contact between the print and the drying surface. Care should always be taken to insure that the print is firmly squeegeed onto the ferrotype plates. The cure is resoaking in glossing solution and drying again.

Prints can also be matte-dried on flat or drum-type dryers by placing the emulsion away from the drying surface. You should not attempt to dry glossy or matte RC prints on a heated dryer unless a layer of cloth separates the paper from the heated surface.

Let me point out the importance of thorough washing of the print after the fixing bath. Any hypo left in the print will be transferred to the apron on the drying equipment. This causes ugly brown stains on the apron material which can contaminate other prints dried later. Hypo on the apron material transferred to a thoroughly washed print can cause that print to become stained as time goes by.

Even if your washing and drying technique is faultless, remove and clean your dryer apron every three or four months if the equipment gets considerable use. Don't throw the apron in your home washing machine because it will undoubtedly shrink and you may not get it back on the dryer. The material should be dry-cleaned. Don't be upset with your local dry-cleaner when you get the apron back and still see the stain marks. The chemical residue will have been removed, but those brown stains are permanent reminders of your carelessness.

As you use your dryer you will find the apron will shrink and possibly not completely cover the drying surface as it did when it was new. Replacement aprons are available from either your camera store or the dryer manufacturer at a reasonable price. I'd replace the apron after about a year's use to ensure you have the benefit of the total drying surface. A print on the drying surface but not covered completely by the apron will probably not gloss well on the portion that is uncovered.

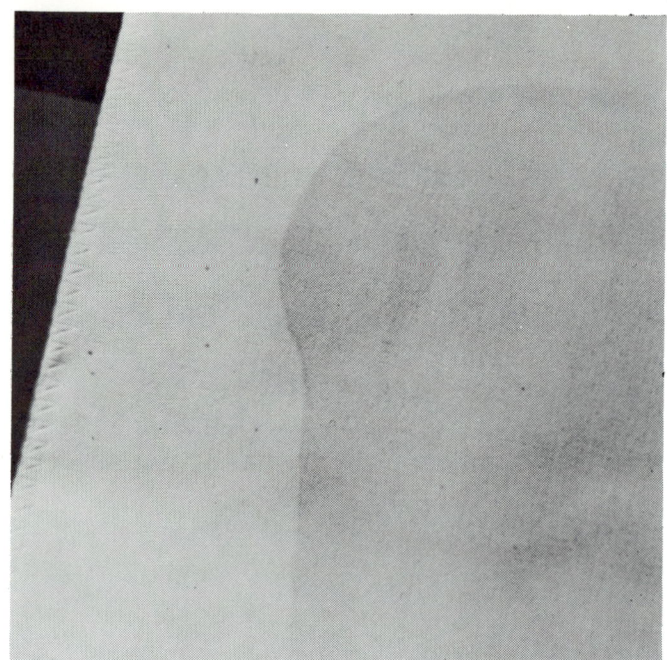

Stains on drying aprons are caused by insufficiently washed prints. Dry-cleaning the apron probably won't remove the stains.

Drying RC Papers—Resin-coated paper, generally called RC paper, has a plastic material as a base. The advantages are that the prints require much less fixing and washing time because the base does not absorb the chemicals, the print is much more durable and less susceptible to damage. But, as with many plastic materials, it is easily damaged by exposure to high heat.

RC prints are best air-dried. When the print is removed from the wash water, a soft photographic sponge can be used to remove excess water. The print can then be laid emulsion side up, on a lintless bath towel and allowed to dry at room temperature. Or, dry them face up on plastic screens. Drying time is normally quite short.

This material dries with a natural gloss which may be increased to some degree by using a low heat source such as a hair dryer to pass warm air over the print surface. This also reduces drying time to two or three minutes and may improve the gloss. Don't try to dry RC prints on regular high-heat drying equipment. It's likely the material will melt and adhere to the drying surface and become impossible to remove. If you do most of your darkroom work during summer months, or live in a tropical climate, walk outside with your washed print and wave it in the warm breeze for two to three minutes and your drying is complete. This limits you to drying only two prints at a time unless you have several friends with empty hands who don't mind standing in public and waving pictures at each other.

Drying Color Prints—Color prints are usually made on RC paper and dried as described in the preceding paragraphs.

Color prints may be dried in the same drying equipment used for black-and-white. The emulsion of the color material is thicker than b&w and more sensitive to heat. Therefore, it must be dried at a lower temperature and at a slower drum speed or for a longer period of time.

If you want to gloss-dry non-RC color papers, you are in for a hassle! Drum dryers must have their drums really polished and waxed. If the drum is not absolutely perfect, the emulsion will stick to the drum—no if's, and's, but's or maybe's—it's gonna stick! Drum dryers sold for color use are terribly expensive as compared to those for b&w because the drum has to be of a lot higher quality to allow drying color prints without sticking. If you have some of the older non-RC glossy paper, find a color dryer you can borrow to dry them on. Otherwise, air-dry them face up on plastic screens or in a blotter roll and forget about the high gloss. You'll be glad you did!

PRINT SPOTTING

Print spotting is what you do to eliminate white spots on the print caused by dust, lead, stippled pinholes or any foreign material on the negative at the time of enlargement. It is simply applying dyes to the emulsion side of the dry finished print. One of the best dyes is Spotone, manufactured by Retouch Methods Co., Chatham, New Jersey. Your camera store has it.

Spotone comes in six dye shades labeled: 0, 1, 2, 3, B and S. Instructions tell which shades to mix to match your printing paper tones. You mix the liquid dyes as recommended and apply them to the print emulsion with a brush. You'll need six sable brushes in sizes 000 to 3.

The secret of effective print spotting is *not* to attempt to cover each white spot with a single dye application. Patience will be rewarded. Begin by dipping your brush in the dye mixture, then diluting in a few drops of clean water. Apply the brush tip to the print with a smooth, gentle touch, taking care to avoid brushing over the edge of the white spot to be eliminated. If you brush over the edges, you add dye where the print already has the correct tone and requires no further darkening. In this case, the original white spot remains proportionately lighter and nothing will be gained.

It takes several seconds for the print emulsion to swell from the fluid and accept the dye. Too concentrated a dye solution may suddenly be absorbed by the print emulsion and produce a dark spot which may be troublesome to remove. *Build up dye saturation slowly.* After working with one particular spot, move to another and allow the dye to set in the first spot. Return to each spot later and add a bit more dye until the offending white matches the tone and density of the surrounding area. THEN STOP! Don't give the spot one more dab for good measure. It will usually be the last straw—the one step beyond.

If you find it necessary to spot the surface of a glossed print, you'll find it helpful to dilute the

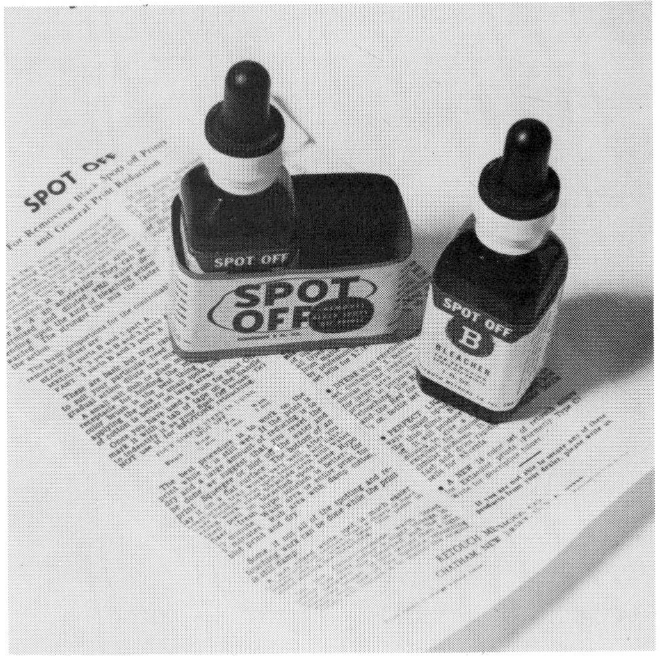

In case you missed a pinhole with the stippling tool, you can save the day with Spot Off. Follow directions packed with the bottles and remember to re-wash the print to avoid any further bleaching.

Spotone dyes are used to cover white spots on prints caused by dust. Apply it with a fine-point brush, letting the dye density build up slowly. The manufacturer provides instructions about how to mix the dyes for a perfect match with the paper you are using.

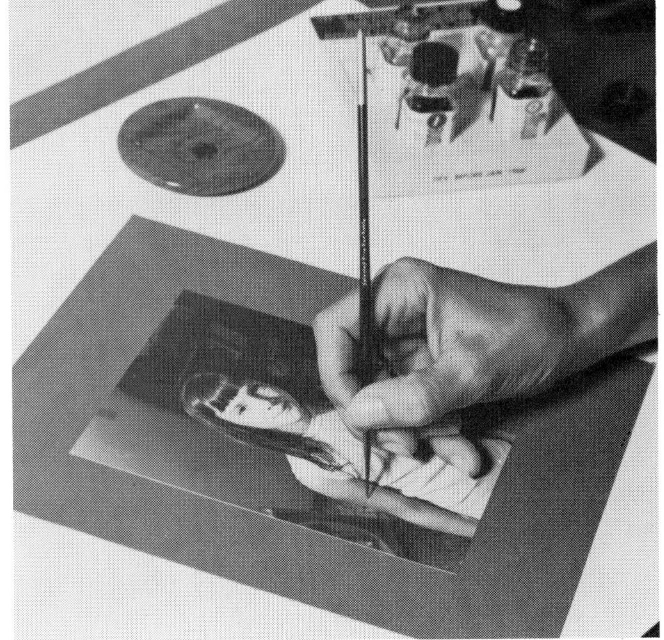

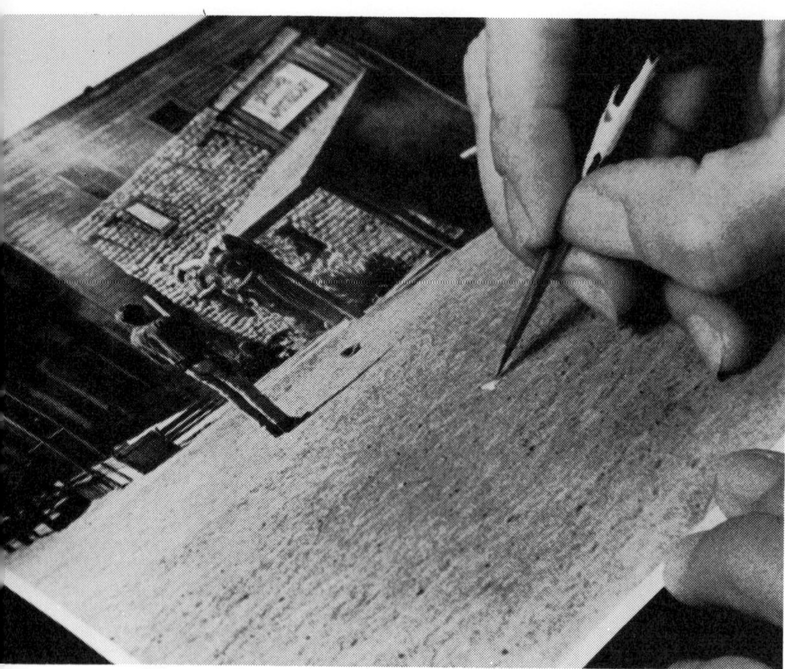

When dying a pin-hole or white spot, work in from the edges, taking care to stop while it still looks just a bit light, especially on large spots.

KEEP THE ETCHING KNIFE SHARP! A dull blade may damage the negative beyond repair. Use a stand magnifier. Make frequent test prints to be sure that too much emulsion hasn't been removed.

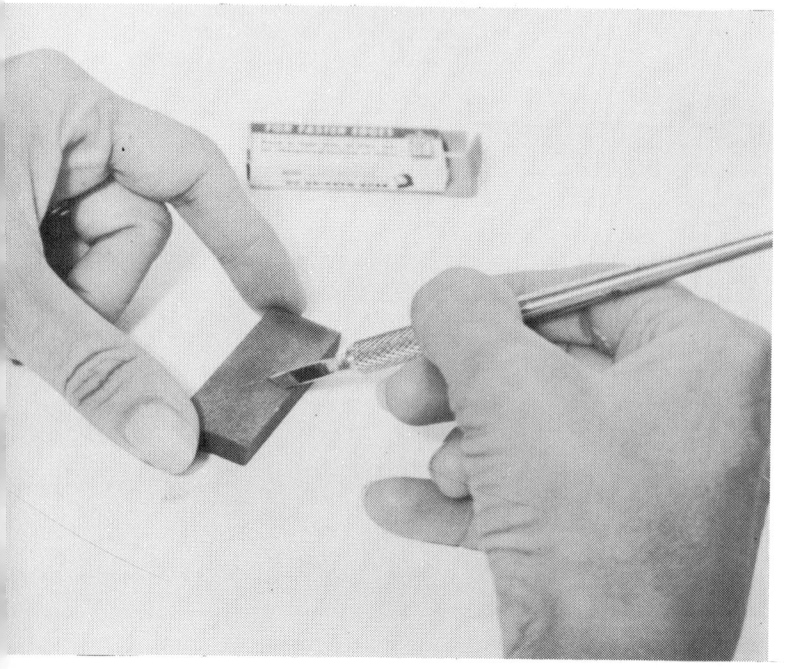

dye on the brush with a few drops of 1% acetic-acid solution rather than clear water. This allows the emulsion to swell and accept the dye more easily.

When spotting prints made with RC paper the brush must be almost dry. If an area does not want to accept the spotting color, wipe the entire surface of the print with the acetic-acid solution and then proceed to do your spotting. This may give a glossy print an unglossed semi-matte surface which I'll tell you how to fix in just a minute.

A word of caution: Don't attempt to spot glossed prints any more than necessary as the spotted areas lose the slick finish and give the appearance of poor drying technique.

Should you become carried away with this artistic magic and find you've gone too far on a spot, you may be able to save the print anyway by removing dye. The makers of Spotone recommend you try eight drops of ammonia mixed with four ounces of water, applied by brush and the excess blotted. Follow with plain water and blot. You may be one of those fortunate individuals who can remove the dye by wiping immediately with a finger dampened with saliva. In either case, good luck!

Hopefully, you have built up the dye to just what you want and your problem with white spots is cured. Now you may find you have a small black pinpoint or two which you wish to eliminate. The makers of Spotone offer a product called Spot Off for such situations. Spot Off is a pair of bottles labeled A and B. B is a bleach. A is an accelerator and these liquids are mixed according to the instructions included and used for immediate bleaching or slight lightening of large areas. Once the mixture is applied, a cotton ball soaked in water and rubbed over the treated area will stop the bleaching action. This product is effective, but can be difficult to control if care isn't exercised. After using Spot Off, be sure to wash the print again, then dry it. Then use Spotone to spot the light area to the desired tone.

Color prints may be spotted by using Kodak Retouching Colors. Apply them in the same manner as Spotone is applied to a black-and-white print. Care must be taken when spotting color prints to make sure that the dyes are mixed to correspond to the coloring of the area around the spot to be covered.

PRINT ETCHING

Tiny black spots can also be removed from the surfaces of some photographic papers by etching the spot with a sharp knife. You can also lighten or remove lines and skin blemishes from prints by etching. I find a pointed X-acto blade or even a sharp single-edged razor blade works fine for this. You have to be super careful because it is so easy to lift the thin emulsion off the paper base. When you do it, you have an ugly spot which is just about impossible to fix. The idea is to use the knife point to scrape away a portion of the emulsion thickness—but don't dig completely through the emulsion into the paper base. The knife is lightly drawn across the spot in a series of strokes, each one slightly separated from its neighbor. This reduces the density of the spot so it is almost not noticeable. If more is needed, go over the spot in a different direction, perhaps at right angles to your original scrapes. Be gentle. Take it easy. Don't wreck your print. You can nearly always get rid of spots this way, especially on glossy paper or glossy paper dried to a semi-matte finish. It is more difficult on matte papers because the emulsion seems to be less tolerant of these scrapes. Practice on scrap prints and test strips to get good at this.

What you do with etching is break up the black spot or offending area into a series of black dots on a white background. This makes the dot less noticeable because it takes on a gray appearance to the eye. The more scratches you put across the area, the less black remains, and the lighter the spot becomes. The black which remains is still just as black as ever, but you don't care because you eye doesn't see it that way. If you make the spot too light and you haven't gone completely through the emulsion, go back with the Spotone to get it right.

I wouldn't try to etch *color* prints with a blade!

REPAIRING SURFACE DAMAGE

If you have made corrections by spotting or etching the surface of a glossy print, these corrections may be very noticeable. One way to

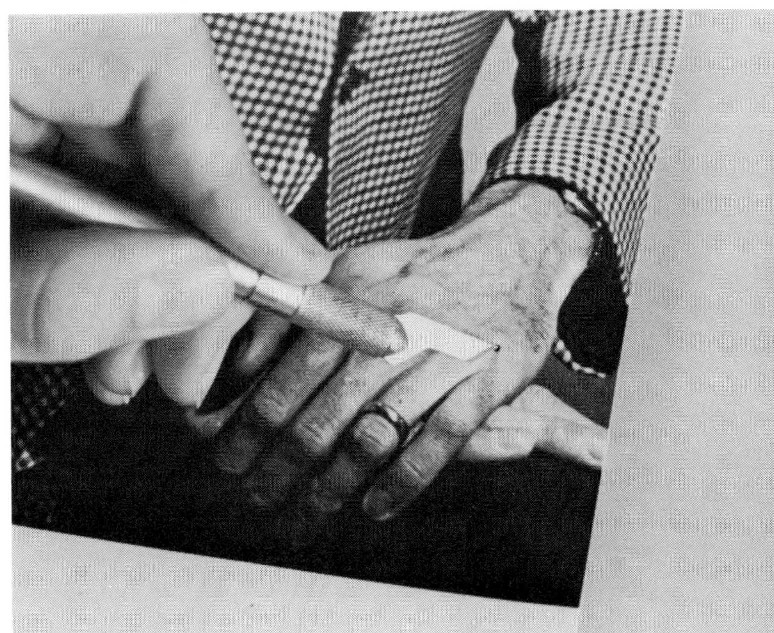

A razor blade or SHARP X-acto knife can be used for print etching to remove small black spots. Draw the blade smoothly towards you. Take the spot off a bit at a time, never dig at it. The slight blemish left may be covered by a coating of matte or glossy spray applied to the entire print.

improve the situation is to spray the surface of the print with a glossy lacquer-type finish such as Krylon Crystal-Clear protective spray. This may be available in your camera store, but if you don't find it there, try an art supply place. Krylon is also available in a semi-gloss or matte finish which can be used to repair the surfaces of matte prints. These finishes dry quite fast but I recommend you spray them on in a well-ventilated area, then allow them to dry where dust won't fall on the surface.

REDUCING DENSITY

A negative which has been overexposed, overdeveloped or possibly both, may be saved by the use of a chemical bleach known as a reducer. Reducers remove some of the silver from the negative enabling you to change contrast, obtain some detail in dense blocked-up areas, eliminate detail where it is not wanted, darken the sky and can get rid of small areas of negative fog. It can be of great help, but don't rely on a reducer to save you always. It is an aid which can help you during those rare times when you weren't paying attention when making an exposure or while processing your film. It will not make a really bad negative good, but it should make it printable.

The most readily available product of this type is Kodak Farmer's Reducer. It is supplied in powder form to make solutions A and B. Solution A is potassium ferricyanide and solution B is sodium thiosulfate, which as you remember, is hypo. When A and B are mixed together, the solution has a very short life, so don't mix them until you are ready to start work.

Use the solution in a small white tray so you can easily see the reduction take place. Follow the instructions in the chemical packet carefully and watch what you are doing. The reducing action takes place quickly so don't let your attention wander. It's better to reduce a bit less than you want than to go too far.

Small spots on the negative can be reduced by applying the solution to the desired area with a fine brush. By using a brush or cotton swab, you can also reduce areas of a print with the same A and B solution. This can be of great help if you have a print which is a bit dark in the highlights. Try using it to brighten up small bright spots in a print to increase the contrast and add brilliance to the picture.

The chemicals are packed to make one quart. Get some, it's handy.

INTENSIFICATION

Correcting excess density through the use of reducers works well and can be very beneficial when necessary. However, the use of intensifiers is another story. Here you are trying to add to something you are lacking. Thin, underexposed or underdeveloped negatives can be helped to a certain degree by using a chemical agent such as Kodak Chromium Intensifier, which is a solution of potassium bichromate and hydrochloric acid. The prepared chemicals bleach the negative image, which after thorough washing according to the recommendations in the packet, is redeveloped.

With the exception of silver intensifier, all others produce a discoloration of the image. Some reduce the permanency of the negative image over a period of time. All can be hazardous to handle so take care. If you absolutely have to use an intensifier, remember that it works better in cases of underdevelopment than when you have missed out by underexposure. Nothing will build up what wasn't there in the beginning.

Good luck!

NEGATIVE RETOUCHING

Portraits are the most common subjects for retouching and very few portraits are made which cannot be helped some by the addition of a little lead to the negative.

The materials necessary for retouching are:

A good stand magnifier
Lead holders
Leads in Grades 2B to 6H
Fine sandpaper
A negative holder
Retouching fluid
Cotton balls
Stippling tool
Etching knife
Light box
Spotting dyes
Bleach

If your local photo dealer doesn't carry these items, try a good art-supply store. Between the two of them, they should be able to furnish or order everything you need.

Negative retouching can eliminate unwanted blemishes and dark lines from the subject's face. These appear on the negative as spots or lines of decreased density. Retouching lead is used to build

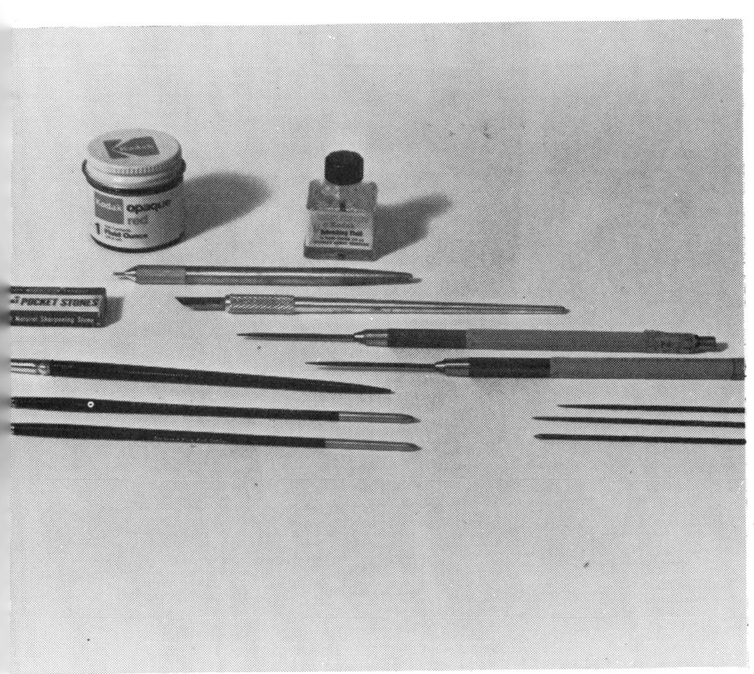
Tools used in retouching negatives and prints: Opaque, retouch medium, stippling tool, etching knife, brushes and lead holders.

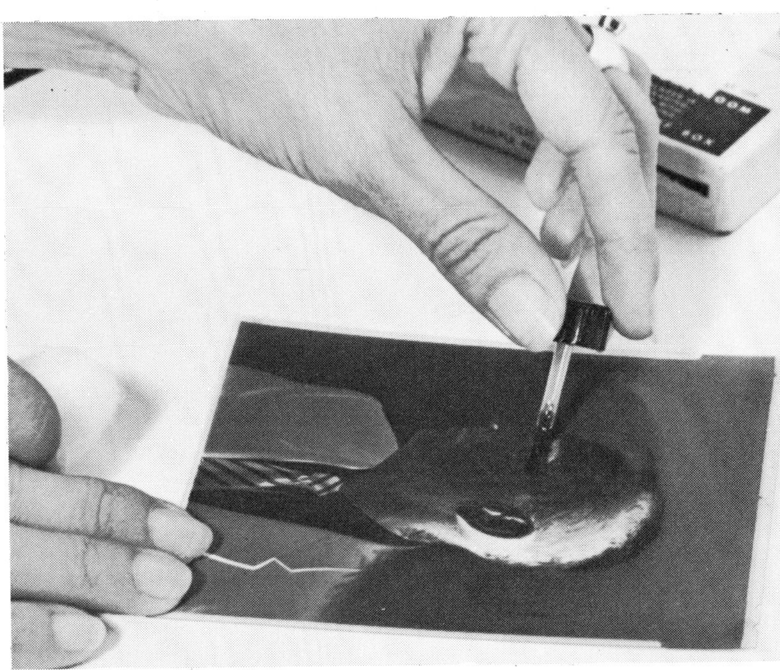
Retouching medium is applied to the emulsion side of the film to provide a "tooth" to which the lead will adhere.

Remove excess retouch medium with a cotton ball. The fluid dries quickly, so don't tarry or it will leave a streaky appearance.

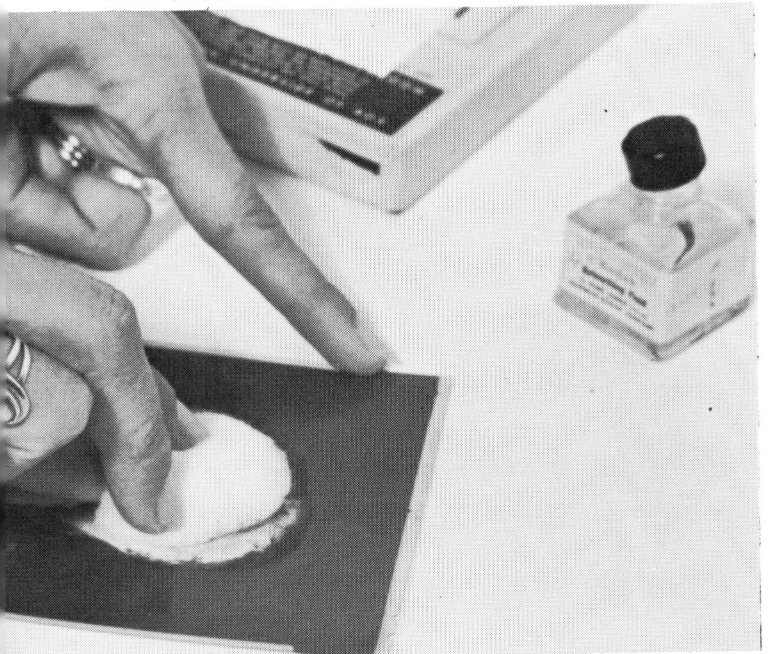

An empty 4x5 box makes an excellent holder for film retouching. In both top and bottom of the box cut an area slightly smaller than the size film you are using.

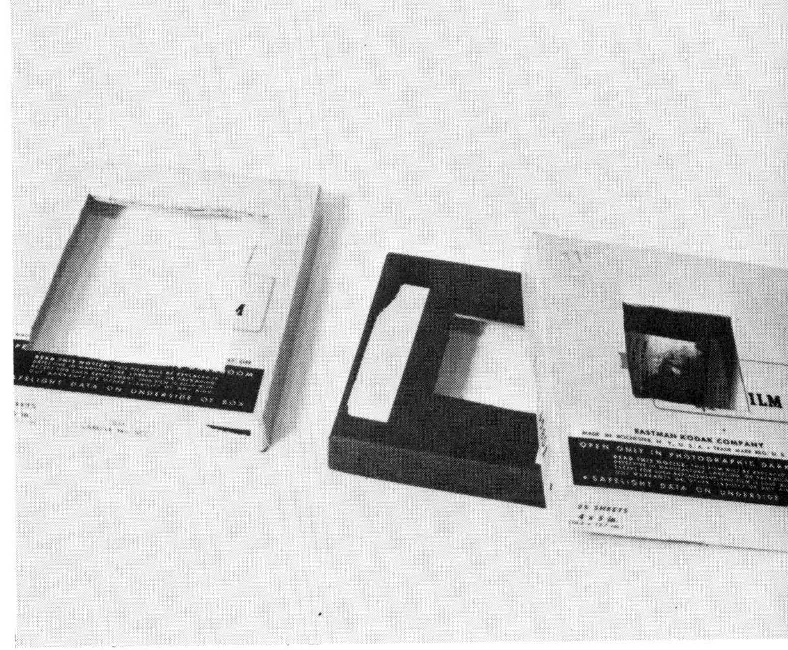

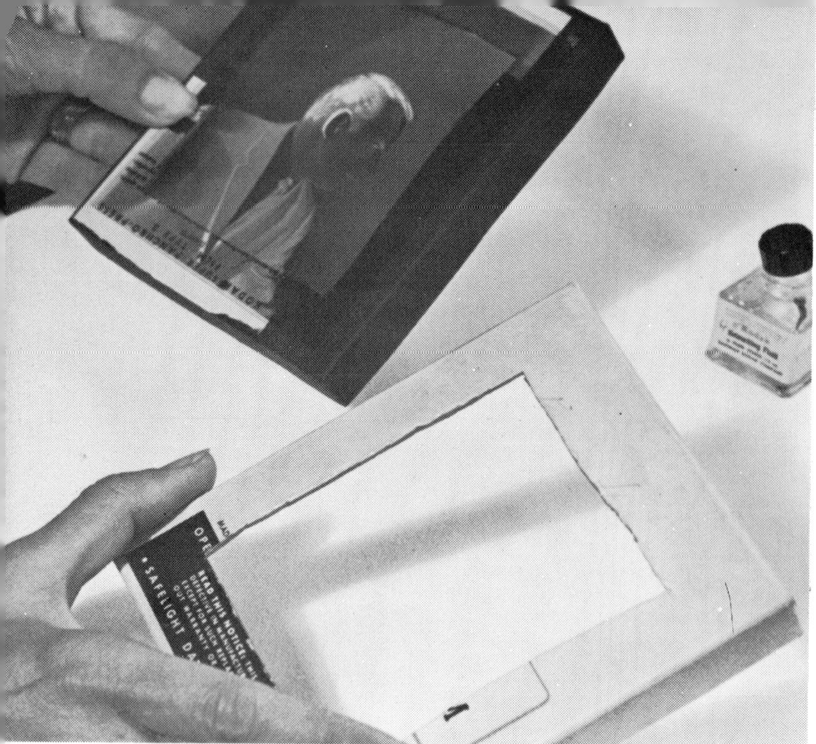

Place the film to be retouched on the back of the bottom half of the "holder" with the emulsion side up, and . . .

up these spots and lines so they have the same density as the surrounding areas. Although the procedure is simple, it requires practice so the applied lead is not noticeable when you print the neg. Poor retouching is worse than no retouching. Today, most people are less conscious of age lines and tend more toward the natural look. Nonetheless, a friend with a temporary blemish at the time the shutter is clicked will appreciate that blemish not showing on the print.

Unless you have a good eye and steady hand, it's terribly hard to retouch a 35mm negative. If you must, take the portrait so the subject's face fills most of the frame and keep your retouching efforts to a minimum. Remember that you'll be printing at considerable magnification and anything you do on the negative may be quite evident unless you are really eagle-eyed and steady-handed.

Lead is applied to the emulsion side of the negative. For it to adhere well, the negative is first coated with a thin layer of retouching fluid to give the emulsion a "tooth" to which the lead will cling. Using the applicator brush, cover the emulsion side with a light coat of the fluid. With a clean cotton ball, gently wipe off the excess, using a circular motion. The fluid dries quickly

. . . cover with the box top. The film will be held secure and flat.

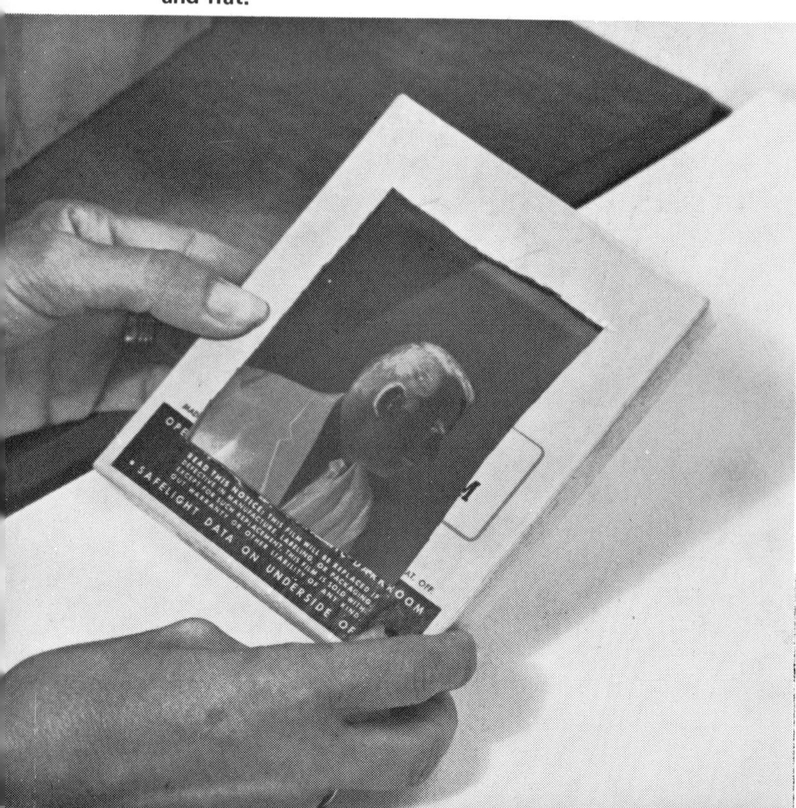

A piece of fine sandpaper folded in half makes an inexpensive and very effective lead sharpener. Move the lead in and out while using a rotating motion. The sharper the point, the smoother the retouching marks will appear.

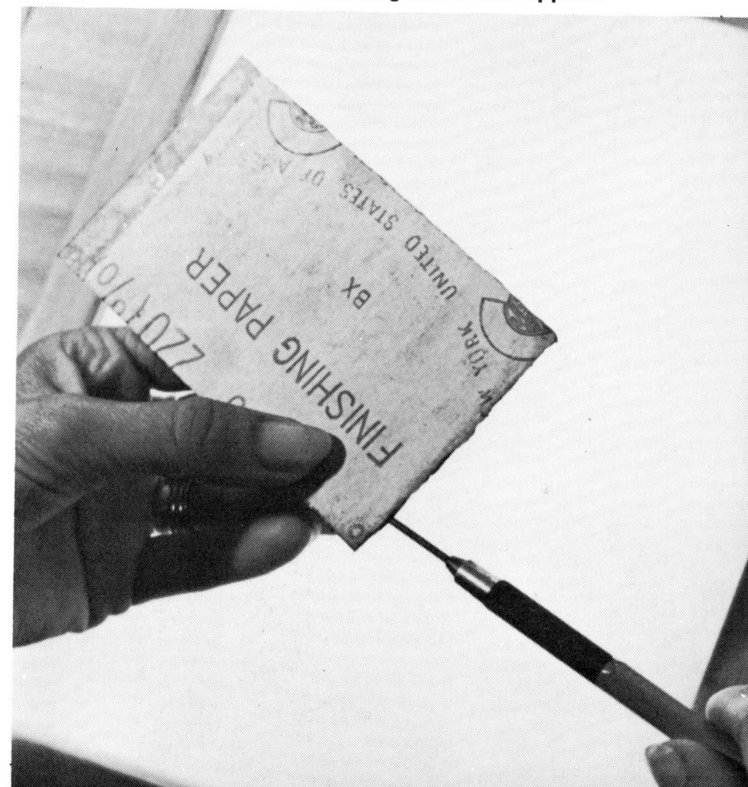

and the surface should appear smooth and even after drying.

An empty 4x5 inch film box with a cut out area slightly smaller than the negative to be operated on serves nicely as a film holder. Place the negative in the holder with the emulsion toward you and lay the whole arrangement on an evenly lighted viewing surface. Tape the negative into the holder with photographic masking tape or ordinary drafting tape.

The lead must be kept extremely sharp during the entire procedure because you are working with delicate thin lines and spots. A piece of fine sandpaper folded in half is your sharpener. Hold the sandpaper between the thumb and index finger while inserting the lead into the fold with a revolving action. This gives the lead a very fine, sharp point. Repeat this often during the retouching.

Using a gentle pressure, apply the lead to the desired area with a continuous figure-8 pattern. Use light strokes and slowly build up the density. Leads marked B are soft and will adhere quickly while the H leads build density slower. When the density of the retouched site matches that of the surrounding area, stop. A quick test print will show how well your lead stayed within the desired area and how smooth the stroke appears. If the lead shows as obvious white lines or blotches, give the negative another application of retouching medium to remove all lead and start over.

With practice you will be better able to judge pressure, stroke and density while using leads. Don't be overzealous and remove too many features from the face. Your friend will thank you for a little visual flattery, but not for changing her or his entire appearance.

PINHOLES

A problem you will encounter somewhere along the line is that of pinholes. Reasons for pinholes have been discussed in a previous chapter, but they still manage to pop up from time to time. These tiny clear dots on the negative print black. It's much easier to deal with them at the negative stage than after they are on the print.

A stippling tool is basically a pen-type holder and a sharp steel needle. You use it by pressing the needle firmly—not vigorously—in the center of the pinhole on the base side of the film. This alters

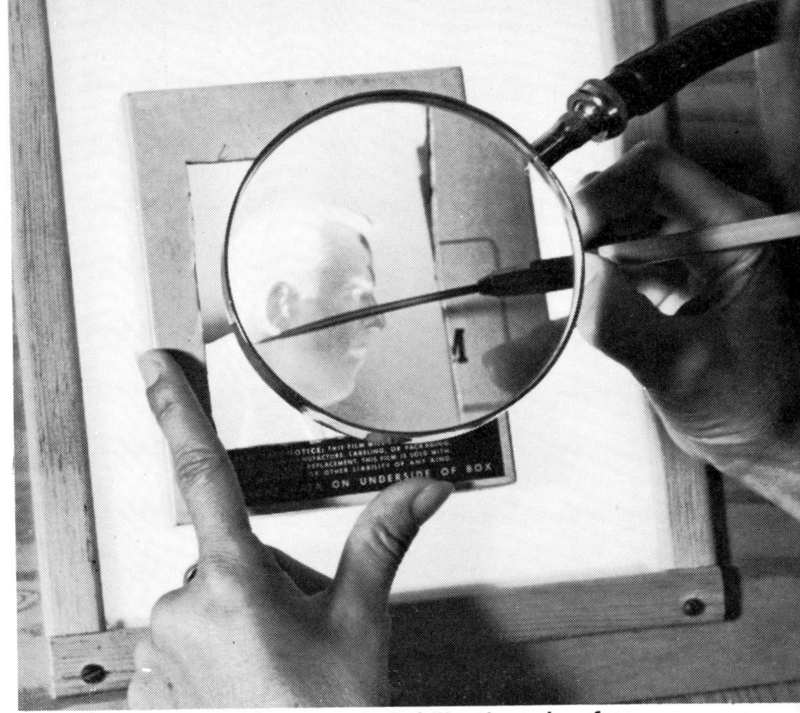

Place the negative holder on an angled illuminated surface and look through your stand magnifier as you apply the lead to the desired area . . .

. . . in an even, continuous figure "8" stroke. Continue this until the lead appears as the same density as the surrounding area. Here's the 8 pattern highly enlarged. Make a quick test print to see how well you did.

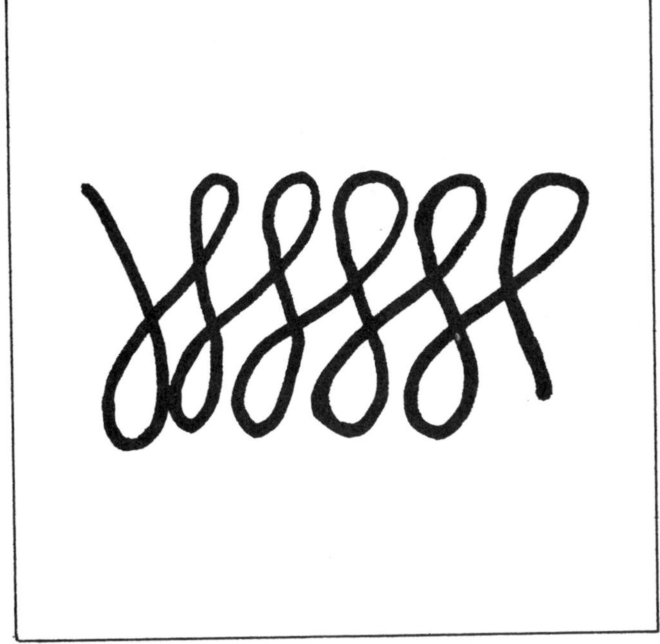

the base surface and changes the direction of the light passing through the film in the enlarger. Now, the pinhole will print as a *white* dot rather than as black. This, as with minor lead-application errors, can be easily taken care of by print spotting.

I always recommend taking as many corrective steps as possible at the negative stage to keep print retouching at a minimum.

ETCHING

An etching knife is a handy tool which, when used incorrectly may have a devastating effect. The knife is used to scrape away emulsion from negative film where areas of gross overexposure occur. These are areas of great density which will appear as stark white, detail-less portions of the print. Etching away some of the excess emulsion allows you to make a print with a more pleasing appearance.

This technique is generally used to eliminate a stray highlighted hair which escaped combing or unusual reflections in eye glasses or eyes. Without having to give it much thought, you should realize you are asking for trouble with this tool in your hand. The knife *must be as sharp as possible* and you have to use an extremely delicate touch. This is tougher than shaving, a nick here won't heal by tomorrow! Go too far or carelessly and you've made yourself a great deal of work on print retouching. Practice on unwanted negatives before you lay it on a once-in-a-lifetime portrait of your mother-in-law!

ADDING DENSITY

Neo-coccine, sold by Eastman as Kodak Crocein Scarlet, is a thin reddish liquid used primarily to lighten shadow areas which would otherwise print too dark or black. It can also be used to add density to a highlight area to add sparkle to a print without destroying detail in the print. It is applied to the emulsion side of the negative, either by brush or cotton swab, depending on the image size to be covered. Apply it directly from the bottle and let it build slowly on the negative. It's wise to make a test print now and then to determine the correct amount of added density. This material is easy to use because it is absorbed slowly by the negative and there's very little danger that you'll overdo it.

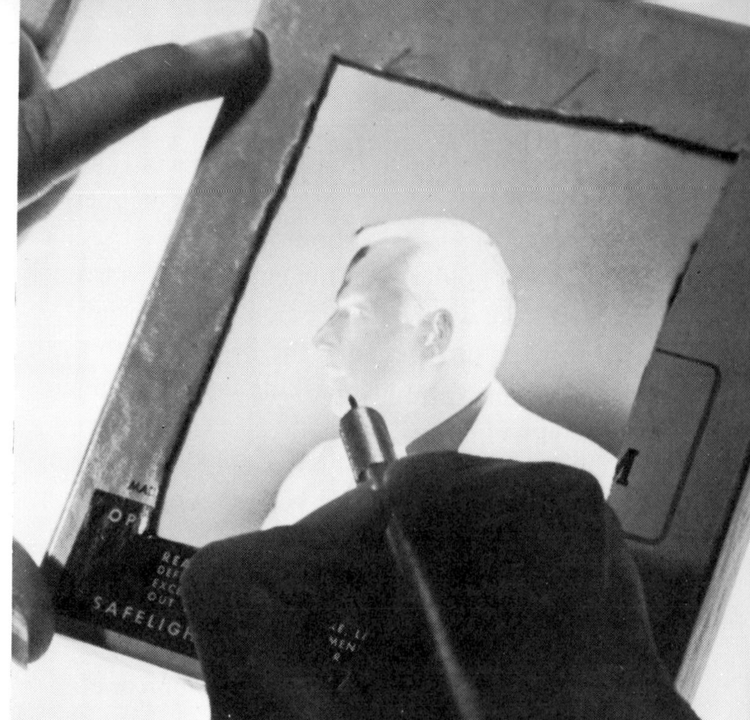

The stippling tool is used on the BASE side of the negative with a firm yet gentle hand. It's a little frightening to be digging holes into the film, but it works wonders eliminating pinholes which would otherwise print as black dots. Take it easy. One punch should do it.

OPAQUE

Kodak Opaque come in either red or black and does just what the name implies. It completely blocks light from passing through the film areas to which it is applied. Opaque is put on the base side of the film, using a brush.

It is most generally used on negatives of extreme contrast to block pinholes or any unwanted object in the scene. Because it is completely light-proof, it is not suited to normal continuous-tone negatives. Opaque is water-soluble and can be washed off if you make a mistake.

COLOR NEGATIVES

Color negatives are retouched the same as black-and-white.

Retouching on color negatives, for the most part, can be done with the same lead as used for black-and-white negatives. Areas of decreased density which need an application of lead do not require addition of color, only of density.

Normally, the only time a color lead will be necessary will be to correct small blemishes on skin areas. A skin blemish will appear as a greenish spot on the negative and a red retouching lead will correct the problem.

It is extremely difficult to use an etching knife on color negatives due to their thicker layered emulsion. If at all possible, try to make the corrections by spotting the print.

PRINT MOUNTING

From time to time, you will make a print which you feel is worthy of display. To display a photograph, mount it on a stiff support. Practically any rigid or semi-rigid material can be used but it's a good idea to choose material made for that purpose. Examples include Strathmore's 100% rag, acid-free Museum Mounting Board and Bainbridge Museum Board. Strathmore board may be available at your camera or art supply store, or write Strathmore Paper Co., Front Street West, Springfield, MA 01089. Charles T. Bainbridge & Sons is at 12-26 Cumberland St., Brooklyn, NY 11205.

Colored poster boards are not good support material because they usually contain dyes which will affect the photograph's permanence in time.

Several materials are available to stick the print onto the support and again, those made for this purpose should be used. Don't use glue for this procedure as it will most surely cause stains or fading in time due to chemical reaction. It has been common practice in the past to use rubber cement for mounting prints and this has been an acceptable method in most cases. Rubber cement, although readily available and easily applied, tends to lack the permanency of some other materials. And, some users say they get stains on their prints after several years.

Dry-mount tissue is the most common material used by professional photographers and your local picture-framing shop which most likely offers print-mounting services. Dry-mount tissue is thin paper coated with a wax-like substance which melts between the print and support when heat is applied. It creates a tough bond.

If you are mounting 8x10 or smaller prints, a regular household flat iron can be used very effectively. The print to be mounted must be completely dry. Do not trim the borders.

A sheet of mount tissue the same size as the print should be "tacked" to the back of the print by a slight pressure with the tip of the iron. Now

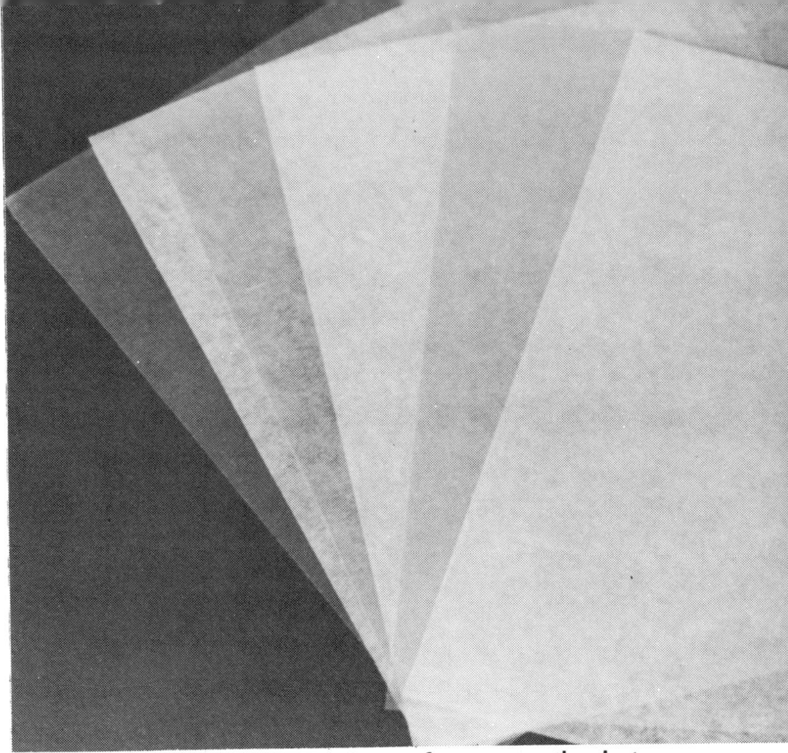

Dry-mount tissue requires heat in one form or another but is the most effective way to adhere a print to a support. It will not chemically affect the print material as will most glues, and is smoother and more permanent than tape. A special low-temperature kind is used to mount RC prints.

Tacking dry-mount tissue is best done with a tacking iron, illustrated on page 151. More readily available is the household flat-iron. Set the heat on *synthetic* and using a figure X, tack the mount tissue to the back of the print. If the tissue sticks to the iron, set the heat control to the next higher setting. RC prints will require a cooler setting. Experiment with scrap prints or test strips to get the temperature right.

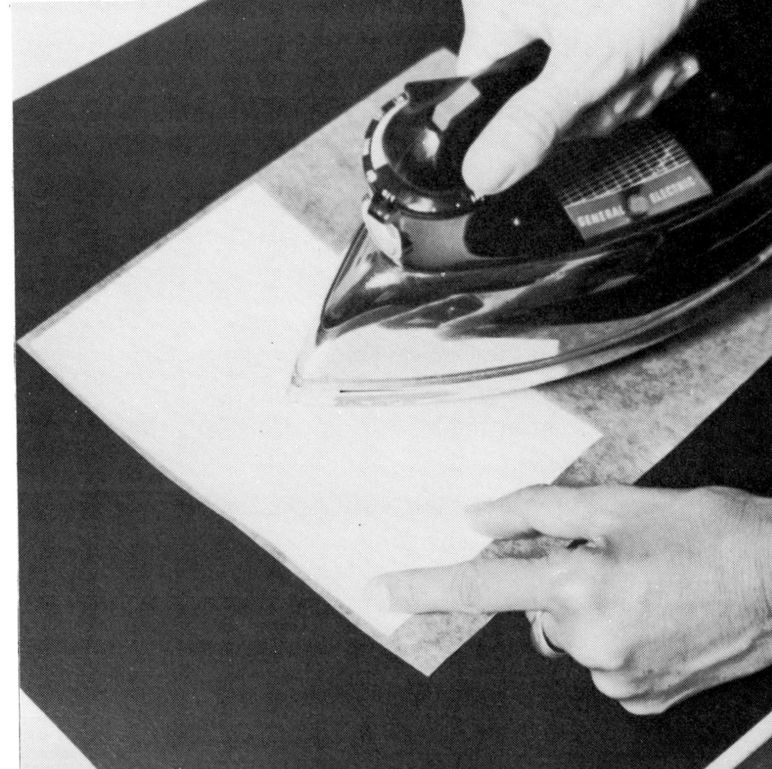

trim the borders, using your darkroom paper trimmer or a sharp X-acto knife and ruler. Because the tissue was tacked to the print, both are trimmed to the same size. This keeps thin strips of mount tissue from extending beyond the edge of the print.

Lay the print face up on the support you have chosen and determine the placement which is most pleasing. Tack down two corners of the dry-mount tissue to the support. Just hold the edge of the print up as you touch the tip of the iron to the tissue. Now your print is positioned.

Double-check the placement of the print on the support. Cover the print with clean paper—or print paper—to protect the print emulsion from direct contact with the flat iron. Firmly go over the entire print area with an even ironing

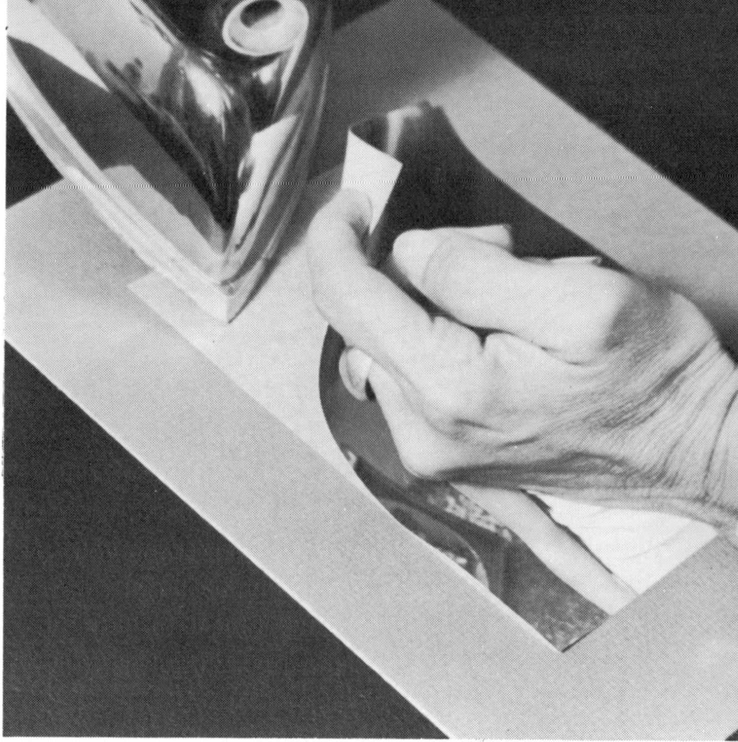

Place the tissue-backed print in position on the support and tack down the two top corners. This holds the print in position during actual mounting.

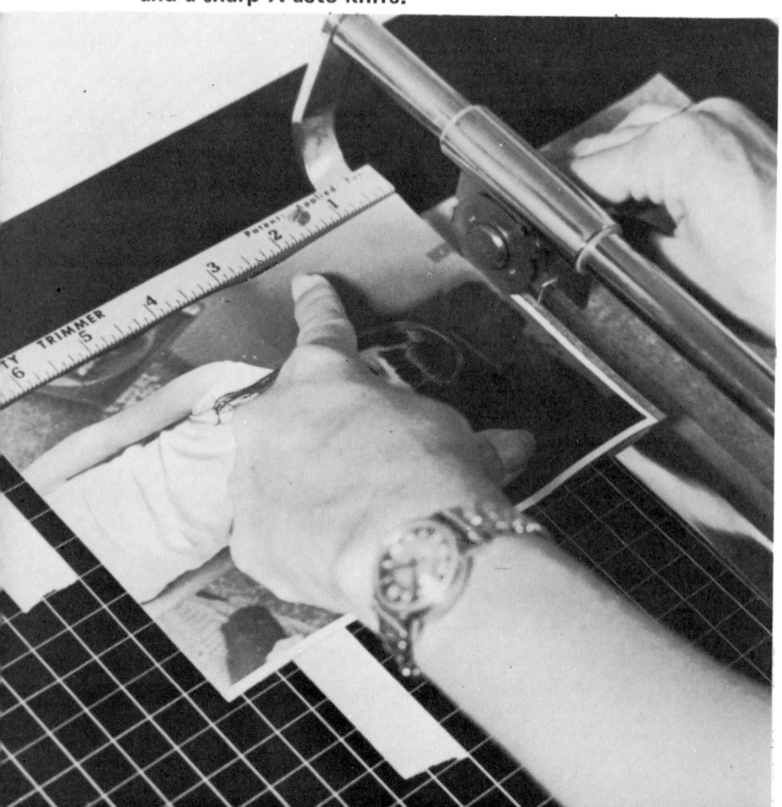

With the tissue tacked to the print, trim the borders using either a photographic paper trimmer or a metal-edge ruler and a sharp X-acto knife.

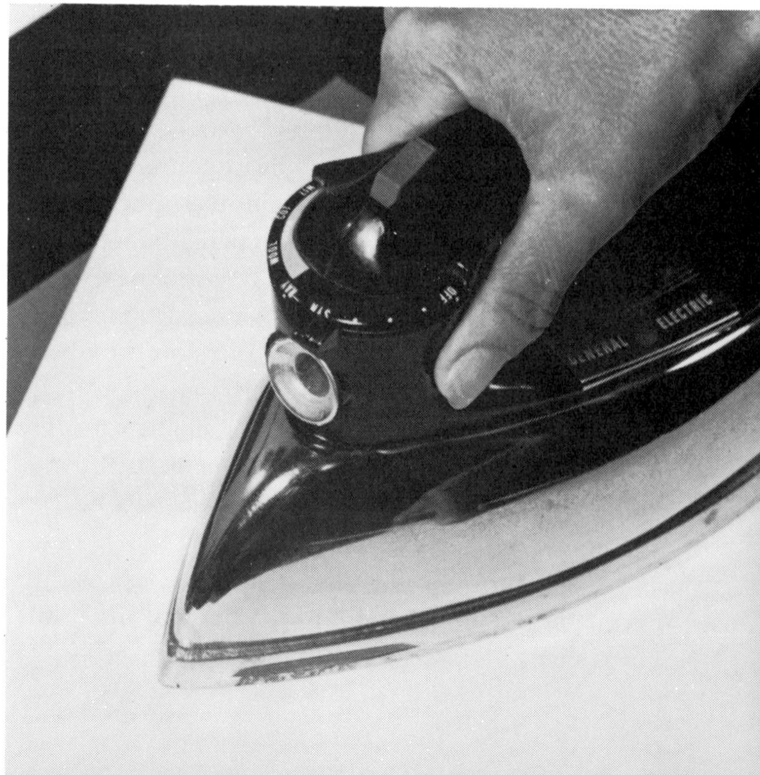

Using a discarded photographic print—one you know was properly washed and dried—a size larger than the print you are mounting—apply heat with an even motion. Don't let the iron set in one spot or you may scorch your picture. Lift the cover paper and check frequently to make sure you are not missing any areas. Put cover-print emulsion against emulsion of print being mounted.
Do a test first with scrap prints when mounting RC prints.

action until the mount tissue has completely melted and the print is in complete contact with the support. This should take about 30 to 40 seconds. If you are mounting double-weight prints, it will take slightly longer to transfer the heat through the print to the mount tissue.

If the tissue doesn't adhere to the support it's because you haven't given the iron sufficient time to transfer heat completely through the print-tissue-support sandwich. The iron should be set in the SYNTHETIC range, a low-heat setting. If your prints are not sticking to the mount, don't just raise the iron to a higher temperature. First try moving the iron more slowly and leave it over the areas of non-stick for a somewhat longer time. Then place large heavy books or other weights atop the mounted print and leave them there until the mounted print has cooled thoroughly.

Be careful when raising the temperature of the iron or you may find the mounting tissue sticks only to the mount—or the print emulsion scorches—or both.

Be very sure that the support, the face of the print and the paper protection sheet are all completely free of dirt. Any small piece of material which is trapped between the print and the support will cause a small raised spot which will be readily visible on your finished product. Don't make the mistake of using newspaper under the iron or your print will include the morning news.

Prints much larger than 8x10 inches should be mounted with the use of a press. A mounting press completes the procedure in one action, more evenly and much faster than you can do with a flat iron. Most picture-framing shops and many camera stores have a mounting press and offer this service at a reasonable cost.

Another mounting material, made by Falcon Safety Products, Inc., is called Perma/Mount. This double-face adhesive material has a peel-off protective cover. Complete instructions are provided on the package. It is easy to use, permanent and requires no special equipment. You can use it to mount photographs on virtually any support material *without heat.*

Perma/Mount is ideal for mounting resin-coated prints, where too much heat may destroy the print. RC papers can be dry-mounted with a mounting press, but only with extreme care so

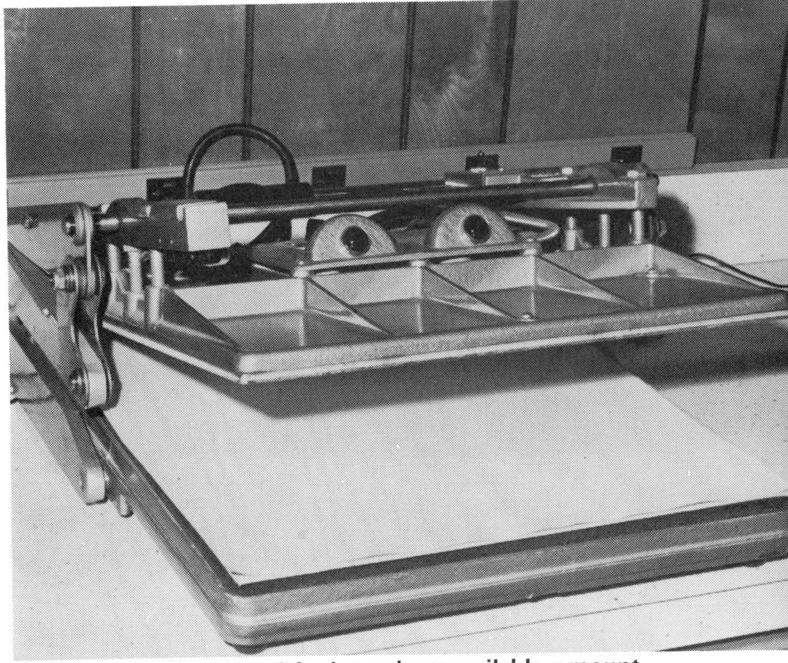

If you use mount tissue, it's nice to have available a mount press such as this one by Seal, Inc. It applies heat evenly over the entire print surface and makes mounting a "one-shot" process. It is a relatively expensive luxury item for the home darkroom. Your camera shop, school, or camera club may have one you can use.

Falcon Perma/Mount is easy to use and requires no heat or special tools. This double-sided adhesive material will mount a print on practically any surface. It comes in the following sizes: 8x10, 11x14 and 16x20 inches.

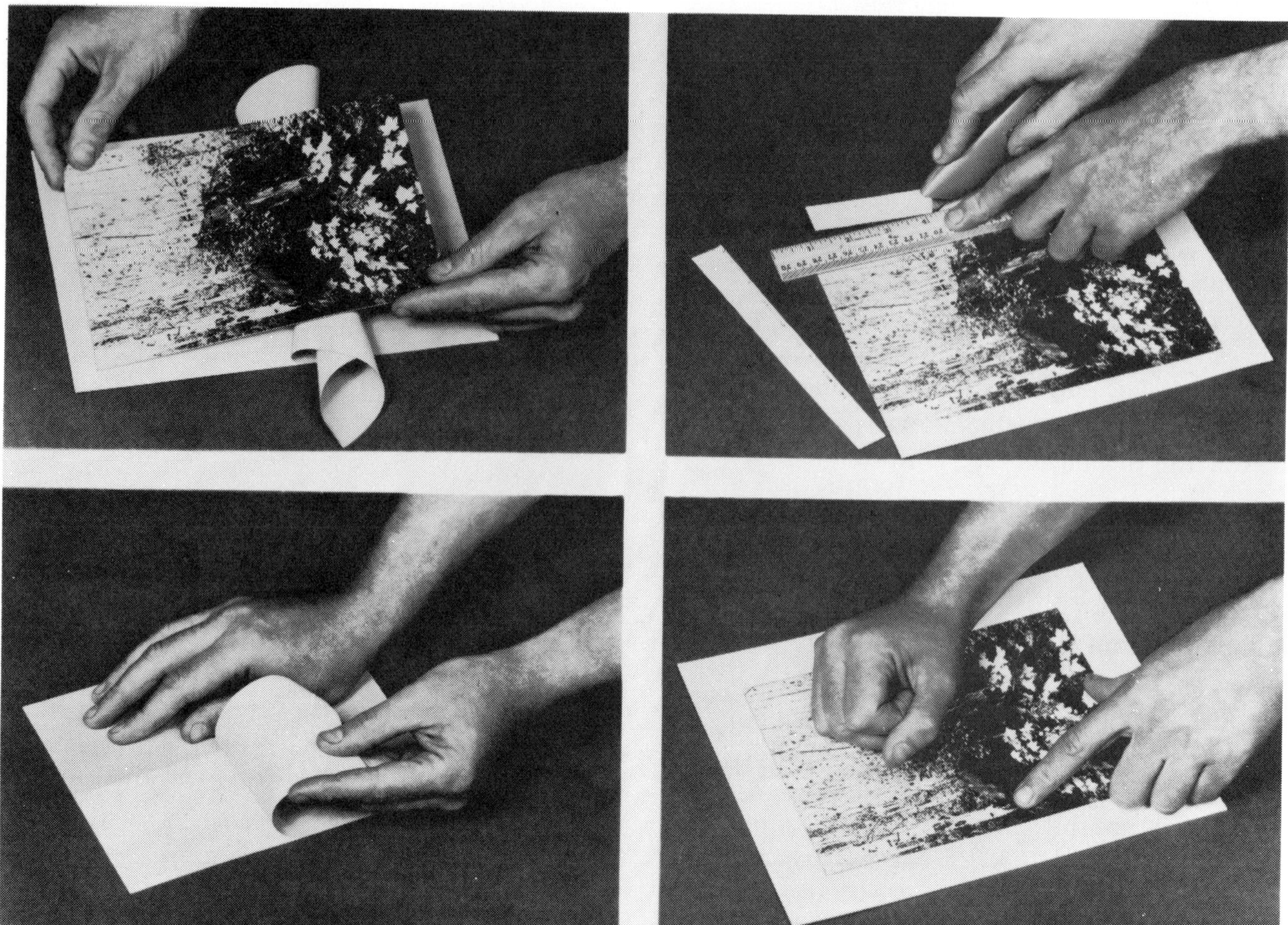

Falcon Permamount double-side adhesive sheets allow photo mounting without heat. Here the print is laid on top of an oversize Permamount sheet as the protective backing paper is pulled away. Then the print and adhesive are trimmed. The second protective sheet is pulled off. Apply the print to the mounting board and firmly press down to ensure good adhesion.

you don't melt the resin coating. It is necessary to have an extremely accurate heat setting on the mounting equipment and to follow the paper manufacturer's recommendations exactly concerning the temperature settings. You should use low-temperature dry-mount tissue especially made for RC papers by SEAL and Kodak.

With the exception of the rubber-cement method, the mounting techniques I have mentioned are permanent. Once the print has been mounted on the support, it is extremely difficult—if not impossible and disastrous—to remove the print. So take your time and be sure that your print is located exactly where you want it on the support before final heat or pressure is applied.

If it appears that, with all of your care, the print is mounted off-center or at an angle, the remedy is to trim the support material. If this should be necessary, the support will wind up smaller than you planned. If you had planned to stick the whole thing in a frame, you've got a problem. This could make it necessary to have an off-sized frame made, which will probably be costly and not worth the time you saved hurrying the placement of the print on the support. Or, you might use another color cardboard to make a mat surrounding your too-small photo with mount. Ingenuity will win out if you put your brain to it.

The same materials and techniques as used with black-and-white may be used when mounting color prints. The only exception is that the heat applied with the use of mount tissue should not exceed 210° to 230°F (99° to 110°C), when using paper-base or RC color material. Make sure the print and the protective paper used between the print and the mount press or flat iron are completely dry. If they are not, the print emulsion

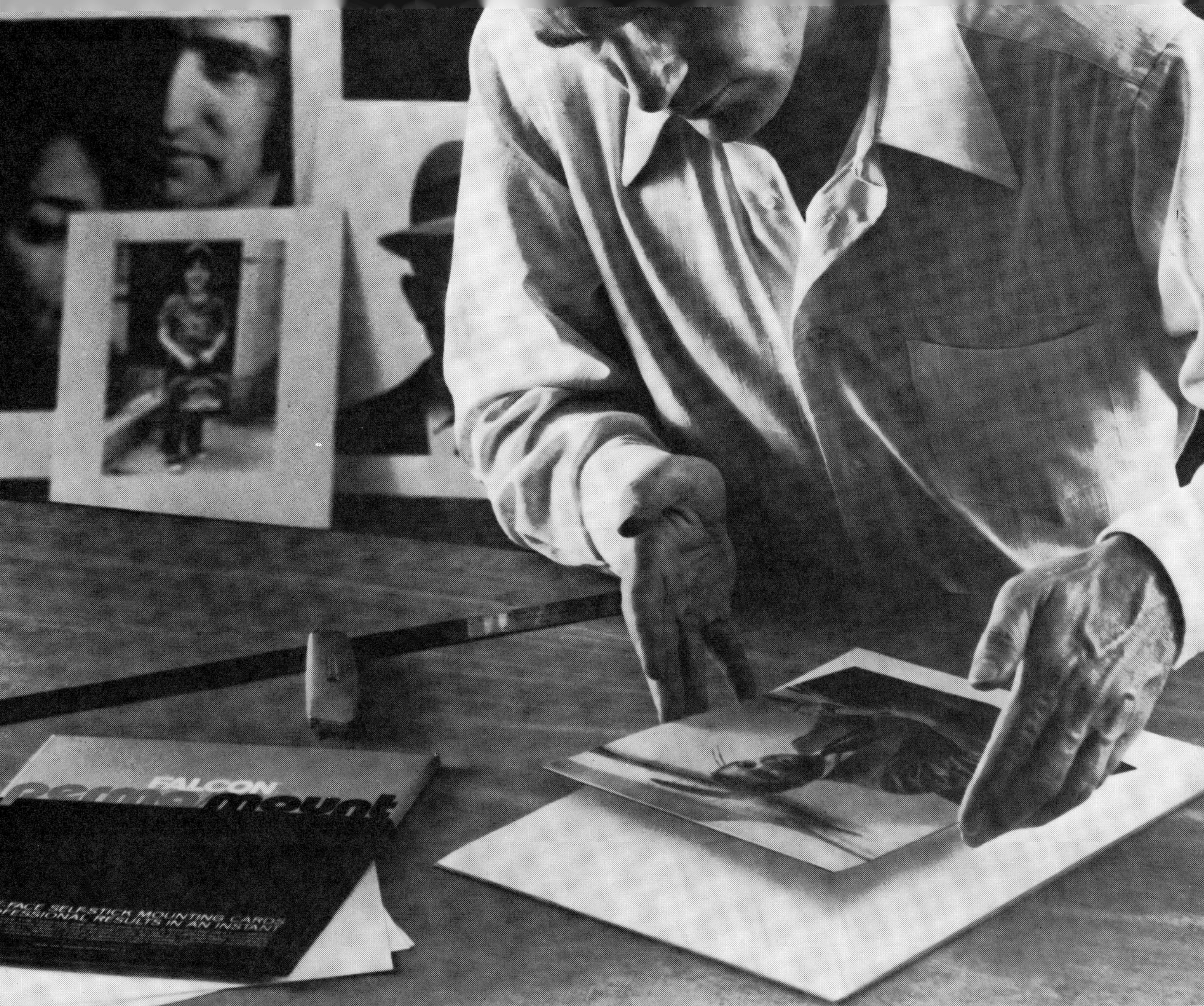

Permamount lets you mount black and white or color prints without being concerned about broiling or bubbling the surface with too much heat. An excellent alternative to dry-mount tissue when you don't have appropriate dry-mount equipment with good temperature controls.

will stick to the protective sheet and cause irreparable damage to the photograph. RC papers require strict adherance to the manufacturer's recommendations concerning temperature when used with mount tissue.

THEY'LL THINK YOU'RE GREAT!

One thing about mounting your prints—people begin to get the idea you are serious about your hobby and are starting to approach it professionally.

Once you have a few mounted prints hanging on your walls at home, in your office, or on display at church or your school, you'll probably start working harder to make better pictures. You'll expose and compose the initial shot more carefully, and spend more time making the prints so you and your friends will begin to get more enjoyment out of your hobby—which is what it's all about, after all!

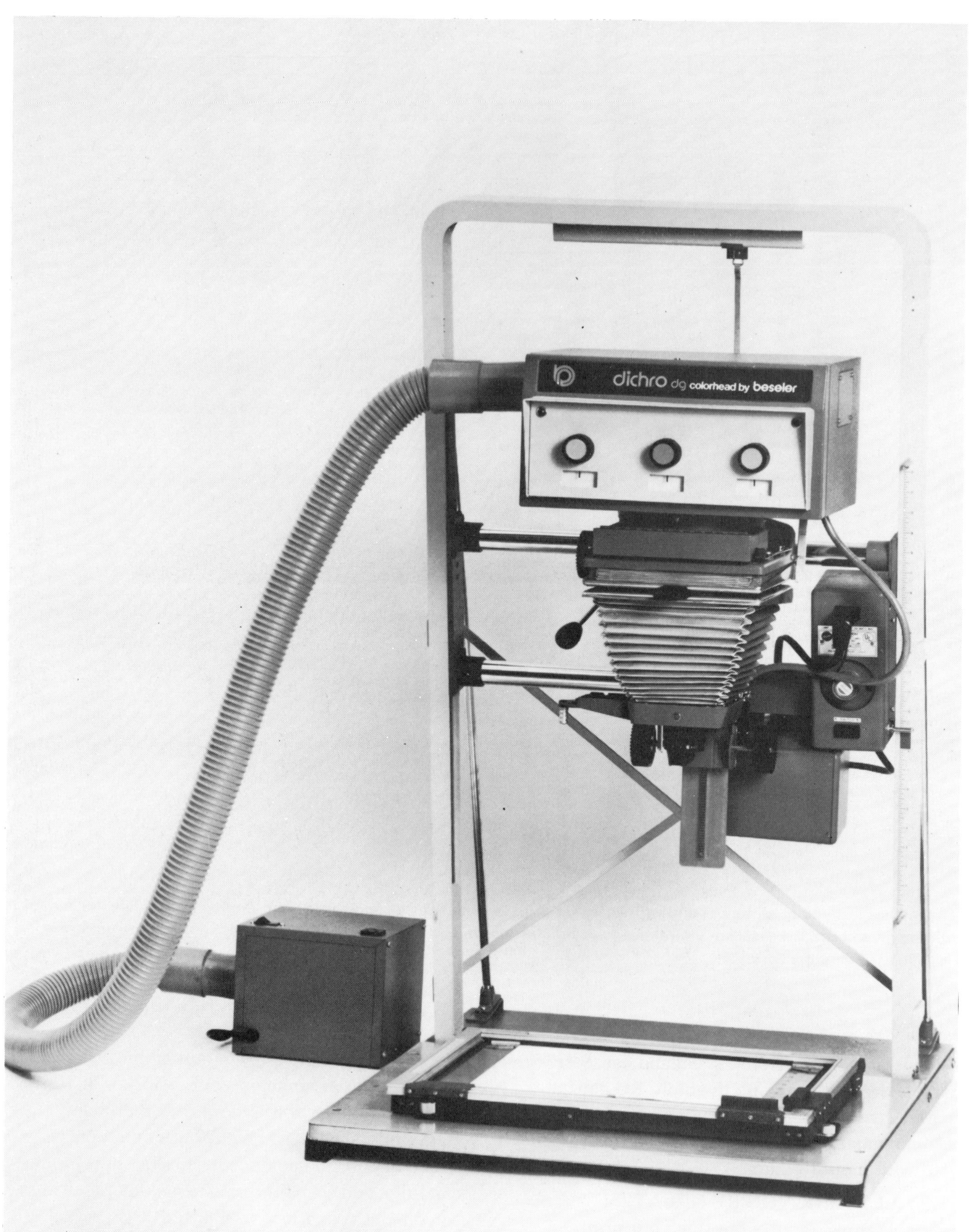

I put this in just to make you drool. Beseler's 45 MXD with Dichro dg Colorhead would make you the envy of all your photographer friends. Unless you are going professional, something less fancy would let you make a lot of color prints with the difference in cost.

Your Darkroom

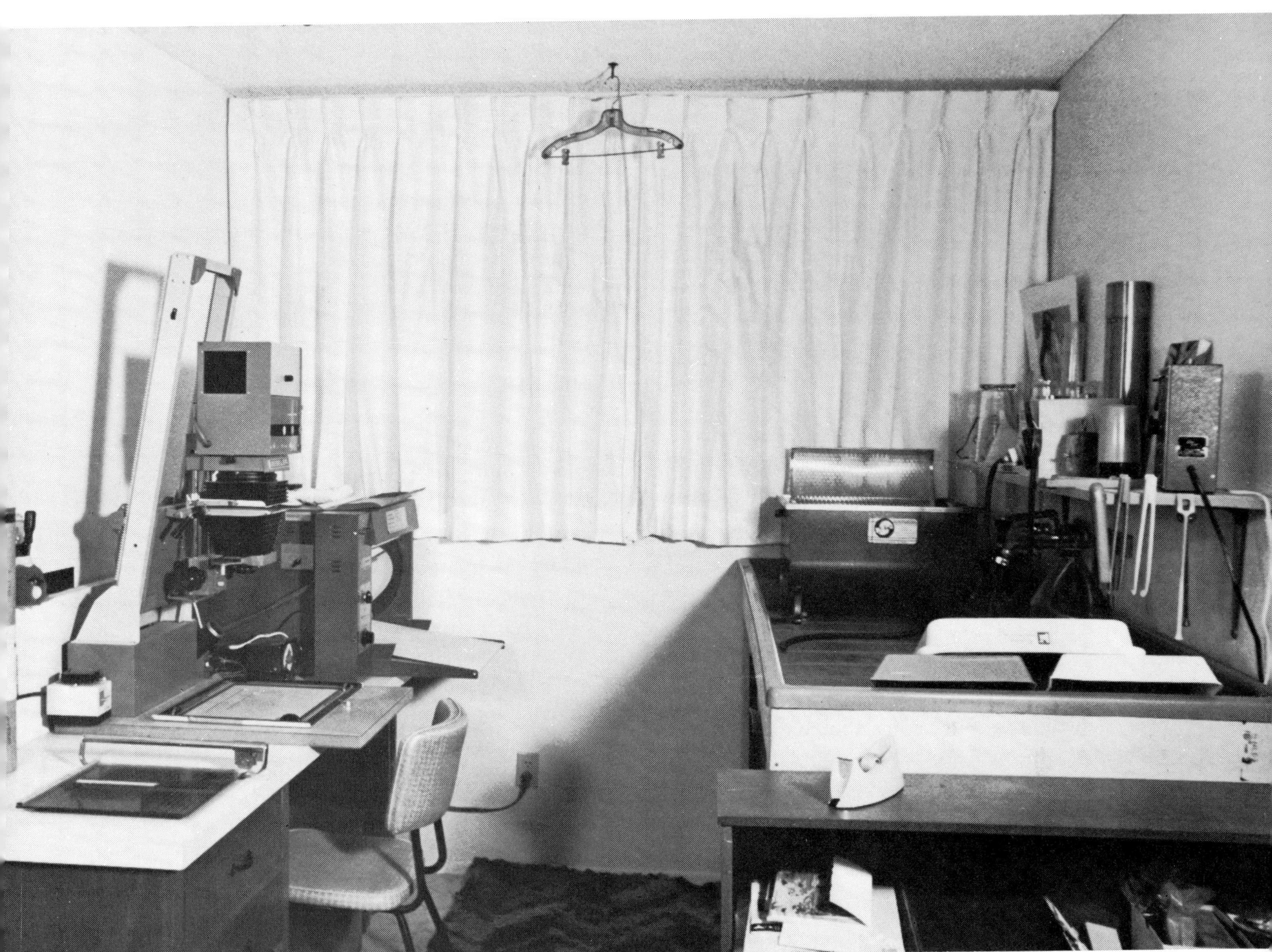

My home darkroom setup. The wet side with the processing sink and print washer is across the room and separate from the dry work side which maintains the enlarger, dryer and counter top areas. This particular space is 8′ x 8′, but much less area can prove workable. With portable, fold-up equipment, a darkened bathroom or kitchen may prove ideal. If you are fortunate enough to have this much space to go "all out," give careful attention to storage and shelf locations.

The term darkroom means just that: a dark room! Whether it's a room designed just for the purpose or a bathroom or kitchen, it must be possible to make it dark. No light can be allowed to enter through the walls, around doors, windows or through air vents. The materials you will be using—film and printing paper—are sensitive to light and should be exposed to light only with a camera or enlarger.

If you have a space which is not too terribly cramped and can be made light-tight, you're in the darkroom business.

Things to consider are plumbing accessibility, including a drain, adequate electrical outlets, heating and cooling, and some creature comforts such as a record or tape player. Because you periodically choose to seal yourself up in a room without companionship, that doesn't mean you necessarily desire the hermit's way. After all, you're into this for enjoyment, even if you do make a few bucks on the side, so by all means—enjoy! I know a man who watches television in his darkroom while he prints. The screen has the appropriate filter, of course.

Let's decide right now what you are going to do with your darkroom. Will you be using it only during the dark hours? If so, it should be an easy proposition to arrange for total darkness. Some heavy material such as a bedspread hung over the windows of the room should do the trick. Remember to check around the doors for light leaking in from other rooms. To be on the safe side, try to arrange a room away from the street so headlights of passing cars won't be a bother.

If you plan to use the room during the day, it's a bit tougher. ALL doors and windows must be made light-tight. Windows may be covered with heavy aluminum foil to reflect light but you will still notice small pinholes, which may be eliminated by hanging heavy black fabric from the wall. Check with a sewing supply or department store for an item called VELCRO. A strip of this material attached to the wall and another sewn to the black fabric allows a solid support for the material which may also be removed easily at will.

Once you have made the necessary arrangements, close yourself up in the room with all doors closed, sit down and wait for five to ten minutes. Look carefully around you and try to pick out objects in the room. If after ten minutes, when your eyes have grown used to the dark, you still can see nothing, you're in great shape. If after this time you can still make out shapes—even dimly—don't despair—you can probably still use it for print making.

Loading film into the developing tank requires TOTAL darkness. When printing, some very dim stray light is allowable as long as it is indirect and doesn't fall on sensitive materials. There's an alternative for the film-loading problem. You don't have to create a light-tight room—you can buy a completely portable one which you can store in a drawer when it's not being used. It's called a changing bag. Use the biggest one you can find because that makes it easier.

BATHROOM AS A DARKROOM

This is a community facility. So, unless you live alone, remember this room is subject to use by others without very much prior notice. If you can get it completely dark, it's probably OK to use for loading the film reel and getting it into the tank, but consider figuring out a way to darken the kitchen so you can use that area with its sink for the rest of your film-developing and printing activities.

A bathroom is not too much short of an ideal darkroom location except for the time/use factor. It is equipped with hot and cold running

What to use—Weatherstripping can be placed along the bottom of doors and around the edges. You may have to adjust the lock so the door closes tighter against its frame. It is not unusual to have to use black felt around the door frame so the door closes against the felt to block off light leaks. Windows can be closed with pieces of plywood painted black on the edges and perhaps edged with felt. You should have a way of latching the plywood in place on the window so it can't fall away from the window unexpectedly. You might want to paint the window side of the plywood flat-black so light will tend to be trapped instead of bouncing around the window frame and past the plywood.

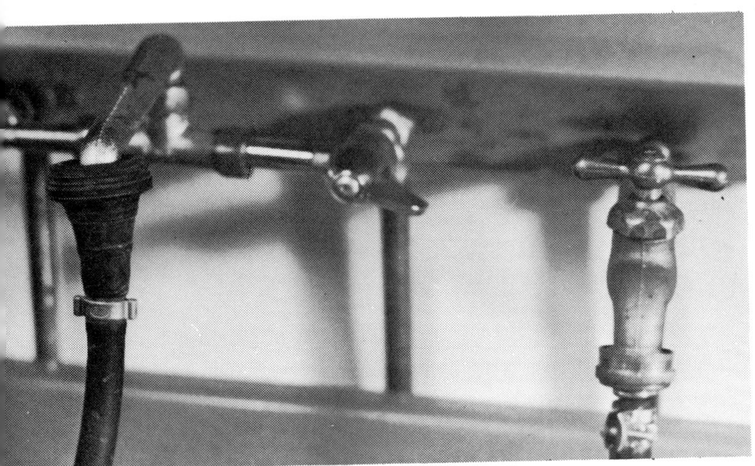

When building a processing sink, arrange the plumbing with a separate faucet for connection to the print washer and a mixing faucet for temperature control. A thermostatic mixing valve is nice if you can afford it.

water, drains, the normal household heating and cooling, sometimes a ventilating fan and usually only one window. A piece of ¾-inch shop-grade plywood, cut to the width of the outer dimension of the bathtub and a foot short of the length, will provide space for an enlarger or contact printer and several 8x10 inch trays. To be sure no chemicals are splashed onto the easel or enlarger baseboard, a partition about 10-inches high should be set between enlarger and tray areas. Working from the level of a bathtub top can prove a little unhandy unless you can find an old milking stool.

Rather than try to fill and empty a bathtub every few minutes, I recommend placing a large tray and Kodak Tray Siphon in the bathtub under the plywood workbench for print washing. Set the tray on a box so it will be high enough for the lower edge of the siphon to clear the bottom of the bathtub.

DARKROOM IN A CLOSET

With some ingenuity a clothes closet can be converted into a darkroom. It will take considerable planning and design on your part. Whether you have a standard 3x4-foot closet or a deluxe walk-in type will make a big difference. With some forethought in both construction and equipment purchase, you will be able to work in either one. The problems you must consider are electrical outlets, ventilation and the ability to arrange wet and dry areas so they do not overlap.

Probably the best use for a closet—aside from hanging clothes—is for loading film into the developing tank. In case you didn't manage to get to your camera store and pick up a changing bag as discussed earlier, consider the closet. But, before you try loading film, make sure that the door is light-tight. You will probably have to lay a large bath towel at the bottom of the door.

OTHER DARKROOM LOCATIONS

Unless you have good temperature control, do not locate your darkroom in an attic. It will be too hot in the summer and too cold in the winter. An unfinished basement is usually too damp the year 'round, and too cold in winter. Dampness causes mildew and can severely affect sensitive materials. If you have a finished basement with either a normal or manufactured temperature from 70° to 75°F (21° to 24°C) this is an ideal spot. Plumbing and electrical fixtures are usually readily available in a basement.

Outside storage rooms are usually subject to temperature extremes and are not generally suited to our purpose.

LOCK ON THE DOOR

I think it is a good idea to load film and make prints in a room where *you* can lock the door. There's just no way to save film or photographic paper when someone flings the door open and floods the room with light—even *dim* light! Putting a sign on the door is helpful. But, if someone is in a hurry to come into a room, chances are that the sign won't even be noticed. If you are going to use a room for darkroom work, get a latch on the door, preferably high enough so children won't be able to lock themselves in accidentally. My darkroom has a sign on the door, handwritten by my eight-year old daughter which reads do not dusturb. Because she is naturally very proud of her own handiwork, she takes heed to the warning when posted. Just an example of how letting your family get involved with your interests can be of help in little ways.

CHANGING BAG

If you don't have a room which can be made totally dark for film loading, here's your alternative. Known since Hector was a pup, alive and well and living at your camera dealer's, is ye olde changing bag. Perhaps your grandfather had one and by golly, it's still the same item. It consists of two large bags, one inside the other. The inner bag is made of a rubberized material and the outer one of heavy fabric. Both in basic black. Each bag has a zipper at the end and each runs in a different direction. The other end has two arm holes with elastic cuff bands. Buy a new one because they do get pinhole light leaks when they are old.

Very simply, the bags are unzipped, the assorted paraphernalia for loading film placed inside, the zippers closed, arms inserted through holes and film smoothly loaded onto the reels and into the tank. If you live in a warm clime, try to pull off this operation fairly quickly. The bag is not air-conditioned and perspiration on the film is no help.

WORK SURFACES

Professional and many home darkrooms include a large sink. This can be a working sink complete with hot and cold running water, drain, and a mixing faucet—perhaps even thermostatically controlled. A sink with running water for washing the film or prints and various utensils is helpful, *but not essential.* Lots of photographs are made where indoor plumbing is not part of the available equipment. A few buckets of clean water can provide all the water that's needed.

If you do have the space, consider building a dry sink out of plywood. Make the sides high enough so water and chemicals won't splash onto the floor—10 inches or so is good. Slope the bottom of the sink—whether wet or dry—so that the liquids will run to one end to a drain or for sponging up with a minimum of effort. Coat your sink with epoxy paint or fiberglass. If you use fiberglass, build the sink outside and do all the necessary sanding on it before you bring it into the house or darkroom.

STORAGE

Within six months, you'll begin to wonder. Within one year, you won't believe it. Where did it all come from? I can't explain to you how much "good things and stuff" you are going to accumulate, but I can prepare you by telling you to plan your storage space with great forethought. This is especially true if you are working in a kitchen, bathroom or other non-permanent location. In such cases, everything must be put away—after thorough cleaning of each item—and stored until the next session. Try to find a locking closet, preferably not exposed to temperature extremes.

I say a locked closet is essential. A quick check of the current price for print paper will make you realize why. Just one inquisitive person who doesn't take time to read the warning about opening under the proper safelight can put you deep in debt with your camera merchant. Also, chemicals are toxic and should be kept out of the hands of children.

SHELVES

If you are building a darkroom, shelves are a must both above and below your work area. Bottles and chemicals can go below the work surface or sink. Timers, processing tanks and other light-weight items can be stored above. Paper can be stored near the enlarger where it is readily at hand. If your darkroom is cold enough so you have to use an electric heater, by all means keep photo-sensitive materials as far away from the heater as possible. Perhaps you're using a portable darkroom which must be disassembled and stored after each printing session in a bathroom or garage. A standard linen closet with shelves from floor to ceiling should be just the ticket for out-of-the-way storage. That is, if your family will let you get away with it!

In lieu of inside storage space, an outside store room will serve the purpose provided the temperature does not get over 80°F (27°C) in the summer or cold enough in the winter so that solutions will freeze; 55°F (13°C) is a minimum temperature for storage of photographic chemical solutions.

With the exception of the enlarger and possibly a dryer, all other darkroom equipment is flat enough so it can be stored under a bed.

VENTILATION, COOLING & HEATING

Let's talk a minute about ventilation. If you are trying to work in a very hot room, your chemicals will keep getting warm—and so will you! Perspiration will drip onto negatives just as you are getting off the last speck of dust. It can be pretty miserable. If you have an area which can be cooled off with a small air conditioner, buy one. This small investment will give a lot of comfort, even when you are using the room for something else.

There are darkroom ventilators which can be put in a wall or door. Some include electric fans to push air into or out of the room. If you have to install a vent or blower, be sure it is baffled so light can't get in. Some bathrooms have built-in ventilating fans and if you can stand the noise, they work fine.

If you need heat in the room, it's a bit different. First, watch where you put an electric heater and be sure it is not close enough to anything which could catch fire. Second, it creates a red glow which is not allowed when loading film. At a distance of ten feet or if it is shielded someway, it probably won't harm printing materials. But, BE SURE! Test it in the same manner as you test a safelight. You may just have to wear a heavier sweater and two pair of socks.

WHAT COLOR WALLS?

Skip this discussion if you are using a room which is not being set up just for dark room use. A closet, bathroom or kitchen which is only used occasionally as a darkroom can have whatever color walls are already there.

Typically, the beginner thinks all walls in a darkroom should be painted black. White or light-gray paint is much better. Stop and consider: White is only white in the presence of light. So in the absence of light—as in your darkroom—white is no different than black.

It may be wise to paint the wall black directly behind your enlarger—or hang a piece of dark non-sheen cloth there. Most enlarger negative carriers leak some white light which could conceivably reflect enough from a white wall to cause a slight fog—areas of increased density—on your print material.

SAFELIGHT & INSPECTION LIGHTS

Safelights are discussed elsewhere in this book but I do want to mention one or two things under this darkroom section. Safelights are available in many sizes and shapes. Some hang from the ceiling or screw in the wall. Others set on a shelf. I have found that a safelight which reflects from a wall and ceiling is the most useful overall illumination. Because the light is bounced from wall and ceiling, you can use a higher wattage lamp in the fixture to get better overall, yet safe, light distribution. This light is used for general darkroom illumination while making black-and-white prints. A smaller direct safelight above the processing tray area is still advisable.

For inspection of negatives and prints following processing, it is wise to have normal room

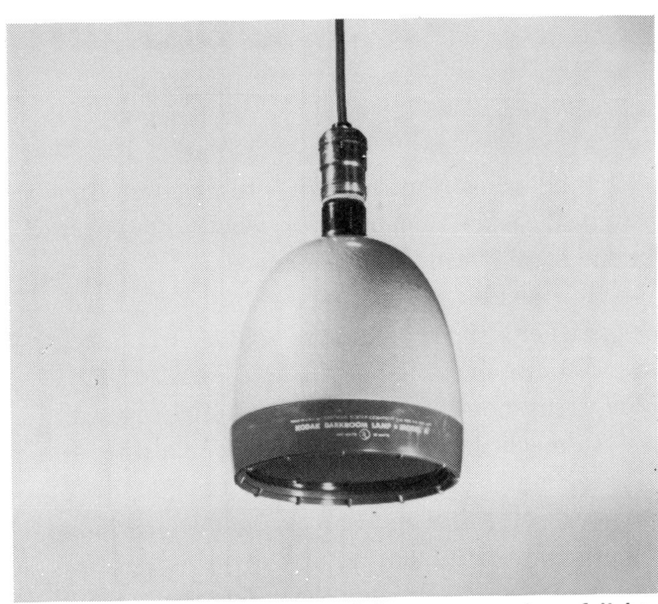

KAS-4 Kodak Safelight is one of the most popular safelights. Several are often used to provide illumination whenever it is needed. An adjustable-mount version is shown in the photo below.

light above the sink or processing area. The switch for such light should be convenient but not so convenient so it can be brushed on accidentally during film or print processing.

REFRIGERATOR

If you have any extra space in the family refrigerator, you will soon commandeer this. Film can be wrapped in plastic bags and stored in either the freezer or regular refrigerator section. The same can be done with photographic papers. Just remember to take it out a couple of hours before use. Keeping photo-sensitive materials cold prolongs their life. If you are building a darkroom from scratch, put a refrigerator in it or nearby. That's one way to make sure you have usable film and print supplies as well as cold liquid refreshment nearby when you crave a tall cool one!

DEHUMIDIFIER

Some areas have high humidity. You don't want that in your darkroom. If you have set up your darkroom in a damp basement, install a dehumidifier. Extremely high humidity has really bad affects on your equipment, film and paper. If your darkroom is air-conditioned or does not suffer from abnormally high humidity, forget the dehumidifier. Extremely dry air in a darkroom causes as many problems as high humidity. Dry air causes unbelievably bad dust problems and static electricity to the point of frustration.

Colorfilm Processing

Processing your own color film can produce pain or pleasure, depending on what you expect as an end result from the experience.

In previous chapters you've noticed I have been rather strict regarding the choice of materials to produce a pleasing photograph. That's the purpose of my book, to explain *one* straight-forward way to reach the goal. I'm changing that direction in this chapter because there are cross-matches between color film and process chemicals which I believe are worth mentioning. At the end of the chapter I give *my* conclusions and recommendations.

Let's look at the "plain/pleasure syndrome."

Pain: Home processing can be more costly than commercial processing.

• More time is required than black-and-white processing.

• More care and control are required than in black-and-white processing.

Pleasure: Home processing can be less costly than commercial processing.

• Greater quality control is obtained.

• Results are seen in hours rather than days.

The cost factor is significant. Depending on the film to be processed, the chemical kit required, the size of the kit available and the number of rolls to be processed, cost can be 50 cents to $36 per roll. It's silly to mix a $10 chemical kit, process one roll of film and watch the solutions deteriorate setting on the shelf. Each kit can be used to process a recommended number of rolls. Processing substantially less film means an increased cost per roll, which is probably unwarranted. The lowest cost per roll is achieved by using the kit to its full recommended capacity.

Color-chemical kits have a much shorter shelf life than chemicals for black-and-white film processing. I think it is wise to mix a color kit only when you will have enough exposed film to use the kit close to its recommended capacity.

It takes quite a bit longer to process color film as compared to black-and-white film. But, due to the vast improvements in color technology it takes considerably less time than it did just a few years ago. Processing times have been cut drastically, as has the number of chemicals necessary.

If you are a careful worker, you can achieve the ultimate in quality control by processing your own color film. No more nightmares about automatic machines going berserk or losses in the mail! No more junior-technician fingerprints in the center of the slide; no more damage to treasured images by labs who run your semi-dry film through what I call *automatic-gouging machines*. However, if you do goof, you have only yourself to blame. And things *can* go wrong; temperatures of developer solutions are not at all tolerant of variations. Color film is thicker and more susceptible to physical damage than black-and-white materials.

One more good reason for trying your own color processing is you do not need to invest in equipment you don't already have for processing black-and-white film. Tanks, reels and assorted what-nots you've been using are all that's required. Let's double-check the list:

Chemical kit for the type film to be processed
16 oz. developing tank
2 35mm Developing reels or 1 120 reel
Thermometer
16 oz. graduate (for negative-processing kit)
Timer
Exposed film
Film hanging clips
Enough brown plastic bottles for the particular kit used
Plastic funnel
Rubber gloves
Tray for water bath
Music and refreshment of your choice

The choice of plastic bottles will vary according to the number of chemical steps required and the size of the processing kit. I recommend the Falcon *air-evac* collapsible bottles for the developer solutions. Even though they are more expensive than standard bottles, they provide the best-possible protection against developer deterioration due to air trapped in the bottle.

If you're still interested, press on and let's look at the procedures. First, the color-negative process:

C-41 FLEXICOLOR BY KODAK

The Flexicolor process is used with the most commonly available color-negative films: Kodacolor II, Kodacolor 400, Vericolor II Types S & L, Fujicolor II Types S & L, Fujicolor II 400, Sakuracolor II and Boot's Colourprint II. The kit contains four chemicals and the total processing time in fresh solutions is 24.5 minutes. The one-pint (16 oz.) complete kit is the most useful size for the home darkroom and will process 12 rolls of 135-36 film. Again, I refer you to the instruction pamphlet where you should particularly notice:

- Precautions for handling. Some chemicals are POISON; some are skin irritants. Wear rubber gloves.
- The bleach, fixer and stabilizer have twice the capacity of the developer, so two units of developer are provided. Mix and use one until it's exhausted, then use the remaining one.
- Storage life of mixed developer solution in full glass bottles is only six weeks.
- Developer time increase table.
- READ THE INSTRUCTIONS COMPLETELY!

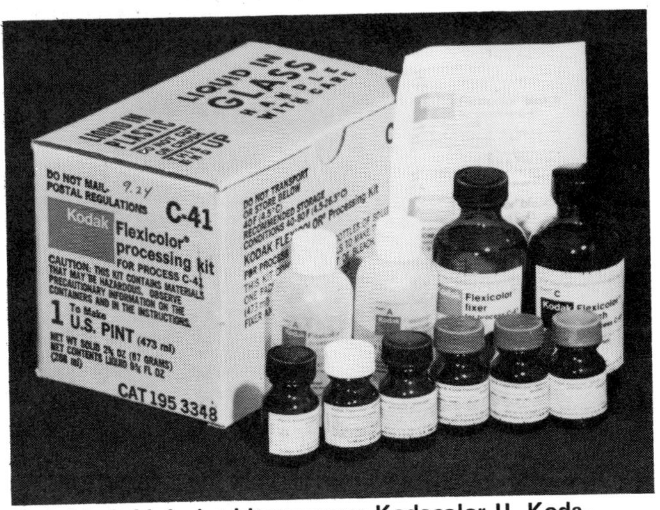

Kodak's C-41 1-pint kit processes Kodacolor II, Kodacolor 400, Vericolor II and any other color-negative materials compatible with the process.

Now, let's go through the process, step-by-step:

1. Mix solutions according to instruction pamphlet. Pour solutions into clean, labeled bottles and cap tightly.
2. In total darkness, load exposed film onto reels, place in developing tank and close lid securely. Turn on room lights.
3. Bring developer temperature to 100 ± 1/4°F (37.8 ± 0.15°C).
4. Set timer for three minutes and 15 seconds. Put on your rubber gloves.
5. Pour Developer solution into tank.
6. Start timer.
7. Rap tank sharply on the bottom and agitate for 30 seconds.
8. Place the tank in 100°F (37.8°C) water bath for 13 seconds.
9. Agitate for 2 seconds, return tank to water bath for 13 seconds and continue in this manner until 10 seconds before completion of development.
10. Empty and drain tank for the last 10 seconds.
11. Set timer for 6 minutes, 30 seconds.
12. Pour Bleach solution at 75° to 105°F (24°–40°C) into developing tank. Start timer.
13. Agitate for 30 seconds.
14. Place tank in 100°F (37.8°C) water bath for 25 seconds, then agitate 5 seconds. Continue this procedure until completion of the step, allowing 10 seconds for draining.
15. At completion of bleach step, you may remove the developing-tank lid and CONTINUE WITH THE FILM UNCOVERED IN NORMAL ROOM LIGHT.
16. Wash film in running water at 75° to 105°F (24°–40°C) for 3 minutes, 15 seconds. As the open tank is filled, agitate vigorously for 2 seconds and quickly dump and drain water for 10 seconds. Continue this procedure until time has elapsed.
17. Set timer for 6 minutes, 30 seconds.
18. Pour Fixer solution at 75° to 105°F (240°–40°C) into developing tank. Start timer.
19. Replace tank lid and agitate for 30 seconds.
20. Place tank in 100°F (37.8°C) water bath for 25 seconds then agitate for 5 seconds. Continue this procedure until completion of the step, allowing 10 seconds for draining.
21. Remove tank lid.
22. Wash film in running water as in Step 16.
23. Set timer for 1 minute, 30 seconds.
24. Pour Stabilizer solution at 75°–105°F, (24°–40°C), into developing tank. Start timer.
25. Replace tank lid and agitate for 30 seconds. No further agitation is required.

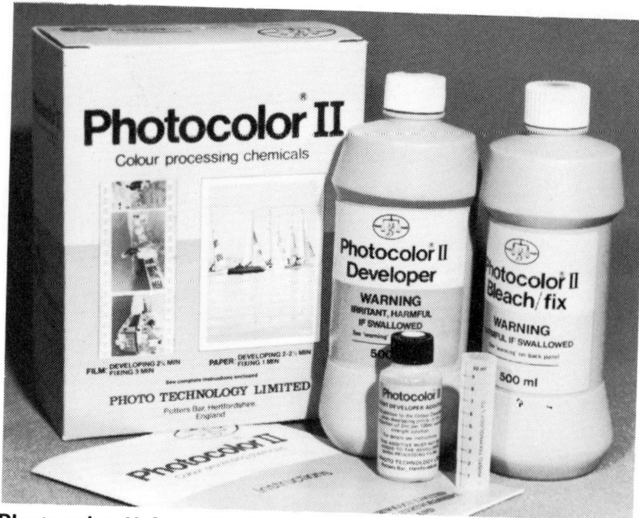

Photocolor II from England offers an easy two-solution process which provides the fastest developing times for color negatives AND color prints made from negatives.

> **DEVELOPER KIT COMPARISON**
>
> All of these kits will process Kodacolor II, Kodacolor 400, Vericolor II Types S & L, Fujicolor II Types S & L, Fujicolor II 400, Sakuracolor II, Boots' Colourprint II or any other film designed for processing by the Kodak C-41 or equivalent process.
>
> **KODAK C-41**
> 1 pint
> 12 rolls 135-36
> 4 chemical steps
> 24.5 minutes @ 100 ±1/4°F (38°±1.7°C)
> 2 water washes
> Approximate cost per roll $.963
>
> **BESELER CN2**
> 1 pint
> 6 rolls 135-36
> 3 chemical steps
> 29.5 minutes @ 75±1°F (24±.6°C)
> 20.6 minutes @ 85±1/2°F (30±.3°C)
> 1 water wash
> Approximate cost per roll $.926
>
> **PHOTOCOLOR II**
> 500cc
> 15 rolls 135-36
> 2 chemical steps
> 12.25 minutes @100°F (38°C)
> 2 water washes
> Approximate cost per roll $1.66
> Photocolor II can also be used to process Kodak Ektacolor 37RC and 74RC, Sakuracolor and Agfacolor Type 4 color printing papers.

26. Remove film from the reels and hang to dry in dust-free area at 75°–105°F (24°–40°C) DO NOT SQUEEGEE THE FILM.

The way I wrote it, it took 26 steps to plough through a four-chemical process and looks pretty formidable. It's really easier than it looks at first glance. Everything is in the instruction pamphlet. I just laid it out step-by-step. It's simple: Take care with temperatures and agitation rates and you'll have the cleanest roll of color negatives you've ever had.

PHOTOCOLOR II

This product is worth considering because it lets you buy one kit to process color-negative film AND prints made from color negatives. That eliminates the problems of mixing and storing several different process kits for different procedures. Photocolor II can be used to process any film suitable for C-41 type processing.

It is a two-solution, easy-to-use process which is twice as fast as the other two C-41 processes I mention. Film takes only 12-1/4 minutes for the complete process, including washing. Rubber gloves are recommended to avoid skin damage.

The instruction booklet—one of the best I've seen—suggests using 100°F (38°C) for processing, but a time/temperature chart lets you compensate for temperatures ranging from 95°–104°F (35°–40°C). This kind of latitude can be especially helpful when temperatures are not cooperating.

I am straying from my basic concept of telling you only one way to do each thing. Why? Because I think you may want to consider using Photocolor II where the tradeoffs are in its favor—where the higher cost is offset by faster processing time and the ability to use one set of processing chemicals for both negatives and prints.

BESELER CN2 PROCESSING KIT

Now I want to take you on a quick trip through a third color-negative kit, namely the Color by Beseler CN2 processing kit. This kit is available in a one-pint size and will process six rolls of 36 exposure, 35mm film designed to be processed by C-41 type chemistry. The process uses three chemical steps and may be used at either 75° or 85°F (24° or 30°C). Processing times are 29 minutes and 30 seconds at 75°F (24°C), or 20 minutes 30 seconds, at 85°F (30°C). Rubber gloves are recommended to avoid skin damage. The procedure for the CN2 kit is essentially the same as for the Kodak C-41 kit—except for temperature and agitation rate—both are fully explained in the instruction pamphlet.

Any of these three chemical kits give you well-processed color negatives when used with care according to the manufacturer's instructions. I am not changing the view I've expressed throughout this book—that it's generally the best idea to avoid confusion by using film and processing supplies by the same manufacturer. I mention the alternative method by Beseler because I believe the temperature factor is worth consideration.

As you can see from the comparison, the CN2 process uses lower temperatures than the C-41 process. I've found the average home darkroom owner has minimal control of critical temperature, especially *higher* temperatures. Assess your own situation and proceed accordingly.

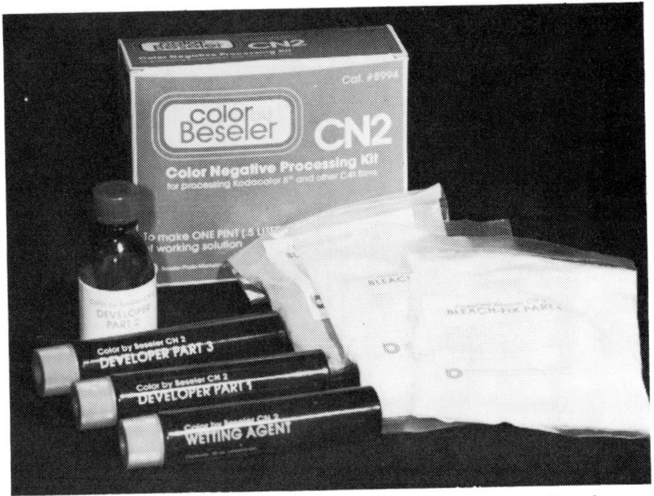

Color by Beseler CN2 processes Kodacolor II, Kodacolor 400 and other color-negative films designed for the C-41 process.

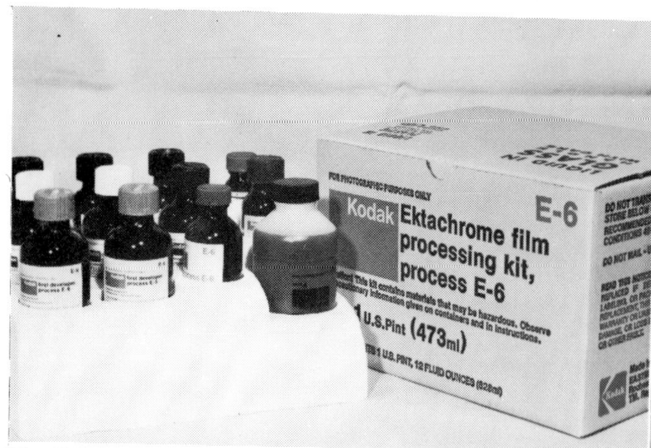

The E-6 Ektachrome processing kit in the 1-pint size is just right for the home darkroom. Remember the kit includes twice the amount of First Developer and Color Developer concentrates. Pay attention when mixing.

SLIDE-FILM PROCESSING

Now, on to the realm of slide-film processing.

First, if you're a long-time Kodachrome fan, go take photographs, because you can't process your own slides. Only Eastman Kodak and a handful of labs are set up for Kodachrome and the necessary chemicals are not available to the home user. The most-common slide films the user may process are:

Kodak: Ektachrome 64 (ER) and (EPR)
Ektachrome 50 (EPY)
Ektachrome 200 ED) and (EPD)
Ektachrome 160 Tungsten (ET) and (EPT)
Ektachrome 400 (EL)
Fuji: Fujichrome 100

Available processing kits for these films include E-6 kits made by Kodak, Unicolor and Beseler.

This chapter does not deal with film characteristics but let me say, if you are a long-time Ektachrome user, don't be dismayed about the introduction of the new films, because they are faster, finer-grained and have better color rendition than the films they are replacing. You'll like them.

A pamphlet packed with the pint-size E-6 kit is easy to understand. It includes basic step-by-step instructions for processing in small tanks. It also tells you how to push-process Ektachrome film.

You'll be using your 16-ounce steel tanks and 135-36 reels with Ektachrome 64 (ER), 200 (ED), and 160 (T). You can also use this E-6 kit to process the professional Ektachromes 50 (EPY), 64 (EPR), 160 (EPT) and 200 (EPD). The kit also processes duplicating films 5071, 7071 and 6121.

Do us both a big favor and read through these instructions before you begin *anything.* Be aware beforehand of what's expected in the way of temperature control and be prepared to process exactly as described.

• Mix chemicals in the standard manner.

• Read all directions first:

• Get your gear together, your blood pressure in check and let's go:

1. In total darkness, load the exposed film on the developing reels and put them in the tank in the usual manner. Cover tank and turn on lights.

2. Bring temperature of First Developer to 100±0.5°F (37.8±0.3°C).

3. Set timer for 7 minutes and put on your rubber gloves.

4. Measure 16 ounces of First Developer into graduate.

5. Pour First Developer into tank and start timer.

6. Rap tank bottom on sink or table to dislodge air bubbles.

7. Agitate continuously for 15 seconds.

8. Place tank in water bath at 100±0.5°F (37.8±0.3°C).

9. Agitate 2 seconds every 30 seconds until 10 seconds from end of step.

10. Empty solution into First-Developer bottle.

11. Set timer for 2 minutes.

12. Start timer and with tank lid in place, wash film in running water at 92°–102°F (33.5–39°C). Fill tank through top opening, agitate for 10 seconds and drain. Continue until 10 seconds from end of wash step.

13. Set timer for 2 minutes.

14. Pour Reversal Bath at 92° to 102°F (33.5–39°C) into tank.

15. Tap bottom of tank again to dislodge air bubbles. Place tank in water bath at 100°F (37.8°C). No further agitation for this step.

16. At the end of reversal-bath step, return solution to proper bottle and remove tank lid. REMAINDER OF THE PROCESS MAY BE CARRIED OUT UNDER NORMAL ROOM LIGHTS.

17. Set the timer for 6 minutes.

18. Pour Color Developer at 100±2°F (37.8±1.1°C) into tank. Start timer. Agitate for 15 seconds and place tank in water bath. Agitate for 2 seconds every 30 seconds until 10 seconds from end of step.

19. Drain tank back into Color Developer bottle.

20. Set timer for 2 minutes.

21. Pour Conditioner at 92°–102°F (33.5–39°C) into tank. Start timer. Rap tank to dislodge air and place tank in water bath at 100°F (37.8°C). No further agitation during this step.

22. Drain solution into Conditioner bottle at 10 seconds before end of step.

23. Set timer for 7 minutes.

24. Pour Bleach at 92°–102°F (33.5–39°C) into tank. Start timer. Agitate for 15 seconds, place tank in water at 100°F (37.8°C). Agitate for 2 seconds every 30 seconds until 10 seconds before end of step.

25. Drain Bleach back into bottle.

26. Set timer for 4 minutes.

27. Pour Fixer at 92°–102°F (33.5°–39°C) into tank. Start timer. Agitate for 15 seconds. Place tank in water bath at 100°F (37.8°C). Agitate for 2 seconds every 30 seconds until 10 seconds before end of step.

28. Drain Fixer into the proper bottle.

29. Set timer for 6 minutes.

30. Start timer and wash in running water at 92°–102°F (33.5°–39°C) using one complete fill-and-dump cycle each 30 seconds.

31. Set timer for 1 minute.

32. Pour Stabilizer at room temperature into tank. Start timer. Rap tank to dislodge air bubbles. No further agitation in this step.

33. Return Stabilizer to bottle. Remove film from reels and hang to dry in dust-free area. DO NOT SQUEEGEE FILM.

If this is your first experience with color-slide processing, don't be alarmed at the strange overall color cast on the wet film. It all dries out and everything appears as you expect.

The whole process sounds tricky but, in action, is pretty simple if you've kept your times and temperatures on the nose. Believe it or not, it's taken me longer to write this than it will for you to run the process. I've processed many rolls of the E-6 Ektachromes exactly as described and have been quite pleased with the results.

The pint-size E-6 kit processes 8 rolls of 135-36 or 12 rolls of 135-20 Ektachrome.

As complete as the instruction sheet is, if you haven't had experience mixing color chemicals before, you may wonder why a bit more isn't mentioned about the number of chemical bottles packed with the kit. You will notice you get two small bottles labeled *First Developer,* two marked *Color Developer Part A* and two marked *Color Developer Part B.* You actually have enough chemical concentrate to mix twice as much first developer and color developer as you have for the other solutions. The reason is that these developers are more quickly exhausted than the other solutions.

When mixing the kit, use one bottle of First Developer concentrate to make a pint of working solution. Save the second bottle until later. Now mix one bottle of Color Developer Part A and one bottle of Color Developer Part B and save the other bottles until later. After processing half of the total film capacity of the kit, dump the First Developer and Color Developer and mix fresh solutions with the bottles of concentrate you so cleverly saved. Now you can continue processing with fresh developers until the kit capacity is reached.

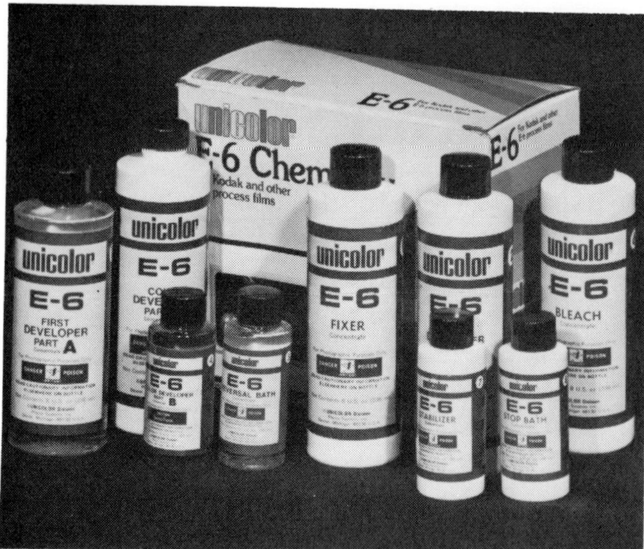

Unicolor E-6 Chemistry kit comes in a 1-quart size and includes these chemicals. You only mix those chemicals you need, thereby prolonging kit life and saving money if you process only a roll or two at a time.

UNICOLOR E-6 PROCESS KIT

Unicolor's E-6 process kit is only for processing E-6 process films. Unicolor E-6 has some real advantages. It comes in a one-quart kit, involves seven chemical steps with three water rinses and requires a total of 27 minutes. You mix only as much chemical as you need to process the number of rolls you have exposed. That means that you don't have to mix the entire kit at once, use it only slightly and agonizingly watch it deteriorate on the darkroom shelf. That's a real cost-per-roll factor in your favor.

According to the rather complete instruction pamphlet packed with the kit, the concentrated solutions kept in bottles with air squeezed out, last at least one year. The one-quart kit will process 8 rolls of 135-36 exposure film.

The instruction pamphlet is interesting in the information it provides. It contains:

- Mixing directions
- Unicolor film-drum instructions
- Conventional film-tank instructions
- Capacities
- Push-processing instructions
- Processing problem solving
- Cautionary information and simple, easy reading;

TAKE ADVANTAGE OF IT.

The processing is relatively standard. Read completely through before the instructions before beginning the proces. Pay particular attention to temperature and agitation recommendations so you'll know what to expect. Unlike the Unichrome process, Unicolor E-6 features a reversal bath; a chemical reversal rather than a physical reversal by re-exposure to light; a little added benefit.

I believe the Unicolor kit will be a real winner for the home user due to the company's standard of quality with previous products, a smaller kit size, relatively short process time and the lower cost-per-roll factor.

You've already read the procedure for the Kodak E-6 process and here's where I differ from the other chapters in this book. I'm going through the step-by-step routine with the Unicolor E-6 process and let *you make your own choice between the two processes.*

1. Mix chemical solutions according to instruction pamphlet. Mix only as much working solution as required for the amount of film to be processed. Squeeze the air from the bottle of concentrate and cap tightly. Put the funny-looking concentrate bottle on the shelf.

2. Bring First-Developer temperature to 100° F (37.8° C).

3. Set timer to 6 minutes and 30 seconds.

4. Pour First Developer into developing tank. Start timer.

5. Agitate first 15 seconds and place tank in 100° F (37.8° C) water bath. Agitate 2 seconds each 15 seconds for remainder of step. Allow drain time before completion of step—10 seconds.

NOTE: At this point you have a choice to make. If you will be processing again within two weeks, you may want to save the working solution for reuse. If so, drain the working solution from the developing tank into a clean, labeled bottle, squeeze the air out and cap tightly. Remember to use within two weeks. This will allow you maximum kit capacity and lowest cost per roll.

Put an expiration date on the bottle as memories sometimes fail.

Or do as I prefer. Dump the used working solution down the sink drain. This one-shot procedure decreases the total kit capacity and somewhat raises the cost per roll, but each time I run the process, I know I'm using good, fresh chemicals and that I can retain maximum reproducible quality. Meanwhile, back at the ranch. . .

6. Drain developing tank as you decide from above note.

7. Set timer for 2 minutes, start timer.

8. Rinse in running water at 92°–102°F (33°–39°C). Fill and drain tank continuously for 6 complete cycles.

9. Set timer for 2 minutes.

10. Pour Reversal Bath at 92°–102°F (33°–39°C) into developing tank. Start timer. Agitate for 10 seconds. No further agitation in this step is required.

11. Drain Reversal Bath from tank in accord with the procedure for First Developer.

REMAINDER OF PROCESS CAN BE CARRIED OUT IN NORMAL ROOM LIGHT.

12. Set timer for 6 minutes.

13. Pour Color Developer at 99°–101°F (37.2°–38.3°C) into developing tank. Start timer. Agitation for this and all remaining steps is identical to that of the First Developer in step 5.

14. Drain tank and set timer for 1 minute.

15. Pour Stop Bath at 92°–102°F (33°–39°C) into developing tank. Start timer.

16. Drain tank. Set timer to 2 minutes.

17. Start timer. Wash film in running water at 92°–102°F (33°–39°C) for six complete fill/drain cycles.

18. Set timer for 3 minutes.

19. Pour Bleach at 92°–102°F (33°–39°C) into developing tank. Start timer.

20. Drain tank. Set timer for 2 minutes.

21. Pour Fixer at 92°–102°F (33°–39°C) into developing tank. Start timer.

22. Drain tank. Set timer for 2 minutes.

23. Start timer. Wash film in running water at 92°–102° F (33°–39°C) for six complete fill/drain cycles.

24. Set timer for 30 seconds.

25. Pour Stabilizer at room temperature into developing tank. Set timer. Agitate 10 seconds only.

26. Drain tank. Remove film from reels. DO NOT SQUEEGEE. Hang film in dust-free area to dry.

Pretty simple, no? Yes!

PUSH PROCESSING

Extended processing, or *push processing,* as it is commonly known, is one of the big benefits of processing your own color-slide film. The idea is to expose film at an ASA rating higher than that set by the manufacturer. This enables you to expose at higher shutter speeds or smaller lens apertures in low-light-level situations. In essence, you are *underexposing* the film and, therefore, must correct the situation by compensation through development variations. Very simply, underexposure must be corrected by *overdevelopment.* This works well to a certain point. Beyond that, film images suffer increased contrast, increased grain and shifts in color balance.

Many commercial labs will not handle extended processing and those that do charge extra for the special service.

Films for this purpose are those with the highest normal sensitivity ratings. It makes no sense to extend a slow film to a higher rating when higher-rated films are easily available. Two films which readily adjust to higher ASA ratings and extended processing are Kodak's Ektachrome 200 daylight and Ektachrome 160 tungsten films, both E-6 process materials. Ektachrome 200 can be rated at ASA 400, an increase of one stop; or ASA 800, an increase of 2 stops. Ektachrome 160 can be rated at ASA 320 (1 stop) or ASA 640 (2 stops). Compensation in processing is obtained by adjustment of first-developer times in the E-6 process.

The first-developer time is increased in increments as shown in the instructions supplied with the kits.

Remember, underexposure and extended processing cause some increase in grain, loss of deep-shadow detail and possible slight color-balance shifts. The greater the variation from normal, the greater these changes. If you expect and accept the change, the resulting slides can

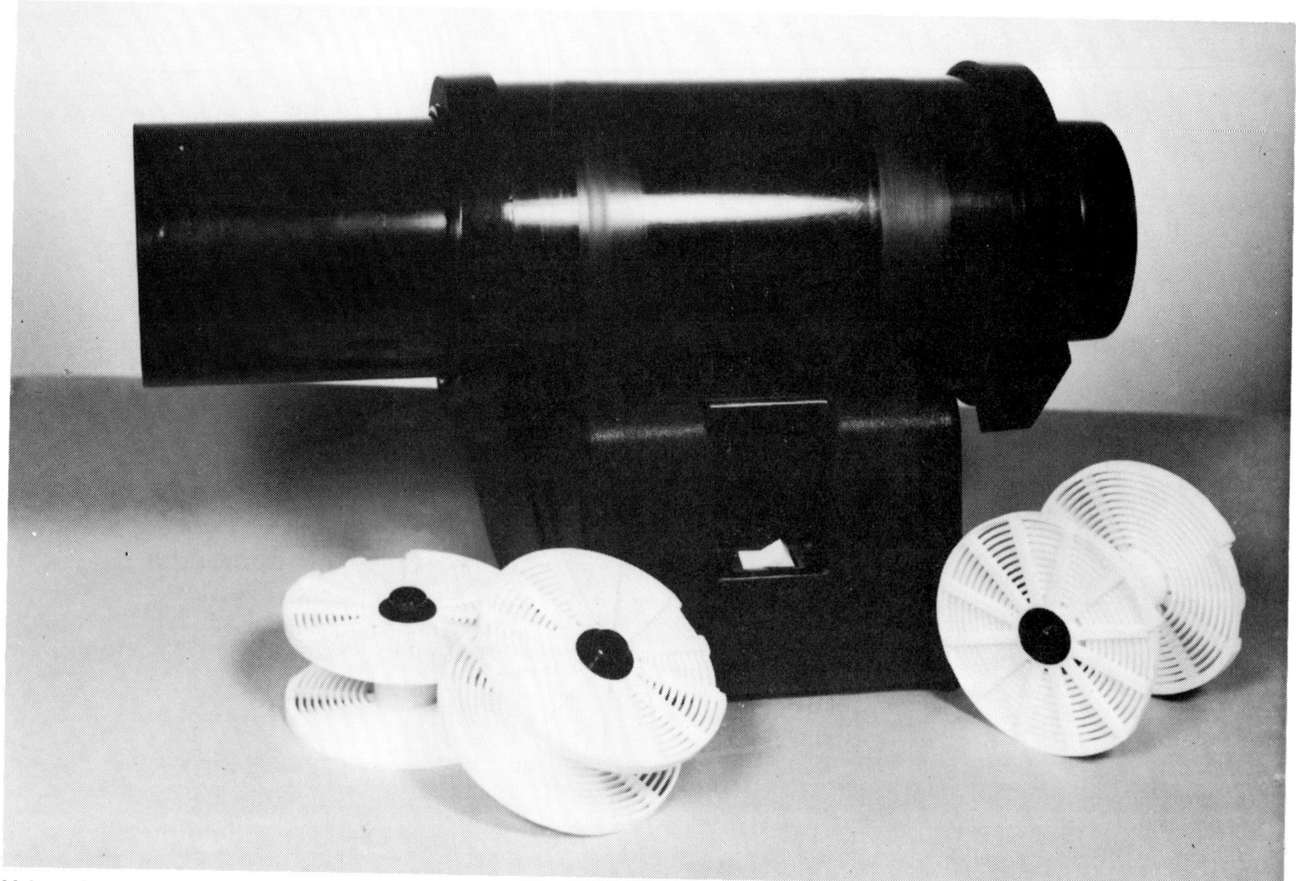

Using the Unicolor Film Drum and Uniroller motorized base is an efficient, time-saving method to clean, consistent color or b&w film processing at a reasonable cost.

be great fun. It takes experience and experimentation; two things you can achieve by doing your own work.

UNICOLOR FILM DRUM

The Unicolor people have come along with a handy film processing unit called the *Film Drum.* The drum is used with a motorized base dubbed the *Uniroller,* and the combination assures consistent and even agitation of roll after roll. As with other drum processors, a great deal of film can be processed at one time using the minimum volume of chemicals. For example, the Kodak E-6 pint kit will allow you to process just two rolls of 35mm film at one time in the standard 16 ounce tank. The same pint of solution will process four rolls at once in the Film Drum.

The Film Drum is a daylight processor. This means that once the film is on the easy-to-load plastic reels and placed in the drum with end cap in place, you can process in normal room light. A movable piston in the drum allows you to load one roll or several, depending on the amount of chemicals used. Unicolor offers plastic film reels in standard film sizes from 110 through 120.

The secret to clean, consistently good processing is the Uniroller base. The motor in the base rotates the Film Drum in one direction, stops and rotates it in the other direction at about ten second intervals. The constant motion of film and chemicals assures even processing action each time. This combination of base, drum, and reels offers semi-automatic film processing at a very reasonable cost.

The instructions packed with the Film Drum are clear and provide concise information concerning solution capacity, and the processing times and steps for a variety of films, including both color slides and negatives. Processing times may be a bit different from those suggested by the manufacturer of the chemical kit you use, but this is because constant agitation is always recommended in the instructions. In addition, some processes use a prewet step before development to assure even processing.

I have discovered a couple extra things that you should be aware of before you use this equipment. Be sure the plastic reels are *completely* dry before trying to load them with film. The smallest bit of moisture causes the film to stick to the reel so that it will neither advance nor unwind. After processing is complete, remove the film very gently. The reel has two sharp tips at the starting point and if you strip the film from the reel too quickly, you may damage the film base by scratching it.

The only other warning concerns dumping and refilling the drum with chemicals. Before you actually process film, practice filling and dumping the drum a few times. Do this in front of your darkroom timer and note the time it takes. I think that Unicolor is a bit optimistic about how long it lasts. When processing four rolls of 35mm film in a pint of solution, you'll find that it takes at least 15 seconds to dump the drum and an additional 10 seconds to refill for the next step.

The equipment offers a good, reasonably priced processing method that allows increased volume without increased time. In these days of both decreased time and dollars, any economy is welcome.

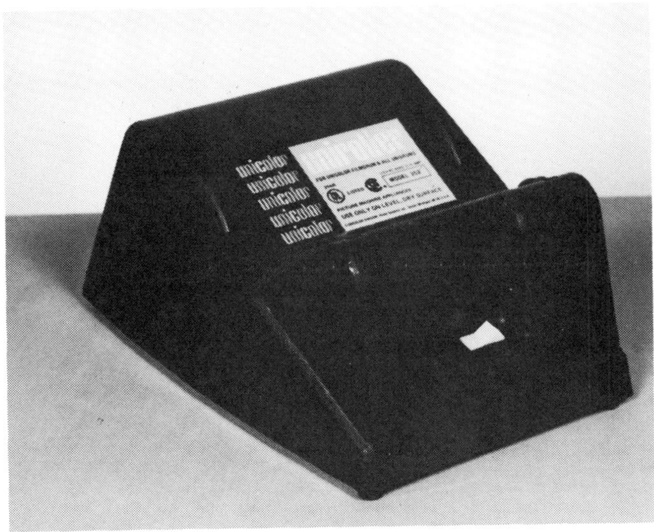

The motorized base is the secret to consistent processing results, roll after roll. It is used to constantly agitate the Unicolor Film Drum during processing.

MOUNT 'EM UP

Once color-negative film is processed and printed, it is filed in the normal manner and left until additional prints are needed. With slide film, you have a different situation. The slide itself is the object for viewing and, unless it is used for the purpose of producing a print, it must be prepared some way for viewing by friends, relatives and other disinterested people. The usual idea is to bind the slide in some sort of a mount and project it on a screen.

There are many different slide mounts on the market. Cardboard, plastic, metal, plastic with glass, and metal with glass are some examples. As you continue making your own slides you will develop your own preferences for slide equipment and supplies.

My recommendation as you start on your way, is to use simple, inexpensive materials such as Kodak Ready-Mounts. They are listed in the Kodak catalog as CAT 145 2283 in the 35mm size, in a box of 100 for about $ .03 each. The mounts

Kodak Ready-Mounts come flat. You fold them after inserting the slide, then seal the edges with heat for slides which look just like those you get from Kodak when you send in film for processing.

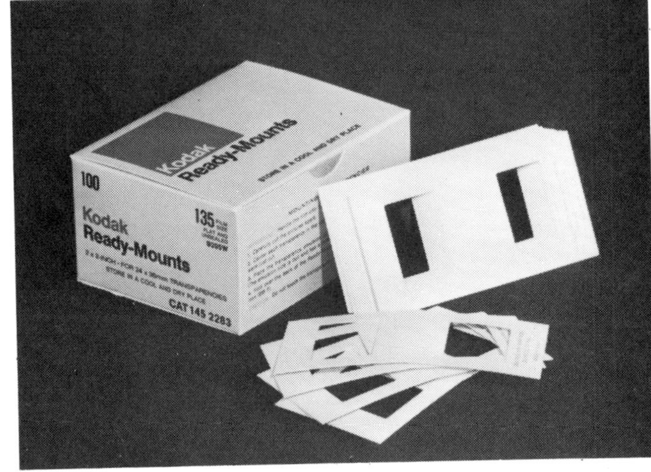

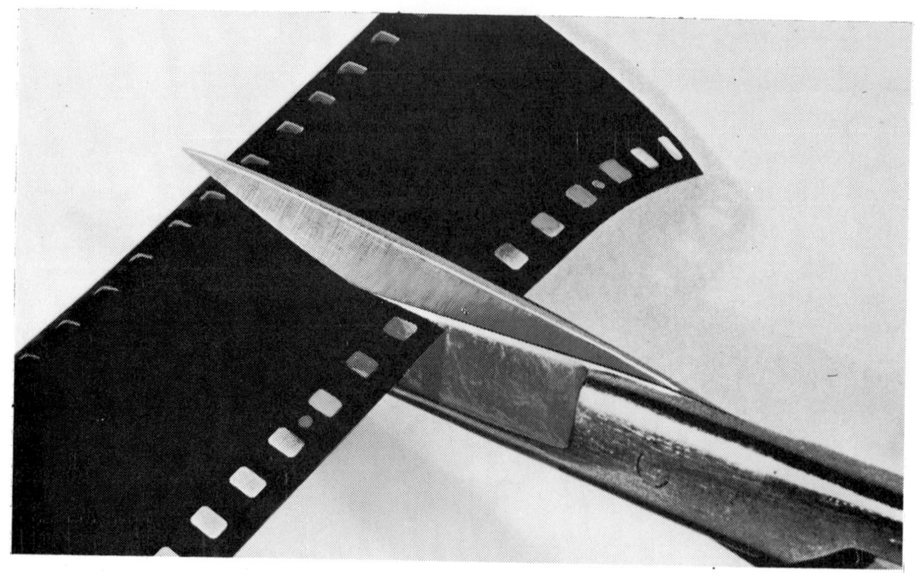

Each frame must be cut apart carefully, and care taken to cut between—not through—sprocket holes. Plastic template supplied with each box of mounts can also be centered over each frame, using the template as a cutting guide.

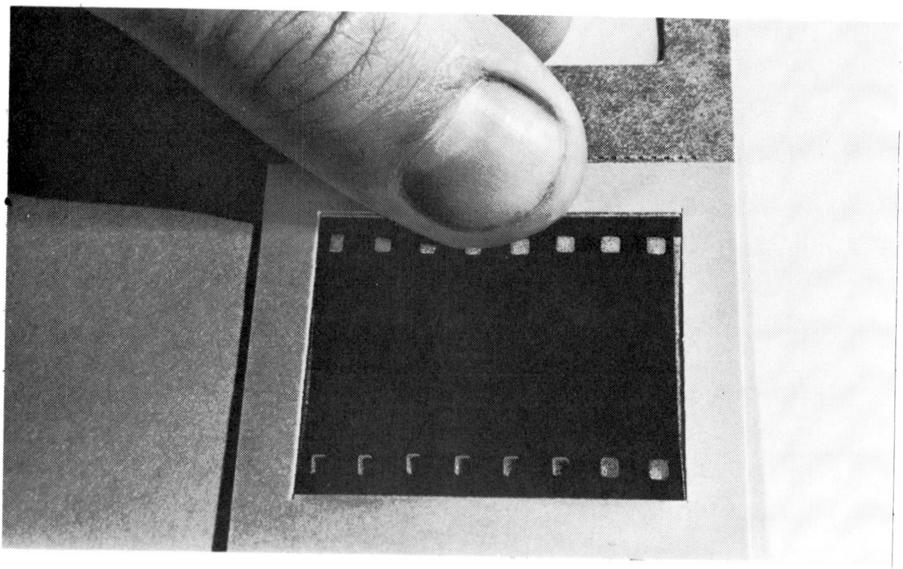

After frames have been cut apart, place the cut film inside the tan-colored adhesive rectangle. Center the film carefully, and do not allow film edges to go beyond the inside margins of the adhesive rectangle. If the film is slightly too large, trim it to the size of the clear-plastic cutting template supplied with the mounts.

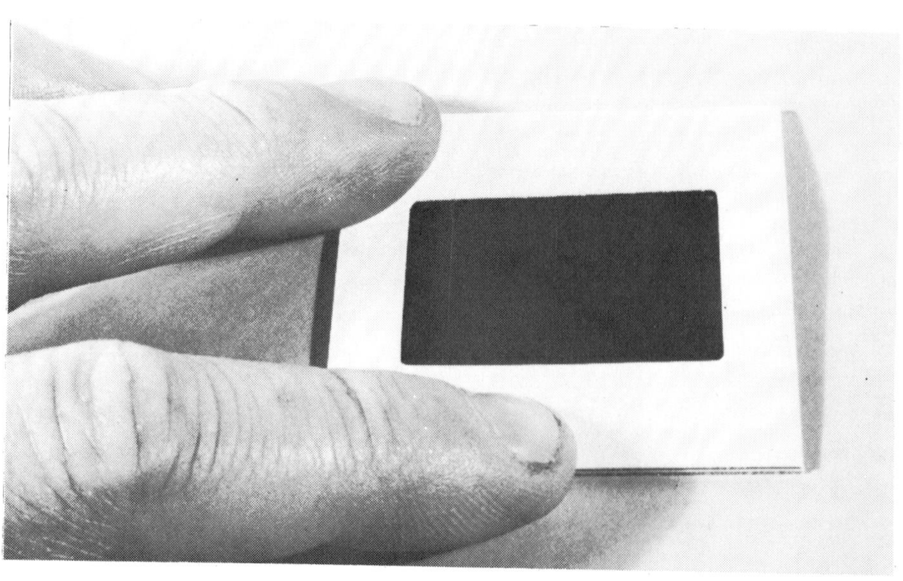

After the film has been properly placed inside the mount, fold over the other half of the mount. The film is now sandwiched inside. Hold the mount closed firmly as shown.

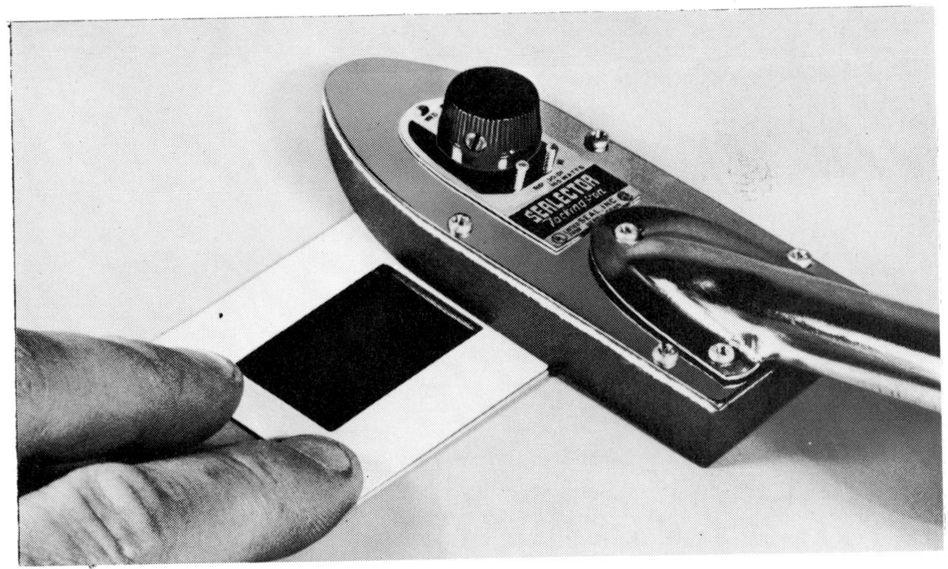

While holding the mount closed, seal the edges with a moderately hot tacking iron—about 225° F. All four edges must be sealed. Be careful not to touch film with iron.

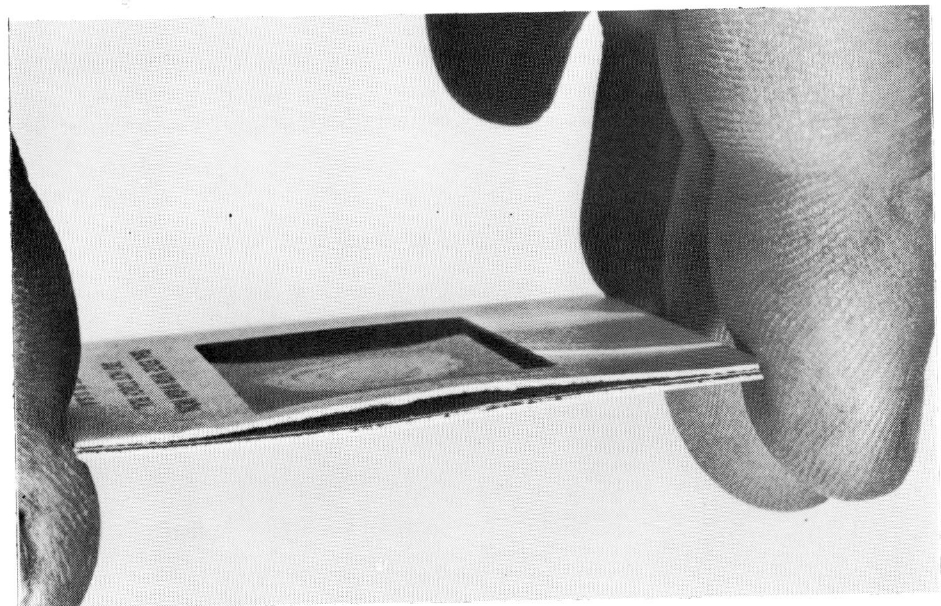

After sealing the mount's four edges, check all edges to see that it has been properly sealed. As shown here, one edge has not sealed, and must be gone over again with the tacking iron.

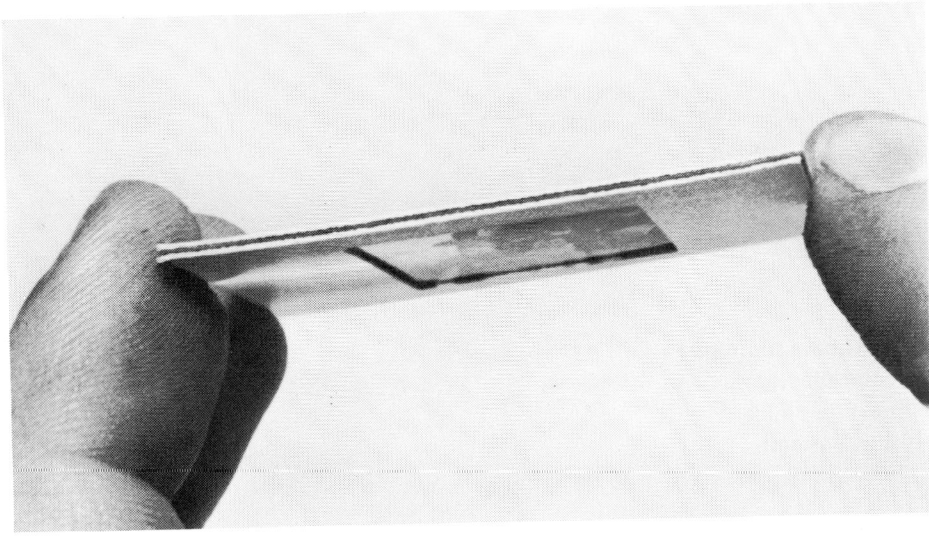

Check the edges of the mount again. Properly sealed mount will be perfectly flat as is this one. No gaps will appear between either side of the mount.

are packed open and flat. Once the slide is in place, the mount is folded in half and heat-sealed with a hot iron.

Here's the procedure:

1. Cut the film frames apart through the black separating lines.

2. Lay the cut frame with emulsion (dull) side down, in the mount. Make sure the frame has been trimmed to fit inside the raised sealing portion of the mount.

3. Fold the mount along the perforated line.

4. Lay the folded mount on a flat, hard surface, with printed side up.

5. Apply a warm iron to all four edges, four or five seconds to each edge. DO NOT TOUCH THE FILM WITH THE IRON. It will melt if you do.

6. Check all edges and make sure they are all tightly sealed. If not, repeat Step 5, and recheck.

That's about it for mounting, except for one final flourish. Mark the mount for proper orientation for projection. Nothing ruins a slide show like an image projected upside down or sideways.

Lay the mount on your table or view box, so the picture is correct; right side up and proper side-to-side. Place a mark of some sort in the lower-left corner. I make my mark by pressing a good pencil eraser on a stamp pad and stamping the slide mount with a circular mark.

When you're ready for projection, insert the slide into the projector so the mark is at the UPPER RIGHT corner as you face the screen. Works every time.

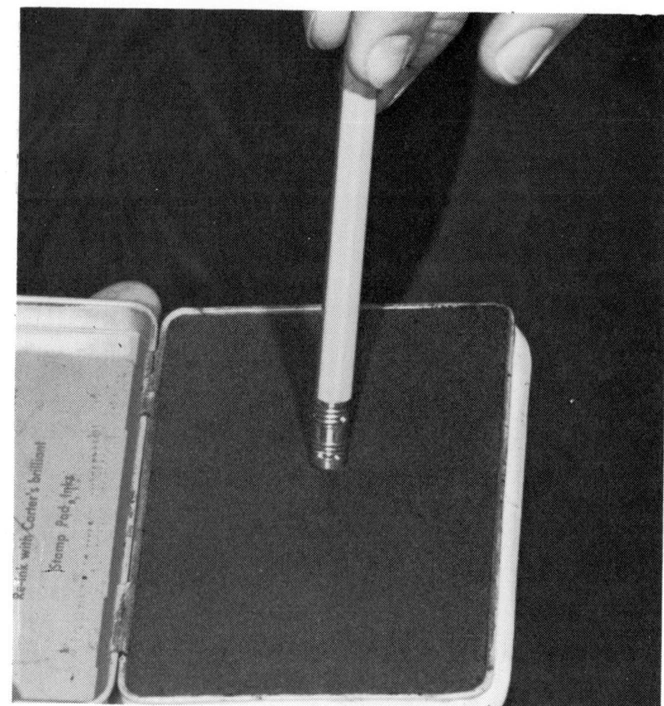

A pencil eraser inked with a stamp pad lets you mark each slide to ensure correct insertion into your projector slide trays.

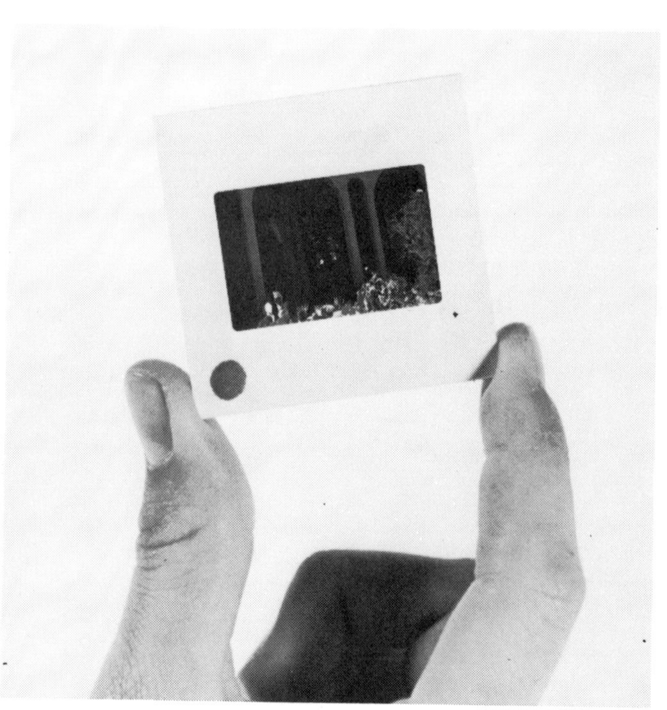

Finished, you did it yourself! Finished mount looks like those you get from Kodak, except this costs half what you pay Kodak for mounting. Plain mounts have room for your name stamp so you can advertise yourself. Note ink dot in lower-left corner which helps get the slides into your projector correctly. Look at slide correctly from base (not emulsion) side and apply dot as shown here.

Printing Your Own Color

Every darkroom owner dreams of the day he/she will be capable of developing color film and making color prints. Many people never attempt it because it can be an awesome proposition. You probably know of someone who tried to handle color and had little or no success. A little disappointment goes a long way towards keeping the photographer discouraged . . . and all his/her friends, too.

If you tried color years ago and had less than favorable results, now is a good time to try again. Equipment and materials have changed from expensive and time-consuming, to reasonably priced and rapid-acting. Several years ago it took an hour just to process a test print to find out how far out of color balance your print really was. Now you get your test print in a mere seven minutes. One product produces a processed, ready-to-dry print in two minutes.

Two methods of color printing in general use today are the *additive* and the *subtractive* methods.

Additive colors are red, green and blue which, when added together in equal parts, produce white. When using the additive method of color printing, the negative is placed in the enlarger and projected onto the print paper. Three exposures are made—one through each of the additive primary color filters.

The subtractive method of printing is more popular than the additive method because it requires only one exposure through the color negative. Therefore, I will discuss primarily the equipment, materials and technique of the subtractive method of color printing. A very good discussion of color vision and the theory of color is in Carl Shipman's H. P. Book *Understanding Photography.*

Subtractive colors are cyan, magenta and yellow. Filters in these colors are used to subtract a color from white light. When all three filters are used together in the proper balance the result is black.

The relationships among these six colors, three primary and three complementary colors, are really simple once you understand them. It's worth taking a minute to get acquainted with them.

We say that red, green and blue light all mixed together give white light because if you do mix those three colors of light the result will *appear* white to the human eye. That's as much reason as anybody needs. If the three colors together look white, then the three colors together must make white light.

You can also demonstrate that the three primary colors of light can be mixed together in different proportions to create all possible colors of light. For example, if you have the right amounts of each color to make white and then you use less red in the mixture the light changes color. It seems to have more blue and green just because it really has less red. The visual color effect is bluish-green. Or greenish-blue, take your pick.

The end result of all color processes is colored light into your eye which can always be considered as some combination of the three primary colors. Your eye will see some color depending on the relative amounts of the three primary colors of light that are present.

Any color process can therefore be considered as merely some clever way to control the amount of each primary color of light that the viewer gets to see. The process must control the amount of red, green, and blue.

The commonest thing around that controls the color of light is a piece of colored glass—we call it a *filter.* If you look at a filter and it appears to be red, it's because red light is coming through the glass. When illuminated by white light, a red filter is evidently *stopping* the other two primary colors, blue and green.

That's exactly what we want to do, except we also need filters which will stop only one color, not two. If you have a filter that *stops* only red, then the colors green and blue must come through the glass. When you see green and blue light mixed together, your main problem is you don't know what to call it. Its name is *cyan.*

The color *cyan* is said to be the *complement*

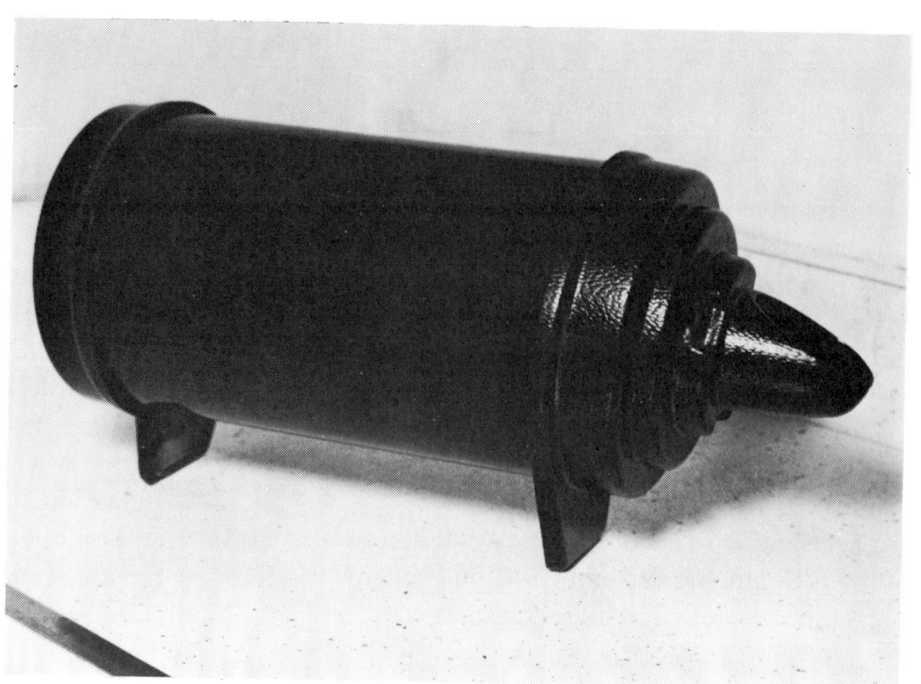

The Unicolor processing drum. Other manufacturers make similar drums of the same basic style. Some use less processing chemicals than others.

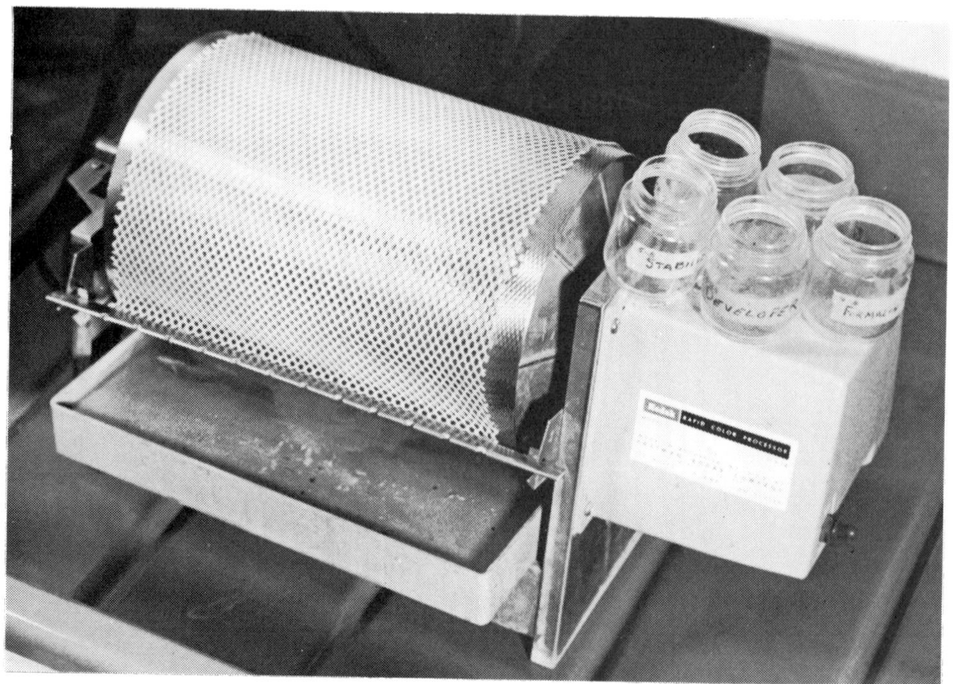

Kodak Model 11 Rapid Processor uses CP-5 chemical kit to process prints in 7 minutes. Each step uses only 4 ounces of solution. Empty baby-food jars make excellent holders for processing chemicals.

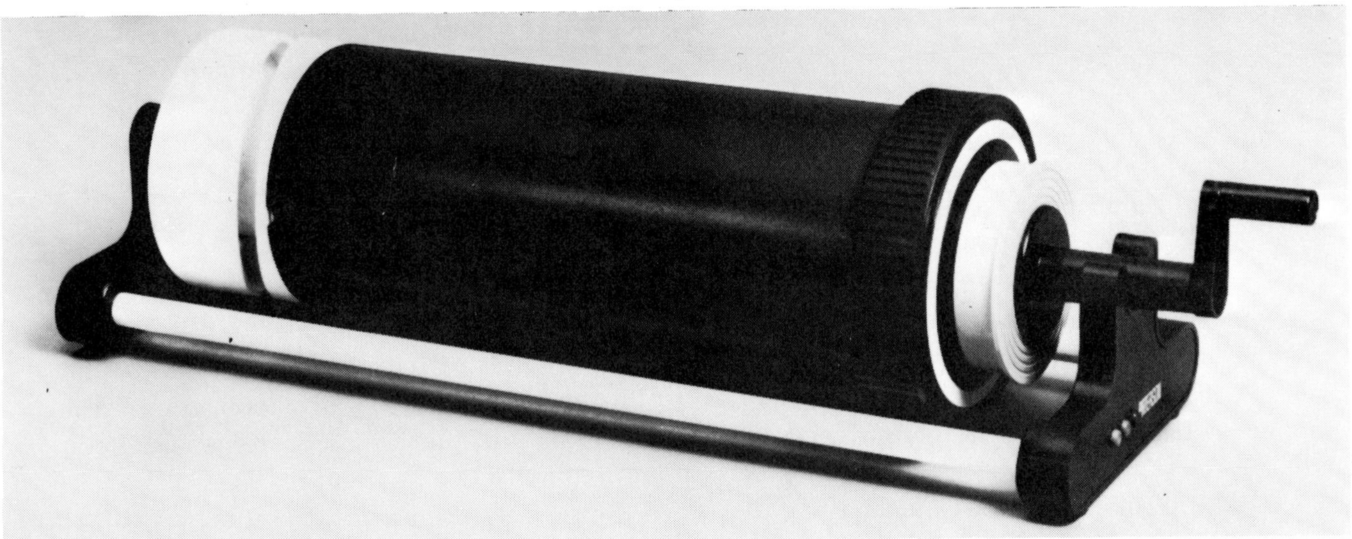

Paterson color print processing drum has its own crank and supporting cradle. Cam device on end ensures good chemical agitation.

of the color *red,* mainly because there is no red there.

If blue is removed from white light, red and green remain and when mixed together they create the color sensation of yellow light. Therefore a yellow filter stops blue light and *yellow* is the complement of *blue.* You know what to call yellow when you see it.

The complement of *green* is *blue* and *red* which when mixed together create a shade of purple called *magenta.*

Color slides and color prints have three layers of emulsion. Each layer controls the amount of a primary color of light by stopping some of that primary color. Therefore each layer is the complementary color of the primary color which it stops. In other words, the layer which controls the amount of red light is itself cyan-colored.

Color slides and prints cause the sensation of white by letting all three primary colors of light pass through the emulsion in equal amounts so the result looks white to your eye. Gray is produced the same way except there is less light of each color but still equal amounts. Black is produced the same way except there is no light of each color.

When you set up your darkroom for making black-and-white prints, you acquired nearly everything necessary to print color. With the addition of a set of color-printing filters, your present enlarger should do nicely.

Processing of the exposed paper may be done either in your standard darkroom trays or in inexpensive plastic drums such as those made by Arkay, Beseler, Colourtronic, Kindermann, Paterson, Premier, Unicolor and probably others I haven't learned of yet. Or, when you really get interested and have the cash to spare, the Kodak motorized drum processor or the Agnecolor Processor should be considered.

A No. 10—dark amber safe-light filter may be an asset, although its use must be limited strictly according to the paper manufacturer's recommendations.

The enlarger must be equipped with a heat-absorbing glass to eliminate the chance of damage to the color negative. The modern color-head enlargers come equipped with this glass. You can buy one for an older enlarger from your local photo dealer or write the manufacturer.

If your enlarger is not equipped with built-in filters, but has a filter drawer, you will need a set of Color Printing—CP—filters ranging in density from 0.05 to 0.50 in each of the colors—cyan, magenta and yellow.

If your enlarger has neither built-in filters nor a filter drawer, you will need a set of Color Compensating—CC—filters in the same density range. CC filters are slightly more expensive but are optically correct and may be used beneath the enlarging lens. Do not use the less expensive CP filters anywhere other than the filter drawer between the light source and the negative.

Regardless of whether you are using CC or CP filters, a 2B Ultraviolet-absorbing filter is necessary and will be used with all filter packs. If you were clever enough to look forward to the day you would be making your own color prints, then you may have purchased one of the color-head enlargers with built-in dichroic filters with dial or lever controls. These enlargers are already equipped with the necessary heat-absorbing glass and ultraviolet 2B filter.

Of additional importance is the fact that the dichroic filters will not fade with use as do the CC and CP filters, thereby aiding the repeatability.

Repeatability can often be a problem in making color prints. A voltage stabilizer for the enlarger can be of great value. Household electrical current is subject to constant fluctuation, due not only to the use of appliances in your own home, but also by the activities of your neighbors. A voltage stabilizer will insure uniform and predictable exposures. It will also put another sizable dent in your bank account. One of the smallest and least expensive devices is the Vivek Regulator which offers 1% regulation for up to 750 watts over a line-voltage range of 105-129 volts AC.

COLOR FILM PROCESSING

There are many manuals written on the complexities of color. My goal is for you to experience the thrill of making your first color print in as simple a way as possible, so let's assume you already have a color negative from a roll of film you've previously shot and processed or had processed. If you want to experience the fun of processing your own color film, go back to the previous chapter on Color Film Processing. Starting on page 143 you learn how to process Kodacolor II color-negative film to make negative-to-positive prints I will talk about first. On page 146 you get the facts on processing Ektachrome for slides to use in making positive-to-positive prints, as I describe later.

Those procedures seem rather long compared to black-and-white film, but it's considerably faster than sending it to a commercial processor, especially if you've been mailing your film away. Remember—processing your own materials gives you complete control over the quality of your work. It is terribly discouraging to have a commercially done roll of film returned damaged because of an equipment failure, or carelessness on the part of a lab technician. Try to get any satisfaction when that happens!

The first thing you notice when viewing the dry film is an overall orange color called a *color mask*. It gives better colors in the print, even though it makes the negative look strange. The color-masking process is all automatic and you don't have to worry about it.

Proofing—Now you must determine which negative you want to print first. Until you become used to viewing color negatives, it can be a bit frightening. In addition to the overall orange cast, all colors are changed from those in the original scene. You are now seeing only complementary colors. All original-scene reds are now cyan, blues are yellow and greens are magenta. Everything changes again when you make a print, so don't spend time trying to interpret color. Instead, judge contrast and density just as you do with black-and-white films.

This is most easily done by making a contact proof sheet using Kodak Panalure paper as described on page 48. This conversion to black-and-white from color lets you see which negatives are correctly exposed. After you have made several color prints, you will probably want to make color contact sheets. This will give you a fair idea of which negatives, if any, have a bad color balance and will vary considerably from your normal filter requirements while printing.

But at this time, stick to black-and-white proofing. Using a magnifier, choose a negative from the proofs which is properly exposed, sharply focused and contains a variety of colors—as best you can recall. Select one of interest to you because this will be your standard reference negative in the future. It will be used to determine differences in printing filters when changing to packages of printing paper of different color values and printing speed. It will also help keep check on your printing techniques and equipment.

COLOR PRINTING EQUIPMENT

You've chosen a well-exposed, sharp, colorful and interesting negative and are ready to print. Let's go over a checklist of what's needed.

Enlarger with color head—or filter drawer above negative carrier—or filter holder to attach beneath lens.
Heat-absorbing glass.
Timer.
Thermometer.
Voltage stabilizer—I consider this essential but you might be able to get along without it if you print at a time when the line voltage is fairly stable.
CP filters for filter drawer; CC filters beneath lens.
CP2B filter.
Color printing paper—Kodak Ektacolor 74RC, 8 x 10 inch
Color paper processing chemicals—Kodak Ektaprint 2, one-gallon size.
No. 10—dark amber—safelight—optional.
3 print processing trays
2 1-gallon brown plastic bottles
Rubber gloves.
Facility for print washing.
Notebook and pen for record keeping.

Enlarger—If your enlarger has built-in dial-type filters you are ahead of the game as this gives a greater degree of filtration than normally possible when using individual filters. And there's no need to handle filters which are always subject to damage. You will also not need the CP2B ultraviolet-absorbing filter or heat-absorbing glass.

Do not use an enlarger with a cold-light source. These fluorescent-type lamps are low in the red component of white light and require abnormally high filtration to correct.

Heat-Absorbing Glass—Necessary if you are using an older enlarger or one not having a "color head." The glass goes above the condenser lens or in the filter drawer above the negative to protect the negative from heat damage during focusing and exposure.

Timer—The system of timing exposures for black-and-white printing exposures is satisfactory for color as long as it's dependable. A portion of print processing is done in total darkness so you'll need a timer which can be seen or reset to signal in the dark.

Thermometer—Keep one handy for routine checks. Color is more sensitive to temperature variations than black-and-white materials.

Voltage Stabilizer—The amount of light produced by an enlarger depends on the AC line voltage. Unless you use a voltage stabilizer, the line voltage fluctuates depending on time of day and what appliances are in use in your house. These voltage fluctuations will prevent you from giving correct exposure even when you have made test prints to find what the exposure should be. Solve the problem by buying and using a voltage stabilizer for your enlarger.

CP FILTERS—Color printing—CP—filters are used above the negative carrier out of the optical system of the enlarger. Because they are not in the image optical path, they are of lower quality than color-compensating filters. They correct color of the light before it goes through the negative and lens. You'll need cyan, magenta and yellow in densities of 5, 10, 20, 40 of each. I recommend red in densities 20 and 40 also. These acetate filters are inexpensive.

Filters you use at the camera for improving b&w exposures don't seem to have much logic in their nomenclature—81B, 2A, and so forth.

Filters for color printing have a nice neat system of identification. There is a number and a letter. The number is *density* and the letter is the *color* the filter appears to have when you look through it at white light. A 10Y is yellow-looking with a density of 0.10. That density is to the color or colors stopped by the filter—the complement.

A higher number says the filter is more dense and appears to be a stronger shade of color. 20R is more dense than 10R. The numbers add together if you put two filters together in the filter pack. Stack 20R and 5R and you get 25R.

CC Filters—Color Compensating—CC—filters are very high quality for use in the image optical path of enlarger or camera. They can be held beneath the enlarger lens in a filter holder. These gelatin filters are more expensive than CP filters. You need filters in cyan, magenta and yellow in densities 05, 10, 20, 30, 40, 50 of each color. Red in 20 and 50 densities is also recommended.

It is important to use as few filters in combination as possible beneath the enlarger lens. This prevents loss of image sharpness caused by light bouncing around on filter surfaces.

These filters are in the path of the projected negative image—KEEP DUST, SCRATCHES AND FINGERPRINTS OFF THE FILTERS!

CP2B—This filter absorbs ultraviolet from the

projector lamp and must be used with any CP or CC filter pack.

Color Printing Paper—I recommend Kodak Ektacolor 74RC paper, which is designed for printing with color negatives. This resin-coated paper processes and dries quickly. DO NOT DRY THIS PAPER ON HEAT EQUIPMENT. The F surface air-dries to a high gloss. It is also available in silk and smooth-lustre surfaces. Store the paper in its foil bag at 50°F (10°C) or lower.

Color Paper Processing Chemicals—Ektacolor 74RC paper is processed in Kodak Ektaprint 2 Chemicals. The two-step processing takes just 8 minutes. Detailed instructions in the developer package must be followed *exactly*. Smallest size available is one gallon.

No. 10 Safelight Filter—A No. 10—dark amber—safelight filter with a 7-1/2-watt bulb may be used at a distance of not less than four feet for a period of not longer than 3 minutes total during dark time.

Print Trays—Three print trays one size larger than the print to be made are necessary.

Rubber Gloves—Good idea to prevent skin irritation. Latex surgical gloves are best.

Facility for Print Washing—One wash step is required and the equipment you use for black-and-white prints should be satisfactory. Don't use a drum-type washer if you are processing more than one color print at a time because the tumbling action can damage print emulsion from a sharp corner of another print.

Notebook—Record-keeping is very important when working with color. Data must be kept regarding filter combinations, exposure times, aperture settings, paper balance and magnification. Test prints are of no value if you forget the factors it took to produce them.

THINK IT THROUGH

How about a little more basic theory—you'll need some understanding of what's about to happen. As I've mentioned, white light is made up of equal parts of red, green and blue. The complementary colors are cyan, magenta and yellow, respectively. Make a sketch of the diagram on page 161 and hang it on the wall near your enlarger. It will help keep your thinking straight.

Remember, you are working with the single-exposure *subtractive* method. Each of the subtractive filters—cyan, magenta and yellow—when introduced into the path of white light, absorbs all or part of its complement and passes the other two primary colors. Therefore, a yellow filter passes red and green while subtracting blue. Each complementary color is made up of the color on each side of it on the triangle. By using only yellow and magenta filters, it is possible to control all the other colors.

Now comes the tricky part which causes the most problems for beginning color enthusiasts. Everything seems to work just backward from what you want to believe. Remember how the negative colors were the complements of the colors in the original scene? The paper will produce an image in colors complementary to those of the negative. Original yellow reproduced blue in the negative which produces yellow on the print.

A simple way to look at it: A color filter over the lens of the *camera* causes the resulting print to have the same overall color as the filter. A yellow filter makes a yellow picture. However, there are two steps in the process—the negative and then the positive—and the emulsion records the complementary color in each case. Yellow of the original scene becomes blue on the neg. When used to expose a print, blue from the negative becomes yellow again on the print.

When you are correcting color balance of a print, you are introducing the color filter between the negative and the positive so there are not two changes in color, from complement back to complement. There is only one.

Therefore yellow added to the *printing* light causes *less* yellow on the print. Another way to describe the same result is to say that yellow added to the printing light causes more of its complement—blue—to appear on the print. But the result is the same, it looks like there is less yellow.

I just discussed the effect of adding more yellow filtering in the printing light. Suppose you are set up with a strong yellow filter and then change it to a light yellow filter. That would mean *less* yellow in the printing light. Mentally shift gears from the paragraph above, consider the effect of reducing the amount of yellow in the filter

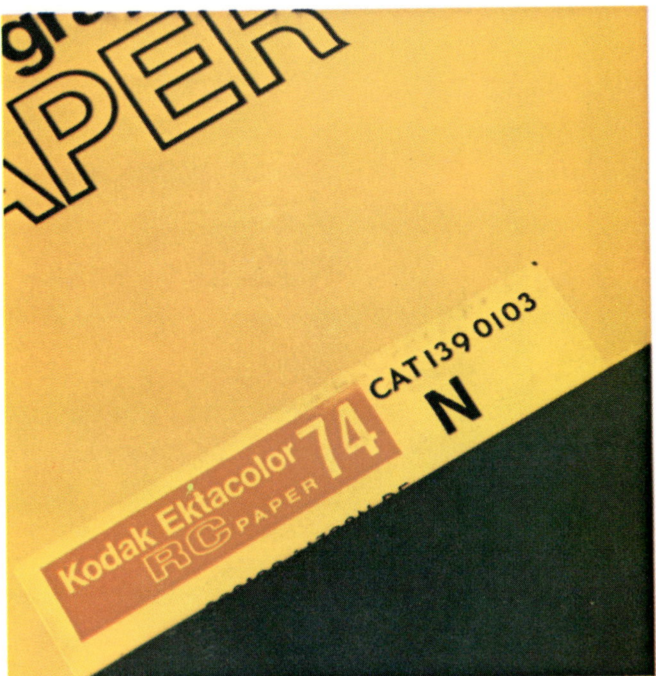

Kodak Ektacolor 74RC paper, available in a glossy (F), smooth lustre (N) and silk-finish (Y) surfaces is used for making color prints from color negatives.

The Beseler 23C with dichroic color head has a dial-in filtration system. Speeds printing time. Filters are fade-proof.

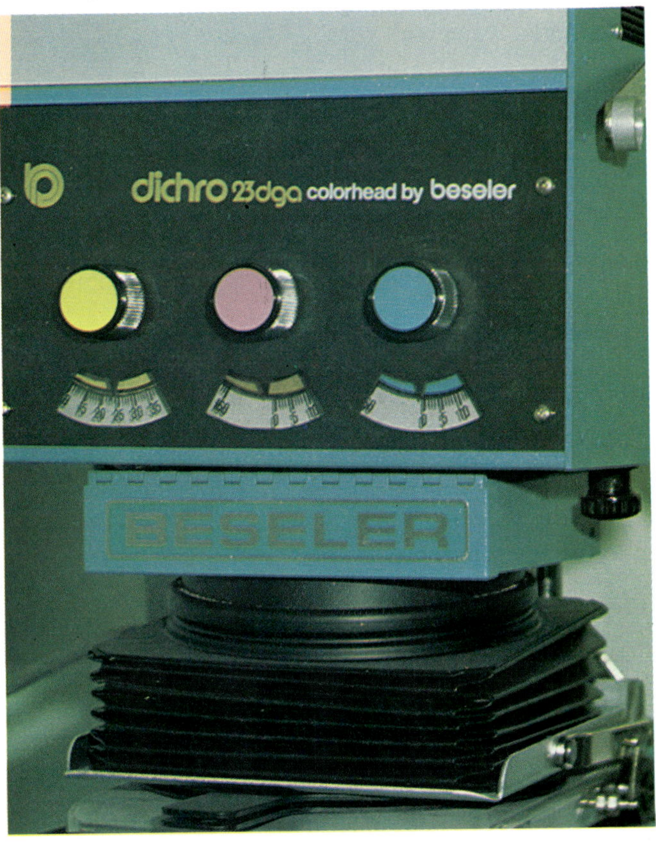

between negative and printing paper.

Less yellow in the filter causes the visual effect of *more* yellow on the print. You can cause that same visual effect by adding a blue filter to the printing light because the complement of blue is yellow.

You can always achieve a visual effect in two ways by using a color *or* its complement. If you get the effect by using more of a certain color, you will get the same effect by using less of its complement.

Reread this a few times, look at the color triangle and let it sink in.

Back with me now? Good, I'll put it in more specific terms. You can make color corrections with only two colors—yellow and magenta. The chart below is based on those two colors.

COLOR PRINT CORRECTION TABLE

Print Is Too	Add Filter	Subtract Filter
Yellow	Yellow	
Blue		Yellow
Red	Yellow & Magenta	
Cyan		Yellow & Magenta
Green		Magenta
Magenta	Magenta	

Use this table when printing from color negatives.

The additive primaries are indicated by the solid line and the subtractive primaries by the broken line. Make a sketch of the diagram and keep it close to your enlarger for reference.

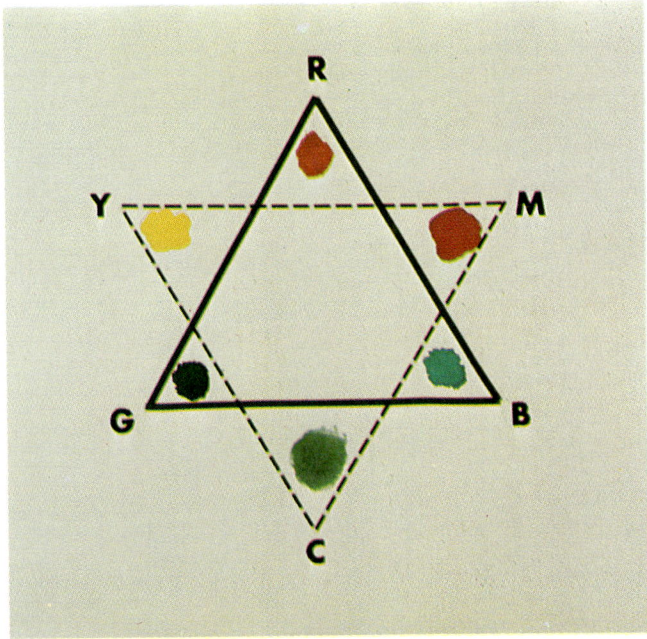

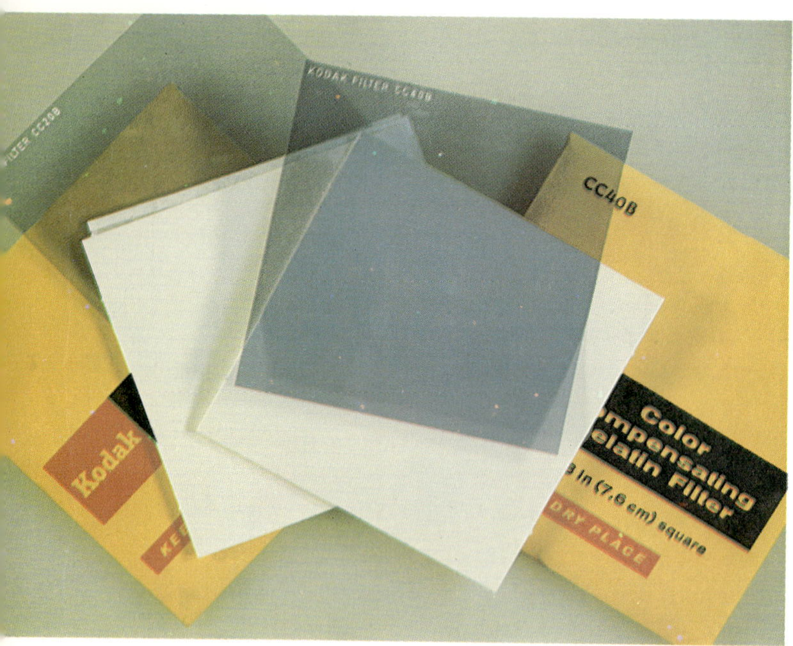

Color compensating (CC) filters are made to very high standards and may be used in the optical path for color printing.

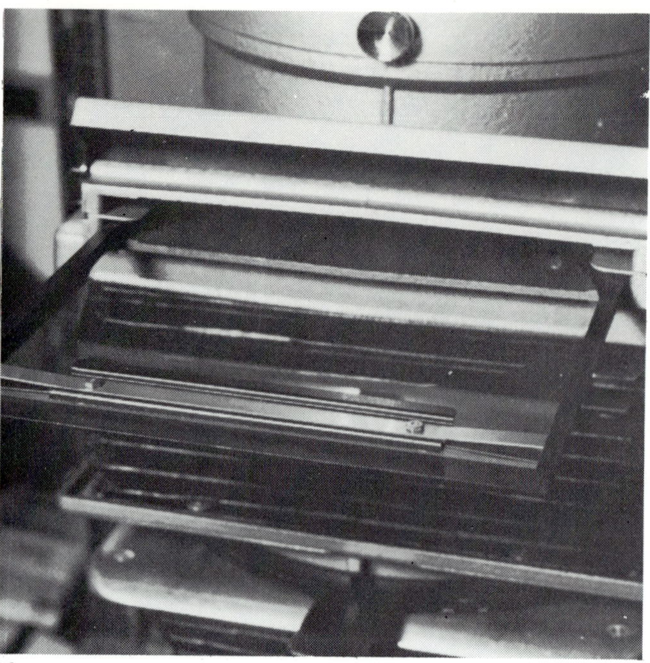

Your enlarger may have a filter drawer rather than built-in filters. This condenser head on a Beseler CB-7 is designed to accept . . . .

With a slight amount of trimming, 3-inch square Kodak CC filters may be held in place below the enlarger lens with a holder such as used for Kodak Polycontrast black-and-white printing filters. Always try to keep the number of filters below the lens to three or less.

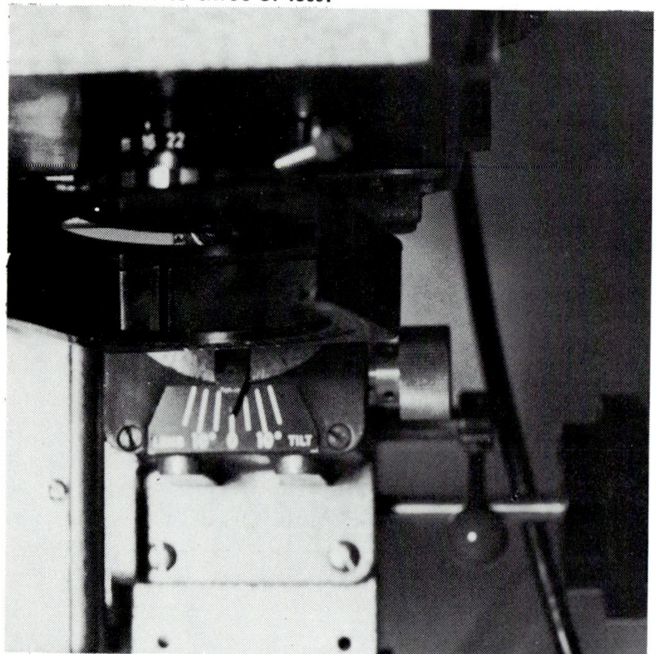

6-inch square Kodak CP filters. Color printing (CP) filters are not optically perfect and must be placed ABOVE the negative stage, usually in a filter drawer.

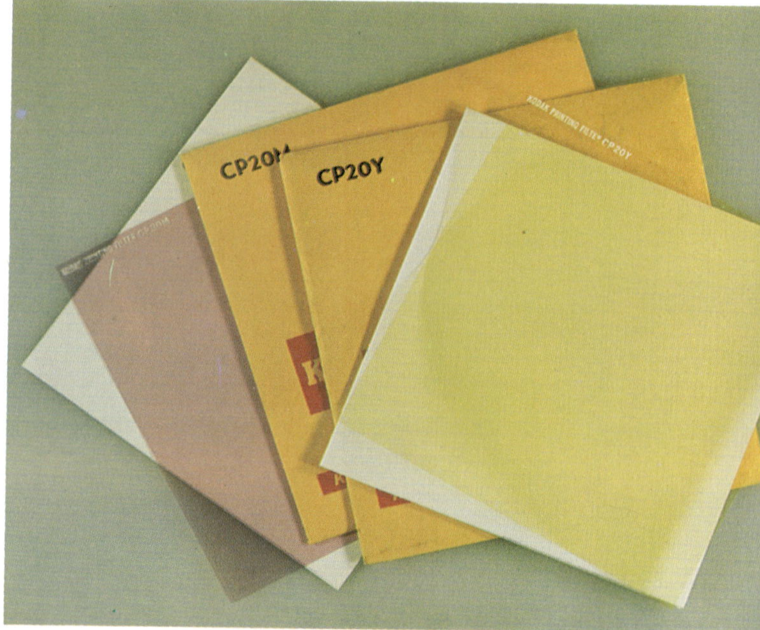

Yellow and magenta in equal parts produce red: 20Y + 20M = 20R. To keep the number of filters to a minimum, I suggested buying a couple of red filters. For instance, if you need a filter pack of 40Y + 40M, you would use these CP filters: 40Y + 40M. By using only one 40R filter, you achieve the same results with one less filter. That is because 40R = 40Y + 40M.

It's difficult to remember that by adding a filter color you get less of that same color in the print, but that's a simplified idea of how it works. With a bit of experience, it will all fall into place.

HOW TO PRINT COLOR

You have all the equipment and materials I've mentioned including the negative to be used as standard. Time to make the first print!

1. You've been keeping the paper in your refrigerator, so allow about two hours for the paper package to come to room temperature.

2. Label bottles. Prepare processing chemicals and set aside in brown plastic one-gallon bottles.

3. Set up processing trays and get the wash arrangement ready.

4. Place negative in enlarger and with darkroom light off, compose and focus to use a full 8x10 inch sheet.

5. Turn on darkroom light and add filters to enlarger. Place CP or CC filters in the appropriate location or dial-in filtration on color head. Use a starting filter pack of 50Y + 50M.

6. Set the lens aperture to *f*-11.

7. Bring the chemicals to a temperature of 91°F (32.8°C) in the trays.

8. Close and lock the darkroom door and turn off the light. Remove a sheet of paper and place it in the easel. Using the test-strip method, make exposures of 5, 10, 15, 20 and 25 seconds.

9. Remove the paper from the easel and in total darkness, process according to the summary of steps included with the print developer.

10. Allow the print to air dry. The slight bluish cast it has while wet will disappear when it dries. Evaluate the print for exposure and color balance. Determine the correct exposure time from the five strips on the sheet. The color balance or lack thereof should be obvious. If the strip with the correct or near-correct exposure is very close to the colors you desire, the perfect print may be near at hand.

Drum Processing Ektacolor 74RC—Perhaps you would rather use one of the processing drums mentioned on page 157 than go through the hassle of using trays in total darkness. If so, the process is quite different. The manufacturer of the tube provides instructions concerning the amount of solution necessary to process paper in particular sizes and quantities. Here are the chemical steps as outlined in Kodak Publication Z-207.

Step	Time	Temperature
1. Prewet with water	30 seconds	91°F (32.8°C)
2. Developer	3½ minutes	91°F
3. Stop bath*	30 seconds	91°F
4. Wash	30 seconds	91°F
5. Bleach-Fix	1 minute	91°F
6. After Bleach-Fix, continue wash steps in appropriate size tray.		
7. Wash	30 seconds	91°F
8. Wash	30 seconds	91°F
9. Wash	30 seconds	91°F
10. Wash	30 seconds	91°F
Total	8 minutes	

All the above times include a ten second drain.

*The acetic acid stop bath is prepared by mixing 32 ounces of water with 1 ounce of 28% acetic acid. To make 28% acetic acid, mix 8 parts water with 3 parts glacial acetic acid. ALWAYS ADD ACID TO WATER, NEVER WATER TO ACID.

Here's a little tip to save you a few cents and help keep your sense of order. When you open the box of Ektaprint 2 developer, you will notice mixing instructions for drum processing, which when followed gives 102 ounces of solution rather than 128 ounces you expect to find in a gallon. The reason for concentrating the developer a bit is that it must be a bit stronger because the first processing step is a water prewet. The prewet is absorbed into the paper emulsion and causes the developer to become diluted.

Here's the tip. Instead of Ektaprint 2 Developer, buy Ektaprint 300 Developer, which is made for machine processing. Mix to make the full 128 ounce gallon, and use it just as if you were using Ektaprint 2. Now when you reach the end of the developer gallon, you have also reached the end of the gallon of Ektaprint 2 Bleach-Fix.

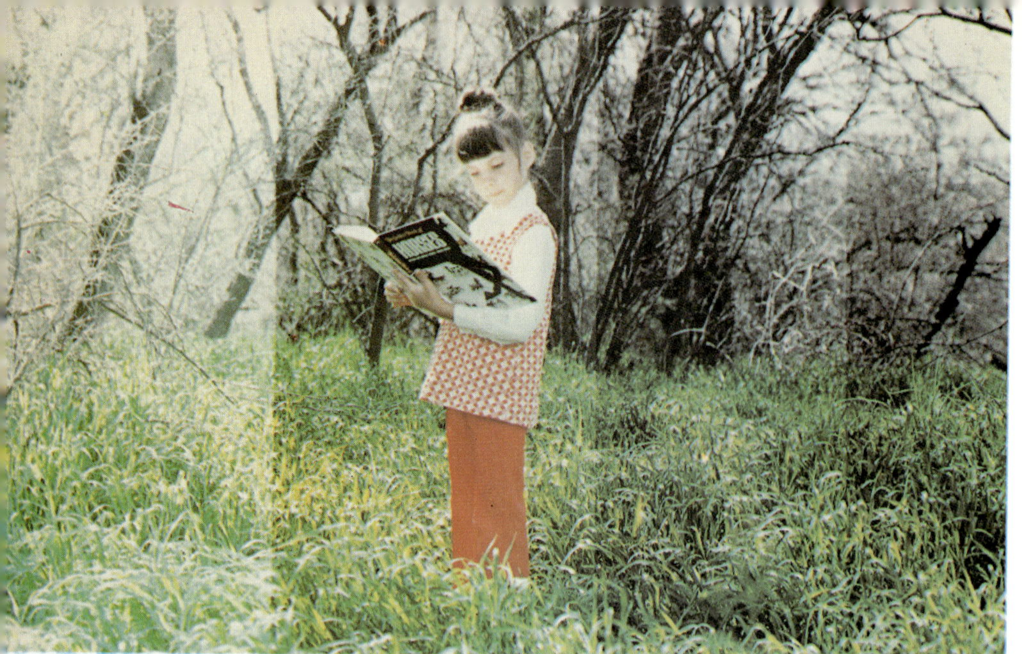

Print 1—Color print test strips are made the same way as b&w ones. Exposures here are 5, 10, 15 and 20 seconds. 15 seconds looks about right. Check for color balance as you look for the correct exposure.

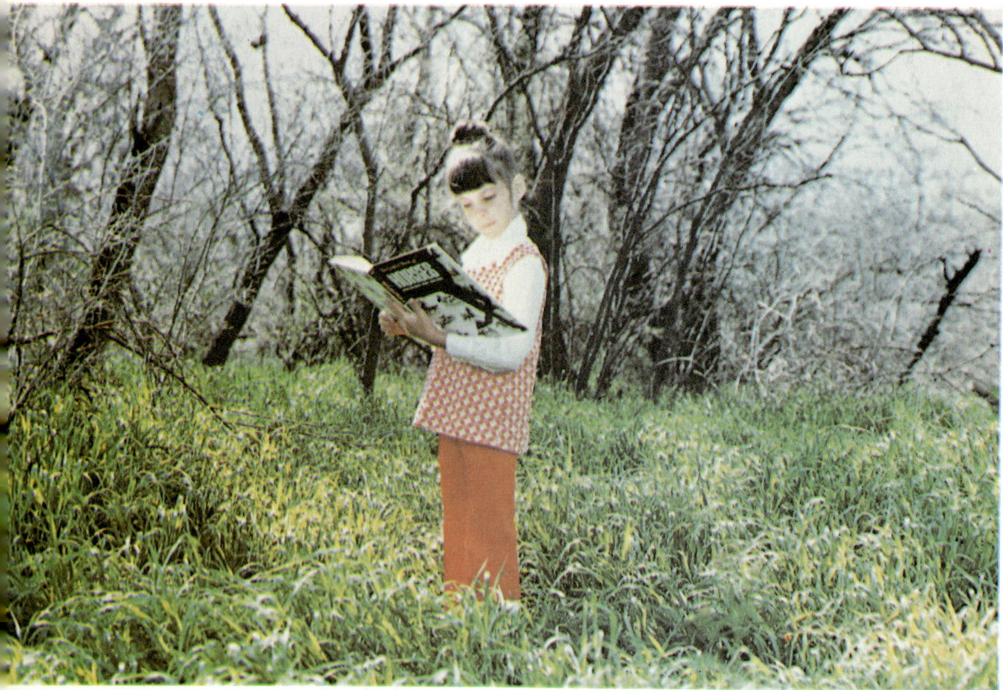

Print 2—15 seconds at *f*-8 with 80Y + 45M filter pack. It's an acceptable print but I'd prefer the grass to be darker.

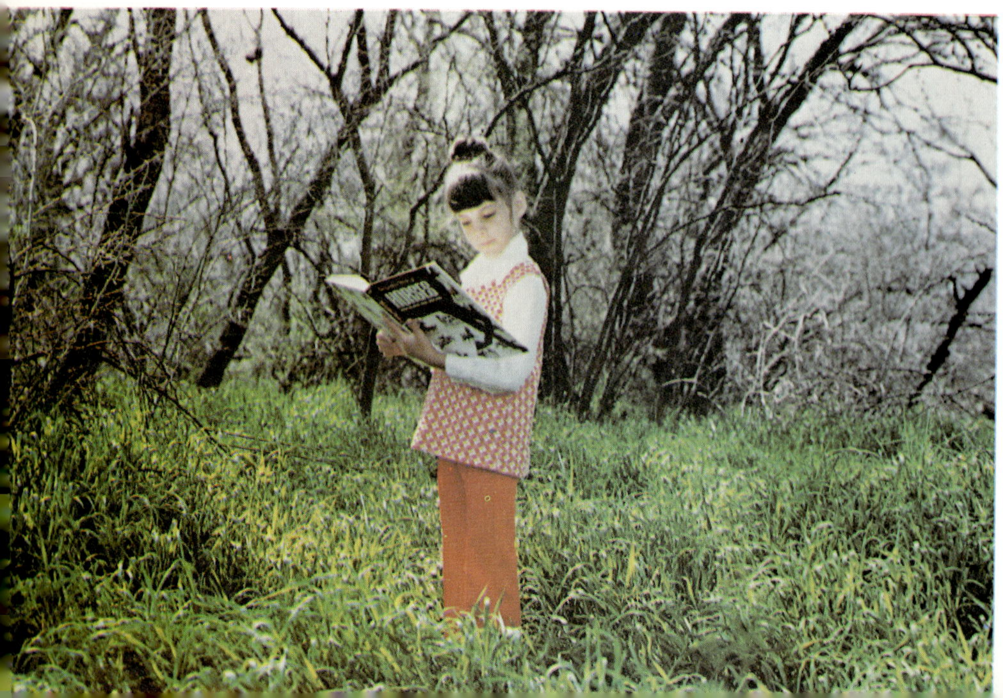

Print 3—same as 2, except I added exposure to the bottom and corners to increase the color saturation a bit.

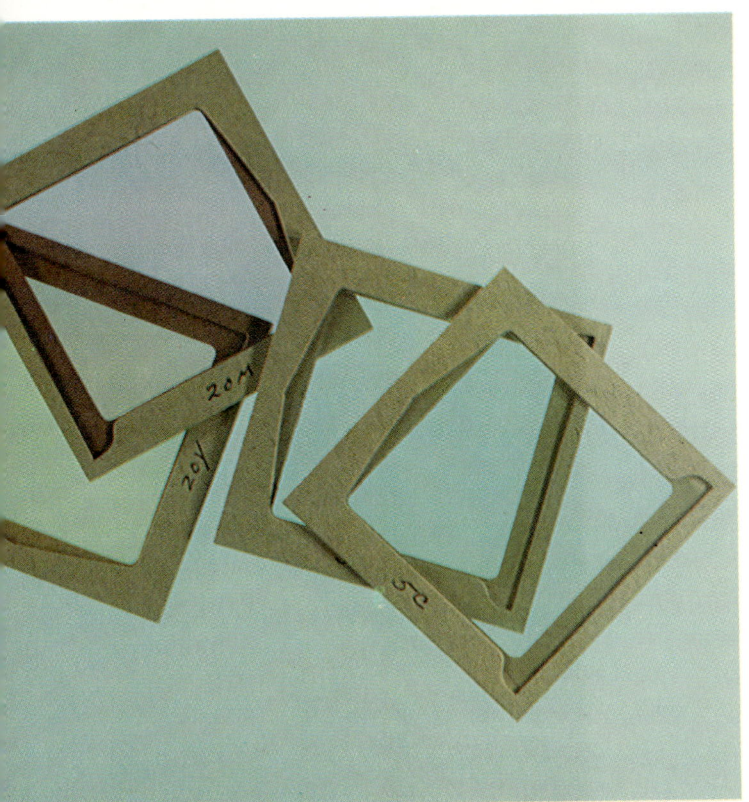

Kodak's Viewing Filter Set includes mounted filters in 5, 10, 20 and 30 densities of cyan, magenta, yellow, green, blue and red. These are especially handy for determining the filter pack changes you need to make your final print.

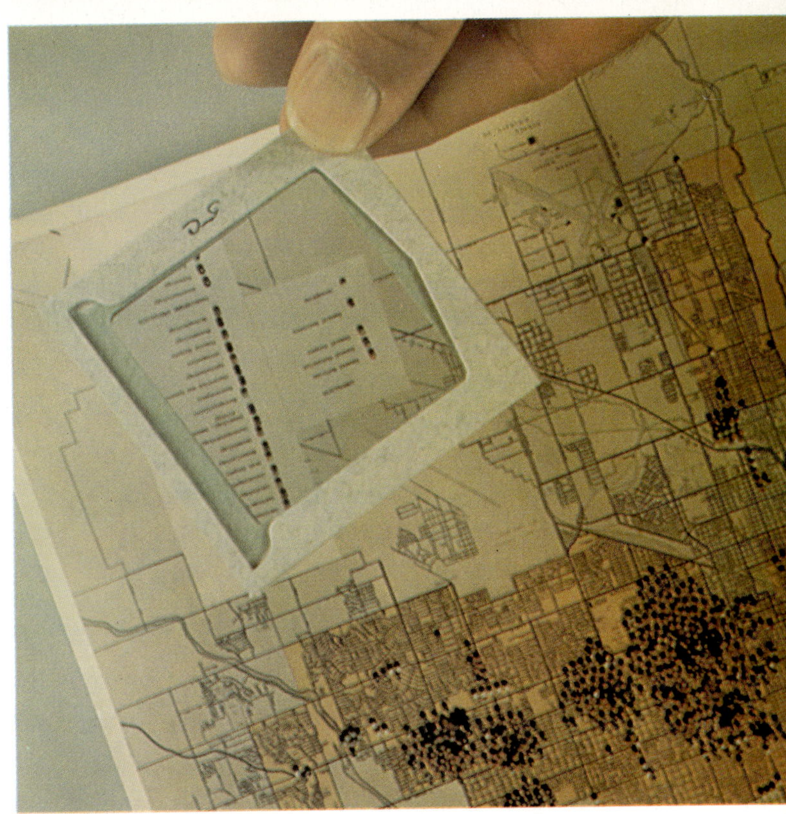

Be sure the print is well lighted and that you are not viewing the shadow of the filter itself. Correct the printing filter by only 1/2 the viewing-filter density you believe gives the best color balance.

Hints for staying sane while processing color prints—Part of this processing business takes place in the dark. You have to be fully aware of where each chemical is and the time in solution for each. Kodak's Ektaprint 2 Kit requires only two solutions with a total dark time of only 4 minutes.

It's easy to set your luminous-dial timer to the times required and transfer the print to the next bath at the right moment.

Here's how to make it all fool-proof and enjoyable, too. With a tape recorder set on RECORD, go through the entire print-processing period in your living room as you read the process steps and watch a timer. Notify yourself on tape at the precise time to drain and transfer the print. During the quiet time, turn the record player up and include some of your favorite music. Allow about 15 seconds at the beginning of the tape so you'll have time to get yourself set for the first solution when you start the recorder. Keep the recorder handy and each time you print, use it to give yourself precisely timed verbal directions. Simple and accurate.

Decide which direction the color shift has taken and refer back to the table I gave you. If the print is too red, you must what? Right—add yellow and magenta. If it's too blue, subtract yellow. Recheck the table and keep the triangle in mind, and you will keep the colors straight.

If the color balance is just slightly off on the print, only a small change in filtration will be necessary. Probably no more than a 10 filter. If it is grossly off, you may have to make several attempts to get the color where you think it should be.

There is a method of viewing prints to determine necessary filter changes and even though it costs a few dollars, it may well save you time and money in wasted trial prints. I suggest you buy Kodak's Viewing Filter Set.

To use these filters to determine filter changes necessary during the enlarging, decide which color you wish to eliminate. Let's suppose the print is too blue. View the print through the complementary color—yellow—selecting the filter density which gives the print the proper balance. Hold the filter near your eye so white light strikes the print and reflected light from the print goes through the filter to your eye. If you lay the filter on the print, its density is effectively doubled because light goes through it twice.

Suppose the print colors appear correct when viewed through a 20Y filter. Going back to our table, when the print is too blue, you know you must subtract yellow. The density of the viewing filter is not the right correction because the action of the printing filter on the print paper is greater than the effect you see by viewing the print. Change the filter pack by **half** the density of the viewing filter. In this case the viewing filter is 20Y, so the filter pack change is to subtract 10Y.

ALWAYS ADD OR SUBTRACT HALF THE VALUE OF THE VIEWING FILTER IN THE COLOR STATED IN THE COLOR PRINT CORRECTION TABLE ON PAGE 161.

Record everything you have done to this point in your notebook. Oaths muttered under your breath when you saw the test print need not be recorded. Everything else should be. Note exposure times, filter pack, lens aperture, magnification, paper balance from paper package, process chemicals and negative identification. Your entry will look something like this:

STANDARD NEGATIVE KODACOLOR II
File No. 5-74-22C
Ektacolor 74RC Paper 8x10"
White Light Data: CC: -20M
CC: +10Y
Ex. Factor: 90
Lens: 50mm set at *f*-11
Exposures of 5, 10, 15, 20, 25 seconds
Enlarger height for full print: 22"
Process: Ektaprint 2
Filter pack: 50Y + 50M
Had pot roast for dinner: too well done.
Print too blue.
Exposure of 15 seconds best.
Viewing filter: 20Y

You notice in the notes, I mention *white-light data.* This information is printed on the paper package sealing wrapper. It is the manufacturer's clue to how this package differs in white-light response from the package you just finished and which—until this point—was your "standard." Each batch of paper is slightly different from a batch with another emulsion number. Always check the white-light data on each new package and use this procedure to determine the filter requirements for the new paper:

1. Subtract the white light data for the old paper from the filter pack used to print your standard negative. Example:

Print 1—95Y + 45M turns print too blue. If print is too blue, *subtract* yellow from filter pack.

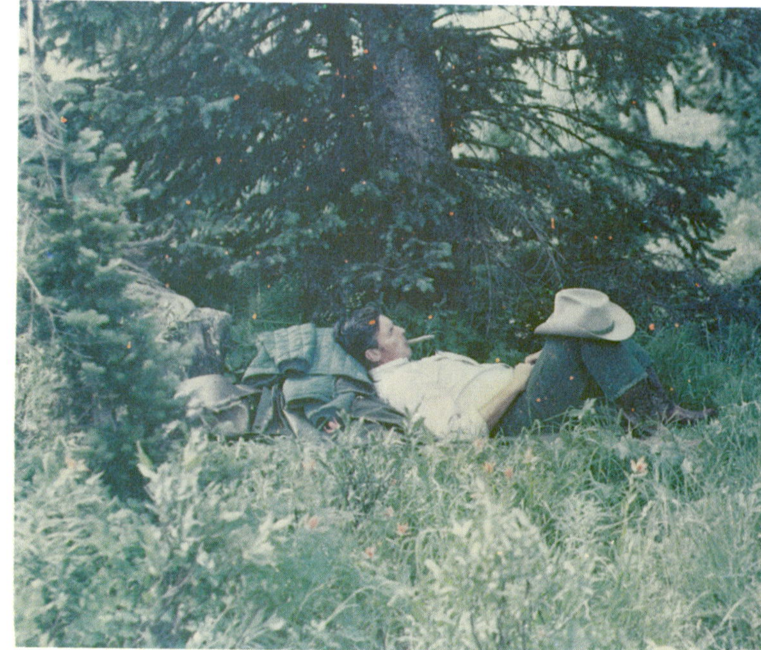

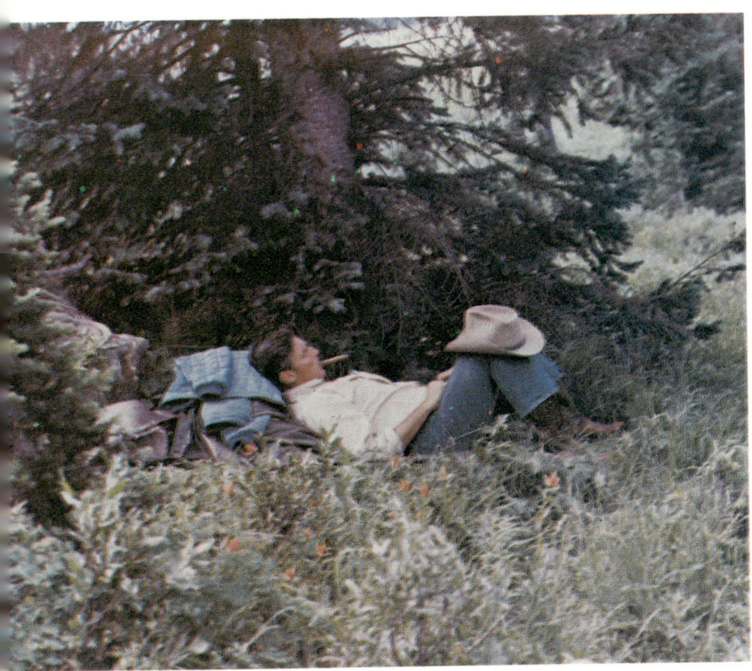

Print 2—75Y with magenta undercorrected at 20M gives overall magenta tint. Print too magenta, *add* magenta to filter pack.

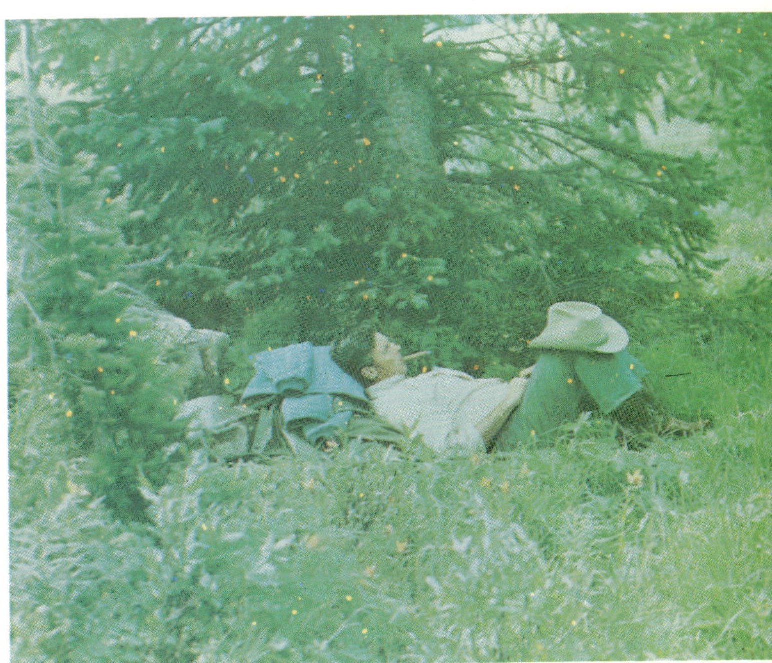

Print 3—75Y and magenta overcorrected at 60M shifts tint to green. Print too green, *subtract* some magenta from filter pack.

Print 4—55Y + 45M gives too little yellow correction and print turns yellow. Print too yellow, *add* yellow to filter pack.

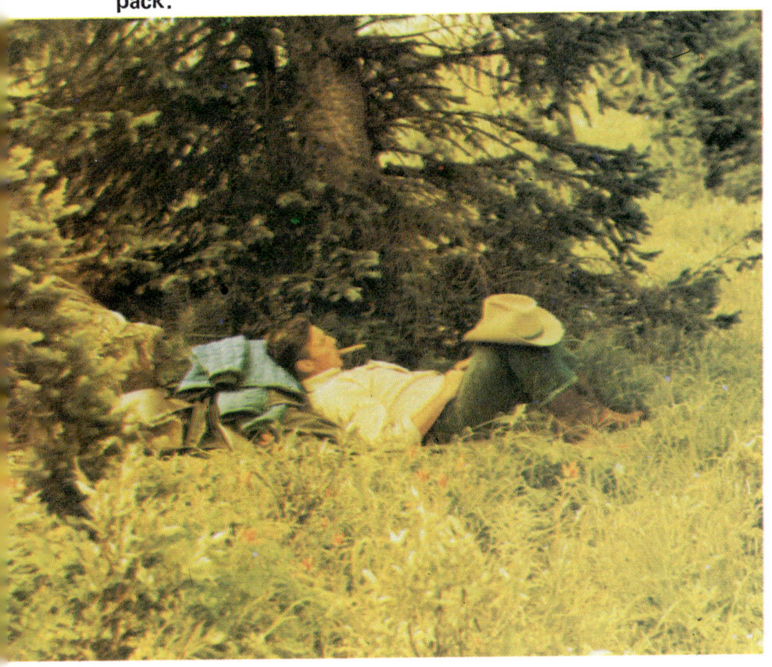

Print 5—75Y + 45M gave me the print I wanted. Check this against the other examples to see how filter changes affect color balance. Exposure of 15 seconds and *f*-11 lens setting are the same for each print. Only one color was changed in the filter pack in each case.

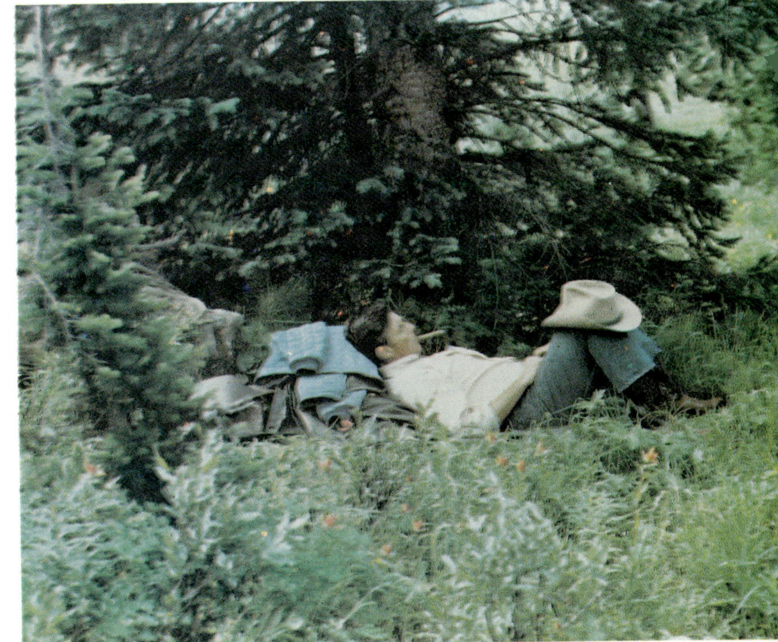

Filter pack	70M	30Y	
WLD	10M	10Y	
	60M	20Y	Basic filter value

2. Add the white light data for the new paper to the basic filter value. Example:

Basic value	60M	20Y	
New WLD	-10M	20Y	
	50M	40Y	New basic pack

Test this new basic filter pack on your standard negative. The test print you get should be very close to the prints made on the previous batch of paper. Calculate the exposure difference with this formula:

$$\text{Exposure time for new paper} = \text{Exposure time for old paper} \times \frac{\text{Exposure factor new paper}}{\text{Exposure factor old paper}}$$

Example:

$$15 \text{ seconds} \times \frac{90}{100} = 13.5 \text{ seconds}$$

This is the exposure time to try with your standard negative.

That pretty well covers anything you need to know concerning the test strips. It only takes a minute or two and will be invaluable the day you want to reprint a negative. Keep records on *all* negatives printed.

You've decided what changes to make in the filter pack and which exposure is best. Go back to step 5 in the procedure and continue from there, using the exposure time you want in step 8. This first trial print should be quite close to the proper color balance. If the test strip was only slightly off you may have the perfect print now. If not, the print may still be somewhat off balance and you'll need to check the print with the viewing filters once more and adjust the filter pack a bit more. If this is necessary, repeat the previous steps until you are satisfied with the color and exposure on the print.

You should be pretty close to the target now. While you are studying the print for any minor corrections in exposure and color, also look for areas which can be helped by dodging or burning-in. The same manipulations you've used on black-and-white prints, are possible with color. But don't use the dodging tool made of colored plastic. Enough light passes through to cause a strong color shift in the dodged area. Remember, color-print paper is sensitive to all colors of light.

Record the data for each trial print and be especially sure to note the information concerning the final print. After you get it all worked out, keep your standard negative handy and print it again from time to time. If you are unable to repeat the results of this print you've just made, even though you may have had to recalculate for a change in paper batches, check the condition of the filters and enlarging lamp.

Each new package of paper will probably be marked with white-light data which differs from the package you were using previously. A data sheet is provided, giving information on filter pack adjustments for a change in emulsion number. Make these adjustments and print your standard negative, using the corrected filter pack. It should be a very close match each time. If it does not, check your calculations, equipment and the age of the chemicals to determine the cause.

PHOTOCOLOR II

Back on page 144 in the color-negative-processing discussion I mentioned Photocolor II, an unusual British-made processing kit which can be used to process both color-negative film AND prints made from color negatives.

This kit works with Kodak Ektacolor 74RC, Sakuracolor and Agfacolor Type 4 printing papers. Processing details are in the very complete instruction book accompanying the kit. You can process a print in just 4 minutes and 40 seconds at 100°F (38°C)—almost twice as fast as some other kits. Temperatures can range from 90°–100°F (32°–38°C) with a time adjustment as shown in a graph in the instructions.

I recommend Photocolor II where its attractive advantages of faster processing time and the ability to process both color prints and negatives offset its higher cost of approximately $1.03 per drum-processed print and 67¢ per tray-processed print (costs for solutions only).

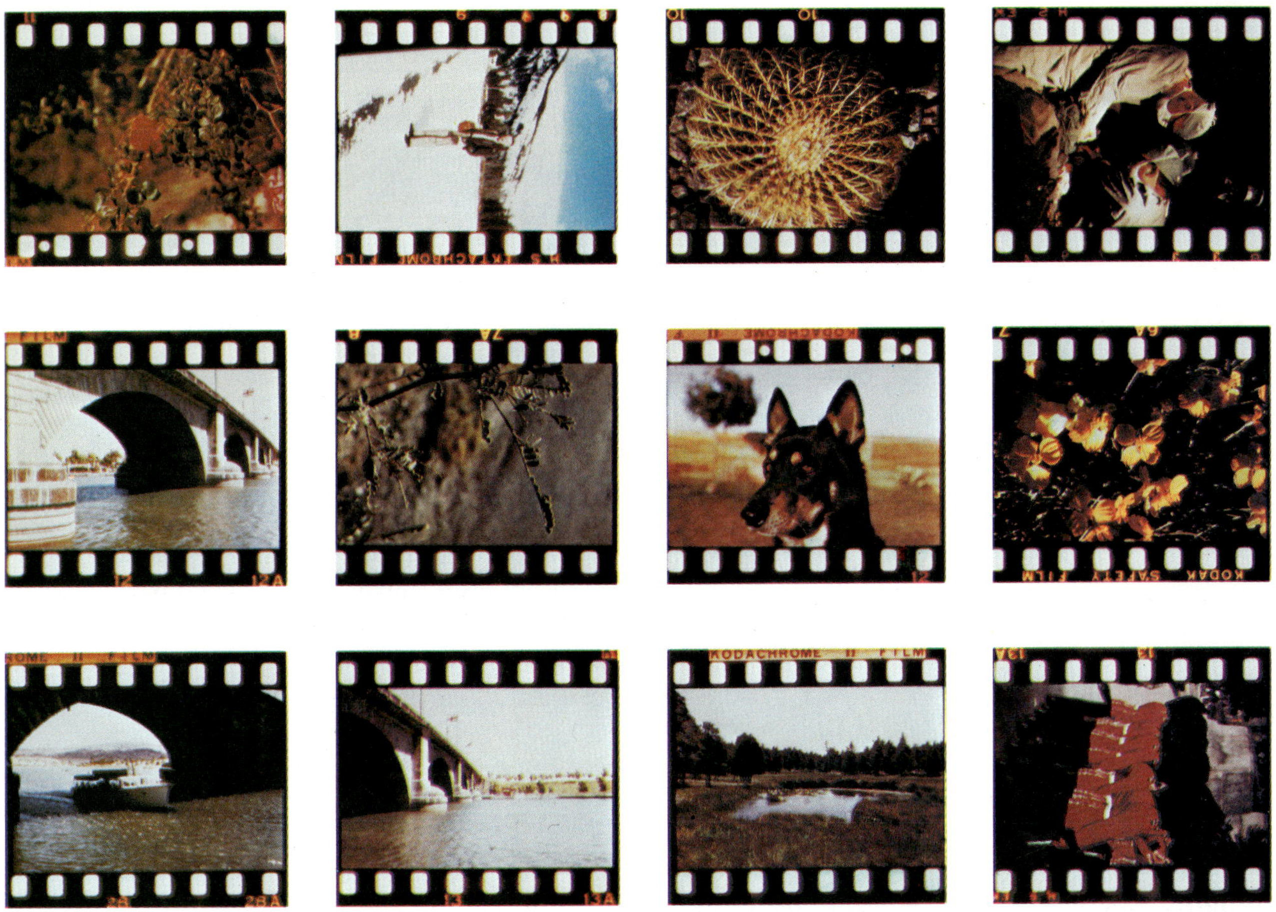

Proof sheets made from slides are helpful in determining exposure and color balance. The contact is made just as if you were using b&w negatives. Though the slides are not equal in density, all provide adequate information on which you can base exposure and print manipulation needs.

PRINTING FROM SLIDES

Many people prefer to shoot slide film rather than negatives. Each exposure appears as a finished product when the slide film is processed.

Slide processing can be done in the home darkroom with all but a few films. The data sheet included with the film tells you if it can be processed by the user, and what chemical kit is necessary. The equipment required is the same as for negative films.

Slide film is a reversal material, meaning that it starts out as a negative and is changed to a positive during the developing process. In the past this was accomplished by re-exposing to a white light during processing to make the positive image. Today re-exposure is not necessary because the reversal is done chemically.

Making prints from slides may be your thing. You will be exposing the printing paper to a positive image on the slide so the printing paper must also be reversal type, just as the slide film is. The only fundamental difference is transparency film has a transparent base; reversal color printing paper is on an opaque reflecting base. Here's a list of what you will need to print from positive transparencies:

Slide—transparency—material of your choice.
Processing equipment as described previously, plus 2 more brown plastic bottles.
1 package Kodak Ektachrome RC paper, Type 2203
Kodak Ektaprint R-1000 Chemical Kit—1 gallon size.

This material is exposed using the same filtration system as negative film. Make a test strip using a full sheet of 8 x 10 paper at *f*-11 for

Print 1 directly below is a test with 10, 20, 30 and 40-second exposures. Remember when printing from slides, less exposure darkens the print. Best exposure appears to be 20 seconds to produce clear whites and best overall color saturation.

Print 2 at right is straight print at 20 seconds exposure using paper maker's recommended 15Y + 20M filter pack.

Print 3 at bottom right centers attention on red jackets and white belts. I darkened lower left corner and marching feet by dodging to hold back light from that area. It got just 5 seconds of the 20-second exposure.

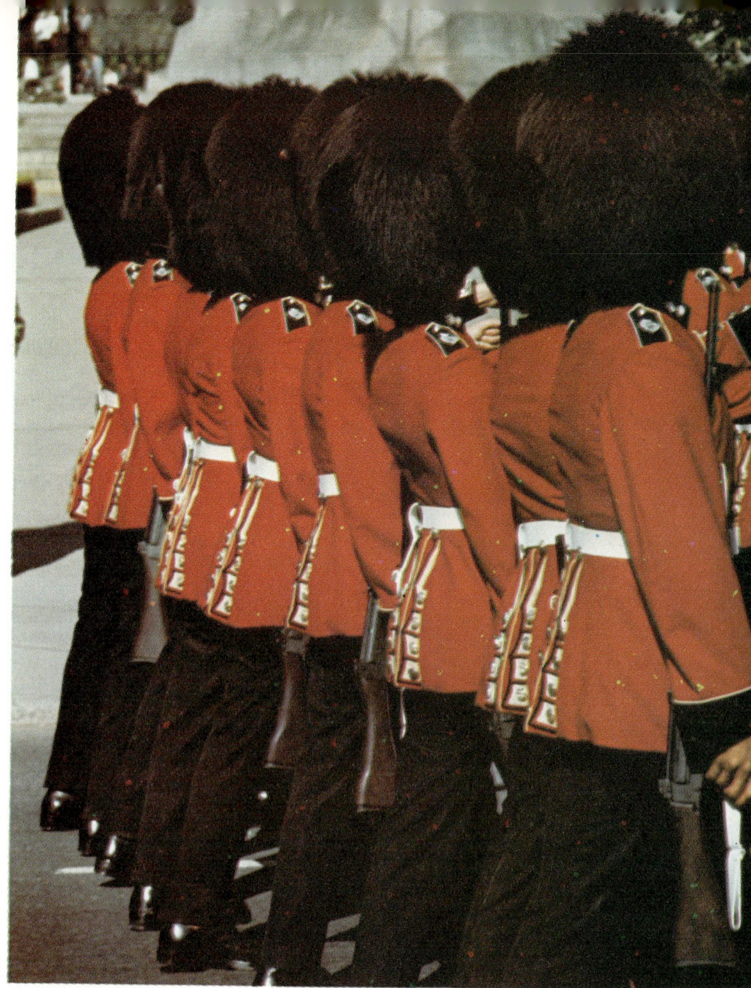

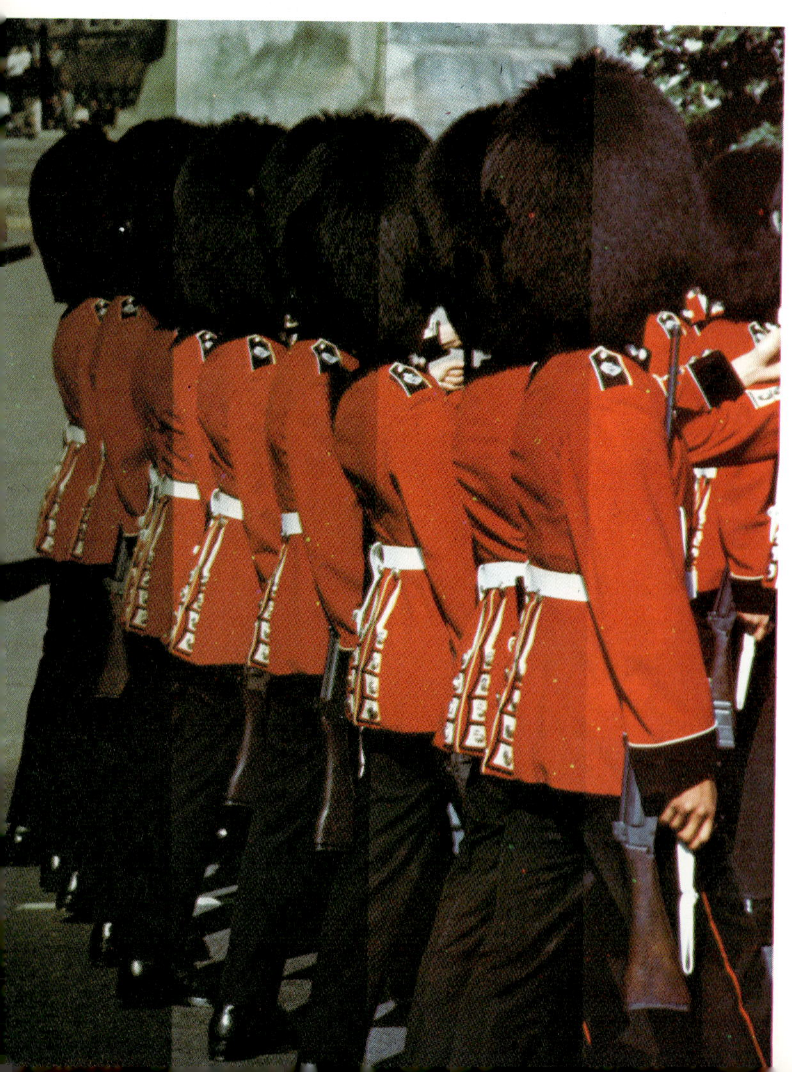

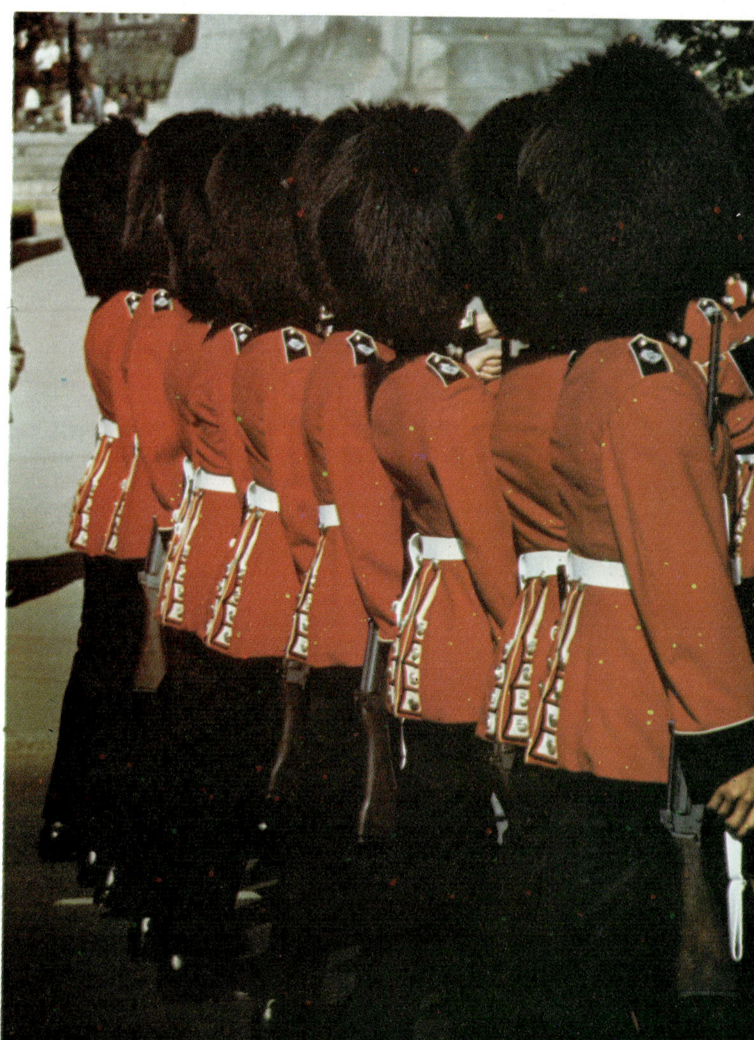

exposures of 5, 10, 15 and 20 seconds. Start with a filter pack of 20Y + 10M. Here's a rundown on the processing steps when using a drum or tube processor:

Prewet with water	1 minute
First developer	2 minutes
Stop Bath	30 seconds
Wash	1 minute
Wash	1 minute
Color developer	2 minutes
Wash	30 seconds
Bleach-Fix	3 minutes
Wash	30 seconds
Wash	30 seconds
Wash	30 seconds
Stabilizer	30 seconds
Rinse with water	15 seconds
Total time	13¼ minutes

All solutions and washes 100°F (38°C)
All times include ten second drain
Dry—100° to 105°F (38° to 40°C)—air dry or hairdryer.

Now evaluate the print for exposure. Think about reversal materials. The more exposure—the lighter the print; the less exposure—the darker the print. The exact opposite of printing negative-to-positive. Overexposure produces a light, washed-out print and underexposure gives you a dark print lacking shadow detail. Got it? Good!

Because you are now working with reversal emulsion—really a negative followed by a positive in one procedure—the filters work differently. Adding a color to the filter pack adds that color to the print. It is the same as using a filter in front of the camera lens when making an exposure using a slide film. Use viewing filters as mentioned before, to determine the change in the filter pack, and consult the chart below.

REVERSAL PRINT CORRECTIONS

Print	Add	Subtract
Yellow		Yellow
Blue	Yellow	
Red		Yellow & Magenta
Cyan	Yellow & Magenta	
Green	Magenta	
Magenta		Magenta

Use this table when printing from color slides.

You'll be pleased with the results when you arrive at the color balance you desire. Sharpness, contrast and detail are magnificent. It's a nice process—faster and cheaper than making a negative from the slide and then printing that as most commercial labs do. If slides are your thing, but you want an occasional print, it's well worth it.

FANCY GOODIES

I should mention the equipment you drool over if you have a friend who is a professional. There is equipment available to expose and process several thousand prints daily, but unless you wish to go into this business on a commercial basis, you're not interested.

About the only exotic piece of gear you may want is a color analyzer. Good ones range from the relatively inexpensive Beseler PM Model to the top-of-the-line Macbeth. Analyzers are miniature computers. Once you achieve perfect color balance, you feed that exposure and filter information into the analyzer and it will tell you how to print each succeeding different negative If you make color prints each evening or each weekend, think about purchasing an analyzer, but don't choke on the price.

Other color materials and processes are available, including those by Unicolor, Beseler, Cibachrome and more. Processing methods use cylinders, tubes, canoes and motorized or manual drums. The procedure I have suggested is simple, efficient and inexpensive. The basics of color printing remain the same. Only the physical items differ.

Once you have gained a bit of experience and have mentally sorted out the fundamentals, the choice of equipment and processing is yours.

If you want complete control over what you produce, it will cost you: Less in dollars, more in time, but it's worth it to—DO IT IN THE DARK!

Chromega

PRE-SOAK TEMPERATURE NOMOGRAM

No need to heat chemicals to manufacturer's specified working temperature. Just use the chemicals at room temperature with a hot water "presoak" at the beginning of the process. The temperature of the presoak bath is determined by the ambient temperature of the working solutions as specified on the chart below.

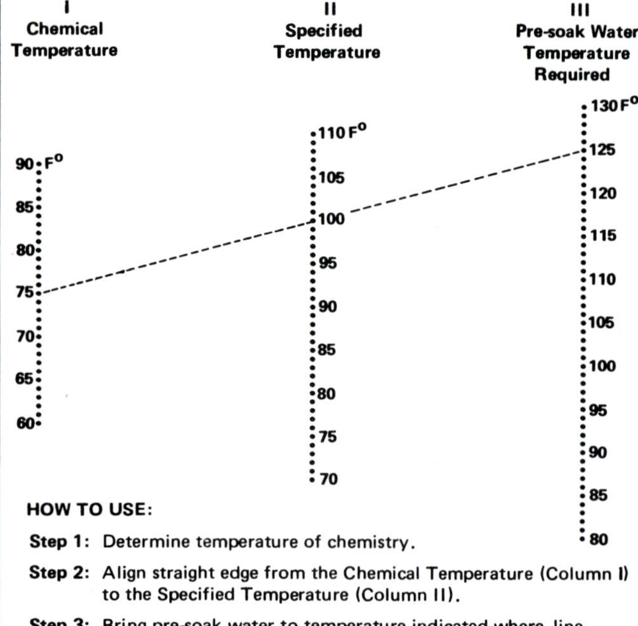

HOW TO USE:

Step 1: Determine temperature of chemistry.

Step 2: Align straight edge from the Chemical Temperature (Column I) to the Specified Temperature (Column II).

Step 3: Bring pre-soak water to temperature indicated where line intersects (Column III).

EXAMPLE: Broken line on Nomogram indicates chemicals at 75° requires 125° pre-soak temperature water.

This nomogram courtesy Simmon-Omega, shows how you can handle color printing a little easier by pre-soaking the print in warm water, regardless of the temperature of the chemicals.

Print 1 using paper maker's recommended 15Y + 20M filtration closely matching original slide.

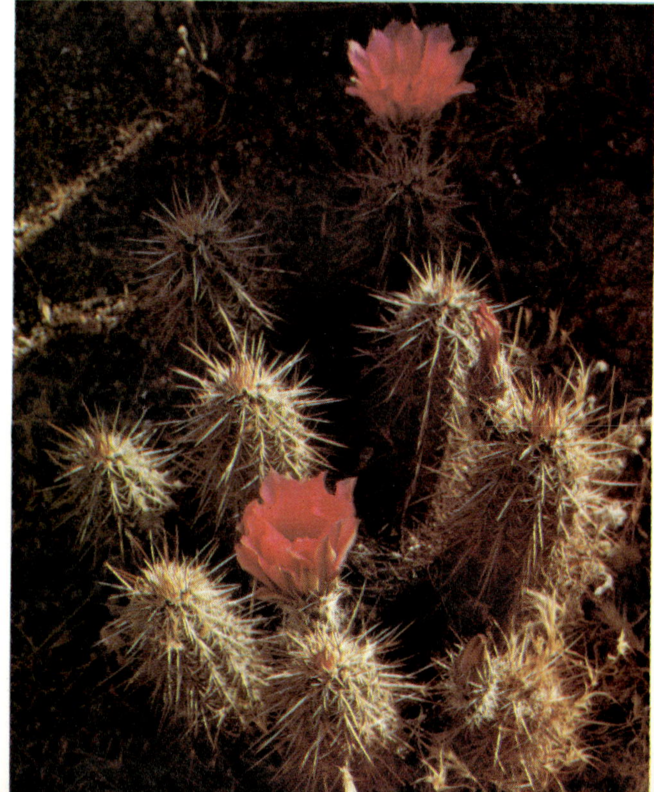

Print 2 had same exposure as 1 with no yellow and 20M. Print lacks yellow. Red blossom picks up a bluish cast.

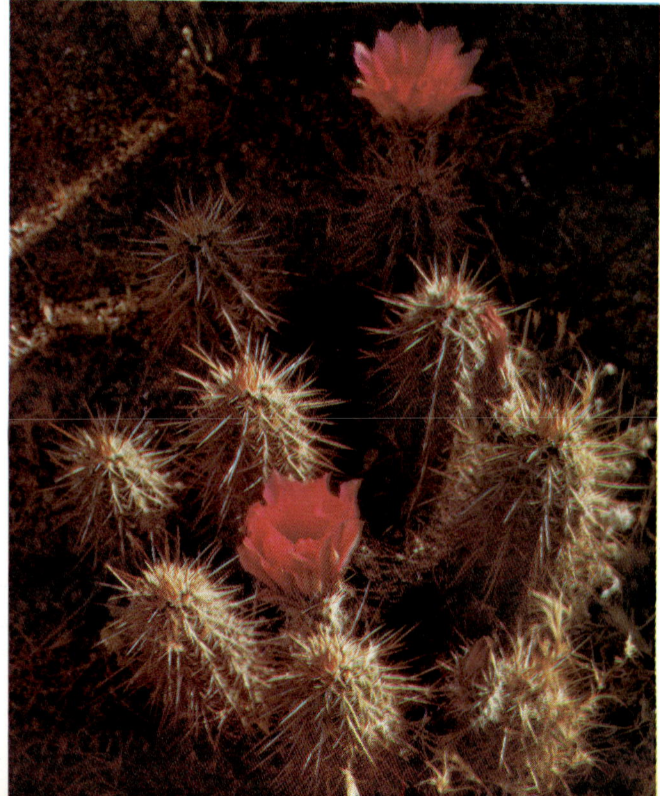

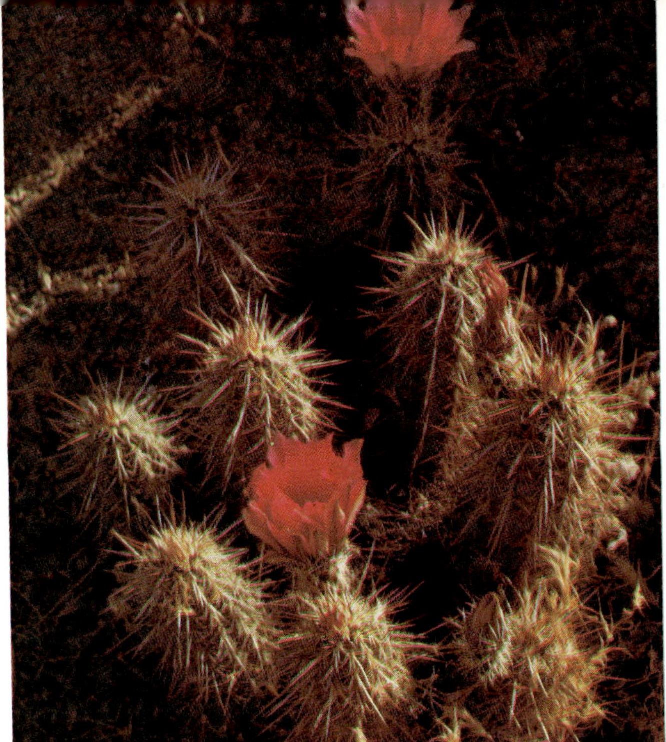

Print 3 used 15Y + 5M to get less magenta and more green appearance. A change of 15 filter density makes a much less noticeable difference when compared to negative-to-positive printing. Also notice the slight density change when adding or subtracting filters.

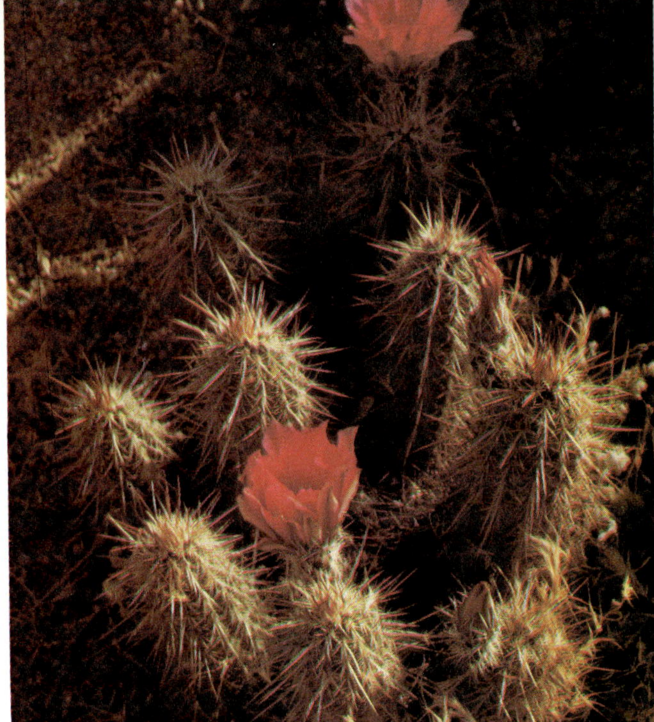

Print 4 used 30Y + 20M. In positive-to-positive printing, adding a color to the filter pack adds that color to the print. Print is now starting to turn yellow as I added more yellow to the filter pack.

All prints in this series were exposed 35 seconds at *f*-3.5. Notice minimal density differences, even with filtration changes. Positive-to-positive printing takes considerably more exposure-time and filter-pack variance to produce a noticeable change than negative-to-positive printing.

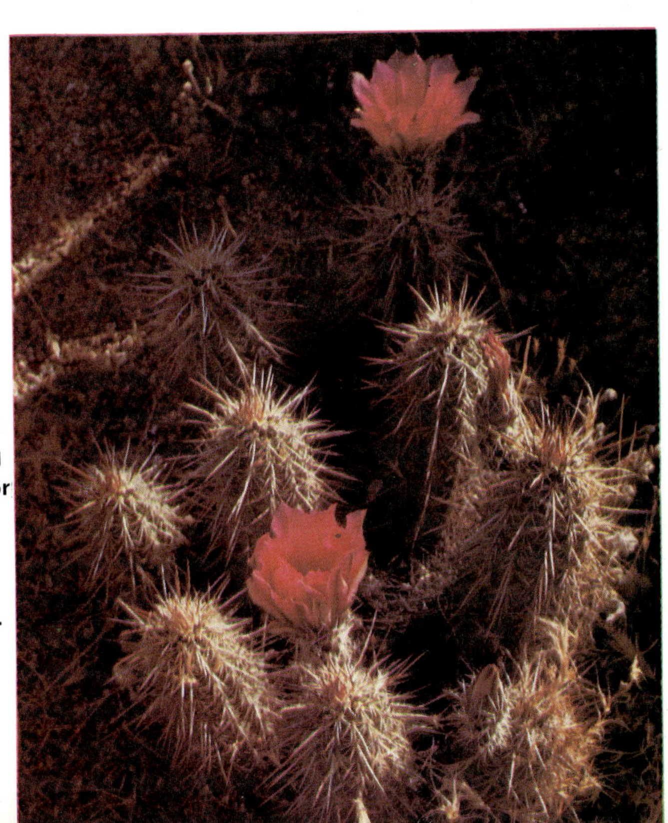

Print 5, final in the series, used 15Y + 35M. Color balance now has an overall purple shift. This series proves printing color from negatives or slides is a personal thing. The color balance I prefer might not suit you. You might prefer slightly more yellow, blue, magenta or green. Addition or subtraction of a filter from the pack lets you quickly and easily alter the color balance to the exact hues you desire. Don't be afraid to experiment and never settle for "close enough." Make the work suit you. After all, it's to enjoy!

CIBACHROME COLOR PRINTS

Cibachrome is a process for producing prints directly from transparencies. It's a relatively new process, having been introduced in the U.S. by Ilford, Inc., in 1974. The product line includes 4x5, 8x10, 11x14 and 16x20 printing paper, chemical kits in 2-quart and 1-gallon sizes, processing tubes, a printing-filter set, exposure monitors, process thermometer, print manual and print-surface sprays.

The advantages of Cibachrome, as stated by the manufacturer, are greater sharpness, better color saturation and greatly increased resistance to fading. Resistance to fading is accomplished by incorporating pure azo dyes into the emulsion during manufacturing, as opposed to all other processes which form the color image during processing. Cibachrome images are supposed to last up to ten times longer than other color-print materials.

Print material is of the resin-coated type, handled in a three-step-plus-wash 12-minute process. Printing paper is labeled *Cibachrome Color Print Material Type A*, and the chemical kit is designated *Chemistry Kit Process P-12.* The handiest kit for home use, I think, is packaged to make two quarts of working solution and may be mixed in one-quart portions if you desire. The kit processes 20 8x10 prints and contains five liquid chemicals, two bags of dry chemical and one bag of bleach-neutralizer powder. Also provided is a set of three plastic cups marked 90ml (about 3 ounces) and designated Developer, Bleach and Fixer, along with the always desirable instruction sheet.

Ilford, Inc., is pretty good about instructions all the way around. Sheets are packed with paper, with chemicals and a separate color-print manual is offered. The paper and chemical sheets are clear and straightforward, providing all the information you require to complete the print-making process. Pay special attention to the cautionary material on the back of Bleach Package 2A. The paper package also includes an exposure mask to be used for print testing and evaluation so you can make four test exposures on one 8x10 sheet of paper.

The Color Print Manual is a much more detailed literary work of 24 pages, plus four tear-out wall charts giving information regarding filter packs, color correction, processing data and a magnification and exposure guide. The manual is well done and if you intend to really get into Cibachrome, I consider it a necessary item.

The equipment required is all standard: Enlarger, printing filters, bottles for solutions, thermometer, timer, trays or process tube. A word of caution: I suggest you either begin with tray processing or purchase the Cibachrome process tube. Tubes by other manufacturers may not be suitable with this material. Tubes with insertable rod dividers will cause streaks and uneven processing at the print ends. If you are just starting with Cibachrome, or are only giving it a quick try, use trays. If you decide to stay with the material, you can buy one of their tubes later.

A process temperature of 75 ± 3°F (24 ± 1.5° C) is recommended. The manual, however, provides informationfor processing at both 68°F and 82°F (20°C and 28°C) as well. Temperature control is quite simple, especially with the ±3°F (± 1.5°C) latitude. Let's run through the process once, using the recommended 75 ± 3°F (24 ± 1.5° C) latitude temperature and the tray method. Read through carefully first, as I'm going to insert a few notes from time to time.

1. Expose print per instructions with the paper. A trial filter pack is suggested for each type of transparency material used.
used.

NOTE: Cibachrome paper construction makes it difficult to determine emulsion side from backing. The maker suggests you hold the paper close to your ear and run your clean, dry finger across the surface. A slight "whisper" is heard on the backing side—nothing on the emulsion side.

2. Pour working chemical solution at 75 ± 3°F (24 ± 14°C) into trays for Developer, Bleach and Fix. The first two steps are in total darkness. WEAR RUBBER GLOVES!

NOTE: Instructions call for 3 ounces of solution for an 8x10 sheet of paper. I'm a bit chicken and use 4 ounces. That gives you fewer prints per kit, but I'd rather have good prints than have to throw out any damaged by chemical starvation.

3. Set timer for 2 minutes.
4. Place exposed print paper in Developer

tray in TOTAL DARKNESS. Start timer. Agitate continuously until 15 seconds prior to completion of step.

5. Drain print to completion of step.

6. Set timer to 4 minutes.

7. Place print paper in Bleach tray. Start timer. Agitate continuously until 15 seconds prior to completion of step. Room lights may be turned on after three minutes.

8. Drain print to completion of step.

9. Set timer for 3 minutes.

10. Place print paper in Fix tray. Start timer. Agitate continuously for the full 3 minutes.

11. Drain print for 15 seconds.

12. Set timer for 3 minutes. Start timer.

13. Wash print in 75°F (24°C) running water.

14. Squeegee print surface and lay print out to dry.

15. Pour all used solutions into a 1/2-gallon or larger plastic bucket. Add 1 level teaspoon of neutralizing powder for each print made. The solution will fizz and bubble. Don't cover the bucket. Pour solution down the drain only after the fizzing stops. Do this with adequate ventilation because the fumes are quite offensive.

16. Clean up your mess and prepare to evaluate the print when it's dry.

If you noticed an offensive odor when going from Developer to Bleach, or Bleach to Fix, add a 15-second water rinse between each step during future runs. It only adds 30 seconds to the process and makes things easier on the sinuses as well as helping to eliminate any chance of chemical streaking.

That's the process.

Once you have evaluated the test print for exposure and color balance, you can determine the necessary adjustments and go on to the next print. Cibachrome material has far greater latitude than the color materials you may have been using. A filter change of at least .15 will be necessary to cause a noticeable color difference. Likewise, exposure changes should be made in terms of a whole *f*-stop, either increase or decrease. A half-stop adjustment will rarely be sufficient.

PERSONALLY SPEAKING . . .

Cibachrome has become popular and found a strong following. Dealers tell me the materials sell well and afford them many return sales. Cibachrome devotees are struck by the relative ease of handling, wide exposure and filter latitudes, color brilliance and promise of fade-resistance. All much sought after qualities indeed. However, like many around me who make much more than the occasional weekend print, I have tried the process extensively and laid it aside. Not because the process isn't good, certainly, because it most definitely is; but rather because of the drawbacks I find related to my personal work and feelings.

Although the color offers great brilliance, I find it unnatural and overdone. Until recently, I was also bothered by the extremely high surface gloss, which required me to use an extra step applying Cibachrome Matte Paint Spray or Velvet Lustre Print Spray at extra cost. In the summer of 1979, however, a new paper surface was introduced which eliminates the problem. It is called *Cibachrome-A RC Pearl,* and it features a smooth lustre, semi-matte finish. It eliminates high reflectance problems.

Although the price of the Cibachrome color-print material has been reduced sharply since its introduction, the paper still costs almost twice as much as other color-print papers.

The greatest problem I find is the odors during the process, especially the bleach and neutralizers. The instructions used to warn about the need for ventilation, but no longer. I stress the use of much more darkroom ventilation than usual when handling these chemical solutions. Ordinary darkroom ventilation may not be sufficient for some people. The fumes can really be stunning. I have been told recent users found less odor than with the original chemicals. My 1977 trials with a fresh, just-delivered kit were unpleasant. Just to make sure you understand the potential problem with powerful unpleasant odors, go through the motions of handling the neutralizer and bleach solutions in your darkroom with the door closed. Keep the lights on and let someone else know what you are doing so they can help you if *you* are susceptible to the fumes. Not *everyone* is susceptible to the fumes.

I've mentioned the disadvantages I've found, but certainly there are many advantages to Cibachrome users. By all means, try it at least once. It is interesting and the results are definitely striking. It may be just *your* cup of tea.

Index